D1144495

BASIC CORPORATE TAXATION

BASIC CORPORATE TAXATION

by

Douglas A. Kahn

The Institute of Continuing Legal Education

Hutchins Hall • Ann Arbor, Michigan

First Printing January 1970

Second Printing April 1970

Library of Congress
Catalog Card Number
71-628299

Printed in the United States of America by
R. W. Patterson Printing Company, Benton Harbor, Mich.

TABLE OF CHAPTERS

3-27-2X

873

TABLE OF CONTENTS

viii

xii

Introduction

The purpose of this book is to provide a concise explanation of the basic aspects of federal corporate taxation and to introduce the reader to the advantages and pitfalls of the more popular corporate buy-out and business planning arrangements. The book is intended primarily for the nontax specialist, but hopefully it will prove to be a useful desk book for both students and specialists. I have not sought to write an exhaustive treatise; rather, it has been my intention to restrict the book to a manageable content that will provide the reader with an overview of the corporate tax structure and an insight into the nature of many specific problems which he may face so that he can isolate those issues and research them in depth.

In structuring the content of the book, the tax material was not organized to conform with the life-cycle of a corporation. I am convinced that the alternative routes available in organizing a corporation can best be understood in the perspective of the tax consequences attendant to the distribution of assets from a corporation to its stockholders, since the choice of the form of corporate organization frequently hinges on those consequences. Of course, business, nontax considerations often control or at least influence the selection of the structure of a corporation, and they are also discussed herein.

The book first considers the tax consequences that attend distributions of corporate property to shareholders. This material includes *inter alia*: discussion of cash and in kind dividends; earnings and profits; stock redemptions; rules of attribution of stock ownership; stock dividends; section 306 stock; redemption of a deceased shareholder's stock under § 303; several methods of liquidation; and collapsible corporations. The book also covers corporate divisions, nonacquisitive reorganizations (*i.e.*, recapitalization, and changes in corporate identity, form or place of organization) and acquisitive reorganizations. With that tax background in focus, the book then addresses the tax, corporate law, and funding problems attendant to an entity or cross-purchase buy-out agreement to purchase the stock of a deceased shareholder. The book next discusses:

the tax aspects of exchanges of property between shareholders and a controlled corporation; the basic operation and requisities of an election under Subchapter S; and the operation of § 1244 on certain common stock, and the means of electing § 1244 coverage. Finally, some of the tax and business planning considerations attendant to the formation of a new corporation and to changes in the capital structure of an existing corporation are examined.

Several important areas of tax law have been omitted or discussed only briefly in compliance with my desire that the material be restricted to a manageable content. There is no discussion in the book of: multiple corporation problems; consolidated returns; and the acquisition by one corporation of the tax attributes of another business. Also, I have limited the book's scope to ordinary domestic corporations; and consequently there is no discussion of special corporations such as: life insurance companies; regulated investment companies; real estate investment trusts; Western Hemisphere trade corporations; China Trade Act corporations; and foreign corporations. Moreover, there is no detailed discussion of personal holding companies or the accumulated earnings tax. While the book makes occasional reference to those latter two concepts, most of the material will not require knowledge of them; and I believe that they are discussed sufficiently herein to permit comprehension of the material to which they are relevant. In that regard, the book provides considerable discussion of the accumulated earnings tax provisions as they relate to corporate buy-out agreements.

By way of introduction to corporate taxation, I have sketched below the general attitude of the federal tax law to a corporate entity. First, however, it should be noted that the corporate tax laws do not apply exclusively to incorporated organizations; they also apply to insurance companies, joint stock companies and associations—*i.e.*, an organization whose attributes resemble an incorporated entity.[1] While the Service initially resisted the attempts of professional corporations and associations to be classified as corporations for tax purposes, it has now conceded that issue.[2]

A corporation is a separate tax entity which is required to file returns and pay income taxes in a manner that is fairly similar to

---

1 I.R.C. § 7701(a)(3). *See* Treas. Reg. § 301.7701-2.
2 T.I.R. 1019 (Aug. 8, 1969) P-H 1969 Federal Taxes ¶ 55, 334.

the requirements imposed upon individual taxpayers. The gross income of a corporation is determined under I.R.C. § 61 just as it is for an individual; and the taxable incomes of both individuals and corporations are determined under I.R.C. § 63. The deductions permitted a corporation are frequently the same as those permitted individuals, but there are a number of differences. For example, a corporation is not granted a standard deduction or a personal exemption; so every dollar of income recognized by a corporation will constitute taxable income to it unless the corporation can itemize specific deductions to offset its income. The so-called "non-business deduction" granted individual taxpayers under § 212 does not apply to corporations. Also, under present law, corporations are not granted the 50% deduction allowed other taxpayers under § 1202 for the excess of net long-term capital gains over net short-term capital losses; but corporations are allowed to elect the alternate tax for such excess long-term capital gains established in § 1201. There are many other differences, too numerous to list here; but in principle the federal taxes apply in the same manner to both corporations and individuals.

Once the taxable income of a corporation is established, it pays a tax under current rates of 22% on all its taxable income and it pays an additional tax (a surtax) of 26% on its taxable income in excess of $25,000.[3] Thus, a corporation pays a tax of 22% on its first $25,000 of taxable income, and it pays a tax of 48% on its taxable income in excess of $25,000. At this time, the corporation must also pay an additional surtax equal to 10% of its customary tax bill under a temporary surtax measure which has been imposed on all taxpayers.[4] Also, the corporation may be subject to certain specific surtaxes such as a personal holding company tax[5] or an accumulated earnings tax[6] when applicable, but those taxes apply to a relatively small percentage of corporations. Of course, tax rates are not immutable, and the rates may well be changed at any time.

Unlike the partnership or to a lesser extent a trust or estate, the corporation does not serve as a tax conduit for passing its in-

---

3 I.R.C. § 11.
4 I.R.C. § 51 added by § 102 of Public Law 90-364 (June 28, 1968).
5 I.R.C. § 541.
6 I.R.C. § 531.

come to its beneficiaries. The corporation must pay taxes on its income less its allowable deductions; and a corporate distribution of earnings to a shareholder *qua* a shareholder does not provide any deduction for the corporation even though it will usually constitute income to the shareholder. This phenomenon is sometimes characterized as a "double tax" or a "dual tax."

> Ex. The X Corporation had taxable income of $20,000 in its taxable year 1965. During 1965, X distributed $10,000 cash to its sole shareholder A. X will pay a 22% tax on its full income of $20,000—*i.e.*, a tax of $4,400. Nevertheless, A will be required to include the $10,000 distribution received by him in his gross income.[7]

Actually, this dual or double tax phenomenon is not as horrendous as it might first appear. Instead of paying dividends, the X Corporation might employ A and pay him a salary of $10,000 per year. A reasonable salary for services is deductible by the corporation as a business expense.[8] As an employee, A becomes eligible for several employee benefits which are granted favored tax treatment—*i.e.*, the corporation may pay A's medical insurance premiums or reimburse him for his medical expenses or those of his immediate family;[9] the corporation may include him in coverage under a group term life insurance plan;[10] and the corporation may include him in an employee qualified deferred compensation plan.[11] Moreover, the corporation might simply accumulate its income and reinvest the proceeds remaining after taxes, since the corporation's tax bracket will frequently be lower than its shareholders' and consequently, it can retain a greater percentage of its earnings than they could if they were to recognize its earnings directly. In this latter case, however, the corporation must beware of the imposition of an accumulated earnings tax or a personal holding company tax which was designed to prevent such accumulations but is not entirely successful in doing so.

In some instances a qualified corporation may elect under Subchapter S to pay virtually no taxes and to have its income taxed

---

7 In miniscule mitigation of A's treatment, A may be permitted to exclude $100 from his gross income. § 116.
8 I.R.C. § 162(a)(1).
9 I.R.C. §§ 105 and 106.
10 I.R.C. § 79.
11 I.R.C. §§ 401-404.

directly to its shareholders. The qualification for Subchapter S treatment and the operation of that provision are described in Chapter V.

I wish to thank Mr. Mark Spiegel and Mr. Robert Weinberg for their assistance in the preparation of this book. I also wish to express my appreciation to my colleague, Professor Stanley Siegel, who has contributed many helpful comments and suggestions.

September 21, 1969   Douglas A. Kahn

I

Corporate Transfers: Tax Impact on Shareholders

A. CORPORATE DISTRIBUTIONS WHICH ARE NOT MADE PURSUANT TO A COMPLETE LIQUIDATION

The tax consequences to a shareholder for receiving corporate assets depend upon several factors: (i) the amount distributed to the shareholder (for distributions in kind, the computation of the amount distributed will depend upon whether or not the shareholder is also a corporation); (ii) whether the distribution was made to the shareholder in his capacity as a shareholder; and (iii) whether the distribution to the shareholder constitutes a "dividend" for federal tax purposes. It should be emphasized that for tax purposes, the word "dividend" is a term of art specifically defined in the Code. The tax definition of a dividend is totally independent of the characterization of corporate distributions to shareholders for state corporate law purposes.[1] It is quite possible for a transaction to constitute a dividend for tax purposes and not be so characterized for corporate law purposes; and, conversely, a dividend under state corporate law does not necessarily constitute a dividend for tax purposes. Unless indicated otherwise, as used hereafter, the term "dividend" shall refer to a dividend for federal tax purposes.

Dividends received by shareholders constitute ordinary income

---

1 For a thorough discussion of the various state laws concerning corporate dividends, *see* 7 CAVITCH, BUSINESS ORGANIZATIONS, Chapters 140 and 141.

to them.[2] In each taxable year, an individual shareholder may exclude from income $100 of dividends received from most domestic corporations.[3] Ordinarily, a corporate shareholder receiving a dividend from a domestic corporation is granted an income tax deduction equal to at least 85% of the amount of the dividend.[4] In certain prescribed situations, the corporate shareholder is permitted to deduct an amount equal to the entire dividend received.[5]

1. Distributions to shareholders of cash or property (other than stock of the distributing corporation) when such distributions are not made pursuant to a redemption or purchase of the distributing corporation's outstanding stock

(a) Amount distributed. Cash distributions to both individual and corporate shareholders create no special problems, and the amount of such distributions is equal to the dollars involved.[6] However, distributions of property in kind cause complications, and the amount of such distributions is not always equal to the fair market value of the property. The reason for this complication is that adjustments must be made to prevent a tax windfall when the shareholder recipient of the distribution is a corporation. Since a shareholder is taxed on the amount of dividends received, it is appropriate to grant the shareholder a tax basis in the property received equal to the amount included in

---

2 I.R.C. § 301(c)(1). All citations herein to "I.R.C." refer to the INTERNAL REVENUE CODE OF 1954.

3 I.R.C. § 116(a). This exemption is subject to the limitations described in I.R.C. § 116(b) and (c), which preclude dividends from certain corporations, including tax-exempt corporations and real estate investment trusts, from the tax exclusion granted under § 116(a). A "domestic corporation" is one organized or created in the United States or under the law of the United States or of any state or territory. I.R.C. § 7701(a)(4).

4 I.R.C. § 243(a)(1). This deduction is subject to the limitations imposed under I.R.C. § 243(c) and § 246. For a brief discussion of Section 243 and other special deductions granted to corporate shareholders, see BITTKER AND EUSTICE, FEDERAL INCOME TAXATION OF CORPORATIONS AND SHAREHOLDERS (2d. ed., 1966), §§ 2.22 and 2.25, pp. 49-52 and 56-60.

5 I.R.C. § 243(a)(2) and (3). § 243(a)(2) applies to small business investment companies; and § 243(a)(3) applies to dividends paid among members of an "affiliated group" (§ 243(b)(5)) if an election has been made under § 243(b).

6 I.R.C. § 301(b)(1)(A) and (B). Distributions to a shareholder for purposes unrelated to his stockholding (e.g., as a creditor) are not dividends. Treas. Reg. § 1.301-1(c).

his gross income because of that distribution. However, a corporate shareholder is normally granted an 85% deduction for dividends paid to it,[7] and if the corporate shareholder were also given a basis in the distributed property equal to its fair market value, the dividend provisions could be used as a device for "stepping-up" the basis of property held by the subsidiary at a relatively small tax cost. For example, if Corporation X owns 100% of the stock of Corporation Y, and Corporation Y has a depreciable building which has been owned by Y for more than 10 years, with a fair market value of $50,000, but with an adjusted basis of only $5,000, there might be a sizable tax advantage to distributing that building to Corporation X as a dividend if the basis could thereby be increased to the present value of $50,000. In such event, Corporation X would have dividend income of $50,000 with an 85% deduction of $42,500, so that for the net cost of $7,500 ordinary income, Corporation X would increase the depreciable basis of the building by $45,000 (from $5,000 to $50,000). Consequently, when the shareholder is a corporation, the tax law limits the increase in basis of property transferred to it with respect to its stock to gain recognized by the distributing corporation;[8] and as an equitable corollary, the amount included in the corporate shareholder's gross income is similarly limited. Thus, the measure of the amount distributed to an individual shareholder is the amount of money plus the fair market value of other property received; but the measure of the amount distributed to a corporate shareholder is the amount of money received plus the *lesser* of either (i) the fair market value of other property received, or (ii) the basis in the hands of the distributing corporation of such other property plus gain recognized by the distributing corporation because of such distribution.[9] Under § 301(b)(2), the amount of such distribution shall be reduced (but not below zero) by the amount of liabilities of the corporation assumed by the shareholder in connection with the distribution and by the amount of liability to which the distributed property was subject immediately before and immediately after the distribution.

---

7 *See* note 4 *supra* and text accompanying that note.

8 I.R.C. § 301(d)(2).

9 I.R.C. § 301(b)(1)(A) and (B).

Ex. (1) Corporation X has two shareholders, individual A and Corporation B. Corporation X has unimproved Blackacre with a fair market value of $10,000 and a basis of $2,000. Corporation X distributed $10,000 cash to A and Blackacre to B. The amount distributed to A is $10,000 and the amount distributed to B is $2,000 (the basis of Blackacre).[10] On the other hand, if the distributions were reversed so that $10,000 cash were distributed to B and Blackacre were distributed to A, then the amount of each distribution would be $10,000.

Ex. (2) Corporation X is wholly owned by Corporation B. X owns unimproved Blackacre with a fair market value of $10,000 and a basis of $15,000. X distributes Blackacre to B. The amount of that distribution is $10,000 since the fair market value is less than the basis of the distributing corporation.

(b) Definition of "dividend." The tax characterization of a transaction as a dividend is significant because dividends are taxed to the shareholder as ordinary income.[11] A dividend for tax purposes is defined in § 316 as "a distribution of property made by a corporation to its shareholders" out of either earnings and profits [12] accumulated after February 28, 1913,[13] or out of current earnings and profits for the taxable year.[14] The "distribution of property" referred to in the above definition includes distributions of any property except stock in the distributing corporation or rights to acquire such stock.[15] The extent to which a distribution to a shareholder constitutes a dividend turns upon the amount of earnings and profits allocated to that distribution under a bifurcated standard, *viz.*, (i) the current earnings and profits of the distributing corporation for the taxable year (determined at the end of the taxable year) are first allocated pro rata to the distributions made during the current taxable year,

---

10 This assumes that Corporation X recognized no gain because of making the distribution.
11 I.R.C. § 301(c)(1).
12 The phrase "earnings and profits" is a term of art for federal tax purposes and is discussed below in paragraph (d).
13 This peculiar date was chosen because the sixteenth amendment to the Constitution became effective on February 25, 1913, and consequently the end of the month was chosen as a dividing line.
14 I.R.C. § 316(a).
15 I.R.C. § 317(a).

and (ii) if the total distributions during the taxable year exceed the current earnings and profits, then the earnings and profits accumulated after February 28, 1913, are allocated to such distributions according to the order of time of distribution.

Ex. (1) At the end of business on December 31, 1964, X Corporation, which reports on a calendar year basis, had an accumulated deficit for its earnings and profits of $20,000. On January 10, 1965, X Corporation distributed $10,000 cash to Shareholder A. From January 1, 1965, to that date, the X Corporation had earned nothing. On December 30, 1965, the X Corporation distributed $10,000 cash to Shareholder B. Between January 10 and December 30, the X Corporation had earned a $10,000 profit, and the current earnings and profits of the X Corporation for the year 1965 (computed at the end of the year) was $10,000. Since there were earnings and profits in the current year, those current earnings must be allocated pro rata to the distributions made during the year 1965, notwithstanding the fact that the corporation had accumulated a deficit prior to the year 1965.[16] Therefore, 50% of the current earnings and profits ($5,000) is allocated to A and 50% is allocated to B, and consequently, both A and B have dividend income of $5,000. The remaining $5,000 each received by A and B are not dividends.

Ex. (2) Y Corporation had accumulated earnings and profits on December 31, 1965, of $1,200. For the taxable year 1966, the Y Corporation had current earnings and profits of $10,000. On June 6, 1966, the Y Corporation distributed $3,000 cash to Shareholder C; and on November 8, 1966, the Y Corporation distributed $9,000 cash to Shareholder D. The $10,000 current earnings and profits are allocated 25% ($2,500) to the June 6 distribution to C and 75% ($7,500) to the November 8 distribution to D. The $1,200 accumulated earnings and profits is then allocated to the distributions in the order made, i.e., $500

---

16 It is worth noting that for state corporate law purposes, the standards for declaring a dividend in most states turn upon the corporation's earned surplus, a concept different from but analogous to earnings and profits; and some states employ a bifurcated earnings test (so-called "nimble dividends") somewhat similar to that used in federal tax law. *See* 7 CAVITCH, BUSINESS ORGANIZATIONS, Chapter 140.

is allocated to the balance of the distribution made to
C ($3,000–$2,500 current earnings and profits), and
the remaining $700 of accumulated earnings and prof-
its is allocated to the November 8 distribution to D.[17]
In tabular form, the allocation is as follows:

Date	Amount Distributed	Allocation of Current e & p	Allocation of Accum. e & p	Total e & p Allocated
June 6	$3,000	$2,500	$500	$3,000
Nov. 8	$9,000	$7,500	$700	$8,200

Ex. (3) As of December 31, 1965, Z Corporation had
accumulated earnings and profits of $12,000. The Z
Corporation operated at a deficit in the year 1966,
and had a deficit earnings and profits for that taxable
year of ($10,000). On July 2, 1966, the Z Corporation
distributed $10,000 cash to Shareholder E. Since Z
had no current earnings and profits in the taxable
year 1966, only Z's accumulated earnings and profits
were available for allocation, and the amount of accumulated earnings and profits must be determined as of
July 2, 1966, the date of distribution. The earnings
and profits accumulated at the beginning of the year
($12,000) must therefore be reduced by the actual op-
erating deficit suffered between January 1 and July 2
(the date of distribution); or if the actual operating
deficit for that period cannot be demonstrated, then a
percentage of the deficit for the entire year shall be
attributed to that period, and the proration shall be
made according to the number of days in the year
prior to the date of distribution. Accordingly, if the
actual operating deficit for that period cannot be determined, then 50% (182 days/364 days) of the
($10,000) annual deficit shall be allocated to that
period, and the Z Corporation is deemed to have had
$7,000 ($12,000–$5,000) in accumulated earnings and
profits at the date of distribution.[18] Accordingly, only
$7,000 of the amount distributed on July 2 is a divi-
dend.

(c) Disguised and constructive dividends. A shareholder may have
dividend income even though there has not been a direct distribution of property to him. The "disguised" or "constructive" dividend may arise where a closely held corporation confers an

---

17 *See* Treas. Reg. § 1.316-2(c) Ex.
18 Treas. Reg. § 1.316-2(b).

economic benefit on a shareholder. For example, a bargain sale by a corporation to its shareholder might constitute a corporate distribution to the shareholder in the amount of the difference between the purchase price and the fair market value of the property sold, and would constitute a dividend to the extent that earnings and profits are available.[19] Also, "loans" purportedly made to a shareholder may be disguised dividends if there is no intention that the so-called "loans" ever be repaid.[20] An excessive salary paid to a shareholder employee or his relative may be treated as a dividend to the extent that the payment exceeds a reasonable wage.[21] These are merely a few examples of disguised dividends, and the reader should be alert for possible application of that principle in any transaction which benefits a shareholder at a cost to the corporation.[22] However, the Government has not always been successful in its attacks on such transactions. For example, the Tax Court held that there was no dividend to a shareholder despite the corporation's failure to charge interest on a large bona fide loan to him.[23]

(d) Earnings and profits. One of the mysteries of federal income taxation is that the substantial verbiage contained in the Internal Revenue Code does not include a definition of the term "earnings and profits," even though the determination of the amount of earnings and profits is crucial to the question of whether corporate distributions shall be characterized as dividends. While § 312 of the Code does provide some illustrations of adjustments to be made in earnings and profits (hereinafter referred to as "e & p"), that section is by no means exclusive.

The basic purpose of e & p is to serve as a measuring rod of

---

19 Treas. Reg. § 1.301-1(j). For a corporate shareholder, where the adjusted basis of the distributed property is less than its fair market value, the amount of the distribution is the difference between the adjusted basis of the property in the hands of the distributing corporation and the amount the corporate shareholder paid for the property.
20 *See, e.g.,* Commissioner v. Makransky, 321 F.2d 598 (C.A. 3 1963). Of course, the actual intention of the parties is a question of fact.
21 Treas. Reg. § 1.162-8.
22 For a list of additional examples and a discussion of this issue, *see* BITTKER AND EUSTICE, FEDERAL INCOME TAXATION OF CORPORATIONS AND SHAREHOLDERS (2d ed., 1966), § 505, pp. 165-173.
23 J. Simpson Dean, 35 T.C. 1083 (1961). The majority of the Tax Court grounded its decision on the probable tax deductibility of interest payments if interest had been charged the shareholder.

the amounts available to a corporation for distribution to its shareholders without impairing its capital. Thus, e & p is analogous to the corporate law concept of earned surplus. However, the adjustments made to e & p and earned surplus are frequently different, and it should never be assumed that a corporation's earned surplus is identical to its e & p. For example, stock dividends will usually reduce the corporation's earned surplus, but unless taxable under I.R.C. § 305(b), they will have no effect on e & p.[24]

Any item included in a corporation's gross income and recognized for tax purposes will increase the corporation's e & p. However, increases to e & p are not linked solely to taxable income, since property received tax-free by the corporation is nevertheless available for distribution to shareholders without impairing capital. For example, interest[25] from municipal or state obligations[26] or receipt of life insurance proceeds[27] will increase e & p.[28] However, realized gain of a corporation on which taxation is deferred by operation of a nonrecognition statute[29] will not increase e & p, since to do so would cause a double increment when the gain is subsequently recognized.[30]

A corporate expenditure or loss will reduce the corporation's capacity to make distributions to its shareholders, and consequently such expenditures or losses frequently reduce e & p even

---

24 Treas. Reg. § 1.312-1(d).
25 Receipt of such interest is excluded from gross income by I.R.C. § 103.
26 Treas. Reg. § 1.312-6(b) requires the inclusion of such tax-exempt interest in the corporation's earnings and profits.
27 Life insurance will be exempt from income tax under I.R.C. §101(a) in most circumstances. But note the "transfer for value" rule in § 101(a)(2), and the exceptions to that rule set forth in § 101(a)(2) (A) and (B).
28 The amount of the increase to e & p caused by the receipt of life insurance proceeds is unresolved. In Rev. Rul. 54-230, 1954-1 C.B. 114, the Service stated that e & p was increased by an amount equal to the excess of the life insurance proceeds over the amount of premiums paid for the policy. For a criticism of that ruling, see BITTKER AND EUSTICE, FEDERAL INCOME TAXATION OF CORPORATIONS AND SHAREHOLDERS (2d ed., 1966), § 5.03, p. 157, n. 16. This issue is discussed *infra* at pp. 207-208 in relation to the entity buy-out of the stock of a deceased shareholder.
29 *E.g.*, I.R.C. §§ 1031, 1033, 108 and 361. But note that I.R.C. § 381 may cause changes in the e & p of a corporation acquiring the assets of another corporation in certain tax-free exchanges; these changes in e & p reflect a carry-over of the e & p of the acquired corporation.
30 I.R.C. § 312(f)(1).

where they are not deductible from gross income for income tax purposes. Some examples of nondeductible expenditures and losses that reduce e & p are: (i) capital losses in excess of capital gains;[31] (ii) losses incurred between related taxpayers disallowed deductibility under § 267;[32] (iii) premiums on life insurance disallowed deductibility under § 264;[33] and (iv) federal income tax liability.[34] Of course there are many other such items.

Some items which are deductible for income tax purposes will not reduce e & p to the same extent, *e.g.*, percentage depletion.[35]

An actual distribution of property to a shareholder with respect to his stock will reduce the e & p of the corporation (but not below zero) by the amount of money distributed or the adjusted basis of the property distributed in kind.[36] The amount of the reduction is modified[37] if the property is distributed subject

---

31 Treas. Reg. § 1.312-7(b). The excess capital loss is not allowed as an income tax deduction (I.R.C. § 1211); while the disallowed loss may be carried forward for five years (§ 1212(a)(1)), it may never be deducted if the corporation does not recognize capital gains in that five-year period. Since losses reduce e & p in the year in which they are incurred, the income tax deductions allowable for capital loss carry-overs and net operating loss carry-overs do not reduce e & p in the year in which deductions are allowed.

32 Treas. Reg. § 1.312-7(b).

33 The reduction in e & p generally has been limited to the excess of the premiums over the increment in the policy's cash surrender value. *See* BITTKER AND EUSTICE, FEDERAL INCOME TAXATION OF CORPORATIONS AND SHAREHOLDERS (2d ed., 1966), § 5.03, p. 160, n. 25.

34 The question of the proper year for deducting the federal income tax liability for a cash basis corporation is unsettled. *See* Drybrough v. Commissioner, 238 F.2d 735 (C.A. 6 1956) for one view. *See* Katcher, *What Is Meant By Earnings and Profits,* 18 N.Y.U. TAX INST. 235, 242-244 (1960) for an excellent discussion of this issue.

Federal income tax liabilities of an accrual basis taxpayer are deducted from e & p for the taxable year to which the tax liability relates. Deutsch, 38 T.C. 118 (1962). Moreover, the taxpayer's subsequent discovery of a tax deficiency will reduce e & p for the year to which the deficiency relates. Deutsch, *supra.* Indeed, the recovery of a tax refund (other than a refund due to facts arising after the year in question) may well increase e & p for the year to which the refund relates. *Compare* Western Wheeled Scraper Co., 14 B.T.A. 496 (1928) *with* Sweets Co. of America, Inc., 8 T.C. 1104 (1947). [These latter two cases both involved determinations of accumulated e & p for purposes of the excess profits tax.] There is a thorough discussion of those issues in Zarky and Biblin, *The Role of Earnings and Profits in the Tax Law,* 18 U.S.C. TAX INST. 145, 156-160 (1966).

35 Treas. Reg. § 1.312-6(c)(1). In such cases depletion must be separately computed on a cost basis, and the cost depletion will reduce e & p.

36 I.R.C. § 312(a).

37 I.R.C. § 312(c).

to a liability or the distributing corporation recognized a gain because of the distribution.[38]

> **Ex.** In 1965, Corporation X had accumulated e & p of $80,000. In the taxable year 1965, Corporation X had no earnings or deficit. During 1965, Corporation X distributed Blackacre to Shareholder A, who is an individual. The fair market value of Blackacre at the date of distribution was $50,000, the basis of X in Blackacre was $30,000, and Blackacre was transferred subject to a mortgage of $10,000. The amount distributed to A is $40,000 (fair market value less the mortgage (I.R.C. § 301(b)(1)(A) and (b)(2)), and he has dividend income in that amount. However, the e & p of X is reduced by only $20,000, *i.e.*, the basis of Blackacre (I.R.C. § 312(a)(3)) less the mortgage (I.R.C. § 312(c)(1)).

The determination of e & p is a highly complex matter, and the above material does not encompass all of the problems involved.[39] Additional references to e & p are made subsequently in this book in connection with specific transactions.

(e) Distributions to shareholders in excess of earnings and profits. The amount distributed to a shareholder in excess of the current and accumulated earnings and profits (hereinafter referred to as "the excess distribution") of the corporation is treated as follows: (i) the excess distribution reduces the basis of the shareholder's stock in the corporation, and to the extent that such basis is available, the excess distribution is not included in the shareholder's gross income;[40] (ii) if the excess distribution is greater than the shareholder's basis in his stock, then the difference is exempt from tax to the extent that it reflects earnings of the corporation accrued prior to March 1, 1913, but to the extent that the difference does not reflect pre-March 1, 1913, earn-

---

38 Gain might be recognized to the corporation under §§ 1245(a), 1250(a), 311(b) and (c), and 341(f). *See* Chapter II *infra*.

39 Among the many source materials available in this area, *see* Katcher, *What Is Meant By Earnings and Profits*, 18 N.Y.U. TAX INST. 235 (1960); Zarky and Biblin, *The Role of Earnings and Profits in the Tax Law*, 18 U.S.C. TAX INST. 145 (1966); and BITTKER AND EUSTICE, FEDERAL INCOME TAXATION OF CORPORATIONS AND SHAREHOLDERS (2d ed., 1966), § 5.03.

40 I.R.C. § 301(c)(2). Treas. Reg. § 1.301-1(f), Ex. (1).

ings, it will be treated as gain from the sale or exchange of property.[41] Thus, in most instances, the difference between the excess distribution and the shareholder's basis in his stock will be included in the shareholder's income as capital gains.

> **Ex.** On January 1, 1965, Corporation *X* had no accumulated earnings and profits. For the year 1965, *X* had current earnings and profits of $5,000. On July 5, 1965, *X* distributed $15,000 to Shareholder *A*. *A* had a basis of $3,000 in his stock of *X*. *X* was not in existence in the year 1913, so no pre-1913 earnings were available. Consequently, *A* recognized ordinary dividend income of $5,000, *A*'s basis in his stock of *X* was reduced from $3,000 to zero, and *A* recognized $7,000 as capital gains income.

(f) Basis of property distributed to shareholders. A shareholder's basis in property received from the corporation is dependent upon whether or not the shareholder is itself a corporation. The basis of property distributed to noncorporate shareholders is equal to the fair market value of the distributed property.[42] The basis of property distributed to corporate shareholders is the lesser of (i) the fair market value of the property, or (ii) the adjusted basis of the property in the hands of the distributing corporation increased by the amount of gain recognized by the distributing corporation as a result of making the distribution.[43] Note that the basis of the property distributed to a shareholder is identical to the amount deemed to be distributed to the shareholder under § 301(b), except that no adjustment is made because of liabilities assumed or accepted by the shareholder.

2. Distribution in redemption of a shareholder's stock

The net result of a shareholder of a closely held corporation selling a portion of his stock to the corporation may more closely resemble a dividend than a sale and will be treated accordingly.

> **Ex.** *A* owns the entire 200 shares of outstanding stock of the *X* Corporation. The *X* Corporation has accumu-

---

41 I.R.C. § 301(c)(3). Treas. Reg. § 1.301-1(f), Ex. (1).
42 I.R.C. § 301(d)(1).
43 I.R.C. § 301(d)(2). *See* Chapter II *infra* for a discussion of the gain recognized by a corporation as a result of making a distribution.

lated earnings and profits of $200,000. *A* sells 100 shares of his stock in *X* to the *X* Corporation for $150,000. Thus *A* owned 100% of the outstanding stock of the *X* Corporation before and after the sale, and the net effect of the "sale" was that *A* withdrew $150,000 from the corporation. The $150,000 would constitute a dividend to *A*.

Prior to 1954, purchases of its own stock by a corporation were treated as sales unless "essentially equivalent to the distribution of a taxable dividend." Decisions holding that a redemption was not essentially equivalent to a dividend analyzed the redemption from two different viewpoints: (i) from the point of view of the shareholder to determine whether the distributions were substantially disproportionate since proportional distributions resemble a dividend; and (ii) from the point of view of the corporation to determine whether there was a legitimate business purpose for making the redemption. While the essentially equivalent test has been retained, the present Code provides additional tests, the satisfaction of which precludes dividend treatment. Some of these additional tests look at the position of the shareholder whose stock is being redeemed, and some of the tests look at the position of the distributing corporation.

I.R.C. § 302(d) provides that unless a specific statutory exception is applicable, a corporation's redemption[44] of a shareholder's stock will be treated as a distribution to the shareholder under § 301[45] rather than as a purchase of the stock. The several specific statutory exceptions are discussed in succeeding paragraphs; but since the application of many of those exceptions depends upon the amount of stock actually or constructively owned by the shareholder involved, the rules of attribution of stock ownership are discussed first.

Before considering attribution, however, the problem of "disappearing basis" should be resolved. If a portion of a shareholder's stock is redeemed by the corporation, and the amounts received from the corporation are characterized as dividends under

---

44 For tax purposes, a "redemption" of stock is a corporation's acquisition of its own stock from a shareholder in exchange for property, irrespective of whether or not the acquired stock is cancelled or retired. I.R.C. § 317(b).

45 A distribution under § 301 will constitute a dividend to the extent that earnings and profits are allocable thereto.

§ 302(d), the shareholder no longer owns the redeemed stock, and for some time there was concern that the shareholder's basis in the redeemed shares would be lost. The Regulations have relieved much of those fears by providing that the shareholder's "lost basis" shall be allocated to other stock in that corporation held by the same shareholder.[46]

> **Ex.** X redeems 100 shares of its stock from A, its sole shareholder, for $50,000. A had a basis of $20,000 in the redeemed stock, and he had a basis of $14,000 in his remaining stock of X. The $50,000 paid to A was determined to be a dividend to A. A's $20,000 basis in the redeemed shares is allocated to his remaining shares of the company for which he has a $34,000 basis after the redemption is completed.

(a) Attribution of one person's or entity's stock ownership to a different person or entity. When stock ownership is a factor in determining corporate tax consequences, not only will the stock owned by the specific shareholder be significant, but frequently the stock owned by a person or entity having a close relationship to the specific shareholder may also be considered. Whether a person has constructive ownership of stock not directly owned by him is determined by technical statutory rules of attribution, and the tests employed are objective rather than subjective. For purposes of determining whether a stock redemption is a sale or a § 301 distribution, the rules of attribution set forth in I.R.C. § 318 control. The reader should be forewarned, however, that the Code does not employ the same attribution rules for all provisions which turn on stock ownership. For example, constructive stock ownership for purposes of determining whether a corporation is a personal holding company is determined under different rules of attribution[47] than those in § 318.

Unless rules of attribution are specifically made applicable to a provision of the Internal Revenue Code, no constructive ownership (other than sham arrangements which involve actual rath-

---

46 Treas. Reg. § 1.302-2(c). If all of a shareholder's stock were redeemed, the lost basis may be allocated to other stock of the corporation not held by the shareholder, the ownership of which is attributed to the shareholder under § 318, Treas. Reg. § 1.302-2(c), Ex. (2).

47 I.R.C. § 544.

er than constructive ownership) will pertain to that provision.[48] Indeed, § 318(a) specifically applies only to those provisions "to which the rules contained in this section are expressly made applicable." In some instances a provision of the Code will adopt rules of attribution contained in another section, but will establish specific modifications.[49]

Section 318 provides for attribution in four separate settings:

(i) Family attribution: an individual is deemed to own the stock owned[50] by his spouse, children, grandchildren and parents;

(ii) Attribution from an entity to its beneficiaries or owners:

(aa) Stock owned by a partnership or estate is considered to be owned proportionately by its partners or beneficiaries.

(bb) Stock owned by a trust is considered to be owned by the beneficiaries of the trust in proportion to their actuarially determined interest; but if all or part of the trust income is taxed to the grantor of the trust under I.R.C. §§ 671-677, then all or part of the stock held by the trust is deemed to be owned by the grantor.

(cc) A portion of stock owned by a corporation will be deemed owned by a shareholder having more than a 50% interest in the corporation in proportion to the shareholder's percentage interest in the corporation. The percentage interest in the corporation is determined by the value of the stock involved rather than by voting power.

(iii) Attribution to an entity from its beneficiaries or owners:

(aa) Stock owned by a partner or beneficiary of an

---

48 *E.g.,* for purposes of determining stock ownership on transfers to a controlled corporation (I.R.C. § 351), there is no attribution of stock.

49 *E.g.,* § 304(b)(1) adopts the rules of attribution contained in § 318 with certain modifications; and § 341(d) adopts most of the rules of attribution contained in § 544(a) with certain modifications; and § 341(e)(8) adopts the rules of attribution contained in § 267(c) with certain modifications.

50 Throughout § 318, reference is made to "stock owned, directly or indirectly," but the meaning of indirect ownership is not clear. Since § 318 refers to stock owned "by or for" an individual or entity, it applies to equitable ownership of stock.

estate is deemed to be owned by the partnership or estate.

(bb) Stock owned by the beneficiary of a trust (other than certain employees' trusts) is deemed owned by the trust, except that the stock owned by a *contingent* beneficiary, the value of whose interests in the trust is actuarially determined at 5% or less, is ignored.[51]

(cc) Stock owned by a shareholder having 50% or more in value of the stock of another corporation is considered to be owned by the latter corporation.

(iv) Options: the holder of an option to acquire stock is deemed the owner of the stock which is subject to the option.[52]

The rules of § 318 are applied strictly, and if parties do not come within those rules, there is no attribution among them. For example, under § 318 there is no attribution among brothers.[53]

A troublesome aspect of the § 318 attribution rules is that, with certain exceptions, a party is deemed to have actual ownership of stock that has been attributed to him, and therefore the attributed stock may then be re-attributed to a third party.[54]

> **Ex.** *A* is a beneficiary of a trust owning 100 shares of stock in *X* Corporation. *A*'s actuarially determined interest in the trust is 75%. Therefore, *A* is deemed to own 75 shares of the stock of *X* held by the trust. Since *A* is regarded as the *actual* owner of those 75 shares, the ownership of the 75 shares will be re-attributed from *A* to his wife, *W*. Thus, the trust owns 100 shares of *X*, and both *A* and *W* are each deemed to own 75 shares of *X*.

There are two circumstances in which constructively owned stock will not be re-attributed to a third party. Stock which is constructively owned by an individual because of *family* attri-

---

51 The determination of the actuarial value of a beneficiary's interest in an estate or trust shall be made according to the methods established (including the table of factors) in Treas. Reg. § 20.2031-7 for ascertaining estate tax values. Treas. Reg. § 1.318-3(b).

52 Warrants and convertible debentures are treated as options. Rev. Rul. 68-601, I.R.B. 1968-47.

53 Attribution rules provided by several other sections of the Code apply to brothers. *E.g.,* § 544(a)(2), and § 267(c)(4).

54 I.R.C. § 318(a)(5)(A).

bution rules is not re-attributed from that individual to another member of his family;[55] but such stock may be re-attributed from that individual to an entity (such as a trust of which the said individual is a beneficiary). Under a 1964 amendment to the Code, stock which is attributed to an entity from a beneficiary or owner shall not be re-attributed from the entity to another beneficiary or owner;[56] this amendment eliminated the previously troublesome problem of so-called "sideways attribution."

> **Ex.** *A* and *B* are equal beneficiaries of an estate which has 100 shares of stock of the *Y* Corporation. *B* individually owns 40 shares of stock of the *Y* Corporation. Fifty of the 100 shares of *Y* stock held by the estate are constructively owned by *A*, and are re-attributed from *A* to his wife, *W*. However, the 50 shares constructively owned by *W* are not re-attributed to *S*, *W*'s son by a prior marriage, since *W*'s constructive ownership was the product of family attribution. The 40 shares of *Y* stock held by *B* are attributed to the estate, which therefore is deemed to own 140 shares of *Y* stock. None of the 40 shares attributed to the estate are re-attributed to *A*, however.[57]

(b) Redemptions which are treated as a "purchase"[58] of stock rather than as a dividend.

(i) *Standards set at the shareholder level.* The Code defines three circumstances where a shareholder's position *vis-a-vis* his fellow shareholders is so changed by a redemption that it is treated as a purchase of that shareholder's stock.[59]

   (aa) *Not essentially equivalent to a dividend.* The

---

55 I.R.C. § 318(a)(5)(B).
56 I.R.C. § 318(a)(5)(C).
57 Prior to the 1964 amendment, one-half (20 shares) of the shares constructively owned by the estate would have been re-attributed to *A*. Thus, there would have been a "sideways" attribution from one beneficiary of an estate (or trust or partnership) to another beneficiary. This "sideways" attribution was eliminated by the 1964 amendment.
58 The word "purchase" is used in this book to distinguish a distribution that is not subject to the provisions of § 301 from a distribution that is covered by § 301. In fact, a redemption of stock is not regarded as an *actual* sale or purchase, but where the distribution is not subject to § 301, the tax result is the same as if it were an actual sale.
59 I.R.C. § 302(b)(1), (2) and (3). In addition, § 302(b)(4) excludes from dividend treatment the redemption of stock by certain railroad corporations pursuant to a plan of reorganization under Section 77 of the Bankruptcy Act.

first of these circumstances is an adoption of the pre-1954 test, *viz.*, redemptions "not essentially equivalent to a dividend" are treated as purchases. The courts are split in their interpretation of that phrase. One line of cases has followed a strict "net effect" test, *i.e.*, whether the circumstances resulting from the redemption are significantly different from the circumstances that would have resulted if a dividend had been distributed.[60] Under this test, a pro rata or nearly pro rata redemption of a shareholder's stock will not qualify,[61] but the extent to which a redemption must be disproportionate is unclear.[62] A second line of cases has adopted a "business purpose" test, *i.e.*, whether the redemption was designed to serve a legitimate business purpose of either the corporation itself or of the shareholders.[63]

A recent case[64] illustrates both the usefulness of the "not essentially equivalent" test and the risks inherent in relying on that test for business planning purposes. In the *Antrim* case, there were four shareholders of a corporation, all four of whom owned preferred stock, and three of whom had actual or constructive ownership of common stock. The corporation redeemed all of its preferred stock. The amount received by the shareholder (hereinafter referred to as X) who did not own any common stock in the corporation was thus received in complete termination of

---

60 This "interpretation" amounts to little more than a restatement of the statutory language "not essentially equivalent to a dividend."
61 Treas. Reg. § 1.302-2(b).
62 The attribution rules of § 318 are considered in determining the extent to which a redemption was disproportionate, Treas. Reg. § 1.302-2(b). *See* Estate of Arthur H. Squier, 35 T.C. 950 (1961) (Acq. 1961-2 CUM. BULL. 5) for an example of a case in which a redemption qualified as not essentially equivalent to a dividend even though attribution was enforced. For a narrow construction of the "essentially equivalent" test and an application of attribution rules, *see* Levin v. Commissioner, 385 F.2d 521 (C.A. 2 1967).
63 *See* Ballenger v. United States, 301 F.2d 192 (C.A. 4 1962); and Davis v. United States, 23 A.F.T.R.2d 69-1028 (C.A. 6 1969). The Supreme Court has granted certiorari in *Davis*. Resort to the corporation's purpose appears inappropriate since Section 302 was purportedly designed to consider the transactions from the shareholder's point of view; but this objection may be more juristic than substantial since the test could usually be applied to § 346(a)(2) with identical result.
64 Commissioner v. Estate of Antrim, 395 F.2d 430 (C.A. 4 1968), *affirming* ¶ 67,060 P-H Memo T.C.

his stock interest in the corporation, and consequently was exempted from dividend treatment by Section 302(b)(3).[65]

The ratio of the amounts paid to each of the other three shareholders (A, B and C) in redemption of his stock to the total amount paid to all four shareholders was substantially disproportionate to their respective percentage holdings of common stock. However, the Commissioner contended that the redemption of the preferred stock from A, B and C constituted a dividend to them because the appropriate reference for determining the ratio was the amount paid to A, B and C (*i.e.*, the amount paid to X should be excluded from consideration), and if the amount paid to X was excluded, the allocation of payments among A, B and C was fairly close to their respective percentage holdings of the corporation's common stock. The court held that the amount paid to X should not be disregarded in determining equivalence merely because X's redemption was expressly excluded from dividend treatment by another subsection of the Code (§ 302(b)(3)), and accordingly the court upheld the taxpayers' claim for capital gains treatment. Presumably, the preferred stock redeemed in *Antrim* was not "tainted" by § 306.[66] The merit of the court's decision has been buttressed by a recently promulgated Revenue Ruling[67] stating that the redemption of all of a corporation's preferred stock (other than "section 306" stock) will not constitute a dividend where there was no proportional relationship of stock ownership (actual or constructive) between the outstanding common and preferred shares.[68]

As the *Antrim* case suggests, the uncertainty of the standard employed in the "not essentially equivalent" test would inhibit the adoption of many legitimate redemption plans. In order to alleviate this *in terrorem* consequence, the Code has provided two objective tests, the satisfaction of either of which will qualify the redemption for nondividend treatment. These objective tests are sometimes referred to as "safe harbors."

(bb) *Substantially disproportionate redemptions.* Un-

---

65 *See* pp. 20-23 *infra.*
66 *See* pp. 51-58 *infra* for a discussion of "section 306 stock."
67 Rev. Rul. 68-547, I.R.B. 1968-42, p. 8.
68 *See* H. Rept. 1337, 83d Cong., 2d Sess., p. 35 (March 9, 1954); and Levin v. Commissioner, 385 F.2d 521 (C.A. 2 1967).

der § 302(b)(2), if the redemption of any one share-holder's stock complies with certain prescribed mathematical tests demonstrating that the redemption is substantially disproportionate, the redemption of that shareholder's stock will constitute a purchase. The standards which the shareholder must satisfy to qualify[69] are:

(1) Immediately after the redemption, the shareholder must own less than 50% of the voting power of all classes of stock entitled to vote;

(2) The percentage of outstanding voting stock[70] of the corporation owned by the shareholder immediately after the redemption must be less than 80% of the percentage of outstanding voting stock of the corporation owned by the shareholder immediately prior to the redemption.

(3) The shareholder's percentage of outstanding common stock of the corporation (whether voting or non-voting) before and after the redemption must also meet the 80% requirement set forth in the preceding paragraph.[71]

Ex. (1) The X Corporation has 400 shares of common voting stock outstanding; A owns 200 shares and B owns 200 shares. A and B are not related parties. The X Corporation has earnings and profits of over $50,000. The X Corporation redeems 100 shares of A's stock for $20,000 cash. A owns less than 50% of the voting stock of X immediately after the redemption, and consequently the first test of § 302(b)(2) is satisfied. A owned 50% of the voting stock of the corporation immediately before the redemption, and he owned $33\frac{1}{3}$% (100/300) after the redemption. Since his percentage after the redemption ($33\frac{1}{3}$%) is less than

---

69 For purposes of applying these tests, the attribution rules of § 318 are employed in determining stock ownership. § 302(c)(1).

70 Voting stock refers to stock having the present right to vote. Stock which is permitted to vote only on the occurrence of some contingency or event is not treated as voting stock until the contingency or event occurs. Treas. Reg. § 1.302-3(a).

71 If there is more than one class of common stock, the 80% requirement shall be measured according to the fair market value of the common stock. I.R.C. § 302(b)(2)(C).

80% of his interest before the redemption (80% x 50% = 40%), the redemption of A's stock is deemed a purchase rather than a dividend.

Ex. (2) If in the preceding Example, A were the father of B, the redemption would have constituted a dividend since A would then be considered the owner of B's 200 shares under § 318(a)(1). Thus, A would be deemed to own 400 of the 400 outstanding shares before the redemption (100%), and he would be deemed to own 300 of the outstanding 300 shares (100%) after the redemption.[72]

Section 302(b)(2) applies only to redemptions of voting stock or to redemptions of both voting and nonvoting stock, but it does not apply to redemptions of solely nonvoting stock (whether common or preferred).[73] It also does not apply to any redemption that will not be substantially disproportionate with respect to the shareholder's stock because of a plan contemplating subsequent redemptions of other shareholders' stock.[74]

(cc) *Termination of shareholder's interest.* Section 302(b)(3) provides that a redemption of a shareholder's stock will constitute a purchase if the redemption terminates the shareholder's stock interest in the corporation.

Ex. (1) X Corporation has outstanding 400 shares of common voting stock and 200 shares of preferred nonvoting stock. The 400 shares of common stock are owned by A, and the 200 shares of preferred stock are owned by B. A and B are not related parties. X redeems B's 200 shares of preferred stock for $10,000 cash. Section 302(b)(2) is inapposite because only nonvoting stock was redeemed.[75] However § 302(b)(3) is applicable, and the redemption will be treated as a purchase.[76]

---

72 It is virtually certain that the "not essentially equivalent" test established in § 302(b)(1) would not be applicable in the above circumstances. Thomas G. Lewis, 35 T.C. 71 (1960).
73 Treas. Reg. § 1.302-3(a).
74 I.R.C. § 302(b)(2)(D).
75 Treas. Reg. § 1.302-3(a).
76 The tax treatment of the redemption may also be subject to the provisions of I.R.C. § 306 if the preferred stock were "section 306 stock," but even if that were the case, the applicability of § 302(b)(3) precludes the operation of § 306(a). *See* § 306(b)(1)(B).

Ex. (2) The Y Corporation has 800 shares of common voting stock outstanding, and has accumulated earnings and profits of $160,000. Grandfather Jones owns 200 shares of Y's stock; Son Jones, the son of Grandfather, owns 200 shares of Y's stock; Granddaughter Jones, the daughter of Son Jones, owns 200 shares of Y's stock; and the remaining 200 shares are owned by the O Corporation. All of the outstanding stock of the O Corporation is owned by Son Jones. The Y Corporation redeems the 200 shares of Y stock owned by Granddaughter Jones for $100,000 cash. The entire $100,000 paid to Granddaughter will likely constitute a taxable dividend. The 200 shares of Y stock owned by Son Jones are attributed to Granddaughter under § 318(a)(1). The 200 shares of Y stock owned by O Corporation are attributed to Son Jones, its sole shareholder, under § 318(a)(2)(C), and those 200 shares are re-attributed to Granddaughter Jones under § 318(a)(1) and (a)(5)(A). The 200 shares of Y stock owned by Grandfather are not directly attributed to Granddaughter.[77] Those shares are attributed to Son Jones, but there is no re-attribution of those shares to Granddaughter.[78] Thus, Granddaughter was deemed to own 600 of the outstanding 800 shares (75%) of Y stock before the redemption, and she was deemed to own 400 shares of the outstanding 600 shares (66⅔%) after the redemption. Accordingly, Granddaughter's stock interest in Y was not completely terminated, and she owns more than 50% of the voting power of Y, and therefore neither § 302(b)(2) nor (b)(3) is applicable. It is possible (but unlikely) that the redemption could qualify as a purchase under § 302(b)(1), *i.e.*, a redemption not equivalent to a dividend.[79]

The Code mitigates the stringent operation of the attribution rules by providing in § 302(c) that the family attribution rules of § 318(a)(1) do not apply to redemptions terminating a shareholder's interest in a corporation if certain requisites are satisfied.[80] These requisites are:

---

77 There is no attribution from a grandparent to a grandchild under § 318 even though there is attribution from a grandchild to a grandparent.

78 I.R.C. § 318(a)(5)(B).

79 *Compare* Estate of Arthur H. Squier, 35 T.C. 950 (1961) (Acq. 1961-2 CUM. BULL. 5) *with* Bradbury v. Commissioner, 298 F.2d 111 (C.A. 1 1962).

80 I.R.C. § 302(c); and Treas. Reg. § 1.302-4.

(1) Immediately after the redemption the distributee has no interest in the corporation (including an interest as an officer, director or employee) other than an interest as a creditor;

(2) The distributee does not acquire any such interest (other than stock acquired by bequest or inheritance) within 10 years after the redemption;

(3) The distributee files an agreement attached to his tax return for the year in which the redemption occurred, in which agreement the distributee promises to notify the district director of any interest he may acquire in the corporation within the 10-year period, and such notification shall be made within 30 days after the interest is acquired.[81]

If the distributee does acquire an interest in the corporation within the 10-year period in contravention of paragraph (2) above, then the provisions of § 302 will not apply, and a tax deficiency may be assessed for the year in which the redemption occurred.[82]

In addition, § 302(c) is not applicable:[83]

(1) If all or a portion of the redeemed stock was acquired by the distributee during the previous 10 years from a person whose stock ownership would be attributed to the distributee under § 318(a); or

(2) If a third person owns stock of the corporation (at the time of redemption) the ownership of which is attributable to the distributee under § 318(a) and such stock was acquired from the distributee within the previous 10-year period unless the acquired stock is redeemed in the same transaction.

Neither of the above two requisites applies if the acquisition or disposition referred to therein did not have federal income tax avoidance as one of its principal purposes.

> **Ex. (1)** *A* owned all 200 shares of outstanding stock of the *X* Corporation. *A* died and bequeathed 100 shares of *X* to his wife, *W*, and 100 shares of *X* to their son, *S*.[84] Subsequently, *A*'s estate was closed, and the shares

---

81 Treas. Reg. § 1.302-4(a).
82 I.R.C. § 302(c)(2).
83 I.R.C. § 302(c)(2)(B).
84 The value (for estate tax purposes) of the 200 shares of *X* was less than 35% of the value of *A*'s gross estate and was less than 50% of *A*'s taxable estate for estate purposes. Consequently, § 303 is not applicable. *See* pp. 31-36 *infra*.

were distributed to *W* and *S*. *X* then redeemed all 100 of *W*'s shares, and she executed an agreement pursuant to § 302(c)(2)(A)(iii). The attribution rules of § 318 do not apply, and the redemption of *W*'s stock is deemed a purchase under § 302(b)(3).

Ex. (2) Consider the same facts as given in the preceding Example (1) except that the 100 shares bequeathed to *S* were instead bequeathed to the Friendly National Bank in trust for *S*. After *A*'s estate is closed and the stock was distributed, the *X* Corporation redeemed from the trust the 100 shares of stock held in trust for *S*. The trustee sought to comply with § 302(c) in order to avoid attribution rules. The Internal Revenue Service has ruled that § 302(c) does *not* prevent attribution in this case and that the trust is deemed to own the 100 shares of *X* stock held by *W*.[85] The Service's position is that § 302(c)(2) renders inapplicable *family* attribution rules pertaining to the party whose stock is redeemed, but it does not preclude the operation of other attribution rules. Here, *S* is considered as owning *W*'s 100 shares because of family attribution, but the stock is re-attributed to the trust under § 318(b)(3) which is not a family attribution provision and therefore is not vitiated by § 302(c).

The Service has construed the requirement in § 302(c) that the distributee not acquire any interest in the corporation for a 10-year period as prohibiting the distributee from rendering any services to the corporation during that period even though the distributee receives no compensation.[86]

(ii) *Standards set at the corporate level.* Distributions to a shareholder made in partial liquidation of the corporation are treated as purchases rather than as a dividend.[87] Partial liquidations are defined in I.R.C. § 346, which provides that a distribution will be in partial liquidation of a corporation if either (1) a distribution is one of a series of distributions made pursuant to a plan of complete liquidation which is effected, or (2) a distribution "not essentially equivalent to a dividend" is in redemption of part of the corporation's

---

85 Rev. Rul. 59-233, 1959-2 C.B. 106.
86 Rev. Rul. 56-556, 1956-2 C.B. 177.
87 I.R.C. § 331(a)(2).

stock pursuant to a plan, and occurs within either the taxable year the plan was adopted or the succeeding taxable year. As used in § 346, the phrase "not essentially equivalent to a dividend" is viewed from the vantage point of the corporation, in contrast to the identical language in § 302(b)(1) which is viewed at the shareholder's level.[88] Thus, the language in § 346 carries forward the doctrine of contraction of corporate business developed in pre-1954 Code cases.[89] For a discussion of what constitutes a corporate contraction, see Bittker and Eustice, *Federal Income Taxation of Corporations and Shareholders* (2d ed., 1966), pp. 309-312; and Portfolio (No. 37-2d) "Partial Liquidation" *Tax Management* (BNA) pp. 20-23.

Although § 346(b) sets forth objective standards, the satisfaction of which will qualify a distribution as a partial liquidation, the failure to comply with § 346(b) creates no inference that the distribution is *not* a partial liquidation. The standards established by § 346(b) are: (i) that immediately prior to the distribution, the corporation conducted at least two trades or businesses, both of which had been actively conducted for five years prior to the distribution and neither of which had been acquired by the corporation during that five-year period in a taxable transaction; (ii) that the distribution is attributable to the corporation's ceasing to conduct one or more of such trades or businesses; and (iii) that the corporation continued the active conduct of at least one of such trades or business after the distribution. A distribution attributable to the corporation's ceasing to conduct a trade or business includes either: (i) a distribution of the proceeds from the sale of such trade or business; (ii) a distribution in kind of the assets of such trade or business; or (iii) a distribution in kind of some of the assets of such trade or business plus a distribution of the proceeds from the sale of the remaining assets of such trade or business.[90] In order to qualify under § 346(b), *all* of the assets (or the proceeds from the sale of the assets) of the terminated trade or business must be distributed to the share-

---

88 *See* S. Rept. No. 1622, 83d Cong., 2d Sess., 49 (1954).

89 *See* Joseph W. Imler, 11 T.C. 836 (1948) (Acq.) holding that the distribution of net fire insurance proceeds received in compensation for the partial destruction of a building by fire was a partial liquidation. *See also* Treas. Reg. § 1.346-1(a)(2).

90 Treas. Reg. § 1.346-1(b)(2).

holders.[91] Unless the distribution to the shareholders is made pro rata, the distribution must be made in redemption of corporate stock to qualify as a partial liquidation.[92]

The liquidation of a passive investment (*e.g.*, a tract containing materials which a corporation leased to a third party, who mined the minerals and paid the corporation royalties therefor, was deemed a passive investment) is not protected by § 346(b), nor does it constitute a corporate contraction under § 346(a).[93]

> **Ex.** *X* Corporation has operated a retail clothing business since 1948. In 1965, *X* purchased the assets of a hardware business for $100,000 cash, and thereafter conducted both the retail clothing business and the hardware business. In 1968, *X* sold the hardware business to a third party and distributed the net proceeds to its shareholders in proportionate redemption of part of their *X* stock. Since the hardware business was acquired by *X* in a taxable exchange within the 5-year period prior to distribution, § 346(b) is inapplicable. However, it is possible that the redemption will qualify as a corporate contraction pursuant to § 346(a)(2).

The requirement of § 346(b) that the two or more businesses or trades have been actively conducted for five years prior to the distribution and that at least one of them be actively conducted after the liquidation is similar to the "active business" test employed in § 355 for corporate divisions.[94] Indeed, the Regulations promulgated under § 346 adopt by reference the Regulations promulgated under § 355 (*viz.*, Treas. Reg. § 1.355-1(c)) for the interpretation of the phrase "active conduct of a trade or business."[95] Among the activities which are excluded from the category of an active business is the ownership of land or buildings substantially all of which are used and occupied by the corporation in the operation of a trade or business.[96]

The deductibility of legal fees and other expenses incurred in

---

91 Oscar E. Baan, 51 T.C. No. 105 (1969).
92 *Id.*
93 Rev. Rul. 56-512, 1956-2 C.B. 173.
94 § 355(b).
95 Treas. Reg. § 1.346-1(c).
96 Treas. Reg. § 1.355-1(c). That Regulation lists additional examples of activities which fail to qualify as an active business.

connection with a partial liquidation is unclear, and the courts are divided.[97]

(c) Redemption of stock—effect on corporation's earnings and profits.

A redemption of stock which constitutes a section 301 distribution has the same effect on the corporation's earnings and profits as does a section 301 distribution to a shareholder which is not made in redemption of stock.[98] A redemption which constitutes a purchase of a shareholder's stock under § 302(a), or a partial liquidation under § 331(a)(2), reduces earnings and profits to the extent that the distribution in redemption is not properly chargeable to capital account.[99] The correct method for computing the amount of reduction is unsettled. A few of the unresolved questions are: (i) Whether the corporation's capital account is to be determined by the fair market value of property and services given the corporation in payment for its stock, or is only the tax basis of the property given the corporation to be taken into account? (ii) What is the effect of the corporation's having several classes of stock with different shareholder rights? (iii) Whether the amount of distribution which reduces earnings and profits is limited to the distributee's ratable share of the corpora-

---

97 *E.g.*, Mills Estate, Inc., 17 T.C. 910 (1951) Non acq. 1951-1 C.B. 7, *reversed and remanded*, 206 F.2d 244 (C.A. 2 1953); Tobacco Products Export Corp., 18 T.C. 1100 (1952) Non acq. 1955-2 C.B. 11; and Gravois Planing Mill Co. v. Commissioner, 299 F.2d 199 (C.A. 8 1962). The Tax Court maintains that the expenses of a partial liquidation must be divided between those items which relate to the distribution of assets and those items which are akin to reorganization expenses, and the Tax Court allows deductions for the former items and not for the latter. *See* Standard Linen Service, Inc., 33 T.C. 1 (1959) (Acq.). However, two courts of appeals have rejected the Tax Court's position and held that all of the expenses of the partial liquidation are deductible or nondeductible depending upon whether the principal purpose of the redemption was to perpetuate the continuing business of the corporation (deductible) or to provide a new structure for the corporation (nondeductible). *See* Mills Estate, Inc. v. Commissioner *supra* and Gravois Planing Mill Co. v. Commissioner *supra*.
98 *See* pp. 9-10 *supra*.
99 I.R.C. § 312(e). Note that a redemption may appear to qualify as a purchase under the auspices of an agreement filed pursuant to § 302(c) and may subsequently be treated as a dividend because the distributee acquired an interest in the corporation within the 10-year period. Query, whether the change in earnings and profits caused by the loss of § 302(c) treatment will be prospective from the date the distributee acquired the prohibited interest?

tion's earnings and profits,[100] or is an amount equal to the difference between the amount received by the distributee and the distributee's ratable share of the corporation's capital account?[101]

> **Ex. (1)** *A* and *B* formed the *X* Corporation and each contributed $10,000 cash for 100 shares of the stock of *X*. After 2 years of operation, *X* had accumulated earnings and profits of $15,000, and the fair market value of *X* was $50,000. *X* then redeemed *A*'s 100 shares of stock for $25,000. If the reduction in earnings and profits of *X* were limited to *A*'s ratable share of the earnings and profits, then the amount of reduction would be $7,500 (50% x $15,000). However, if the reduction in earnings and profits is determined by the difference between the amount distributed to *A* ($25,000) and *A*'s ratable share of the capital account (50% × $20,000 = $10,000), then the $15,000 earnings and profits would be reduced to zero.[102]

(d) Sale of corporate stock to either a subsidiary corporation or a sister corporation. The net result of a shareholder's selling stock of a controlled corporation to a subsidiary of the controlled corporation or to another corporation which is also controlled by the selling shareholder may be similar to a dividend distribution.

> **Ex.** *A* owns the 200 outstanding shares of stock of the *P* Corporation. *P* owns all of the outstanding stock of the *S* Corporation. *A* sells 100 shares of *P*'s stock to *S* for $50,000 cash. The net result of this "sale" is that *A* retains 100% control of *P*, and he has withdrawn $50,000 cash from a subsidiary of *P*.

Reasonably, the transaction described above should be treated no differently than would be a distribution from *S* to *P* of $50,000, and a redemption by *P* of 100 shares of its stock. However, a 1948 Tax Court decision treated a transaction similar to

---

100 *See* Woodward Investment Co., 46 B.T.A. 648 (1942) Acq. 1942-2 C.B. 20. *See* Edelstein and Korbel, *The Impact of Redemption and Liquidation Distributions on Earnings and Profits: Tax Accounting Aberrations Under* § *312(e),* 20 TAX L. REV. 479 (1965).

101 *See* Helvering v. Jarvis, 123 F.2d 742 (C.A. 4 1941). Note G.C.M. 23460, 1942-2 C.B. 190 in which the Service contends that *Woodward* and *Jarvis* are reconcilable.

102 *See* BITTKER AND EUSTICE, FEDERAL INCOME TAXATION OF CORPORATIONS AND SHAREHOLDERS (2d ed., 1966), § 7.85, pp. 323-325.

this as a sale.[103] The Tax Court's treatment of this matter was repudiated by a 1950 amendment to the 1939 Code.[104] At the present, a corporation's purchase of stock of a parent or sister corporation is subject to the provisions of § 304 of the 1954 Code.

(i) *Brother-sister corporations.* If one or more persons are in control[105] of each of two corporations and neither of the two corporations controls the other, and one of the controlled corporations acquires stock of the other controlled corporation from the person or persons in control, § 304 treats the exchange as a transaction subject to the provisions of § 302 (*i.e.*, a redemption of a corporation's own stock). For purposes of applying § 302(b) to determine whether the exchange shall be treated as a purchase or as a section 301 distribution, reference is made to the stock of the issuing corporation (*i.e.*, the corporation whose stock was "sold" by the person or persons in control).[106] However, if the exchange is treated as a section 301 distribution, the determination of whether the distribution constitutes a dividend is controlled

---

103 Rodman Wanamaker Trust, 11 T.C. 365 (1948), *affirmed,* 178 F.2d 10 (C.A. 3 1949).
104 Sec. 208 of the Revenue Act of 1950. The 1950 Act applied only to purchases by subsidiary corporations, but the 1954 Code enlarged the coverage of that provision to encompass brother-sister corporations as well.
105 For purposes of § 304, "control" refers to actual or constructive ownership of stock possessing at least 50% voting power or 50% of the total value of all outstanding shares. Section 318 is applied (without the 50% limitation contained in § 318(a)(2)(C) and (a)(3)(C)) in determining control. Section 304(c). Because of attribution rules, an individual may be deemed to control a corporation in which he has no *actual* possession of its stock. Coyle Jr. v. United States, 21 A.F.T.R.2d 1512 (C.A. 4 1968).
106 I.R.C. § 304(b)(1). In determining whether the exchange comes within § 302(b), the attribution rules of § 318 are applicable, except that the 50% limitation contained in § 318(a)(2)(C) and (a)(3)(C) is disregarded.
  A peculiar aspect of § 304 is that a literal construction of the statute would render the brother-sister provisions meaningless. When one or more persons control both Corporation X and Corporation Y, the stock of Corporation X owned by the controlling shareholders would be attributed to Y under the attribution rules, and similarly the stock of Y would be attributed to X. Thus, X would be deemed a subsidiary of Y, and vice versa. In that event, the parent-subsidiary rules would apply in all circumstances in which § 304 is applicable, and the brother-sister rules would never apply. Presumably, this is a product of a drafting error, and the literal language should not control over the obvious intention of Congress to treat brother-sister corporations differently from parent-subsidiary corporations.

by the earnings and profits of the acquiring corporation (*i.e.*, the corporation that purchased the stock from the person or persons in control).[107]

> **Ex.** X Corporation has 200 shares of stock outstanding and Y Corporation has 500 shares of stock outstanding. X has accumulated earnings and profits of $15,000, and Y has accumulated earnings and profits of $120,000. Neither X nor Y had any current earnings and profits in the year 1966.
>
> **(1)** A owns 100 shares of the 200 outstanding shares of X, and A owns 250 of the 500 outstanding shares of Y. The remaining shares of X and Y are owned by persons who are not related to A. A sells 80 shares of X stock to Y for $50,000 cash. A owned 50% of the outstanding X stock before the "sale." After the sale, A owns 20 shares of X outright, and he has constructive ownership of 40 additional shares of X stock,[108] and consequently his total holding of X stock after the sale is 60 shares. A's 60 shares of X constitute 30% of the outstanding X stock (60/200), and since that is less than 80% of A's percentage holding before the sale, the sale qualifies under § 302(b)(2), and the distribution to A is not a dividend.
>
> **(2)** A owns the 200 outstanding shares of X stock and the 500 outstanding shares of Y stock. A sells 100 shares of X stock to Y for $62,000 cash. A owned 100% of X stock before the "sale," and after the sale he owns 100 shares outright and 100 shares constructively from Y.[109] Thus, A continues to own 100% of X after the "sale," and therefore § 302(a) is not applicable. The $62,000 is a section 301 distribution, and it will constitute a dividend to the extent that Y Corporation (the acquiring corporation) has earnings and profits. Since Y has $120,000 of earnings and profits, the entire distribution of $62,000 to A is a dividend.

(ii) *Parent-subsidiary corporations.* If a corporation (the acquiring corporation) purchases the stock of another corpora-

---

107 I.R.C. § 304(b)(2)(A).
108 The 80 shares of X stock owned by Y are attributed to Y's shareholders according to their percentage interest in the ownership of Y. I.R.C. §§ 304(b)(1), and 318(a)(2)(C). Thus, A is deemed to own 50% of the 80 shares of X held by Y.
109 § 318(a)(2)(C).

tion (the issuing corporation), from a shareholder of the issuing corporation, and the issuing corporation controls[110] the acquiring corporation, the purchase is treated as a distribution in redemption of the stock of the issuing corporation.[111] Thus, for purposes of determining whether the "redemption" qualifies as a purchase under § 302(b), the stock position of the issuing corporation controls.[112] If the distribution to the shareholder is deemed a section 301 distribution, the amount of that distribution which is a dividend is determined as if the amount distributed to the shareholder were instead distributed by the acquiring corporation to the issuing corporation and then distributed to the shareholder from the issuing corporation.[113] Indeed, the Service has ruled that in these circumstances the parent corporation has received a constructive dividend from its subsidiary in an amount equal to the payment made for the parent's stock.[114] The apparent effect of that provision is to impose dividend treatment in virtually all cases where a subsidiary acquires its parent's stock and § 301 is applicable, since the earnings and profits of the parent corporation will determine whether the distribution was a dividend, and the earnings and profits of the parent corporation will be increased by the amount of the distribution which is constructively paid to the parent.[115]

It should be noted that an exchange with a corporation may qualify under both § 351[116] and § 304. For example, *A*, an individual, owned 100% of the stock of both the *X* Corporation and the *Y* Corporation, both of which have large amounts of earnings and profits. *A* transferred *Y* stock to *X* in exchange for *X* stock plus boot of $20,000, and *A* realized a gain of $23,000 on the exchange. Under § 351(b), the amount of gain recognized by *A* is limited to the amount of boot he received—*i.e.*, $20,000, and the $20,000 *recognized* gain would be taxed at capital gains rates. But, under § 304,

---

110 For the definition of "control," *see* note 105 *supra*.
111 I.R.C. § 304(a)(2).
112 I.R.C. § 304(b)(1).
113 I.R.C. § 304(b)(2)(B).
114 Rev. Rul. 69-261, I.R.B. 1969-21, p. 5.
115 It would appear that the only escape from dividend treatment is when the parent corporation has a significant operating deficit in the year of distribution and had no accumulated earnings and profits.
116 *See* Chapter V *infra*.

the $20,000 in boot would be taxed as ordinary income. The Sixth Circuit and the Tax Court have held that § 351 takes precedence over § 304 and therefore that the gain on the exchange is treated as capital gains.[117] The apparent result of elevating § 351 over § 304 is to create a sizable loophole, and if the judiciary does not repudiate this rule, it is likely that the Treasury will seek Congressional action.

(e) Distribution in redemption of stock which was included within the gross estate of a decedent for federal estate tax purposes. In order to assist the representatives of a decedent's estate to satisfy obligations incurred on account of the decedent's death, Congress has granted the redemption of corporate stock which was included in a decedent's gross estate a special exemption from dividend treatment, provided that certain statutory requisites are satisfied.[118] The provisions of § 303 are primarily of importance to owners of stock of a closely held corporation and may permit the withdrawal of funds from such corporation upon the death of a stockholder without causing taxable dividends to the recipient.

Section 303 provides that a corporation's redemption of stock which was included in a decedent's gross estate for federal estate tax purposes will be deemed a distribution in full payment of the stock (and thus excluded from § 301) in the following circumstances:

(i) The estate tax value of the stock of the redeeming corporation that is included in the decedent's gross estate is either greater than 35% of the value of the decedent's gross

---

117 Commissioner v. Stickney, 399 F.2d 828 (C.A. 6 1968). The history of *Stickney* is interesting. After the initial trial, the Tax Court held that § 351 takes precedence over § 304. Henry McK. Haserot, 41 T.C. 562 (1964). On the first appeal, the Sixth Circuit declined to resolve that issue and remanded the case to the Tax Court for a determination of whether the distribution was essentially equivalent to a dividend. Commissioner v. Haserot, 355 F.2d 200 (C.A. 6 1965). On remand, the Tax Court found that the distribution was essentially equivalent to a dividend, but the Court declined to reexamine its prior decision on the priority of § 351. (46 T.C. 864 (1966)). Two tax court judges dissented and stated that § 304 should control. On appeal *sub nom Stickney*, the Sixth Circuit held that § 351 controlled and thus affirmed the original Tax Court decision.

118 I.R.C. § 303.

estate, or alternatively is greater than 50% of the value of the decedent's taxable estate.[119] Under § 303(b)(2)(B), where stocks of two or more corporations were included in the decedent's gross estate, the value of the stocks of those several corporations may be combined in determining whether the 35%-50% test is satisfied, provided however, that only the stock of a corporation which had more than 75% of the value of its outstanding stock included in the decedent's gross estate can be included in the aggregate group.[120] If 75% or less of the value of the outstanding stock of a corporation is included in the decedent's gross estate, the value of that stock cannot be aggregated with the value of the stock of other corporations for the purpose of complying with the 35-50% test.

(ii) Section 303 applies only to distributions made in redemption of the said stock within either:

(aa) The period between the decedent's death and the 90th day after the expiration of the period of limitations provided by § 6501(a) for the assessment of the federal estate tax;[121] or

(bb) If a petition for redetermination of an estate tax deficiency is filed with the Tax Court, and if the Tax Court case constitutes a bona fide dispute in contrast to a suit filed solely to extend the time period in which payments can be made under the protection of § 303,[122] the distribution may be made during the period between the decedent's death and the 60th day after the Tax

---

119 I.R.C. § 2051 defines "taxable estate." The taxable estate alternative can be particularly helpful where the decedent's estate is entitled to marital or charitable deductions.

120 For purposes of determining whether stock included in the decedent's stock satisfies the 75% test, no attribution rules are applicable. Estate of Byrd v. Commissioner, 388 F.2d 223 (C.A. 5 1967).

121 The period of limitation in § 6501(a) runs for three years after the estate tax return was filed, and since the estate tax return is due 15 months after the decedent's death (§ 6075(a)), the corporation has approximately 4½ years to make distribution. The time period for a corporate distribution under § 303 is not shortened when the decedent's estate tax return is filed early because for purposes of computing the period of limitations under § 6501(b)(1), the return is deemed filed on the last permissible day. Rev. Rul. 69-47, I.R.B. 1969-6, p. 16.

122 Treas. Reg. § 1.303-2(e).

Court's decision becomes final.[123] It is noteworthy that only Tax Court litigation can extend the permissible time period; and, consequently, refund suits in the District Court or the Court of Claims have no effect on this period of limitations.

(iii) The maximum amount of corporate distributions that can be excluded from dividend treatment under § 303 is the sum of the death taxes (both federal and state) imposed on account of the decedent's death, and the funeral and administrative expenses which are allowable as estate tax deductions under § 2053 (or § 2106 if the decedent was not a resident and was not a citizen of the United States). While death taxes and funeral and administrative expenses establish the upper limit of the amount of distribution that can be protected by § 303, the amounts received in redemption of the stock need not actually be expended in payment of such taxes and expenses.

Normally, section 303 redemptions will be made of stock held by the decedent's estate, but the dividend exemption provided by § 303 is not limited to such stock. Any redeemed stock which was included in the decedent's gross estate may be covered by § 303 if the terms of that section are satisfied. Thus, the donee of stock which was included in the decedent's gross estate because it was transferred in contemplation of death may use § 303.[124] Also, heirs, legatees, appointees, takers in default of an unexercised general power of appointment, and a trustee of a trust created by the decedent may all use § 303, when applicable.[125] However, there may be shareholders whose stock is redeemed in compliance with § 302(b)(2) or (b)(3) and therefore do not need the protection of § 303; but if the redeemed stock was included in decedent's gross estate and otherwise qualified for § 303 treat-

---

123 The question of when a Tax Court decision becomes final has been considered in tax accrual accounting cases. *E.g.*, Commissioner v. Fifth Ave. Coach Lines, 281 F.2d 556 (C.A. 2 1960), *cert. denied*, 366 U.S. 964 (1961). Generally, the decision will not become final until all appeals have been completed and time to appeal further or seek certiorari has expired.
124 Treas. Reg. § 1.303-2(f).
125 *Id.* If the amount of redemptions of section 303 stock exceeds the allowable ceiling, the method of allocating section 303 benefits among the shareholders is unresolved. *See* BULLETIN OF THE SECTION OF TAXATION (ABA), p. 244 (Fall, 1967).

ment, the amount distributed in payment for that stock will be charged against the maximum amount permitted to be distributed under § 303.[126]

Section 303 is not applicable to redemptions of stock from persons who acquired the decedent's stock by gift or purchase from third parties; nor is § 303 applicable to redemptions of stock from shareholders who received the stock in satisfaction of a specific monetary bequest[127] since they are deemed to have acquired the stock by purchase rather than by bequest. Thus, according to the Regulations, stock distributed by the decedent's estate to the decedent's widow, or to a marital trust in satisfaction of a marital deduction pecuniary formula clause, cannot be redeemed under § 303.[128] Consequently, if the redemption of such stock is contemplated, it would be prudent to redeem the stock from the estate, and then have the estate distribute the proceeds to the widow or to the marital trust.

Where a shareholder receives "new stock" in a corporation, the basis of which is determined by reference to the basis of "old stock" which was included in a decedent's estate and which qualified for redemption under § 303, then the "new stock" may also be redeemed under § 303.[129] Moreover, even if this new stock is "section 306 stock,"[130] § 303 has priority and the redemption will not be treated as a dividend to the extent that § 303 is applicable.[131]

---

126 Treas. Reg. § 1.303-2 (f).

127 *Id.*

128 *Id. But see* United States v. Lake, 406 F.2d 941 (C.A. 5 1969) in which the court refused to apply Treas. Reg. § 1.303-2(f) because the redemption of stock from the decedent's daughter was consistent with the statutory purpose of § 303 even though she did not acquire the redeemed stock directly from the decedent but from a testamentary trust of which she was the beneficiary. *See also* Meyer, *Redemption of Stock in the Close Corporation to Pay Death Taxes,* 27 N.Y.U. TAX INST. 401, 403-405 (1969).

129 I.R.C. § 303(c).

130 *See* pp. 51-58 *infra* for a discussion of section 306 stock.

131 Treas. Reg. § 1.303-2(d). Normally, there will be no problem with § 306 on redemption of shares included within a decedent's estate because such stock will lose its § 306 taint upon the decedent's death. Section 306(c). However, if the corporation recapitalizes after the decedent's death, and the decedent's estate receives a distribution of preferred stock, such stock may be § 306 stock, and the provisions of § 303 could be useful in effecting its redemption.

The corporation may not have sufficient funds available to redeem the stock of a deceased shareholder within the time permitted by § 303.[132] In such event the corporation may be permitted to redeem a portion of the stock by distributing to the shareholder, within the statutory period, personal promissory notes of the corporation, even though the corporation's payment of such notes will be made after the statutory period.[133] In so using corporate notes, maximum caution should be exercised to insure that the distributed "notes" do not constitute equity interests in the corporation (such as hybrid stock), since subsequent payment on the notes may have dire tax consequences if the "notes" are classified as equity interests.[134] Examples of appropriate steps are: the corporation should not establish an overbalanced debt-capital ratio; the maturity date of the notes should be less than five years from the date of issue; the notes should bear reasonable interest; and the notes should not be subordinated to the claims of creditors. Of course, business considerations may outweigh tax caution in determining the attributes of the corporate notes.

It is worth emphasizing that while the rationale for enacting § 303 (and its predecessors) was to provide liquidity for an estate, the operation of § 303 is not limited to circumstances in which liquidity is a problem. Section 303 may be employed to advantage even though the estate has sufficient liquid assets. Moreover, it is not required that the proceeds from a redemption under § 303 actually be used to pay death taxes or administrative and funeral expenses. Consequently, where a significant portion of the value of a decedent's estate is comprised of stock of a

---

132 If a corporation attempts to retain liquid assets in order to fund a contemplated purchase of a shareholder's stock on his death, the corporation may incur a surtax liability under the accumulated earnings tax provisions (§ 531 *et seq.*). *See* Chapter IV *infra.*

133 Rev. Rul. 65-289, 1965-2 CUM. BULL. 86; and Rev. Rul. 67-425, 1967-2 CUM. BULL. 134.

134 For a further discussion of this issue, *see* Chapter IV *infra.* The Service will not rule on whether a redemption qualifies under § 302(b), and therefore presumably will not rule on § 303 either, where the redeemed stock is held as security or in escrow for the payment of corporate notes if there is a possibility that the stock will be returned to the shareholder. Rev. Proc. 69-6 (Sec. 3.01-5), I.R.B. 1969-1, p. 29. The Service has further stated that *ordinarily* it will not rule on the tax effect of a redemption where payment is made in corporate notes payable over a period of time in excess of 15 years. Rev. Proc. 69-6 (Sec. 4.01-3), I.R.B. 1969-1, p. 31.

closely held corporation, careful consideration[135] (both during the decedent's life and after his demise) should be given to the use of § 303. If there is a desire to withdraw funds from a corporation, § 303 provides a relatively painless vehicle.[136] As Dean Willard Pedrick[137] commented in a speech a few years ago, "Section 303 should not be lightly disregarded; it is literally a once in a lifetime opportunity."

In conjunction with § 303, consideration should also be given to those provisions of the Code that permit estate taxes to be paid over a period of years.[138] For a discussion of the interplay between § 303 and one of the deferred tax payment provisions (§ 6166), see Portfolio #91 "Corporate Stock Redemption—Section 303," *Tax Management* (BNA) pp. A31-A33.

(f) Redemption of the entirety of one shareholder's stock as a dividend to the surviving shareholders. A corporation's redemption of the entirety of one shareholder's stock of that corporation will not usually constitute a constructive dividend to the surviving shareholders. See Rev. Rul. 58-614, 1958-2 C.B. 920; and *Holsey v. Commissioner*, 258 F.2d 865 (C.A. 3 1958). See also Rev. Rul. 59-286, 1959-2 C.B. 103. However, in planning for a corporate redemption, care should be taken that the surviving shareholders have no *obligation* to purchase the stock which the corporation plans to redeem; for if they are so obligated, the redemption might be construed as a payment by the corporation in satisfaction of the surviving shareholder's debts, and consequently the payment would constitute a constructive dividend to them. *Wall v. United States*, 164 F.2d 462 (C.A. 4 1947). For a discussion of the potential tax problems of the surviving shareholders, see Bittker and Eustice, *Federal Income Taxation of Corporations and Shareholders* (2d ed., 1966), § 7.25 pp. 294-300.

---

135 For a discussion of planning techniques employing § 303, *see* Chapter VI *infra*.

136 Since the basis of the redeemed stock will be equal to its estate tax value (§ 1014), there will frequently be little or no gain recognized on a § 303 redemption, and the gain that is recognized will constitute capital gains.

137 Dean of the Arizona State College of Law. The author's quotation of Dean Pedrick's statement is based on his recollection of several years' vintage, and is therefore more of a paraphrase than a direct quotation.

138 Particularly, note I.R.C. § 6166, which sets objective standards for its use similar but not identical to those contained in § 303.

(g) Collapsible corporations. When an individual shareholder receives property from a corporation in redemption of his stock under § 302(a) or § 303, or in a partial liquidation under § 346, or a complete liquidation under § 331,[139] the shareholder will usually recognize capital gain in the amount that the fair market value of the property he receives exceeds his basis in the corporation's stock. Typically, the corporation will recognize no income,[140] and the noncorporate shareholder's basis in the distributed property will equal its fair market value. As a consequence of these results, the tax avoidance device of a "collapsible corporation" was developed. The collapsible corporation is formed to produce or purchase an asset, the sale or exploitation of which would create ordinary income, so that the individual shareholders may utilize the corporate entity and the rules of corporate taxation to convert the characterization of the income realized from such assets from ordinary income into capital gains.

The following examples illustrate the manner in which a corporation could be employed for collapsible purposes.

> **Ex. (1)** *A*, an individual, owns a large tract of land which he plans to subdivide, construct homes on each plot, and then sell to customers. If *A* were to proceed with that plan, the gain recognized by him on the sale of each home would be treated as ordinary income. Instead, *A* forms the *X* Corporation and contributes the tract of land to *X* in exchange for *X*'s stock. This is a tax-free exchange under § 351. The corporation then subdivides the tract and constructs the homes. The resulting value of the improved property will usually be substantially in excess of the costs of subdividing and construction plus the basis of the land. The individual shareholder *A* might then cause the complete liquidation of *X*, recognize capital gains income on the difference between the fair market value of the property and his basis in *X*'s stock, and thereby acquire a basis in the improved property equal to its fair market value. The subsequent sale of the properties by *A* for a price equal to their respective fair market values at the date of liquidation will not cause *A* to recognize any gross income since the amount realized will equal his basis. Thus, *A* will have converted the realized gain from the

---

139 *See* pp. 58-59 *infra.*
140 *See* Chapter II *infra.*

properties from ordinary income into long-term capital gains.

Ex. (2) *B*, *C* and *D* are famous movie personalities. They form the *Y* Corporation to produce a film. *Y* produces a film starring *B*, *C* and *D*, who work for *Y* for relatively low compensation. The rental of the film will produce ordinary income. Consequently, *Y* is liquidated, the film is distributed to *B*, *C* and *D* as tenants in common, and they each recognize capital gains in an amount equal to the difference of the value of their respective share of the film and their basis in their *Y* stock. *B*, *C* and *D* then rent the film to various exhibitors or distributors and depreciate their stepped-up basis over the useful life of the film. Thus, their depreciation allowance (which in large part stems from the capital gains recognized by them) offsets the rental income and constitutes a conversion of ordinary income into capital gains.

An alternative device for *B*, *C* and *D* would be to sell their *Y* stock to *E* for an amount equal to the fair market value of the film. *B*, *C* and *D* would recognize capital gains on the sale of their *Y* stock, *E* could then liquidate the *Y* Corporation without recognizing gain since his basis in the *Y* stock will be equal to the fair market value of the film. *E* can then rent the film and depreciate his basis.

These transactions and similar arrangements are subject to attack by the Commissioner as violative of such principles as sham transactions and assignment of income and analogous concepts. However, after several unsuccessful efforts in that direction,[141] the Treasury sought a statutory resolution to this problem. Accordingly, in 1950, Congress added § 117(m) to the Internal Revenue Code of 1939, and that provision, with significant modifications, was adopted as § 341 of the 1954 Code.

Where § 341 is applicable so that a corporation is treated as collapsible, gain recognized by a shareholder from (i) the sale or exchange of his stock of such corporation, or (ii) a distribution in partial or complete liquidation of the corporation, or (iii) a

---

141 Pat O'Brien, 25 T.C. 376 (1955), Acq. 1957-1 C.B. 4; Commissioner v. Gross, 236 F.2d 612 (C.A. 2 1956); and Herbert v. Riddell, 103 F. Supp. 369 (S.D. Calif. 1952). *See* Farer, *Corporate Liquidations: Transmuting Ordinary Income Into Capital Gains,* 75 HARV. L. REV. 527 (1962).

distribution made by such corporation in excess of its earnings and profits and in excess of the shareholder's basis which is treated under § 301(c)(3)(A) as gain from the sale of such stock,[142] will be treated as ordinary income to the extent that such gain would otherwise have been treated as long-term capital gain.[143]

The statutory definition of a collapsible corporation is complex and there are many technical, complex exceptions to collapsible treatment, some of which remove a corporation from the collapsible category and some of which isolate a single shareholder from recognition of ordinary income without disturbing the statutory treatment of other shareholders. This book merely provides a skeletal discussion of the subject; and where there is a possibility of collapsible treatment, the reader should examine writings which deal with this subject in greater detail.[144] The reader should bear in mind that however great was the need for a solution to the collapsible corporation loophole, § 341 was the product of Congressional overreaction; and many legitimate corporate enterprises have been caught in the broad net of § 341 to the surprise and grief of unwary shareholders. The drastic consequences of collapsible treatment and the breadth of its coverage constitute a strong argument for caution and conservative planning.

A collapsible corporation is defined in § 341(b) as a corporation that is formed or availed of:

(i) Principally for the manufacture, construction or production of property; or for the purchase of certain assets, hereinafter referred to as "section 341 assets";

(ii) With a view to (a) a sale, liquidation or distribution be-

---

142 I.R.C. § 341(a). Peculiarly, the statute does not provide explicit coverage for a redemption of a shareholder's stock under § 302(a); but it is most unlikely that such redemptions would be deemed to be outside the scope of § 341.

143 Section 341 has no effect on short-term capital gains recognized by a shareholder. Treas. Reg. § 1.341-4(a).

144 *E.g.,* Bittker and Eustice, *Collapsible Corporations In a Nutshell,* 22 TAX L. REV. 127 (1967); Portfolio, 29-2nd Tax Management, *Collapsible Corporations—General Coverage;* Portfolio, 49 Tax Management, *Collapsible Corporations—Special Exceptions;* Hall, *The Consenting Collapsible Corporation—Section 341(f) of the Internal Revenue Code of 1954,* 12 U.C.L.A. L. REV. 1365 (1965); and Rosenzweig, *Selling or Liquidating a Service Business: Special Problems,* 26 N.Y.U. TAX INST. 1001, 1002-1007 (1968).

fore the corporation has realized a substantial part of the taxable income to be derived from the property and (b) a realization by the shareholders of the gain attributable to the property. The term "section 341 assets" includes inventory property, stock in trade, property held primarily for sale to customers, unrealized receivables or fees, and certain section 1231(b) property.[145] However, property held for a period of three years or more after the completion of the manufacture, construction, production or purchase of property is not a section 341 asset.[146] Note that there is no limitation on the type of property to be manufactured, constructed or produced by a collapsible corporation, only the property to be purchased is limited to section 341 assets.

Since virtually all business corporations are formed or availed of principally for the production, construction or manufacture of property or the purchase of section 341 assets, the question of whether the requisite view exists is frequently crucial. According to the Regulations, the view exists if persons in a position to determine the corporation's policies contemplated that there be a sale, liquidation or distribution before the corporation has realized a substantial part of the gain from the property irrespective of whether such action was contemplated unconditionally, conditionally or merely as a recognized possibility.[147] Obviously, this is a very broad standard. The Regulations also specify that the collapsible view must exist at some time during construction, manufacture, production or purchase of the collapsible property.[148] Thus, if the collapsible view first arises after the collapsible activity is completed (unless the view arises from circumstances which could reasonably have been anticipated), then § 341(b) does not apply. However, several courts have stated that the Treasury's interpretation is too restrictive from the Government's viewpoint and that the requisite view may exist at any time when the corporation is "availed of" for the proscribed pur-

---

145 I.R.C. § 341(b)(3). Section 1231(b) property includes most depreciable property and real estate used in a trade or business. Section 341(b)(3) excludes certain section 1231(b) assets from its reach.
146 I.R.C. § 1223 is used to determine whether the three-year holding period has been satisfied.
147 Treas. Reg. § 1.341-2(a)(2).
148 Treas. Reg. § 1.341-2(a)(3).

poses.[149] Nevertheless, the Treasury has not changed its Regulations. If the requisite view is held by persons in a position to determine corporate policies, a particular shareholder cannot obtain exclusion because he was not a shareholder at that time or did not share in the proscribed view.[150] If the sale or liquidation is caused by unforeseen and nontax related circumstances, such as the illness of a shareholder, the collapsible provisions do not apply.[151]

Section 341 is applicable only if the liquidation, distribution or sale occurs "before the realization by the corporation manufacturing, constructing, producing or purchasing the property of a substantial part of the taxable income to be derived from the property."[152] This limitation raises two questions: (i) what percentage of income is substantial, and (ii) whether the determination of "substantial" is made according to the percentage of income realized by the corporation at the date on which the shareholder's gain is recognized, or according to the percentage of unrealized potential income at that date. Notwithstanding the clear statutory reference to income realized by the corporation, the Regulations state that the proper test is whether a substantial percentage of the income to be derived from the property has not been realized at the pertinent date.[153] The courts are divided in construing the statute—the Fifth Circuit, the Tenth Circuit and the Tax Court rely on the percentage of income realized by the corporation and the Third Circuit relies on the percentage of unrealized income.[154]

> **Ex.** The X Corporation is formed by A and B for the purpose of subdividing a tract of land, constructing homes thereon, and selling the homes. The X Corpora-

---

149 *E.g.,* Glickman v. Commissioner, 256 F.2d 108 (C.A. 2 1958). *Contra,* Jacobson v. Commissioner, 281 F.2d 703 (C.A. 3 1960).
150 Treas. Reg. § 1.341-2(a)(2).
151 Commissioner v. Solow, 333 F.2d 76 (C.A. 2 1964), *affirming* ¶ 63,087 P-H Memo T.C.
152 I.R.C. § 341(b)(1)(A).
153 Treas. Reg. § 1.341-2(a)(4), and § 1.341-5(c)(2).
154 *Compare* Commissioner v. Kelley, 293 F.2d 904 (C.A. 5 1961), *affirming* 32 T.C. 135 (realization of ⅓ of income was deemed sufficient to bar collapsible treatment); and Commissioner v. Zongker, 334 F.2d 44 (C.A. 10 1964) (realization of 34% of income was sufficient); *with* Abbott v. Commissioner, 258 F.2d 537 (C.A. 3 1958). The Service will not follow the decision in *Kelley.* Rev. Rul. 62-12, 1962-1 C.B. 321.

tion constructs the homes; and after selling one-third of the homes and realizing one-third of the potential income from the sale of the tract, the X Corporation is completely liquidated. Assuming the requisite view, the question of whether X was a collapsible corporation may turn on whether it complied with the substantial realization test. Under the Regulations and the position adopted by the Third Circuit, the percentage of unrealized income (⅔) is substantial and the corporation is deemed collapsible. Under the view of the Fifth and Tenth Circuits and the Tax Court, the percentage of realized income (⅓) is substantial and may well exclude X and its shareholders from collapsible treatment.[155]

The effect of a collapsible corporation's sale of its assets pursuant to a liquidation under § 337 is described below in connection with the discussion of the latter section.

Where the amount (both in quality and value) of collapsible property held by a corporation is not in excess of the amount which is normal for its business activities or normal for the purposes of an orderly liquidation if it is in the process of liquidation, and if the corporation has a substantial prior business history involving the use of such property, the corporation will usually not be treated as collapsible.[156]

In addition to the statutory definition of a collapsible corporation in § 341(b), § 341(c) creates a rebuttable presumption that a corporation is collapsible if the fair market value of its "section 341 assets" is (a) 50% or more of the fair market value of its total assets and (b) 120% or more of the adjusted basis of such section 341 assets. For this purpose cash, stock and certain securities and other obligations are disregarded in determining the corporation's total assets. The inapplicability of § 341(c) does not give rise to a presumption that the corporation is not collapsible.

The last three subsections of § 341 provide relief from the

---

155 As to the meaning of "substantial," the realization of 17% was not deemed a substantial part (Heft v. Commissioner, 294 F.2d 795 (C.A. 5 1961)); and the realization of slightly less than 10% of anticipated lease rentals was not deemed substantial. Max N. Tobias, 40 T.C. 84 (1963). As indicated in note 154 above, 33% and 34% of income have been deemed substantial.
156 Treas. Reg. § 1.341-5(c).

harsh treatment of that section. Section 341(d) provides three separate exceptions to collapsible treatment: First, it permits capital gains treatment for a shareholder who at no time after the commencement of the manufacture, construction, production or purchase of the collapsible property either (i) owned or was deemed to have owned more than 5% in value of the outstanding stock of the corporation, or (ii) owned stock that was attributed to another shareholder who then owned or was considered to own more than 5% of the outstanding stock;[157] second, § 341 does not apply to gain recognized during a taxable year where 30% or more of such gain is attributable to noncollapsible property; and third, § 341(a) does not apply to gain realized more than three years after the completion of the manufacture, construction, production or purchase of the collapsible property. The applicability of the exceptions contained in § 341(d) is subject to technical rules, and they should be studied carefully.[158]

Prior to 1958, the operation of § 341 caused shareholders to recognize ordinary income in circumstances where the shareholders would have been entitled to capital gains treatment had they conducted the enterprise in their individual capacities without utilizing a corporation.[159] This demonstrated that § 341 was a case of overkill—*i.e.*, it went beyond preventing the conversion of ordinary income into capital gains and actually served to convert capital gains into ordinary income. In order to ameliorate that consequence, in 1958 Congress added the extremely complex subsection (e) to § 341.

Section 341(e) can apply in four situations: (1) sale or exchanges of stock by a shareholder (other than sales or exchanges of stock to the issuing corporation or to certain related persons defined in the statute); (2) certain distributions in complete liquidation of a corporation pursuant to § 337; (3) certain complete liquidation for which nonrecognition treatment is pro-

---

157 For purposes of § 341(d), the ownership of stock is determined under the constructive ownership rules of I.R.C. § 544 except that the definition of an individual's family is expanded to include the individual's brothers and sisters and their spouses, and also includes spouses of the individual's lineal descendants.

158 *See* Rev. Rul. 65-184, 1965-2 C.B. 91 for an example of the complexity of these exceptions.

159 *See* Braunstein v. Commissioner, 374 U.S. 65 (1963).

vided under § 333; and (4) certain sales or exchanges of property by the corporation under the nonrecognition provisions of § 337. Speaking very generally, § 341(e) will preclude ordinary income treatment and the corporation's recognition of income, in the above four situations, if the amount of unrealized appreciation of those assets of the corporation that would produce ordinary income when sold either by the corporation or by any shareholder holding more than 20% of its stock (or for purposes of a liquidation under § 333, more than 5% of its stock) is no greater than 15% of the corporation's net worth. This general standard, however, is subject to numerous modifications and technical rules as to its application to individual shareholders and to each of the four situations described above.

The complexity of the subsection (e) rule and the fact that its applicability depends upon the resolution of factual issues (*e.g.*, whether either the corporation or any more than 20% shareholder is a dealer in property held by the corporation) will likely inhibit reliance on this provision for planning purposes. Consequently, the *in terrorem* effect of § 341 on legitimate corporate enterprises has probably not been resolved by the adoption of subsection (e).

The nonapplicability of § 341(e) is not to be taken into account in determining whether a corporation is collapsible under the statutory definition of § 341(b).

An additional relief from § 341(a) is provided by § 341(f). Again, speaking very generally, § 341(f) permits a shareholder to sell his stock without fear of having to recognize the gain as ordinary income under § 341(a) if the corporation consents to recognize gain on its real estate and noncapital assets when it disposes of them in a transaction that would otherwise qualify for nonrecognition of gain. The property of the corporations which is marked for gain under this subsection is sometimes referred to as "section 341(f) assets." A consent under § 341(f) does not depend upon showing that the corporation is in fact a collapsible corporation; and if the consent is filed, it cannot be repudiated later because the corporation was not collapsible and therefore the election was unnecessary.

3. Distributions of stock, securities or stock rights of the distributing corporation

(a) **Distribution of stock or stock rights.** A corporation's distribution, with respect to its stock, of its own stock or stock rights to its own shareholders normally will not be included in the gross income of the shareholders.[160] This exclusion from gross income applies whether the distributed stock is preferred or common stock and whether the stock is issued with respect to common or preferred stock. However, under I.R.C. § 306, stock which is so distributed, other than common stock issued with respect to common stock, may cause special consequences upon its disposition by the shareholder.[161] There are only two circumstances[162] in which the corporation's distribution, with respect to its stock, of stock or stock rights will not be excluded from the shareholder's gross income:

(i) Where the distribution is made in discharge of preference dividends for the taxable year of the corporation in which the distribution is made or for the preceding taxable year; or

(ii) Where the distributee was given an election to have the distributions made either (1) in property or (2) in the stock of the corporation (or in rights to acquire the stock); for this purpose it does not matter whether the distributee's election is exercised or exercisable before or after the declaration of the distribution.

Prior to 1969, these two exceptions to tax-free treatment created very few difficulties. However, in 1969, the Regulations promulgated under § 305 were amended so as to broaden substantially the interpretation of these two exceptions where a corporation has more than one class of stock outstanding.

Under the revised Regulations, where a corporation has more than one class of stock outstanding and where one class is entitled to periodic distributions of stock or stock rights, the class

---

160 I.R.C. § 305(a). While there may be constitutional limitations on the power of Congress to tax stock dividends (Eisner v. Macomber, 252 U.S. 189 (1920)), it is clear that Congress is empowered to tax some kind of stock dividends (*e.g.*, disproportionate dividends), and their decision not to do so stems from a determination of tax policy rather than a constitutional restriction.
161 *See* pp. 51-58 *infra.*
162 I.R.C. § 305(b).

of stock entitled to the periodic distribution is deemed preferred, and therefore the distribution of stock or stock rights with respect to that "preferred" stock is taxable as made in discharge of preference dividends.[163] Where one class of common stock is convertible into another class at an established rate of conversion which increases periodically in predetermined increments, each of the periodic increments constitutes a distribution of stock rights to the shareholders of the convertible stock, and this "distribution" is *not* excluded from tax under § 305.[164] Where the conversion ratio is required to be reduced to reflect cash or property dividends paid to the shareholders of the convertible stock, the shareholders of the other stock are deemed to have received a distribution of stock reflecting their increased equity in the corporation, and this distribution is *not* excluded from tax by § 305.[165] The following examples paraphrased from the revised Regulations illustrate the above provisions:

Ex. (1) Corporation Y, a calendar year taxpayer, has two classes of stock outstanding. Class B stock can be converted at the option of the holder into Class A stock. The conversion ratio in the year 1969 is one share of Class A for each share of Class B. However, in each calendar year after 1969, the ratio of Class A convertible into Class B increases 5%. Thus, in 1970, one share of Class B can be converted into 1.05 shares of Class A; and in 1971, one share of B can be converted into 1.10 shares of A. Since this annual increment in conversion ratio is deemed a distribution of stock rights, Class B stock is deemed preferred stock (*i.e.*, stock entitled to periodic distributions of stock or stock rights), and the 5% annual increments are taxed to the shareholders of the Class B stock, as a distribution and discharge of a preferential dividend.

Ex. (2) X Corporation has outstanding Class A and Class B stock. The terms of the Class B stock require that one share of Class A stock be distributed annually with respect to each 20 shares of Class B stock.

---

163 Treas, Reg. § 1.305-3(b)(1). There are exceptions to this strict rule for certain transactions involving convertible stock and stock exchanged for the assets or stock of another corporation. Treas. Reg. § 1.305-3(b)(3) and (4).
164 Treas. Reg. § 1.305-3(b)(2), Ex. (2).
165 Treas. Reg. § 1.305-2(b)(2), Ex. (4).

The B stock is deemed preferred stock, and the annual distribution of A stock is taxed as a distribution in discharge of a preferential dividend.

Ex. (3) Corporation *Z* has two classes of stock outstanding. Each share of Class B is convertible into one share of Class A; however, the ratio is reduced under a formula to reflect cash dividends paid to the shareholders of Class B stock. Thus, where a $1 cash dividend is paid on the Class B stock, the number of shares of Class A stock obtainable on conversion of the B stock is reduced accordingly. The reduction of this ratio increases the equity interest of the A stock in the corporation and therefore is treated as a stock distribution to the shareholders of the A stock. The Regulations state that this distribution will be taxable,[166] presumably because the shareholders of the A stock are receiving a stock distribution rather than the cash distribution made on the B stock as a result of their option not to exchange A stock for B under Section 1036. However, it is not clear where the holders of A stock would derive the power to exchange it for B stock.

The scope of the election exception under the revised Regulations is extremely broad. The Regulations suggest that whenever a corporation has two types of common stock outstanding, and a distribution is made in money or property with respect to the other type, the shareholders have made an election "by virtue of the existence of the two types of common stock,"[167] either of which could have been exchanged tax-free for the other under the protection of Section 1036. The Regulations do not discuss whether the feasibility of such an exchange must be taken into account. The validity of the revised Regulations is questionable,[168] and it appears that the Treasury has requested the adoption of legislation similar to the amendments made to the Regulations,[169] which does indicate some lack of confidence. Nevertheless, it would be prudent to avoid making stock dividends within the ambit of the Regulations if it is desired that the stock

---

166 *Id.*
167 Treas. Reg. § 1.305-2(b)(1).
168 *See* Levin, *New 305 Regs. limit tax advantages of 2-class common stock, but alternatives exist,* 30 J. TAXATION 2, 4-5 (1969).
169 *See* The Wall Street Journal (April 23, 1969), p. 3.

dividends be excluded from gross income under § 305(a).[170]

The new amendments to the Regulations under § 305 do provide a grace period. The new provisions of the Regulations adopted by the 1969 amendments do not apply to distributions made on or before December 31, 1969, on account of stock which was either outstanding or was required to be issued on September 7, 1968.[171] Moreover, the new provisions do not apply to any distributions made on or before December 31, 1968.[172]

If there is an election or a discharge of preference dividends within the meaning of § 305(b), the distribution to the shareholder of the stock or stock rights will constitute a distribution under § 301 to the extent of the fair market value of such distributed stock or stock rights.[173] In that event, the earnings and profits of the corporation will be reduced by an amount equal to the fair market value of the distributed stock or stock rights that are treated as income to the shareholder.[174]

> **Ex. (1)** The total outstanding stock of X Corporation is 100 shares of common stock. A owns 50 shares and B owns 50 shares. The X Corporation declares a stock dividend[175] of one share of $50 par preferred stock for each outstanding share of common. Neither the 50 shares of preferred stock of X distributed to A nor the 50 shares distributed to B are included in the gross income of A or B.[176]

> **Ex. (2)** Assuming the same facts as in Example (1) except that A and B were each given an option by the X Corporation to receive either the 50 shares of $50 par preferred stock or $2,500 cash, and both A and B elected to take the preferred stock. Then, there would be a section 301 distribution in an amount equal to the fair market value of the preferred stock, and the earnings and profits of the X Corporation would be re-

---

170 *See* Levin, *New 305 Regs. limit tax advantages of 2-class common stock, but alternatives exist,* 30 J. TAXATION 2 (1969).
171 Treas. Reg. § 1.305-2(b)(3)(ii); and Treas. Reg. § 1.305-3(b)(5)(ii).
172 Treas. Reg. § 1.305-2(b)(3)(i); and Treas. Reg. § 1.305-3(b)(5)(i).
173 Treas. Reg. § 1.301-1(d). I.R.C. § 305(b).
174 Treas. Reg. § 1.312-1(d).
175 The "stock dividend" referred to in this example is a dividend for corporate law purposes in contrast to a dividend for tax purposes.
176 But upon the subsequent disposition of the preferred stock, A and B must consider the effect of I.R.C. § 306.

duced by an amount equal to the fair market value of the 100 shares of preferred stock.

Ex. (3) The total outstanding stock of X Corporation is 100 shares of common stock and 10 shares of preferred stock. A is the owner of 5 shares of preferred. Each share of preferred stock when issued on September 9, 1969, was convertible into 5 shares of common. At the expiration of each year, the conversion ratio is automatically increased by one share of common for each share of preferred. According to the 1969 amendment to the Regulations, on September 8, 1970, when A's preferred stock is convertible into 5 additional shares of X common stock, A received a section 301 distribution equal to the fair market value of 5 shares of X's common stock.

Ex. (4) C is the president of the Y Corporation, but C owns no stock of Y. Y distributes to C 1000 shares of its stock having a fair market value of $10,000. C has taxable income of $10,000 irrespective of the earnings and profits of the Y Corporation since the distribution was not made to C as a shareholder.

(b) Basis of old and new stock (or stock rights) and holding period of new stock (or stock rights). If a distribution of stock or stock rights is excluded from income by § 305(a), then a portion of the basis of the stock in respect to which the distribution was made is allocated to the distributed stock or stock rights.[177] The basis allocation between the old stock and the new stock (or stock rights) is made according to their respective fair market values determined immediately after the distribution.[178]

For purposes of determining whether capital gains or losses recognized on the subsequent disposition of stock or stock rights acquired in a tax-free distribution under § 305 were long-term or short-term gains or losses, the holding period of such stock or stock rights includes the period for which the shareholders held the stock with respect to which the distribution was made (*i.e.*, the holding period of the "old" stock is tacked on to the holding period of the "new" stock or stock rights).[179] However, if stock

---

177 I.R.C. § 307(a).
178 Treas. Reg. § 1.307-1(a) and 1(b) (Ex.).
179 I.R.C. § 1223(5).

rights are distributed tax-free under § 305, and the distributee exercises those rights and purchases new stock, the holding period of the purchased new stock commences with the date on which the stock rights were *exercised*.[180]

> **Ex.** *A* has owned 100 shares of common stock of the *X* Corporation since 1956, and *A* has a basis of $50 per share (or a total basis of $5,000) in his stock. On February 5, 1964, *X* Corporation declared a stock dividend of one share of $5 par preferred stock for each outstanding share of common stock, and accordingly *A* received 100 shares of $5 par preferred stock. The fair market value of *A*'s common stock immediately after the distribution was $95 per share (a total fair market value of $9,500 for the 100 shares). The fair market value of the $5 par preferred stock at the date of distribution was $5 per share (or a total of $500 for the 100 shares). The $5,000 basis of the common stock is allocated as follows:
>
> Basis of preferred
>
> $$\frac{500 \text{ (fmv pref)}}{500 \text{ (fmv pref)} + 9{,}500 \text{ (fmv com)}} \times \$5{,}000 = \$250$$
>
> basis allocated to preferred or $2.50 basis in each share of preferred stock.
>
> Basis of common
>
> $$\frac{9{,}500 \text{ (fmv com)}}{9{,}500 \text{ (fmv com)} + 500 \text{ (fmv pref)}} \times \$5{,}000 = \$4{,}750$$
>
> basis allocated to common or $47.50 basis in each share of common stock.
>
> On April 4, 1964, *A* sold 5 shares of the $5 preferred stock for $25. *A* had a basis of 5 × $2.50 = $12.50 in those 5 shares and consequently his gain (assuming that § 306 is not applicable)[181] is $12.50, which is taxed as long-term capital gains.

With one exception, the allocation of basis between the old and new stock or stock rights is mandatory. The sole exception is when a corporation distributes stock rights, the fair market value of which at the time of distribution is less than 15% of the fair

---

180 I.R.C. § 1223(6).
181 It is more likely that § 306 would apply here, but for purposes of illustration it is convenient to ignore that section temporarily.

market value of the old stock at such time.[182] In this latter event, no basis will be allocated to stock rights (which will therefore have a zero basis) unless the shareholder elects to allocate basis in the normal manner, and the election can be made only by attaching a statement to that effect to the shareholder's tax return for the year in which the rights are received.[183]

(c) Distributions by corporation of its own securities. If a corporation distributes its own securities (or other evidences of debt) to a shareholder in a section 301 distribution, whether that shareholder be an individual or a corporation itself, the amount distributed for purposes of § 301 is equal to the fair market value of the securities (or other debt instrument).[184] The shareholder's basis in the distributed security, whether or not the shareholder is itself a corporation, is equal to the fair market value of the security.[185] However, the earnings and profits of the distributing corporation are reduced by the *principal* amount of the distributed securities rather than their fair market value.[186]

4. Preferred stock bail-outs and section 306 stock

Since in most instances the distribution of a corporation's own stock does not constitute income to the distributee shareholder, a crafty taxpayer could abuse that exemption were it left unchecked. For example, where A is the sole shareholder of the X Corporation which has accumulated earnings and profits of over $150,000, A could cause the X Corporation to distribute to him preferred nonvoting stock having a fair market value of $100,000,[187] and A could then sell the preferred stock to B, an unrelated party, for $99,000. X would then redeem the preferred stock seriatim over a three-year period. In effect, A would have withdrawn $99,000 from the corporation, and the excess of that amount over his basis would be taxed to him at

---

182 I.R.C. § 307(b).
183 Treas. Reg. § 1.307-2.
184 Treas. Reg. § 1.301-1(d). This regulation is inconsistent with I.R.C. § 301(b)(1)(B) and § 317(a); nevertheless, it is a reasonable construction of the probable intent of Congress.
185 Treas. Reg. § 1.301-1(h). As to corporate shareholders, this regulation is inconsistent with I.R.C. § 301(d)(2), but it also appears reasonable (*see* note 184 *supra*).
186 I.R.C. § 312(a)(2).
187 A would not be taxed on this distribution because of § 305(a).

long-term capital gains rates. The cost to A of transmuting the withdrawal from a dividend, taxed at ordinary income rates, to a capital gain is the extra $1,000 paid to B by the corporation when the preferred stock is redeemed plus the dividends paid to B on the preferred stock during the three-year period prior to final redemption, and that cost is borne by the corporation without tax consequence to A.

In the above example, A adopted a so-called "preferred stock bail-out" for obvious purposes. The Government could attack the transaction as a sham or step transaction, but that contention was not successful in an important case which upheld the taxpayer's use of the bail-out.[188]

Consequently, in the 1954 Code, Congress sought to close that loophole, not by taxing stock dividends, but rather by imposing a "taint" on stock in certain circumstances so that the disposition of such tainted stock might cause the recognition of ordinary income. Section 306 is the apposite provision of the Code and that statute provides the "tainted" stock with the generic name "section 306 stock."

(a) Definition of section 306 stock. Section 306 stock means stock which comes within any one of subparagraphs (i), (ii) or (iii) below.

(i) *Stock dividend*—stock (other than common stock issued with respect to common stock) which was distributed to a shareholder who later disposes of such stock if by reason of § 305(a) any part of the distribution was not included in the shareholder's income.[189]

> **Ex. (1)** The X Corporation has 100 shares of common voting stock outstanding and 100 shares of preferred nonvoting stock outstanding. A owns 50 shares of Class A common stock; B owns 50 shares of Class B common stock; and C owns all 100 shares of preferred stock. The X Corporation has substantial earnings and profits. As stock dividends, X distributed 50 shares of Class B common stock to A; distributed 50 shares of pre-

---

188 Chamberlin v. Commissioner, 207 F.2d 462 (C.A. 6 1953), *cert. denied,* 347 U.S. 918 (1954).
189 I.R.C. § 306(c)(1)(A). The meaning of "common stock" is unclear. *See* Rev. Rul. 57-132, 1957-1 C.B. 115 holding that nonvoting redeemable common was not "common stock" as that term is used in § 306.

ferred stock to *B;* and distributed 50 shares of Class B common stock to *C.* The distributions were excluded from income under § 305(a). The common stock received by *A* is not section 306 stock; the preferred stock received by *B* is section 306 stock; and the common stock received by *C* is section 306 stock.

Ex. (2) In 1964, *D* owned 10 shares of $100 par preferred stock of the *Y* Corporation, and *D* had a basis of $900 in those 10 shares. The preferred stock had a fair market value of $80 per share. The preferred stock is entitled to 5% cumulative dividends (*i.e.,* dividends of $5 per share per year), but the last dividends were paid in 1961. *Y* Corporation has accumulated earnings and profits of $200,000. In 1964, *Y* distributed 10 shares of its common stock to *D*, and each share of common had a fair market value of $30. The distribution satisfied the obligation of *Y* to pay *D* preferential dividends (totaling $15 per share) for the years 1962 through 1964 inclusive. Since $10 of the value of each share of common stock was in satisfaction of *D*'s right to a preferential dividend for 1963 and 1964, that amount constitutes a taxable dividend to *D*.[190] Since that portion of the common stock was not excluded from income by § 305(a), it does not qualify as section 306 stock. The remaining $20 of the value of each share of common stock (including the $5 given in discharge of defaulted preferential dividends for the year 1962) is excluded from income under § 305(a), and therefore constitutes section 306 stock. Thus, one-third of each share of common stock received by *A* is not section 306 stock and has a basis of $10,[191] and the remaining two-thirds of each share of common stock is section 306 stock. The combined basis of the two-thirds portion of the 10 shares that is section 306 stock is $\frac{200}{200 + 800} \times 900 = \$180$. Thus, each share of common stock has a basis of $28— *i.e.,* a $10 basis for the one-third portion that is not section 306 stock, and an $18 basis for the two-thirds portion that is section 306 stock.[192]

(ii) *Stock (other than common stock) received in a corporate reorganization or division.* Where a shareholder dis-

190 I.R.C. § 305(b)(1).
191 Treas. Reg. § 1.301-1(h).
192 Treas. Reg. § 1.306-3(c).

poses of stock (other than common stock) that he previously received pursuant to a plan of reorganization[193] or pursuant to a tax-free (or partially tax-free) corporate division,[194] and where gain or loss from the transaction in which the stock was received was not recognized in whole or in part, then the stock will constitute section 306 stock to the extent that the effect of the transaction was substantially the same as a stock dividend (or where the stock was received in exchange for section 306 stock).[195]

(iii) *Stock whose basis in the hands of the shareholder disposing of the stock is determined by reference to the basis of section 306 stock.* Where a shareholder exchanges section 306 stock for other stock in a tax-free exchange (*e.g.,* a transfer to a controlled corporation),[196] the new stock will also be tainted by § 306.[197] If both this paragraph (iii) and paragraph (ii) are applicable to the same stock, paragraph (ii) has priority.[198] Thus, common stock received in exchange for section 306 stock pursuant to a tax-free recapitalization will not be tainted by § 306.[199]

In no event will stock issued by a corporation constitute section 306 stock if the corporation has no current or accumulated earnings and profits for the taxable year in which the distribution was made.[200] It should be emphasized that this exception of § 306 rests, not merely on the earnings and profits at the time of distribution of the stock, but rather on both the accumulated earnings and profits plus the total amount of the corporation's earnings and profits for the year in which the distribution occurred. However, where a transfer is made to a controlled corporation, and the transferor receives preferred stock in exchange for his contribution (other than a contribution of section 306 stock), the preferred stock will not constitute section 306 stock since the transferor's receipt of the preferred stock is excluded from tax under

---

193 "Reorganization" is defined in I.R.C. § 368(a).
194 The stock must have been distributed under § 355 (or under so much of § 356 as applies to § 355).
195 I.R.C. § 306(c)(1)(B).
196 I.R.C. § 351.
197 I.R.C. § 306(c)(1)(C).
198 I.R.C. § 306(c)(1)(C); and Treas. Reg. § 1.306-3(e).
199 Treas. Reg. § 1.306-3(d).
200 I.R.C. § 306(c)(2).

§ 351 rather than § 305, and the definition of section 306 stock does not include stock received under § 351 except where it is received in exchange for section 306 stock.

The statute has also guarded against certain efforts to circumvent § 306 by using stock rights or convertible stock, or by changing the terms of issued stock.[201]

The tax consequence of a disposition of § 306 depends upon whether or not the disposition is a redemption and whether certain exceptions are applicable.

(i) Where a shareholder disposes of section 306 stock in any manner, other than where the stock is redeemed, then the amount realized by the shareholder shall constitute ordinary income to the extent of the stock's ratable share of the corporation's earnings and profits at the time that the stock was distributed to the shareholder, and the balance of the amount realized shall be treated as a payment for the purchase of the stock and gain will be computed accordingly.[202] In no event will the shareholder recognize a loss on the disposition of section 306 stock.[203] However, the shareholder's unused basis in the section 306 stock will be re-allocated back to the stock with respect to which the section 306 stock was issued.[204]

> **Ex. (1)** A owned 100 shares of common stock of the X Corporation. A received a tax-free stock dividend of 10 shares of preferred stock having a fair market value of $1,000. The basis of the 10 preferred shares (determined under § 307) was $600. The X Corporation had earnings and profits in excess of $200,000. A subsequently sold 5 shares of preferred stock for $650 cash. The 5 shares of preferred stock's ratable portion of earnings and profits at the time of distribution was $500 (i.e., their fair market value). Therefore, $500 of the $650 realized on the sale is ordinary income to A. The remaining $150 is offset against A's basis in the 5 shares of $300 and therefore is not income to him. Accordingly, A also realized a capital loss of $150, but the loss is not recognized.[205] The $150 of unused basis in

---

201 I.R.C. § 306(d), (e) and (g).
202 I.R.C. § 306(a)(1).
203 I.R.C. § 306(a)(1)(C).
204 Treas. Reg. § 1.306-1(b)(2)(Ex. 2).
205 I.R.C. § 306(a)(1)(C).

the section 306 stock is added to *A*'s basis in his common stock,[206]

Ex. (2) Several years later, *A* sold his remaining 5 shares of preferred stock for $1,200. Five hundred dollars of that amount was ordinary income; $300 of the amount realized was offset against *A*'s basis and therefore was not income to him. The remaining $400 of the purchase price is treated as capital gains. The earnings and profits of the corporation are not reduced, and *A* does not receive the $100 dividend exclusion under § 116(a).

While Treas. Reg. § 1.306-1(b)(1) suggests that a pledge of section 306 stock to secure a loan made without personal liability constitutes a "disposition" of the stock, it is difficult to see the significance of that statement since § 306(b)(3) exempts from § 306 any transaction in which gain or loss is not recognized.

In Rev. Rul. 57-328, 1957-2 C.B. 229, the Service ruled that a donation of "306 stock" to a tax-exempt charitable foundation did not constitute a disposition by the donor under § 306(a)(1). Upon a later sale by the charity or upon a redemption by the corporation, the income is recognized by the tax-exempt donee rather than by the donor.[207] However, the Service might contend successfully that the gift and subsequent redemption were the equivalent of a redemption of the stock from the donor followed by a gift of cash to the donee if at the time the gift was made, the corporation was under a binding obligation to redeem the stock from the charity.[208]

(ii) Where a shareholder disposes of section 306 stock through a corporate redemption, the total amount realized constitutes a distribution to the shareholder under § 301.[209] Thus, the distribution will reduce the corporation's earnings and profits; and the shareholder may use the $100 dividend exclusion provided by § 116(a).

---

206 Treas. Reg. § 1.306-1(b)(2) (Ex. 2).
207 *See* Robert L. Fox, ¶ 68,205 P-H Memo T.C. (1968). Since the donee is tax-exempt, its recognition of income has no adverse tax consequences.
208 *Cf.* Rev. Rul. 60-370, 1960-2 C.B. 203. *But compare,* The Humacid Co., 42 T.C. 894 (1964) Non acq., 1966-1 C.B. 4.
209 I.R.C. § 306(a)(2).

> **Ex.** X Corporation has earnings and profits of $2,000, and it issues section 306 stock to A, its sole shareholder. The fair market value of the section 306 stock is $1,000. Several years later, the corporation redeemed A's section 306 stock for $4,000, and the corporation's accumulated and current earnings and profits for the year of redemption was $5,000. A received a dividend of $4,000.

Thus, the amount of ordinary income recognized under § 306 for a redemption of section 306 stock depends upon the corporation's earnings and profits in the year of redemption. However, the amount of ordinary income recognized on the sale of section 306 stock depends upon the historical earnings and profits of the corporation at the time the section 306 stock was distributed. If the terms of section 306 stock were changed prior to disposition thereof, the value of the stock and its ratable share of earnings and profits will be determined at that later date if that nets a higher figure.[210]

(iii) The following transactions are exempted from the reach of § 306:[211]

> (aa) Where the redemption or sale liquidates the entire interest of the shareholder in the corporation. For purposes of determining whether the shareholder's interest was terminated, the attribution rules of § 318 are applicable; but if the disposition was a redemption, the shareholder may use § 302(c) and (b)(3) to avoid § 306 treatment.[212]

> (bb) Where gain or loss is not recognized to the shareholder (*e.g.*, a gift of the stock).

> (cc) Where it is demonstrated to the satisfaction of the Commissioner that both the distribution of the stock and the subsequent disposition or redemption of the stock did not have avoidance of federal income tax as a principal purpose.[213]

---

210 I.R.C. § 306(g).
211 I.R.C. § 306(b).
212 Treas. Reg. § 1.306-2(a).
213 There is no apparent reason for the Code's treatment of a distribution of common stock on preferred as a distribution of section 306 stock. However, in many instances, the subsequent disposition of the common stock will qualify for an exemption from § 306 because no tax avoidance purpose was involved. I.R.C. § 306(b)(4).

(dd) Under § 306(e), an additional exemption is provided where section 306 stock was issued with respect to common stock and was subsequently converted into common stock. However, common stock with conversion privileges is not treated as common stock.

B. DISTRIBUTION OR SALE OF CORPORATE ASSETS PURSUANT TO A COMPLETE LIQUIDATION OF THE CORPORATION

The tax consequences of a complete liquidation depend upon whether: (i) the corporation being liquidated is the subsidiary of another corporation; (ii) certain statutory elections have been made; (iii) a shareholder acquired a controlling interest in the liquidating corporation within a short time prior to the liquidation; (iv) the liquidating corporation is collapsible; and (v) the business of the liquidated corporation is reincorporated. Moreover, if a corporation sells all or part of its assets preparatory to making distributions in liquidation, those sales may be subject to special tax treatment. Before considering these several matters, "complete liquidation" should be defined. For tax purposes, "[a] status of liquidation exists when the corporation ceases to be a going concern and its activities are merely for the purpose of winding up its affairs, paying its debts, and distributing any remaining balance to its shareholders. A liquidation may be completed prior to the actual dissolution of the liquidating corporation. However, legal dissolution of the corporation is not required. Nor will the mere retention of a nominal amount of assets for the sole purpose of preserving the corporation's legal existence disqualify the transaction."[214]

1. Ordinary liquidations

In the absence of a specific statutory exception, a distribution of assets to a shareholder in complete liquidation of the corporation is treated as payment for the shareholder's stock.[215] The amount received by the shareholder in excess of his basis in his

---

214 Treas. Reg. § 1.332-2(c). Presumably, the definition set forth in that regulation is applicable for tax purposes to all liquidations, even though the regulation is promulgated under the statute dealing with the liquidation of certain subsidiary corporations.

215 I.R.C. § 331.

stock will usually be taxed as capital gains.[216] The basis in the hands of the distributee of property in kind distributed in a liquidation is equal to the fair market value of the property at the time of distribution.[217]

Among the several exceptions to the foregoing are:

(a) Liquidation of a collapsible corporation.[218]

(b) In certain circumstances, liquidation of a corporation which is controlled by a parent corporation.[219]

(c) A liquidation made in compliance with Section 333.[220]

(d) The liquidation of a corporation, control of which was acquired by a shareholder within a reasonable period of time before the liquidation occurred.

Prior to the 1954 Code, a judicial doctrine was established that where a party acquired all (or virtually all) of the stock of a corporation for the purpose of liquidating the corporation and thereby obtaining its assets, and then the corporation was promptly liquidated, the substance of the transaction was considered to be a purchase of assets though the medium of acquiring the stock. Consequently, on liquidation of the corporation, no gain or loss was recognized by the shareholder, and the shareholder's basis in the distributed property was equal to the purchase price.[221] Thus, changes in the fair market value of the corporation's assets between the date of purchase of the corporation's stock and the date of liquidation would not affect the tax consequences of the shareholder on liquidation.[222] This judicial principle is commonly referred to as the "Kimbell-Diamond" rule,

---

216 If the stock is not a capital asset in the hands of the shareholder, his gain will be ordinary income.
217 I.R.C. § 334(a).
218 I.R.C. § 341. *See* pp. 37-44 *supra*. All or part of the gain realized on liquidation of a collapsible corporation may be recognized as ordinary income.
219 I.R.C. § 332. *See* pp. 62-70 *infra*.
220 *See* pp. 70-78 *infra*.
221 *See, e.g.,* Commissioner v. Ashland Oil & R. Co., 99 F.2d 588 (C.A. 6 1938), *cert. denied,* 306 U.S. 661 (1938); and H. B. Snively, 19 T.C. 850 (1953).
222 However, in more recent years, an increase in the value of the corporation's depreciable assets may cause the corporation to recognize additional ordinary income under § 1245 and § 1250 upon making a distribution of those assets. *See* Chapter II *infra*.

in deference to a landmark decision on this issue.[223] As applied to the purchase of stock by a corporate shareholder, the "Kimbell-Diamond" rule was codified in the 1954 Code with some modifications.[224] However, the judicial rule continues to apply (without statutory codification) when an *individual* acquires control of a corporation for the purpose of promptly liquidating it, and does so.[225]

(e) A liquidation where the business of the liquidated corporation is continued by another corporation which is controlled by essentially the same persons as controlled the liquidating corporation. The guise of a liquidation could be employed to cloak a dividend distribution with a mask of capital gains were it not for the time-honored precept of substance over form. Two devices which have been tried are:

(i) The X Corporation transfers the operating assets of its business to the Y Corporation in either a tax-free exchange (under § 351) or a taxable exchange for Y's stock pursuant to a plan of liquidation on which gain is not recognized under § 337.[226] The Y Corporation is controlled either by A, the sole shareholder of X, or by X itself. X is then liquidated, and its investment assets and Y stock are distributed to A. A claims capital gains treatment on the liquidation.

(ii) B is the sole shareholder of the X Corporation. The X Corporation is liquidated and its assets are distributed to B. Subsequently, B forms the Y Corporation and transfers to it the operating assets of the business formerly conducted by the X Corporation. B retains the ownership of the investment assets received from X in his individual capacity. B might contend that the liquidation of X caused him to recognize capital gains, and B might further contend that the accumulated earnings and profits of X died with that corporation and that Y commences business with zero earnings and profits.

The net effect of each of the above described transactions is that

---

223 Kimbell-Diamond Milling Co. v. Commissioner, 14 T.C. 74 (1950), *affirmed,* 187 F.2d 718 (C.A. 5 1951), *cert. denied,* 342 U.S. 827 (1951).
224 I.R.C. § 334(b)(2). *See* pp. 68-70 *infra.*
225 American Potash & Chemical Corporation v. United States, 399 F.2d 194, 208 (Ct. Cls. 1968); United States v. Mattison, 273 F.2d 13 (C.A. 9 1959).
226 *See* pp. 78-102 *infra.*

(i) the business of X continues to be conducted in corporate form by a new corporation which is, however, indistinguishable from X, and (ii) the shareholder of X has converted the investment assets of X from corporate ownership to his individual ownership. The Service may contend[227] that the substance of either of those transactions is a reorganization, and that A or B received boot, taxable as a dividend, to the extent that A or B received assets of the X Corporation which were not subsequently reincorporated. Compare *James Armour, Inc.*, 43 T.C. 295 (1964) with *Pridemark, Inc. v. Commissioner*, 345 F.2d 35 (C.A. 4 1965). If the Service is successful in collapsing the transactions and treating them as a reorganization, the earnings and profits of the X Corporation will be carried over to the Y Corporation.[228] Alternatively, the Service may contend that the "liquidation" is a sham and ought to be ignored.

The Service is not always successful in its attacks on a "reincorporation."[229] A lengthy period between liquidation and reincorporation, and the presence of unanticipated intervening events which made reincorporation desirable, would significantly strengthen the shareholder's position.[230] Moreover, there are conceptual difficulties with treating these transactions as reorganizations. For example, the Government has frequently contended that these transactions constitute a "D" reorganization. A "D" reorganization[231] is applicable only where either two corporate entities survive the distribution made to the shareholder, or where the liquidating corporation transferred substantially all of its assets to the surviving corporation.[232] In the typical reincorporation, neither of those tests is satisfied. However, the Tax Court has rejected a literal interpretation of § 354(b) and has held that that statute applies if substantially all of the *operating assets* of the liquidating

---

227 Treas. Reg. § 1.331-1(c) evidences the likelihood that the Service will take that position. *See* Hertz, *Liquidation of a Corporation Business in Kind: Form of Continued Operations; Recapture; Installment; Winding Up; Reincorporation,* 26 N.Y.U. TAX INST. 969 (1968).

228 I.R.C. § 381.

229 *E.g.,* Joseph C. Gallagher, 39 T.C. 144 (1962); and Commissioner v. Berghash, 361 F.2d 257 (C.A. 2 1966); and Simon v. United States, 402 F.2d 272 (Ct. Cls. 1968).

230 *Cf.* Simon v. United States, 402 F.2d 272 (Ct. Cls. 1968).

231 I.R.C. § 368(a)(1)(D) defines a so-called "D" reorganization. *See* Chapter III *infra* for a discussion of "D" reorganizations.

232 I.R.C. §§ 354(b) and 355(b).

corporation were transferred.[233] While that construction rests on an elastic reading of the English language, it does arrive at a sensible result.

The Service may seek to characterize a reincorporation as an "F" reorganization;[234] and in some circumstances the Service may rely on the "C" or "E" reorganization provisions. Frequently, the Government will urge several alternative grounds for treating the transaction as a reorganization. An attempt to avoid the reach of these several reorganization provisions by resorting to straw or sham transactions may arouse the ire of a court and consequently is subject to the risk of causing even more serious consequences to the taxpayers if the matter is litigated.[235]

In any event, where a corporation has been liquidated, the distributed assets ought not be reincorporated without first making a careful appraisal of the risks of dividend treatment. Similar consideration must be given to the sale of corporate assets pursuant to a plan of liquidation when the sale is made to a corporate entity having more than 20% common ownership with the selling corporation.[236]

2. Liquidation of a controlled subsidiary corporation

Since 1935, the tax laws have reflected a congressional policy to permit the liquidation of a controlled subsidiary corporation with-

---

233 James Armour, Inc., 43 T.C. 295 (1964). *See also,* Moffat v. Commissioner, 363 F.2d 262 (C.A. 9 1966); Reef Corporation v. Commissioner, 368 F.2d 125 (C.A. 5 1966); Babcock v. Phillips, 372 F.2d 240 (C.A. 10 1967). *But compare,* Rommer v. United States, 268 F. Supp. 740 (D.N.J. 1966).

234 *See* pp. 148-153, Chapter III *infra.* An "F" reorganization is defined in I.R.C. § 368(a)(1)(F).

235 *E.g.,* Davant v. Commissioner, 366 F.2d 874 (C.A. 5 1966), *cert. denied,* 386 U.S. 1022. *But see* Rev. Rul. 69-185, I.R.B. 1969-16, p. 11.

236 *See* pp. 98-99 *infra.* Rev. Proc. 69-6 (Sec. 3.01-9) I.R.B. 1969-1, p. 30, states that the Service will not rule on the applicability of § 337 to a sale to another corporation where more than 20% in value of the stock of both corporations is owned by the same persons. While it is unlikely that a contention of reincorporation will be successful when the common ownership is less than 50%, the threat of litigation will be sufficient to deter many transactions. In the same spirit, the Service has stated that it will not rule on the tax effect of a liquidation which is preceded or followed by the reincorporation or sale to another corporation of all or part of the business and its assets where the liquidating and transferee corporations have more than 20% in value of their stock owned by the same persons. Rev. Proc. 69-6, (Sec. 301-8) I.R.B. 1969-1, p. 30.

out causing any tax consequences to the parent corporation. This exemption removes a tax impediment to the exercise of business judgment in rearranging the corporate structure of an enterprise, and it conforms with the tax-free treatment provided for certain exchanges made pursuant to a reorganization.

Under the Code, no gain or loss will be recognized to a parent corporation for receiving distributions in liquidation of its subsidiary, provided that certain requisites are satisfied,[237] and in that event the parent corporation will succeed to the tax attributes of the subsidiary, e.g., the parent will absorb the subsidiary's earnings and profits,[238] net operating losses,[239] and will assume the subsidiary's basis in its assets.[240]

(a) Requisites for tax exclusion for parent corporation. The requisites for tax-free treatment for the parent corporation are:

(i) The parent corporation owned at least 80% of the total combined voting power of the voting stock of the liquidating subsidiary and at least 80% of the total number of outstanding shares of nonvoting stock, except that nonvoting, non-participating preferred stock is not taken into account.[241] The parent corporation must have possessed the requisite percentages indicated above for a continuous period commencing on the date on which the plan of liquidation was adopted and terminating on the date on which the subsidiary's assets were distributed to the parent corporation.

In some instances a taxpayer might desire to remove a sub-

---

237 I.R.C. § 332.
238 I.R.C. § 381.
239 *Id.*
240 I.R.C. § 334(b)(1). But note I.R.C. § 334(b)(2) discussed below at pp. 68-70.
241 *See* Treas. Reg. § 1.302-3(a)(3) which states that for purposes of § 302, stock which has voting rights only on the occurrence of an event (such as a default in dividends on preferred stock) is not voting stock until that event occurs. It is likely that this construction of "voting stock" is equally applicable to § 332.

There is some question whether nonvoting participating preferred stock should be excluded from consideration of the second 80% test where, for the period in question, no dividend in excess of the preference was paid. *Compare* Pioneer Parachute Co. v. Commissioner, 162 F.2d 249 (C.A. 2 1947) *with* Erie Lighting Co. v. Commissioner, 93 F.2d 883 (C.A. 1 1937). It would appear that such stock should be included in the computation of the parent's percentage of the number of outstanding shares of nonvoting stock.

sidiary's liquidation from the reach of § 332, *e.g.*, the amount of the parent's investment in the subsidiary may be greater than the present value of the subsidiary's assets, and the parent might therefore wish to make the liquidation a taxable transaction so that it could recognize a loss on the exchange. Query, whether the parent corporation's sale or disposition of some of the subsidiary's stock immediately prior to the liquidation, in order to reduce its stock ownership below the 80% bench mark, will disqualify the liquidation from coverage under § 332?[242]

Where a parent corporation owns less than the required 80% of the voting control and nonvoting stock of the subsidiary, and where shortly prior to liquidation of the subsidiary, the parent corporation acquires sufficient additional stock of the subsidiary to satisfy the 80% tests, there is considerable risk that the plan of liquidation will be deemed to have been adopted prior to acquisition of the additional stock, and consequently, that the parent will not comply with the ownership test for the entire period required by § 332.

(ii)   Either the subsidiary corporation:

(aa) Within one taxable year, distributed its assets in complete cancellation or redemption of all its outstanding stock; or

(bb) Acquired all its outstanding stock in complete cancellation or redemption thereof in accordance with a plan of liquidation under which all the transfers are to be completed within three years after the close of the taxable year in which the first distribution is made under the plan. If the transfers are not completed within the three-year period or if the parent corporation does not retain the requisite percentage of control and ownership during that period, the provisions of § 332 are lost for all distributions to the parent. Accordingly, where liquidation is not completed within one taxable year and the parent corporation seeks the refuge of § 332, the Serv-

---

242 *See* Commissioner v. Day & Zimmerman, Inc., 151 F.2d 517 (C.A. 3 1945); and the discussion of this issue in BITTKER AND EUSTICE, FEDERAL INCOME TAXATION OF CORPORATIONS AND SHAREHOLDERS (2d ed., 1966) § 9.41, pp. 369-370.

ice requires that the parent corporation waive the statute of limitations on assessment and collection for each taxable year within the period of liquidation, and the Commissioner may also require the parent corporation to file a bond containing such terms as the Commissioner specifies.[243]

While the requirement that a plan of liquidation be adopted has been liberally construed,[244] prudence dictates that such a plan be adopted formally by the directors and shareholders of the corporation, and that within 30 days thereafter, the corporation file the information return required by § 6043.[245]

Also, care should be taken to insure that a serial redemption of the stock of a liquidating corporation does not deprive the parent corporation of the requisite percentage of control and ownership prior to the final liquidating distribution.

(b) Tax consequences to minority shareholders. Section 332 provides a tax exclusion only for the controlling parent corporation which complies with the conditions described above. When § 332 is applicable to a parent corporation, but there are also minority shareholders of the liquidating corporation, § 332 does not afford any relief to the minority shareholders.[246] Thus, the minority shareholders will usually recognize gain or loss on their receipt of liquidating distributions; but in some instances, the distributions to the minority shareholders may not cause recognition of gain or loss, e.g., where the minority shareholders make a timely election under § 333,[247] or possibly where the liquidation of the subsidiary takes the form of a statutory merger which qualifies as a tax-free

---

243 Treas. Reg. § 1.332-4(a). For a liberal application of § 332 to a liquidation in which not all of the liquidating corporation's assets were distributed within the three-year period and in which the parent corporation failed to file either a bond or a waiver of the statute of limitation, see Cherry-Burrell Corp. v. United States, 367 F.2d 669 (C.A. 8 1966). However, the special circumstances existing in Cherry-Burrell detract from its precedential significance.

244 See I.R.C. § 332(b)(2); see, e.g., Burnside Veneer Co. v. Commissioner, 167 F.2d 214 (C.A. 6 1948).

245 This information should be filed on Form 966. Treas. Reg. § 1.6043-1(a).

246 Treas. Reg. § 1.332-5.

247 See pp. 70-78 infra.

reorganization.[248] However, § 333 is rarely useful as a liquidating tool.[249]

> **Ex. (1)** On January 1, 1964, the X Corporation had 1,000 shares of common voting stock outstanding. The A Corporation owned 900 shares of X having a basis of $90,000, and B, an individual shareholder, owned 100 shares of X having a basis of $10,000. On March 1, 1964, the shareholders of X resolved that X should distribute all of its assets in redemption of its outstanding stock, and the redemption was completed by August 5, 1964.[250] The A Corporation received distributions in liquidation of property having a fair market value of $135,000; and B received property having a fair market value of $15,000. Section 332 excludes the entire $45,000 gain realized by A from the latter's gross income.[251] However, B will recognize the $5,000 gain realized by him on the distribution. B might elect to be covered by § 333 if the liquidating distributions were made within one calendar month, but even if applicable that provision will be of no benefit to B if X has earnings and profits of any significant amount, or if X has a sizable amount of cash or stocks and securities acquired after 1953.[252]

> **Ex.(2)** The same facts as in Example (1) except that the liquidation of X is accomplished by merging X into A under a state law providing for statutory mergers. Pursuant to the merger, B surrendered his stock in X and received an appropriate number of shares in the A Corporation. A recognizes no gain on the merger under § 332.[253] It is likely that B also recognizes no gain on the exchange of X stock for A stock because of the reorganization provisions.[254]

---

248 I.R.C. § 368(a)(1)(A). While Treas. Reg. § 1.332-2(d) and (e) suggest that for purposes of § 332, an "upstream" merger is treated as a liquidation, there is no suggestion that the same transaction could not also qualify as a reorganization to the extent that § 332 is not applicable.
249 *See* p. 77 *infra.*
250 Where all of the assets of the liquidating corporation are transferred within one taxable year, the shareholder's resolution authorizing the distributions of those assets in redemption of the outstanding stock constitutes an adoption of a plan of liquidation for purposes of satisfying the Code's requirement that one be adopted. I.R.C. § 332(b)(2).
251 The exclusion is mandatory. Section 332 is not an elective provision, and it also excludes realized losses.
252 *See* pp. 70-78 *infra.*
253 Treas. Reg. § 1.332-2(d) and (e).
254 I.R.C. § 354(a), and 368(a)(1)(A).

(c) Liquidation of subsidiary's indebtedness to parent. Where a liquidating subsidiary corporation is indebted to its parent corporation, then all or a portion of the distributions made to the parent constitute payments in satisfaction of the debt rather than distributions in redemption of stock—*i.e.*, creditors of a liquidating corporation have priority over shareholders, and where a shareholder is also a creditor, the priority requires that distributions first be allocated to debt and that only the remaining balance, if any, be available for redemption of stock. Under the 1954 Code, the subsidiary usually will not recognize any gain or loss on the distributions of appreciated or depreciated assets in payment of its debts to its parent.[255] The single exception to the subsidiary's exemption is where the subsidiary is insolvent, in which event the subsidiary can recognize a gain or loss on its distributions in payment of its debts.[256] If the subsidiary is insolvent, and the parent is the principal or only creditor, and the parties prefer that the liquidating distributions not be taxable, the parent could seek the umbrella of § 332 by first either cancelling the debt or contributing sufficient assets to the subsidiary to make it solvent, and thereafter liquidating the subsidiary. However, a cancellation of indebtedness or a capital contribution made shortly before a liquidation would almost certainly be ignored as a sham or step transaction.[257]

Section 332 has no application to a parent's receipt of payment on the subsidiary's debt whether or not the subsidiary is solvent.[258] Where the payment made to the parent exceeds the latter's basis in the debt (*e.g.*, where the parent purchased bonds of the subsidiary at a discount), the parent will recognize a gain. If the payments are less than the parent's basis, the parent is allowed a bad debt deduction or a loss deduction for worthless securities.[259]

---

255 I.R.C. § 332(c).

256 Northern Coal & Dock Co., 12 T.C. 42 (1949) Acq. 1941-1 C.B. 3. The underlying theory for recognizing the subsidiary's gain or loss is that § 332 applies only where distributions are made to a parent corporation as a shareholder, and where the only distributions made are payments of debts, § 332 (and therefore § 332(c)) are inapplicable, and the payments are treated as a normal exchange.

   Note that if § 332(c) is inapplicable, the parent-subsidiary relationship does not bar the subsidiary from recognizing and deducting a loss which was incurred pursuant to a complete liquidation. I.R.C. § 267(a)(1).

257 *See* Rev. Rul. 68-602, I.R.B 1968-47, p. 9.

258 Treas. Reg. § 1.332-7.

259 Rev. Rul. 59-296, 1959-2 C.B. 87.

Where the subsidiary is insolvent and consequently § 332 is inapplicable, the parent is entitled to a loss deduction for the worthless stock of the subsidiary.[260]

(d) Planned termination of parent corporation. In *Fairfield Steamship Corp. v. Commissioner*, 157 F.2d 321 (C.A. 2 1946), Judge Learned Hand, writing for the Second Circuit, stated that an earlier counterpart of § 332 was not applicable to a liquidation of a subsidiary where it was intended that the parent would also be liquidated, because the nonrecognition provision of [§ 332] is premised on the continuation of the business of the liquidated corporation, and therefore does not apply where there is no intention to continue the business. The "holding" in *Fairfield* is difficult to fathom since the issue before the court was the tax consequences to the subsidiary, and there was no apparent relevance to the principle on which Judge Hand based his decision. Indeed, the court promulgated an addendum to its opinion, which shifted the basis of its decision.

The present vitality of the principle enunciated in *Fairfield* is unclear. The Tax Court has suggested that the *Fairfield* principle is limited to situations where both the parent and the subsidiary are to be liquidated,[261] but a recent Revenue Ruling, which discussed the tax consequences of a liquidation under § 332 where both the parent and subsidiary corporations are to be liquidated, made no mention of the *Fairfield* doctrine.[262]

(e) Basis of subsidiary's assets received by parent corporation. Normally, the basis of assets received by a parent corporation pursuant to a § 332 liquidation of its subsidiary is identical to the basis the property had in the hands of the liquidating subsidiary corporation at the time of transfer.[263] The one exception to this transference of basis is provided by § 334(b)(2), the codification of the so-called "Kimbell-Diamond" rule.[264] Section 334(b)(2) provides that the parent corporation's basis in the assets of a subsidiary which were acquired on liquidation will equal the adjusted basis of the sub-

---

260 I.R.C. § 165(g). In this situation, the parent cannot utilize the subsidiary's net operating loss carry-over. Rev. Rul. 68-359; I.R.B. 1968-28, p. 13.
261 International Investment Corp., 11 T.C. 678 (1948), *affirmed,* 175 F.2d 772 (C.A. 3 1949).
262 Rev. Rul. 69-172, I.R.B. 1969-15, p. 10.
263 I.R.C. § 334(b)(1).
264 *See* pp. 59-60 *supra* for a discussion of that rule.

sidiary's stock in the hand of the parent corporation where certain objective conditions exist, *viz.*,

(i) Within a twelve-month period the parent corporation "purchased"[265] stock of the subsidiary having at least 80% of the voting power of all voting stock and at least 80% of the total number of shares of the subsidiary's nonvoting stock (other than nonvoting, nonparticipating preferred stock of the subsidiary); and

(ii) The subsidiary is completely liquidated within two years after the requisite stock was purchased (or if the stock was purchased in several stages, within two years after the date of the last purchase).

> **Ex.** On January 4, 1964, the *A* Corporation paid $200,000 for all 1,000 outstanding shares of stock of the *X* Corporation. On July 12, 1965, the *X* Corporation was liquidated and its assets, in which *X* had a basis of $100,000, were transferred to *A*. *A* has a basis of $200,000 in the assets received from *X*.

Although it had been thought that § 334(b)(2) was exclusive and that the "Kimbell-Diamond" rule had no applicability if a corporation did not comply with § 334(b)(2), a 1968 Court of Claims case held otherwise. In *American Potash & Chemical Corp. v. United States*,[266] the court said that the legislative history of § 334(b)(2) did not indicate a congressional intent to prevent application of the judicial rule when § 334(b)(2) requirements were not met.

The difficulties encountered in allocating basis among the several assets of the liquidating corporation, particularly where one of the assets is good will, are discussed in Crawford, "Allocation of Goodwill in a Section 334(b)(2) Liquidation; Which Method May Be Used?", 26 *J. of Taxation* 204 (April, 1967).

If pursuant to its complete liquidation, a solvent subsidiary corporation makes a distribution to its parent corporation in satisfaction of a debt owed the parent, and under I.R.C. § 332(c) no gain or loss is recognized by the subsidiary on account of such payment, then the basis of such distributed property in the hands of the parent corporation is identical to the basis such property

---

265 The term "purchase" has a restricted definition for this purpose and should be examined carefully. I.R.C. § 334(b)(3).
266 399 F.2d 194 (Ct. Cl. 1968).

had in the hands of the distributing subsidiary corporation. I.R.C. § 334(b)(1).

3. Liquidation where an election has been made under section 333

In certain circumstances the shareholders of a liquidating corporation may elect under I.R.C. § 333 that gain realized from the receipt of liquidating distributions will not be recognized to the extent permitted in that section. While § 333's antecedent was first enacted in the Revenue Act of 1938[267] as a temporary measure for the purpose of encouraging the liquidation of personal holding companies that were subject to a penalty tax on their undistributed earnings,[268] it was soon added to the 1939 Code as permanent legislation.[269] Irrespective of its purpose, the operation of § 333 and its antecedent provisions has never been limited to the liquidation of personal holding companies.

(a) Tax consequences to a shareholder of receiving liquidating distributions where section 333 is applicable. Section 333 provides that a qualified electing shareholder recognizes gain on liquidating distributions made under that section in redemption of shares of stock held by the shareholder at the date of adoption of the plan of liquidation only to the following extent:

(i) The gain realized by a noncorporate qualified electing shareholder on the redemption of each share of his stock will be recognized as ordinary dividend income to the extent of such share's ratable portion of the corporation's accumulated earnings and profits;[270] and if the gain realized on a share of

---

267 Section 112(b)(7) of the Revenue Act of 1938.
268 A personal holding company is defined in I.R.C. §§ 541 et seq., and the tax consequences of coming within that classification are set forth therein. For a discussion of the accumulated earnings tax and of personal holding companies, which concepts have some relation to each other, see BITTKER AND EUSTICE, FEDERAL INCOME TAXATION OF CORPORATIONS AND SHAREHOLDERS (2d ed., 1966), ch. 6, pp. 209-256.
269 Section 120 of the Revenue Act of 1943 added § 112(b)(7), the predecessor of § 333, to the 1939 Code.
270 Each share's ratable portion of the corporation's accumulated earnings and profits is determined as of the last day of the month of liquidation without diminution by reason of distributions made during that month, and by accruing all items of income and expense up to the date on which the liquidating transfers were completed. Only earnings and profits accumulated after February 28, 1913, are included in the computation. I.R.C. § 333(e)(1), and Treas. Reg. § 1.333-4(b)(1).

stock exceeds the share's ratable portion of accumulated earnings and profits, then the difference will be recognized as capital gains to the extent that such share's ratable portion of the amount of money, and stock and securities acquired by the distributing corporation after December 31, 1953,[271] received by the shareholder as liquidating distributions, exceeds such share's ratable portion of the corporation's accumulated earnings and profits.

The gain or loss realized in a § 333 liquidation must be computed separately on each share of stock owned by a qualified electing shareholder, and the loss realized on a share of stock is recognized in full.

> **Ex.** In 1966, X Corporation had 100 shares of common stock outstanding, 80 shares of which were owned by A, an individual, and 20 shares of which were owned by B, an individual. B purchased his 20 shares in 1958 for $100 per share. A acquired 60 shares in 1956 for $80 per share, and A acquired his remaining 20 shares in 1961 for $150 per share. In March, 1966, X distributed all of its assets in complete liquidation, and A and B made timely elections under § 333. X had $1,500 of earnings and profits accumulated after February 28, 1913, at the date of transfer of all its assets. At the date of liquidation, the assets of X consisted of $2,500 cash and unimproved Blackacre having a fair market value of $9,500. X distributed $500 cash and a ⅕ interest in Blackacre to B, and X distributed $2,000 cash and a ⅘ interest in Blackacre to A. Thus, A and B received $25 cash plus an undivided interest in real estate having a value of $95 for each share of their stock. B realized a gain of $20 per share. The ratable portion of accumulated earnings and profits for each share of B's stock was $15, and consequently B recognized ordinary income of $15 per share (or a total of $300 for his 20 shares). In addition, the ratable portion of cash for each share of B's stock which was in excess of such share's ratable portion of accumu-

---

271 The provision concerning stocks and securities acquired after 1953 is intended to prevent the avoidance of recognition of gain on distribution of cash by first investing the corporation's cash in stocks and securities and then distributing the latter. However, by establishing the date 1953 as the cut-off, Congress has demanded an unduly long holding period of stocks and securities, and the statutory adoption of that date has been criticized by the American Institute of Certified Public Accountants. *See* 26 J. OF TAXATION 147 (March, 1967).

lated earnings and profits ($25 cash—$15 e & p) was
$10; but since only $5 of the $20 realized gain per share
was unrecognized after accounting for the $15 ordinary
income recognized as indicated above, B recognized a
long-term capital gain of $5 per share, or a total of $100
capital gain for his 20 shares.

The ratable portion of accumulated earnings and
profits for each share of A's stock was $15 per share;
and of the $25 cash that was distributed in redemption
of each share, $10 was in excess of such share's ratable
portion of accumulated e & p. As to each share of the
60 shares of stock for which A had a basis of $80, A
realized a gain of $40 ($120 amount realized—$80
basis); of this $40 gain, $15 was recognized as ordinary
income, $10 was recognized as long-term capital gains,
and $15 was not recognized at all. Thus, on those 60
shares of stock, A recognized ordinary income of $900 and
long-term capital gain of $600. As to the remaining 20
shares of A's stock for which he had a basis of $150 per
share, A lost $30 per share on their redemption, and all
of that loss (a total of $600) is recognized as a long-term
capital loss.

Note that B is treated harshly by § 333, i.e., his entire
realized gain ($20) was recognized and $15 of it is treated as ordinary income.

(ii) The gain realized by a corporate qualified electing shareholder on each share of its stock will be the greater of either
(aa) such share's ratable portion of accumulated earnings and
profits of the distributing corporation,[272] or (bb) the amount of
money, and stock and securities acquired by the corporation
after December 31, 1953, which was received by such corporate
shareholder as a liquidating distribution in redemption of such
share of stock. The entire gain recognized on each share of
stock will be treated as capital gains, and the amount of loss
recognized on any share of stock will be recognized in full.[273]

Ex. X Corporation has 300 shares of common stock outstanding, 100 of which are owned by the O Corporation.
O has a basis of $10 per share in its 100 shares of X

---

272 See note 270 supra for a discussion of the manner in which earnings
and profits are determined for the purpose of computing recognized
gain under § 333.
273 Treas. Reg. § 1.333-4(c)(1) and 4(a).

stock. In May, 1966, pursuant to a complete liquidation under § 333, X distributed all of its assets, consisting of $3,000 cash and office equipment having a fair market value of $6,000. O received $1,000 cash and office equipment having a fair market value of $2,000 as its share of the liquidating distribution. X had accumulated earnings and profits of $4,500 at the time of distribution. O realized a gain of $20 on each share of X stock. The ratable portion of accumulated earnings and profits for each share of X stock was $15, and the ratable portion of cash distributed to O for each share of X stock was $10. Consequently, O recognized a gain of $15 per share (a total of $1,500 for its 100 shares), all of which is treated as capital gains; and the remaining $500 of gain realized by O is not recognized.

In determining the amount of money received by a shareholder, a distribution of accounts receivable to a shareholder is not deemed a distribution of money.[274]

(b) Basis of assets received by a qualified electing shareholder in a section 333 liquidation. In an ordinary liquidation, the shareholder's basis in assets received as liquidating distributions is equal to the fair market value of the assets.[275] However, where a shareholder received liquidating distributions in redemption of his stock, and where the shareholder realized gain on such distributions, the recognition of which is determined under § 333, then the basis of the assets received by the shareholder is equal to the shareholder's basis in his redeemed stock reduced by the amount of money received by the shareholder and increased by the amount of gain recognized by him.[276] This basis is allocated among the assets received in liquidation according to their respective fair market values.[277]

The allocation of basis according to the fair market value of

---

274 D. Bruce Forrester, 4 T.C. 907 (1945). However, the subsequent collection of the receivables may constitute ordinary income. Osenbach v. Commissioner, 198 F.2d 235 (C.A. 4 1952).
275 I.R.C. § 334(a).
276 I.R.C. § 334(c).
277 Treas. Reg. § 1.334-2. Where property is subject to a mortgage or pledge, only the excess of fair market value over the amount of the mortgage or pledge is taken into account in determining the value of that asset for the purpose of allocating basis, and after the basis has been so allocated, the shareholder adds to the basis of a mortgaged or pledged asset an amount equal to the mortgage or lien.

the distributed assets may result in the vesting of a large portion of the basis in nondepreciable assets. This allocation can be particularly onerous where a business having substantial good will is distributed to shareholders who continue the operation of the business; in that event a portion of the basis must be allocated to good will, [278] and basis allocated to good will is of little use to the shareholders unless they sell the business. Moreover, the necessity of valuing good will creates additional burdens.

Where § 333 is applicable to a liquidating distribution so that the basis of the distributed assets is determined in whole or in part by the shareholder's basis in his stock of the liquidating corporation, then for capital gains purposes, the holding period of the distributed assets in the hands of the shareholder includes the holding period of the distributing corporation's stock held by the shareholder.[279]

(c) Requisites of a shareholder's employment of section 333. The provisions of § 333 are applicable only to "qualified electing shareholders," and consequently it is necessary to consider the meaning of that term. A qualified shareholder must have been a shareholder at the time the plan of liquidation was adopted, and must have filed an election to be covered by § 333 within 30 days after the date of adoption of the plan of liquidation.[280] Failure to file a timely election will prevent a shareholder's use of § 333.[281] Moreover, in many instances, the validity of a shareholder's election turns on whether other shareholders of the corporation have made timely elections. For an election of a noncorporate shareholder to be valid, timely elections must be filed by noncorporate shareholders who at the time of adoption of the plan of liquidation were owners of stock possessing at least 80% of the total combined voting power of all classes of stock held by noncorporate shareholders which stock contained the right to vote in the adoption of a plan of liquidation.[282] For an election of a corporate shareholder to be valid, timely elections must have been filed by corporate

---

278 Rev. Rul. 66-81, 1966-1 C.B. 64.
279 I.R.C. § 1223(1).
280 I.R.C. § 333(d). The election is made on Form 964. Treas. Reg. § 1.333-3.
281 Treas. Reg. § 1.333-3. *See, e.g.,* Shull v. Commissioner, 291 F.2d 680 (C.A. 4 1961); and Harold O. Wales, 50 T.C. 399 (1968).
282 I.R.C. § 333(c)(1).

shareholders, other than an "excluded corporation," which at the time of adoption of the plan of liquidation were owners of stock possessing at least 80% of the total combined voting power of all classes of stock owned by corporate shareholders (other than excluded corporations) which stock contained the right to vote on a plan of liquidation.[283] An "excluded corporation" is a corporation which at any time between January 1, 1954, and the date of adoption of the plan of liquidation was the owner of stock possessing at least 50% of the total combined voting power of all classes of stock entitled to vote on the adoption of such plan.[284] Thus, shareholders are divided into two separate groups, corporate shareholders and noncorporate shareholders, and the determination of the validity of the election for each group is made without regard to the stock holding or elections made by the other group.

> **Ex.** X Corporation has 1,000 shares of common voting stock outstanding. All conditions of § 333, other than the election provisions, were satisfied on liquidation of X.
>
> **(1)** 900 shares of the stock of X are owned by the A Corporation; 90 shares are owned by B, an individual; and 10 shares are owned by C, an individual. B files a timely election to be covered by § 333, but neither A nor C files an election. B's election is valid. B owns stock possessing over 80% of the voting power of the stock owned by the noncorporate shareholders, and consequently his election is sufficient. Distributions to A and C will not fall within § 333, but if C had made a timely election, distributions to him would have been covered.
>
> **(2)** The A Corporation files a timely election. Since A is an excluded corporation, distributions to A cannot be protected by § 333 which is inapplicable.
>
> **(3)** A Corporation owns 600 shares of X; D Corporation owns 250 shares; E Corporation owns 50 shares; B, an individual, owns 75 shares; and C, an individual, owns 25 shares. Only D Corporation and B filed timely elections. Section 333 is applicable to distributions to the D Corporation, but it is not applicable to distributions to B or to any other shareholder. D Corporation owned stock

---

283 I.R.C. § 333(c)(2).
284 I.R.C. § 333(b).

possessing a total combined voting power of greater than 80% of the voting stock held by corporate shareholders (other than *A* which is an excluded corporation). However, *B* held stock possessing only 75% of the combined voting power of the voting stock held by noncorporate shareholders.

The Regulations provide that a timely election cannot be revoked.[285] While one court of appeals decision allowed the shareholders to revoke an election where the actual earnings and profits of the distributing corporation were substantially greater than the shareholders had believed when they made the election,[286] other courts have accepted the regulation.[287]

A stringent requisite of § 333 is that the distribution in liquidation of all of the corporation's assets must be made within one calendar month;[288] and the failure to comply with that provision will preclude all the shareholders from using § 333. The Regulations ameliorate this statutory requisite by providing that a corporation may retain a reasonable amount of cash under an arrangement for the payment of unascertained or contingent liabilities and expenses, even though payment will be made after the calendar month, provided that the arrangement for payment is made in good faith.[289] The Service has further held that the corporation may retain a reserve for payment of attorneys' fees, accountants' fees and other expenses of liquidation if such reserve is established in good faith and is reasonable.[290]

Difficulties in meeting the calendar month requirement may arise from a variety of sources. The corporation may own assets which are difficult to assign (*e.g.*, an exclusive franchise right or

---

285 Treas. Reg. § 1.333-2(b)(1).
286 Meyer's Estate v. Commissioner, 200 F.2d 592 (C.A. 5 1952).
287 Raymond v. United States, 269 F.2d 181 (C.A. 6 1959). However, in such cases the taxpayer's plight will often elicit the court's sympathy, and the court may be more receptive to an argument advanced by the taxpayer that the shareholder's election was invalid for failure to comply with one of the statutory requisites. *See, e.g.,* Harold O, Wales, 50 T.C. 399 (1968).
288 I.R.C. § 333(a)(2).
289 Treas. Reg. § 1.333-1(b).
290 Rev. Rul. 56-286, 1956-1 C.B. 172.

an income tax refund claim).[291] The corporate officer may not be able to locate one or more shareholders, or the corporate assets may not be readily susceptible to a division among the shareholders. In these latter instances, distribution to a trust or an escrow agent may comply with the statute, but care must be taken to comply with § 333 and to avoid pitfalls under other provisions of the Code.[292]

Section 333 is not applicable to the liquidation of a collapsible corporation,[293] unless § 341(e)(3) applies.

(d) Usefulness of section 333. Since the nonrecognition provisions of § 333 have many exceptions and since the rules of allocation of basis may operate unfavorably, the section is of limited usefulness. Some warning signs indicating that § 333 may not be helpful are: (i) a sizable amount of earnings and profits in the corporation; (ii) large amounts of cash, and post-1953 stock and securities in the corporation; (iii) an expectation that the corporate assets will be sold soon after acquisition;[294] (iv) a substantial amount of depreciable property in the corporation which will receive a low basis on a § 333 liquidation; and (v) if the distributing corporation will recognize income on making the distributions in liquidation (*see* Chapter II *infra*), the resulting increase in the corporation's earnings and profits may have an adverse tax consequence to the shareholders.

(e) Liquidation of corporations which became personal holding companies as a result of amendments adopted in 1964. In 1964, Congress amended the personal holding company provisions of the Code so

---

291 31 U.S.C. § 203 imposes restrictions on the assignment of claims against the Government; but there is precedent for allowing such claims to be assigned to shareholders upon liquidation of a corporation. Wells Fargo Bank & Union Trust Co. v. United States, 115 F. Supp. 655 (N.D. Cal. 1953); and United States v. Improved Premises, Etc., 204 F. Supp. 868 (S.D. N.Y. 1962).

292 For a discussion of the difficulties encountered in this area and some possible solutions, *see* Portfolio #58-3rd "Corporate Liquidations under Section 333" pp. A-16 to A-21, TAX MANAGEMENT (BNA).

293 I.R.C. § 341 defines collapsible corporations. *See* pp. 37-44 *supra*.

294 For example, the liquidation of a corporation holding unimproved and highly appreciated land might better be received in a taxable exchange so that the shareholder may obtain a higher basis for the land and recognize less ordinary income when he subdivides and sells it. Of course, attention should also be directed to the collapsible corporation provisions.

that many corporations previously excluded from that classification were no longer so fortunate.[295] Consequently, with certain exceptions, such corporations were forced either to distribute their earnings to their shareholders or to pay a 70% surtax. In order to minimize the tax consequences of liquidating a corporation which prior to 1964 had been operating outside the scope of the personal holding provisions and which was caught by the 1964 changes, Congress provided that where such a corporation was liquidated under § 333, the tax consequences to the shareholders will be lightened if certain requisites are satisfied.[296] For many (but not all) corporations, this relief measure is applicable only to liquidations which occurred prior to January 1, 1967; and in any event the exceptional relief afforded by § 333 is of limited availability.

4. Sale of corporate assets pursuant to a plan of liquidation

Prior to the adoption of the 1954 Code, there was considerable risk of "double" tax consequences on the liquidation of a corporation. While the 1954 Code has ameliorated the tax impact on liquidations, some of the pre-1954 problems persist, and the prior law has continuing vitality. The following example illustrates the nature of these problems.

Ex. *A*, an individual, owns all of the outstanding stock of the *X* Corporation. *A* wishes to liquidate the *X* Corporation and sell its assets.

(1) Under the pre-1954 law, if *X* were to sell its assets to a third party for an amount greater than its basis in the assets, *X* would recognize a taxable gain on the sale. If subsequently *X* were to distribute the proceeds of sale to *A* in redemption of *A*'s stock, that transfer would constitute a taxable exchange as to *A*. Consequently, tax liabilities would be imposed twice on the devolution of *X*'s assets to *A* — once on *X* when it sold the assets and once on *A* when he received the proceeds in liquidation.

(2) If, instead of selling its assets, *X* were to distribute

---

295 Section 219 of the Revenue Act of 1964. *See* Libin, *Personal Holding Companies and the Revenue Act of 1964*, 63 MICH. L. REV. 421 (1965).

296 I.R.C. § 333(g). *See* Libin, *Personal Holding Companies and the Revenue Act of 1964*, 63 MICH. L. REV. 421, 446-448 (1965).

its assets to A in complete liquidation, the transfer would constitute a taxable exchange as to A, who would therefore incur tax liabilities. However, A's basis in the distributed assets would equal their fair market value, and consequently, if A were then to sell the assets to Y, A would not realize any gain on the sale. Thus, by reversing the order of sale and distribution, the net tax impact on the liquidation can be substantially reduced.

There are two obstacles hindering the use of the second alternative as a means of minimizing the tax consequences. First, it is not always expedient to distribute a corporation's assets in kind. Second, and more importantly, the sale of the corporation's assets by the shareholder may be attributed to the corporation under the *Court Holding* doctrine.[297] In *Court Holding*, the Supreme Court affirmed a Tax Court holding that a shareholder's sale of corporate assets received in liquidation of the corporation was in reality a sale on behalf of the corporation and accordingly that the corporation recognized taxable gain therefrom. In that case, the corporation had negotiated the terms of a sale, and then had distributed its assets to its shareholder who consummated the sale. The fears engendered by *Court Holding* were not abated by the Supreme Court's decision in *United States v. Cumberland Public Service Co.*[298] five years later. In *Cumberland*, the shareholders had unsuccessfully sought to sell their corporate shares to a buyer. In turn, the buyer offered to purchase most of the corporate assets from the corporation, but the corporation refused that offer. The corporation's shareholders then offered to acquire the corporate assets and to sell them to the buyer, and upon the buyer's acceptance, the transaction was effected accordingly. The Supreme Court held that the sale in *Cumberland* was not made on behalf of the corporation, and therefore was not taxable to it.

The result of the *Court Holding* and *Cumberland* cases was to attach unwarranted significance to the order in which the corporation's assets were sold and distributed, and to burden shareholders who are contemplating corporate liquidations with substantial doubts as to the tax consequences. In order to cure these prob-

---

297 Commissioner v. Court Holding Co., 324 U.S. 331 (1945).
298 338 U.S. 451 (1950).

lems,[299] Congress adopted § 337 of the 1954 Code, which, where applicable, denies recognition of gains or losses realized by a liquidating corporation on the sale of its assets. Nevertheless, the *Court Holding* and *Cumberland* decisions have continuing relevance; and even today, in some circumstances, it may be advantageous to liquidate a corporation first and then have the shareholders sell its assets. For example, corporate sales and liquidations are often subject to local state income taxes, and many states have not adopted[300] a counterpart to § 337 so that for those states, a sale and liquidation may cause a double state tax incidence unless the corporation liquidates first and the shareholder sells afterwards. Also, in some instances it may not be possible to qualify a liquidation under § 337, or to qualify certain sales of the corporation's assets[301] under § 337, and in either event the *Cumberland* approach might be utilized.

Section 337 is frequently employed, and is one of the most important code provisions concerning corporate liquidations and the sale of an incorporated business. Consequently, the details of that section should be examined carefully.

(a) General operation of section 337. Section 337 provides that if a corporation adopts a plan of complete liquidation on or after June 22, 1954, and all of the assets of the liquidating corporation are distributed within the 12-month period commencing on the date of adoption of such plan, then no gain or loss will be recognized to such corporation from the sale or exchange of corporate property within the 12-month period. The nonrecognition provision of § 337 is mandatory; and where § 337 is applicable, neither gain nor loss can be recognized irrespective of the wishes of the corporation and its shareholders.

---

299 S. Rept. No. 1622, 83d Cong., 2d Sess., pp. 48-49 (1954). In that report, the Senate Committee on Finance stated (p. 49): "The result of [the Court Holding and Cumberland] decisions is that undue weight is accorded the formalities of the transaction and they, therefore, represent merely a trap for the unwary."

300 Where a state has adopted a tax law which conforms with the federal tax laws (*e.g.*, MICH. COMP. LAWS §§ 206.1-206.499 (1948)), the state tax law will usually create no additional planning problems.

301 For example, it may not be feasible to sell the corporation's inventory in a single bulk sale. See I.R.C. § 337(b). The liquidation and subsequent sale of the inventory by the shareholders nevertheless may be attributed to the corporation. *Cf.* United States v. Lynch, 192 F.2d 718 (C.A. 9 1951), *cert. denied,* 343 U.S. 934 (1952).

Ex. (1) X Corporation adopted a plan of complete liquidation on June 12, 1962. On August 12, 1962, X sold Blackacre to A for $50,000, and X had a basis of $20,000 in Blackacre. On February 10, 1963, X sold 100 shares of stock of the Y Corporation to B for $30,000; X had a basis of $33,000 in those 100 shares of Y's stock. X distributed ¾ of its assets to its shareholders on March 5, 1963, and distributed the balance of its assets on May 14, 1963. Neither the $30,000 gain realized on the sale of Blackacre nor the $3,000 loss realized on the sale of the Y stock is recognized by X.

Ex. (2) If, in the above example, ¾ of the assets of the X Corporation were distributed to its shareholders on March 5, 1963, and the balance of its assets were distributed on July 2, 1963 (more than 12 months after the plan was adopted), then § 337 will not apply[302] and both the gain from the sale of Blackacre and the loss from the sale of the Y stock will be recognized.

Even where § 337 is applicable, not all sales or dispositions within the requisite 12-month period are free from tax consequences. Transactions which cause taxable income to the corporation are discussed in paragraph (b) below.

(b) Qualifying for nonrecognition under section 337. As noted above, § 337 is applicable only where:

(i) A corporation adopts a plan of complete liquidation on or after June 22, 1954; and

(ii) All of the assets of the corporation, other than a reasonable amount of assets retained in good faith to satisfy existing liabilities, expenses and claims (including unascertained or contingent liabilities and claims),[303] must be distributed in liquidation within the 12-month period commencing with the date[304] of adoption of the plan of liquidation.

---

302 Section 337 may apply if the assets retained beyond the 12-month period were held in order to satisfy outstanding expenses, liabilities and claims (contingent or otherwise) provided that the amount retained is reasonable and bona fide. Treas. Reg. § 1.337-2(b).

303 Treas. Reg. § 1.337-2(b). Retaining assets to satisfy outstanding obligations involves some risk, however. *E.g.,* John Town, Inc., 46 T.C. 107 (1966).

304 The determination of the date on which the plan of liquidation was adopted has caused some difficulties. *See* Treas. Reg. § 1.337-2(b), and City Bank of Washington, 38 T.C. 713 (1962), non-acq., 1964-2 C.B. 4. This question is discussed at pp. 92-93 *infra*.

Section 337 provides for nonrecognition of gain or loss realized by the corporation from sales of *property* made during the 12-month period commencing with the date of adoption of the plan of liquidation. There are a number of exceptions to that nonrecognition provision.

(i) *Sale of inventory.* A corporation's sale of its stock in trade, or inventory, or property held for sale to customers in the ordinary course of its trade or business will not be covered by § 337 (and therefore gain or loss from such sales will be recognized); except that if substantially all of such property which is attributable to a trade or business of the corporation is sold to one person in one transaction, then § 337 will apply to the sale of such property. The apparent reason for this exclusion is that § 337 was intended to accord tax relief for sales made in the process of liquidating a corporate enterprise, and should not be made available for sales of inventory to customers in the ordinary course of business. Where a corporation is involved in two or more trades or businesses, the inventory, etc., of each trade or business may be sold in a separate bulk sale under the protection of § 337, and the Service's construction of separate trades or business has been reasonably liberal as the following examples paraphrased from Treas. Reg. § 1.337-3(d) indicate. It is assumed in the following examples that the liquidations considered were completed in compliance with § 337.

Ex. (1) Corporation *A* operates a hardware store and a grocery store at different locations. The two stores share a common warehouse, but they handle unrelated items. Within 12 months after adopting a plan of liquidation, *A* sold the entire inventory of the hardware business to *B* in one transaction, and distributed all of its assets (including the proceeds of sale and the inventory of the grocery store) to its shareholders. Since the hardware business is a separate business, the sale of its inventory is covered by § 337 and no gain or loss is recognized on that sale.

Ex. (2) Corporation *B* operates two department stores, each in a different location. Both stores handle the same items and use a common warehouse. If the inventory held in the warehouse which is attributable to each store can be determined, and if all the inventory of one store, including the inventory held in the warehouse on behalf of that store, is sold to one person in one transaction, no gain or loss will be recognized on that sale. However, if the inventory held in the warehouse cannot be attributed to either store separately, and if the inventory of one store, exclusive of the inventory stored in the warehouse, is sold to one person in one transaction, § 337 is not applicable to such sale.

The potential breadth of the "inventory" exceptions to § 337 is indicated by the Tax Court's decision in *Hollywood Baseball Association*, 49 T.C. 338 (1968) (on remand from the United States Supreme Court) that the employment contracts a baseball club had with its players constituted inventory and consequently that sales of the contracts were not protected by § 337.

(ii) *Sale of installment obligations.* Where § 337 is otherwise applicable to a liquidation,

(aa) The sale of an installment obligation which was acquired by the corporation in respect of property sold by the corporation prior to the date of adoption of the plan of liquidation is not covered by § 337, and gain or loss therefrom is recognized;[305]

(bb) The sale of an installment obligation which was acquired by the corporation in respect of the sale of property (other than the sale of inventory or stock in trade, the sale of property in which ordinary income realized under I.R.C. §§ 1245 or 1250 was deferred or the sale of assets subject to recognition of gain under § 341(f)) on or after the date of adoption of the plan of liquidation is covered by § 337; and

(cc) The sale of an installment obligation acquired by the corporation in respect of the sale of inventory or stock in trade is not covered by § 337; except that where substantially all of the inventory and stock in trade of a single trade or business was sold to one person in one

---

305 I.R.C. § 337(b).

transaction within the requisite 12-month period, then
the sale of an installment obligation received as part or
full payment for the bulk sale of such inventory and stock
in trade is covered by § 337 if the sale of such installment obligation is also made within the requisite 12-
month period.[306]

(iii) *Sale of depreciable property.* Prior to 1962, gain realized from the sale of property used in a trade or business
was usually treated as capital gains.[307] With the adoption of
§ 1245 in 1962, and the adoption of § 1250 in 1964, part
or all of the gain from the sale of depreciable property is
treated as ordinary income.[308] For convenience, the amount of
ordinary income recognized under § 1245 or § 1250 is sometimes referred to herein as "§ 1245 gain" or "§ 1250 gain."

Sections 1245 and 1250 state that they apply notwithstanding other provision of the Code.[309] Consequently, even though

---

306 I.R.C. § 337(b)(1)(B) and (b)(2).
307 I.R.C. § 1231.
308 Sections 1245 and 1250 are sometimes referred to as the "recapture
of depreciation" provisions. I.R.C. § 1245 requires the recognition of
ordinary income upon the sale of depreciable personal property and
of certain depreciable real property (other than a building and its
structural components) to the extent that the amount of taxable gain
realized on the sale is attributable to depreciation deductions allowed
the taxpayer while he held the property. Only depreciation for periods
after the year 1961 (or June 30, 1963, for elevators and escalators)
is taken into account.
   I.R.C. § 1250 is similar in principle to § 1245 except that: (i)
§ 1250 applies to depreciable real property which is not covered by
§ 1245; (ii) only depreciation allowed after the year 1963 is taken
into account; (iii) where the real property is held for more than one
year, the amount of depreciation that is recaptured is limited to a
percentage of the excess of the total amount of depreciation taken
over the total amount of depreciation that would have been taken if
the straight line method of depreciation were used (*i.e.,* where the
property is held for more than one year, the recapture provisions
apply only where an accelerated method of depreciation was used, and
then only to a portion of the excess depreciation taken); and (iv) if
the real property is held for over 10 years, none of the depreciation
is recaptured. The scope of § 1250 may be expanded by the proposed
Tax Reform Act of 1969, if it is enacted.
   The application of the recapture provisions of §§ 1245 and 1250
is not limited to sales and exchanges, but those sections also apply
to other dispositions of depreciable property including some dispositions which otherwise would not be taxable transactions. Some examples of this aspect of §§ 1245 and 1250 are noted at pp. 109-111 *infra.*
   The provisions of §§ 1245 and 1250 are complex; for an analysis
of those sections, *see* Portfolio #97 "Depreciation Recapture—*Sections* 1245 and 1250," TAX MANAGEMENT (BNA).
309 I.R.C. §§ 1245(d) and 1250(h).

a corporation's sale of depreciable property is within § 337, the "§§ 1245 and 1250 gain" from that sale will nevertheless be recognized to the corporation.[310]

> **Ex.** In 1963, the X Corporation acquired a machine which it used in its business. The cost of the machine was $5,000. On April 5, 1965, the X Corporation sold the machine for $6,000, and that sale was covered by § 337. X had accrued depreciation deductions of $2,000 at the time of sale, and consequently X had a basis of $3,000 in the machine. X realized gain of $3,000 on the sale, of which $2,000 was § 1245 gain and $1,000 was not. X recognizes the $2,000 § 1245 gain, but § 337 provides nonrecognition for the additional $1,000 realized gain.

The sale of property the cost of which had been fully deducted by the corporation raises an additional question discussed in paragraph (v) *infra*.

When a corporation acquired a depreciable asset, it may have been allowed a tax credit (the so-called "investment credit") for that acquisition.[311] The amount of that credit depends upon the useful life of the property.[312] Consequently, if the corporation disposes of such property prior to the expiration of the minimum holding period required for the amount of credit taken, the corporation will recognize a tax liability as a "recapture" of all or a part of the credit previously taken.[313] The provision for a recapture of an investment credit takes precedence over the nonrecognition provision of § 337.

The Supreme Court's decision in *Fribourg Nav. Co. v. Commissioner*, 383 U.S. 272 (1966) established that a sale of depreciable property for an amount in excess of basis does not require the disallowance of depreciation accrued in the year of sale.

(iv) *Sale of accounts receivable.* Where a corporation which reported its income on the cash method of accounting sold

---

310 Treas. Reg. § 1.1245-6(b).
311 I.R.C. § 38 *et seq.* The investment credit may soon be terminated by Congress. *See* H. Rept. 91-321 (accompanying H. R. 12290) 91st Cong., 1st Sess. (June 20, 1969).
312 I.R.C. § 46(c)(2).
313 I.R.C. § 47.

its accounts receivable and contended that § 337 precluded the recognition of gain from the sale, the Court of Appeals for the Ninth Circuit held that under I.R.C. § 446(b),[314] the Commissioner could require the corporation to recognize the amount received in payment for the receivables as income.[315] A sale of receivables by other cash basis corporations is likely to meet a similar fate.

Where a corporation which reports its income on the accrual method of accounting sells its accounts receivable, there will usually be no gain realized from the such sales since the corporation has previously accounted for the income reflected in the receivables. However, if the corporation had established, and deducted, a bad debt reserve for the accounts receivable it sold, the Service contends that the corporation must recognize the amount of the reserve as income.[316] Indeed, the Service contends that the corporation will recognize such income even where it sells the accounts receivable for an amount equal to the difference between the face value of the receivables and the amount of the bad debt reserve, *i.e.*, the corporation will recognize income on the cancelled reserve, even where its estimate of bad debts proves accurate.[317] The Service's position rests on a "tax benefit" theory; since the corporation deducted the amount of the bad debt reserve from its prior years' income as an estimate of the receivables that would prove to be uncollectible, the disposition of the receivables eliminates the possibility that the corporation will suffer a bad debt loss from them and consequently the corporation must recognize as income the amount previously deducted. Where the amount paid the corporation for its receivables is less than the face amount of the receivables (thereby vindicating all or part of the corporation's estimate of bad debts), the Service maintains that the difference constitutes a loss on the sale of the receivables, and this loss is not recognized under § 337.

---

314 Under I.R.C. § 446(b), where a taxpayer's method of accounting does not clearly reflect his income, the Commissioner may require the taxpayer to change his method of accounting to a method which the Commissioner determines does clearly reflect the taxpayer's income.

315 Family Record Plan, Inc. v. Commissioner, 309 F.2d 208 (C.A. 9 1962), *cert. denied,* 373 U.S. 910 (1963).

316 Rev. Rul. 57-482, 1957-2 C.B. 49.

317 J. E. Hawes Corp., 44 T.C. 705 (1965).

The Service's treatment of bad debt reserves under § 337 is identical to its treatment of such reserves where accounts receivable of a going business are transferred to a controlled corporation under § 351;[318] the cases dealing with this issue under § 351 and § 337 rest on the same principles and, for purposes of precedent, are interchangeable.

The Service's inclusion of an amount equal to bad debt reserves in a corporation's income is reasonable where the accounts receivable are sold at face value, but is doubtful where the receivables are sold for less than face value. Perhaps the Service's position can be rationalized on the basis that if the liquidating corporation had not been permitted by the tax laws to establish a bad debt reserve, which is an estimate of the amount of receivables that will prove to be uncollectible, the corporation would not have enjoyed any deduction for the reserve; and when the corporation sold the receivables, it would have realized a loss (the difference between the face amount of the receivables and their actual value) which would not be recognized under § 337. It might be contended that the granting of permission to establish a bad debt reserve should not permit the corporation to enjoy a tax deduction that otherwise would never be made available to it. The position of the Service has been adopted by the Fifth Circuit and by the Tax Court,[319] but was rejected by the Ninth Circuit,[320] the United States District Court in Colorado,[321] and the United

---

318 *See* Chapter V *infra.*
319 Nash v. United States, 24 A.F.T.R.2d 69-5272 (C.A. 5 1969); Bird Management, Inc., 48 T.C. 586 (1967); and J. E. Hawes Corp., 44 T.C. 705 (1965); and Max Schuster, 50 T.C. 98 (1968) (three judges dissenting); *Schuster* is pending on appeal.
320 Estate of Schmidt v. Commissioner, 355 F.2d 111 (C.A. 9 1966). *Schmidt* involved a transfer to a controlled corporation under § 351. In West Seattle National Bank of Seattle v. Commissioner, 288 F.2d 47 (C.A. 9 1961), the Ninth Circuit held that the bad debt reserve was properly recognized by the liquidating corporation as income, but in that case the receivables were sold for an amount equal to their face value which was greater than their net value. The Government apparently wishes to relitigate this issue in the Ninth Circuit, since it has announced that it will appeal from its adverse judgment in Scofield v. United States, 23 A.F.T.R.2d 69-1447 (C.D. Cal. 1969). *Scofield* also involved a transfer to a controlled corporation under § 351.
321 Mountain States Mixed Feed Co. v. United States, 245 F. Supp. 369 (D. Colo. 1965), *affirmed without consideration of this issue,* 365 F.2d 244 (C.A. 10 1966).

States District Court for the Northern District of Alabama.[322] A recent decision of the Tax Court, however, may render this problem moot insofar as it relates to § 337. In *Coast Coil Co.*,[323] the Tax Court held that accounts receivable constituted installment obligations and consequently that the gain or loss realized from their sale was beyond the scope of § 337 and accordingly was to be recognized by the taxpayer. In the *Coast Coil* case, the Court permitted an accrual basis taxpayer to deduct the loss realized by it on the sale of its receivables for less than their face value. The Tax Court's decision conforms with an earlier Tax Court case[324] which previously had been ignored because it had been affirmed by the Ninth Circuit on different grounds and it was assumed that the Ninth Circuit's failure to discuss this issue constituted an implied rejection of it. The effect of the *Coast Coil* decision on this problem is illustrated by the following example:

Ex. The X Corporation has accounts receivable in the face amount of $30,000. X has established a $5,000 bad debt reserve so that the net amount of its receivables is $25,000. Pursuant to a liquidation under § 337, X sells its receivables to Y for their net amount—$25,000. Under the Service's position,[325] X will recognize $5,000 income under a tax benefit theory since X obtained a $5,000 deduction in anticipation of becoming uncollectible and X can never realize those bad debt losses after having disposed of the receivables. Of course, X's basis in its receivables must then be increased to $30,000, so X realized a $5,000 loss on the sale, but the Service contends that the loss is unrecognized because of § 337. However, the Tax Court's decision in *Coast Coil* requires the recognition of gain or loss sustained on the sale of receivables; and consequently X would recognize $5,000 income under the tax benefit rule and would recognize a $5,000 loss on the sale, and the two will wash out.

---

322 Birmingham Trust National Bank v. United States, 22 A.F.T.R.2d 5202 (N.D. Ala. 1968), *reversed sub nom.* Nash v. United States, 24 A.F.T.R.2d 69-5272 (C.A. 5 1969).
323 50 T.C. 528 (1968).
324 Family Record Plan, Inc., 36 T.C. 305 (1961), *affirmed on other grounds,* 309 F.2d 208 (C.A. 9 1962), *cert. denied,* 373 U.S. 910 (1963).
325 As noted above, the Service's position has been rejected by the Ninth Circuit and by three District Courts.

The Service has appealed in *Coast Coil*, and the ultimate disposition of that case will be very important.

(v) *Sale of assets, the cost of which were fully deducted prior to sale.* The Service maintains that where a corporation sells an item, the cost of which had been deducted in full in prior years, the amount received on the sale is recognized income to the corporation, notwithstanding the provisions of § 337.[326] The Service rests its contention on a "tax benefit" theory. Presumably, the Service's position is limited to the sale of items the cost of which was fully deducted in the year of acquisition as an expense in contrast to items the cost of which was fully deducted over a period of years through depreciation allowances. In any event the recapture provisions of § 1245 will usually prevent a tax benefit on the sale of fully depreciated personal property, but it is unlikely that § 1245 applies to property the cost of which was "expensed" in the year of acquisition.[327]

Both the Tax Court[328] (*Anders*) and the United States District Court for the District of Arizona[329] (*Spitalny*) have rejected the Government's position and held that income from the sale of previously expensed properties was not recognized by the corporation where the sale was covered by § 337. The Tenth Circuit reversed the Tax Court's decision in *Anders* (24 A.F.T.R. 2d 69-5133), and the Government has authorized an appeal in *Spitalny*.

Section 337 is intended to equate the tax consequences to a corporation and its shareholders of the sale of a corporation's assets followed by a liquidation with the tax consequences that attend a complete liquidation, followed promptly by the shareholders' sale of its assets. Consequently, where

---

326 Rev. Rul. 61-214, 1961-2 C.B. 60.
327 The deduction for the cost of an item as an expense is not depreciation or amortization, and only the latter two deductions are recaptured by § 1245. I.R.C. § 1245(a)(2). *See* Rev. Rul. 68-104, 1968-1 C.B. 361 where the Service concluded that property which had a useful life of less than one year was not depreciable and hence did not qualify for the tax treatment accorded by § 1231. *See also* Commissioner v. Anders, 24 A.F.T.R.2d 69-5133 (C.A. 10 1969).
328 D. B. Anders, 48 T.C. 815 (1967), *reversed* 24 A.F.T.R.2d 69-5133 (C.A. 10 1969).
329 Spitalny v. United States, 288 F. Supp. 650 (D. Ariz. 1968).

§ 337 is applicable, gain from the sale of expensed items of property should not be recognized by the corporation, unless the corporation would recognize the value of such items as income if such items were distributed in liquidation to the corporation's shareholders. Perhaps the Service will contend that liquidating distributions of expensed items create income to the distributing corporation, but the author knows of no instance in which that contention was made.

(vi) *Assignment of income, and change of accounting method.* A sale of property under § 337 may nevertheless cause recognition of income to the corporation where the exclusion of income from the sale would contravene other tax principles. We have already noted that the tax benefit theory may cause recognition of income,[330] and that the Commissioner may force the corporation to change its method of accounting to reflect income.[331] The corporation may also recognize income under assignment of income concepts.[332] While a sale of property, the recognized gain from which would be ordinary income to the corporation, may be covered by § 337 (*e.g.*, a bulk sale of inventory), corporations should be wary that the Government may attempt to impose tax consequences on such sales.[333] As indicated above, where gain from a sale reflects previously earned but unrecognized ordinary income,

---

330 See paragraphs (iv) and (v) above.
331 *See* Family Record Plan, Inc. v. Commissioner, 309 F.2d 208 (C.A. 9 1962), *cert. denied,* 373 U.S. 910 (1963).
332 Commissioner v. Kuckenberg, 309 F.2d 209 (C.A. 9 1962). *Kuckenberg* involved the sale of construction contracts by a cash basis corporation where at the date of sale the income from the contracts had been earned but was unpaid. *See also* Central Building & Loan Association, 34 T.C. 447 (1960), where a corporation was held to recognize gain on the sale of a promissory note to the extent of accrued but unpaid interest thereon; and *see* Rev. Rul. 59-120, 1959-1 C.B. 74.
333 In Pridemark, Inc. v. Commissioner, 345 F.2d 35 (C.A. 4 1965), the Fourth Circuit stated that the term "property" in § 337 referred only to capital assets and that the sale of noncapital assets (or at least the sale of items the gain from which would be ordinary income) is not covered by that provision. This statement in *Pridemark* is broader than was necessary for the decision in that case, and probably will not be construed literally in subsequent cases. Nevertheless, it constitutes a warning that should not be unheeded. Indeed, in Coast Coil Co., 50 T.C. 528 (1968), the Tax Court adopted the Fourth Circuit's view and made it an alternative ground for its holding that a corporation's loss on the sale of accounts receivable is not denied recognition by § 337. *See also* Commissioner v. Anders, 24 A.F.T.R.2d 69-5133 (C.A. 10 1969).

the gain will usually be recognized notwithstanding § 337.

(vii) *Involuntary conversions.* Section 337 applies to a "sale or exchange" of property, and there is a question whether all involuntary conversions constitute a sale or exchange.

The condemnation of property is treated as a sale or exchange of the condemned property.[334] The chief difficulty with applying § 337 to condemnations is the determination of when the sale occurred. The Service contends that the sale occurs when title passes to the condemning authority even though the price may not have been determined at that time.[335] The determination of the date title passed is a technical question and in some instances a difficult one to resolve. An early passage of title may cause recognition of income to the corporation if it antedates the adoption of the plan of liquidation.[336]

Initially, the question of the recognition of income from the proceeds of insurance or damages received on account of the destruction of property by fire or other casualty was subject to some doubt, but it now appears settled that § 337 is applicable to such income.[337] While the Service first contended that such income must be recognized,[338] it later reversed its position and conceded that § 337 is applicable.[339]

In *United States v. Morton, Sr.*,[340] the Eighth Circuit held that income from fire insurance proceeds paid during liquidation was not recognized under § 337 even though the fire occurred prior to the adoption of the plan of liquidation.

(viii) *Insolvent corporation.* The Service has ruled[341] that § 337 applies only where there is a distribution of some corporate assets to the shareholders; and consequently, under

---

334 Rev. Rul. 59-108, 1959-1 C.B. 72.
335 *Id.*
336 *E.g.,* Place Realty Corporation, ¶ 62, 144 P-H Memo T.C.
337 Kent Manufacturing Corp. v. Commissioner, 288 F.2d 812 (C.A. 4 1961) reversed a Tax Court holding that income was recognized on such conversions (33 T.C. 930 (1960)) and held that § 337 was applicable. *See also* Towanda Textiles Inc. v. United States, 180 F. Supp. 373 (Ct. Cl. 1960).
338 Rev. Rul. 56-372, 1956-2 C.B. 187.
339 Rev. Rul. 64-100, 1964-1 C.B. (Part 1) 130, revoking Rev. Rul. 56-372.
340 387 F.2d 441 (C.A. 8 1968).
341 Rev. Rul. 56-387, 1956-2 C.B. 189.

the Service's position, where the liquidating corporation is insolvent, gains from sales of its assets will be recognized. There is some inconsistency between this ruling and the policy underlying the income tax exclusion provided for gain realized from the cancellation of the debts of an insolvent debtor.[342] In view of the Service's ruling, it might be in the best interests of the creditors of an insolvent liquidating corporation to forgive a sufficient amount of the corporation's debts to permit a small distribution to the shareholders. The forgiveness of the debts will cause income to be recognized by the corporation only to the extent that the value of its assets exceeds its debts after the cancellation,[343] and even that small amount of income might be excluded under I.R.C. § 108 if an election is made under § 1017. The tax savings on the corporation's sale of its assets (which tax burden must ultimately be borne by the creditors) may more than compensate the creditors for their "generosity," and any assets the shareholders receive will improve their position.

(ix) *Section 341(f) assets.* Section 341(f), which was added to the Code in 1964, permits shareholders to sell stock of a collapsible corporation without incurring ordinary income from the sale, provided that an election is made under that section to "taint" certain corporate assets (called "subsection (f) assets") so that gain will be recognized by the corporation on disposition of those assets.[344] Thus, where a corporation sells subsection (f) assets, gain may be recognized by the corporation notwithstanding § 337.

(c) Determination of the date of adoption of the plan of liquidation. The Regulations[345] provide that the date of adoption of a plan of liquidation *ordinarily* is the date on which the shareholders adopted the resolution authorizing the corporation to distribute all of its assets in redemption of its stock. However, facts might indicate that the plan was adopted prior to the formal resolution of the

---

342 *See* Lakeland Grocery Co., 36 B.T.A. 289 (1937).
343 *Id.*
344 *See* p. 44 *supra.*
345 Treas. Reg. § 1.337-2(b).

shareholders.[346] A corporation might seek to straddle the date of adoption of a plan by first selling depreciated property for a recognized loss and then adopting a plan of liquidation after which its appreciated property may be sold for a nonrecognized gain. In such event, the Service may well contend that the plan was actually adopted prior to the sale of the depreciated assets. Surprisingly, the Service has not had outstanding success in its attacks on straddles.[347]

A related problem arises when the liquidating corporation abandons its initial plan of liquidation and then adopts a new plan. The question of whether the date of adoption of the plan is the date on which the first or second plan was adopted will usually turn on a factual determination as to whether the original plan was actually abandoned.[348]

(d) Collapsible corporations. Section 337 is not applicable to sales by a collapsible corporation,[349] and consequently gain from such sales is recognized. If a sufficient percentage of the assets of the corporation are sold, the corporation will not be collapsible because a substantial part of the income of the corporation was recognized.[350] This could lead to a type of *renvoi* where the recognition of income removes the corporation from the collapsible category; but if the corporation is not collapsible, then § 337 would preclude recognition of the income; but if the income is not recognized, then the corporation is collapsible, etc. The Service short-circuited this merry-go-round in its ruling that in such circumstances neither the non-recognition provisions of § 337 nor the ordinary income provisons of § 341 (the collapsible corporation section) will be applicable.[351]

(e) Liquidation within one calendar month under section 333. Section 337 is not applicable to sales by corporations if § 333 applies to the liquidation of the corporation.[352] Since a successful election under

---

346 In Rev. Rul. 65-235, 1965-2 C.B. 88 the Service held that a plan of liquidation could be adopted for a closely held corporation by an informal meeting of the controlling shareholders. *See also* Mountain Water Co. of La Crescenta, 35 T.C. 418 (1960).
347 *See* Virginia Ice & Freezing Corp., 30 T.C. 1251 (1958); and City Bank of Washington, 38 T.C. 713 (1962), Non-acq. 1964-2 C.B. 4.
348 *See* West Street-Erie Boulevard Corp. v. United States, 23 A.F.T.R.2d 69-1070 (C.A. 2 1969); and Malcolm C. Howell, 40 T.C. 940 (1963).
349 I.R.C. § 337(c)(1)(A).
350 I.R.C. § 341(b)(1). *See* pp. 41-42 *supra*.
351 Rev. Rul. 58-241, 1958-1 C.B. 179.
352 I.R.C. § 337(c)(1)(B).

§ 333 by any shareholder will preclude the corporation's use of § 337, it may be prudent in some circumstances to cause the distribution of the corporation's assets to be made over a period greater than one calendar month so that a group of minority shareholders cannot frustrate the plans of the majority by making an election under § 333.[353]

(f) Short-term gains. During the 12-month period of liquidation, a corporation may buy and sell stocks and securities resulting in short-term capital gains and losses. If the deferral of final distribution is bona fide, these short-term gains and losses will not be recognized by the liquidating corporation.[354]

(g) Sale of assets by a subsidiary corporation prior to a liquidation to which section 332 is applicable. With one exception noted below, the sale of corporate assets by a subsidiary corporation prior to its liquidation under § 332[355] will not be covered by § 337.[356] Section 337 was enacted to relieve liquidations from double tax incidence; and since the liquidation of a controlled subsidiary under § 332 does not cause taxable income to the parent corporation,[357] there is no reason to bar recognition of gains realized on the sale of the subsidiary's assets, and § 337 does not do so. However, § 332 does not provide nonrecognition of gain for minority shareholders;[358] and when the gain on the sale of the subsidiary's assets is recognized, a minority shareholder could suffer the double tax incidence that § 337 was designed to eliminate. Accordingly, the Technical Amendments Act of 1958 added § 337(d) to the 1954 Code, which provides relief for a minority shareholder—*viz.*, the minority shareholder treats his percentage of the tax paid by the subsidiary corporation on sales of corporate assets, from which income would not have been recognized had § 332 not been applicable, as an income

---

353 This would be possible where one group of shareholders is comprised of individuals and the other group is comprised of corporations.
354 Frank W. Verito, 43 T.C. 429 (1965), Acq. 1965-2 C.B. 7.
355 Section 332 encompasses the complete liquidations of a controlled subsidiary corporation. *See* pp. 62-70 *supra* for a discussion of that section.
356 I.R.C. § 337(c)(2).
357 I.R.C. § 332(a).
358 Treas. Reg. § 1.332-5.

tax credit,[359] and a like amount is deemed to have been distributed to him as a liquidating distribution. Thus, the net effect to the minority shareholder is essentially identical to what would have been his position had § 337 applied.

Ex. In the year 1966, the X Corporation had 100 shares of common stock outstanding, 10 shares of which were owned by A, an individual, and 90 shares of which were owned by the O Corporation. Within 12 months of adopting a plan of liquidation, X sold its inventory to a third party in a single bulk sale, and X realized a gain of $100,000 on the sale. X promptly liquidated and distributed its assets to A and O in redemption of their stock. Since § 332 is applicable and therefore § 337 did not provide nonrecognition for the sale, X recognized a gain of $100,000 on the sale, and X paid a corporate income tax of $48,000 thereon.

The total value of the property distributed to A in redemption of his stock was $15,000, and A's basis in his 10 shares of stock was $5,000. Consequently, in the absence of § 337, A would have recognized a long-term capital gain of $10,000 on the redemption, and A would have paid a tax of $2,500 on that gain.[360]

Under § 337(d), A must include in the amount received in redemption of his stock his 10% share of the tax paid by X on the sale of its inventory, *i.e.*, $4,800. Thus, A is deemed to have received $19,800 in redemption of his stock, and the income tax on his $14,800 gain is $3,700. However, A is treated as having paid $4,800 to the Government, and this amount wipes out his tax liability for the sale plus $1,100 of additional tax liability (or if A had no additional tax liability, he is entitled to a refund of $1,100). The net amount realized by A from the liquidation is:

---

359 The mechanics of allowing a "credit" to the minority shareholder is that he is deemed to have paid the Government an amount equal to the "credit" on the last day for which payment of tax for that taxable year is due. I.R.C. § 337(d)(2). A "credit" should not be confused with a deduction; the economic benefit of a credit is equal to the number of dollars of credit allowed, but the economic benefit of a deduction is equal to a percentage of the amount deducted determined according to the taxpayer's tax bracket.

360 The computation of A's tax is based on the assumption that he will employ the 25% alternative tax for capital gains.

$15,000 distributed
+ 4,800 credit
−(3,700) tax liability
_____
$16,100 total

Note that if § 337 had applied to the sale of the inventory by X, the net amount A realized from the liquidation would be identical. A would have received the $15,000 mentioned above. In addition, since § 337 would have relieved X of the $48,000 income tax liability, A would have received his 10% share of that amount, *i.e.*, $4,800. Thus, the net amount realized by A would be:

$19,800 distributed to A
−(3,700) tax liability
_____
$16,100 total

It should be noted that this provision for minority shareholders is not applicable if the basis of a liquidating subsidiary corporation's assets in the hands of the parent corporation is determined under I.R.C. § 334(b)(2).[361]

The one exception to the nonapplicability of § 337 to the liquidation of a subsidiary under § 332 is when the statutory codification (I.R.C. § 334(b)(2)) of the so-called "Kimbell-Diamond" rule is applicable.[362] The rationale of § 334(b)(2) is that where a corporation acquired a controlling interest in the stock of a second corporation for the purpose of liquidating the second corporation and taking over its assets, the substance of the transaction was that the acquiring corporation purchased the assets of the second corporation through the medium of a stock acquisition, and the transaction should be treated as a purchase of assets for purposes of determining basis.[363] Thus, when § 334(b)(2) is applicable, the basis to the parent corporation of the assets of the subsidiary corporation received by the parent as liquidating distributions is equal to the parent's basis in the stock of the subsidiary.

_____

361 *See* pp. 68-70 *supra.*
362 For a discussion of the "Kimbell-Diamond" rule and § 334(b)(2), *see* pp. 59-60, 68-70 *supra.*
363 While the above statement reflects the rationale of § 334(b)(2), the operation of that section turns on technical objective facts rather than on a determination of subjective motivation. *See* pp. 68-70 *supra.*

Congress has sought to conform § 337 with the aims of the "Kimbell-Diamond" rule. Thus, if § 334(b)(2) is applicable in determining the basis of property acquired by a parent corporation on liquidation of its subsidiary, § 337 will apply to provide non-recognition of *gain* realized by the subsidiary on sale of its corporate assets, but such nonrecognition is limited in amount to the difference between (i) the adjusted basis of the subsidiary's stock in the hands of the parent corporation that is allocable to such assets sold by the subsidiary, and (ii) the basis of such assets in the hands of the liquidating corporation.[364] Any gain in excess of that difference will be recognized, and all losses will be recognized. In effect, the Code "steps-up" the basis of assets in the subsidiary corporation to the basis such assets would have had under § 334 (b)(2) in the hands of the parent corporation if such assets had been distributed in liquidation. Strangely, this change of basis in the hands of the subsidiary corporation operates only for purposes of nonrecognition of gain and has no effect on losses incurred by the subsidiary through sales of its assets. Consequently, when § 334(b)(2) is applicable, a subsidiary corporation may recognize the losses realized from the sale of depreciated assets, and may simultaneously sell appreciated assets without recognizing the gain realized on the latter sales; and the deduction allowed for the recognized losses is not reduced by the nonrecognized gains.[365] Clearly, where a liquidation under § 334(b)(2) is contemplated, there are significant tax advantages to having the subsidiary sell depreciated assets prior to the liquidation; for if the assets are distributed to the parent corporation, the parent's basis in the assets will not reflect the depreciation suffered, and therefore the loss will never be recognized.

When the assets of a subsidiary corporation are to be sold, the subsidiary liquidated, and the parent corporation liquidated shortly thereafter, there is a risk that the subsidiary's sale of its assets will not be covered by § 337, and that gain will be recognized on

---

364 I.R.C. § 337(c)(2)(B); and Treas. Reg. § 1.337-4. For purposes of this provision, the basis of the parent's stock is allocated among the subsidiary's assets according to their fair market value on the date that the first item of property is sold, and that allocation remains unchanged unless the parent's stock ownership is altered. Treas. Reg. § 1.337-4(c).

365 United States Holding Co., 44 T.C. 323 (1965), Acq. 1966-2 C.B. 7.

such sale.[366] However, if the *Fairfield* holding[367] were adopted, the liquidation of the subsidiary would not qualify under § 332 where the parent corporation is to be liquidated soon after receiving the subsidiary's assets; and consequently the sale of the subsidiary's assets may be covered by § 337. But the validity of the *Fairfield* doctrine is extremely doubtful; and a recent Revenue Ruling, which discusses several variations of the above situation, does not even mention the possibility that § 332 would not be applicable in such cases.[368] It would be most unwise to rely on *Fairfield* for planning purposes.

From a tax viewpoint, there are two safer courses of action. One is to have both the parent and the subsidiary corporation adopt plans of liquidation, liquidate the subsidiary first, and then have the parent sell the assets, in which event under § 337, the gain from the sales made by the parent corporation (including gain from the liquidation of the subsidiary) will not be recognized.[369] However, the subsidiary must not conduct any negotiations for the sale of its assets before liquidating because, if it does, the Service will contend that the *Court Holding Co.* doctrine[370] then applies to make the subsidiary the actual seller of its assets; and thus the gain thereby imputed to the subsidiary will not be protected by § 337.[371] The second and safest course of action is to liquidate the parent corporation first so that the subsidiary's subsequent liquidation will not qualify under § 332; and therefore gain from sales made by both the subsidiary and the parent will be covered by § 337.[372] There will be only one tax imposed since the basis of the parent's shareholders in the subsidiary's stock received by them in liquidation of the parent will equal the stock's value.

(h) Reincorporations. Section 337 requires that the assets of the selling corporation be distributed in "complete liquidation" of the corporation. Where the liquidating corporation sells assets to an

---

366 As noted above, § 337 will not usually apply to sales of a liquidating corporation where § 332 is applicable to the liquidation.
367 Fairfield Steamship Corp. v. Commissioner, 157 F.2d 321 (C.A. 2 1946). *See* p. 68 *supra.*
368 Rev. Rul. 69-172; I.R.B. 1969-15, p. 10.
369 *Id.* Situation 3.
370 *See* p. 79 *supra.*
371 Rev. Rul. 69-172; I.R.B. 1969-15, p. 10, Situation 4.
372 *Id.* Situation 1.

acquiring corporation, some of the stock of which is owned by the shareholders of the liquidating corporation, there is a risk that the transaction may be characterized as a reorganization and that the distributions in "liquidation" may be deemed "boot" and possibly taxed to the shareholders as ordinary income.[373] It is not settled what percentage of the purchasing corporation must be held by the liquidating corporation's shareholders before a reorganization will be deemed to exist; but the Service has determined that a sale of this kind is a reorganization where only 45% of the purchasing corporation's stock was held by the liquidating corporation's shareholders;[374] and the Service has implied that 20% common ownership is within the danger area by its announced refusal to rule whether one corporation's sales to a second corporation will qualify under § 337 when more than 20% in value of the stock of both corporations is held by the same persons.[375] While it is doubtful that common ownership of less than 50% will be treated as a reincorporation if the matter is litigated, it is usually more prudent to avoid litigation where it is possible to do so.

Where the assets of a liquidating corporation are sold to an acquiring corporation and part of the purchase price is satisfied by the delivery of notes of the acquiring corporation, consideration should be given to the risk that such notes will be deemed hybrid stock or equity investment so that the subsequent distribution of those notes in liquidation will vest the shareholders of the liquidating corporation with an equity interest in the acquiring corporation. In such event the transaction might be characterized as a reorganization and the liquidating distributions treated as boot.

(i) Deductibility of expenses of liquidation. Generally, the expenses of liquidating a corporation are deductible;[376] however, there are special considerations where the expenses are incurred in connection with the sale of corporate assets, gain or loss from which is not recognized under § 337.

---

373 Rev. Rul. 61-156, 1961-2 C.B. 62.
374 Rev. Rul. 61-156, 1961-2 C.B. 62 revoked a more liberal construction previously adopted by the Service in Rev. Rul. 56-541, 1956-2 C.B. 189.
375 Rev. Proc. 69-6 (§ 3.01-9) I.R.B. 1969-1, p. 30.
376 *E.g.,* Pacific Coast Biscuit Co., 32 B.T.A. 39 (1935).

(i) *State income tax liability incurred on sale.* For several years, the Service contended that state income taxes incurred by reason of a sale of corporate assets, gain from which is not recognized for federal tax purposes, are not deductible expenses.[377] The Service based its disallowance of a deduction on I.R.C. § 265 which denies deductibility to expenses incurred in connection with income which is wholly exempt from tax. The Service's position was uniformly rejected in litigation[378] for the reason that § 337 does not render the gain from sales "wholly exempt" from income, but rather provides nonrecognition to avoid double taxation. After several unsuccessful years, the Service conceded that state taxes are deductible.[379]

(ii) *Legal fees and brokerage commissions incurred in connection with sales under Section 337.* The deductibility of legal fees and brokerage commissions incurred in connection with a sale of corporate assets under § 337 is unsettled. It might be expected that such expenses are costs of making the sale and should be offset against the amount realized from such sale, thereby reducing the gain (or increasing the loss) from the sale, none of which would be recognized under § 337. Initially, those expenses were so treated.[380] However, the Courts of Appeals for the Fourth and Tenth Circuits have permitted a liquidating corporation to deduct legal fees incurred in connection with the sale of its assets[381] on the ground that such expenses are part of the cost of liquidation. The Courts of Appeals for the Seventh Circuit and the Eighth Circuit have held that such expenses are not deductible.[382]

---

377 Rev. Rul. 60-236, 1960-2 C.B. 109.
378 *E.g.,* Hawaiian Trust Co., Ltd., Trustee v. United States, 291 F.2d 761 (C.A. 9 1961); and Commissioner v. McDonald, 320 F.2d 109 (C.A. 5 1963).
379 Rev. Rul. 63-233, 1963-2 C.B. 113, revoking Rev. Rul. 60-236.
380 Otto F. Ruprecht, ¶ 61,125, P-H Memo T.C.
381 United States v. Mountain States Mixed Feed Co., 365 F.2d 244 (C.A. 10 1966); and Pridemark, Inc. v. Commissioner, 345 F.2d 35 (C.A. 4 1965). Those cases involved only legal fees, and therefore the courts did not pass on the deductibility of brokerage commissions. *See* Note, 65 MICH. L. REV. 1508 (1967).
382 Alphaco, Inc. v. Nelson, 385 F.2d 244 (C.A. 7 1967), *reversing* 257 F. Supp. 118 (E.D. Wisc. 1966); United States v. Morton, Sr., 387 F.2d 441 (C.A. 8 1968), *reversing* 258 F. Supp. 922 (W.D. Mo. 1966). *See also* Lanrao, Inc. v. United States, 288 F. Supp. 464 (E.D. Tenn. 1968).

Consequently, there is an even split among the Circuit Courts of Appeals that have considered this issue.

(j) Distributions made to an escrow agent or a trustee. In some circumstances a liquidating corporation may possess assets which cannot conveniently be distributed among its shareholders within the requisite 12-month period. For example, the corporation may possess an income tax refund claim or an undivided interest in real property, which cannot be collected or sold within the 12-month period. In such cases the corporation can assign the property to an independent trustee on behalf of the stockholders, and after the trustee has collected the claim or sold the property, the trustee will distribute the proceeds among the shareholders.

The Service has ruled[383] that distribution to a trustee for the stockholders (as indicated above) within the 12-month period would comply with § 337 provided that the trustee is either selected by the stockholders or appointed by a court of competent jurisdiction, and provided that such a plan of liquidation is permissible under state law. In a subsequent ruling,[384] the Service held that the distribution of corporate property to an independent escrow agent appointed by the officers of the corporation for that purpose will qualify under § 337. Care should be taken to insure that there is no possibility that any of the proceeds held in trust or in escrow could become payable to the corporation. The Service has indicated informally that it will issue private rulings on such plans.

A related problem arises when the corporation cannot locate a shareholder in order to make a distribution to him, or several competing persons claim the ownership of the same shares of the corporation's stock. As to missing shareholders, the Regulations (Treas. Reg. § 1.337-2(b)) permit the corporation to make distributions to "a State official, trustee, or other persons authorized by law to receive distributions for the benefit of such shareholders." The trustee plan or escrow arrangement described in the paragraph above might be employed either where there is a missing shareholder

---

383 Rev. Rul. 63-245, 1963-2 C.B. 144.
384 Rev. Rul. 65-257, 1965-2 C.B. 89.

or where the identity of the actual stock owner is unsettled.[385]

A similar problem arises when the corporation plans to make a bulk sale of its assets and minority shareholders object and demand their appraisal rights under local corporate law. In such event it will not usually be feasible to resolve the appraised value of the minority shareholder's stock within a 12-month period, and to comply with § 337, the corporation may distribute assets to an independent escrow agent appointed by the corporate officers or the shareholders.[386] The escrow agreement should provide that any funds remaining after satisfaction of the minority shareholders' claim will be distributed among the other shareholders (rather than be returned to the corporation) and if the escrowed funds are inadequate, the difference will be contributed by the other shareholders, rather than by the corporation.

---

385 *See* Henry Yeckes, ¶ 66,178 P-H Memo T.C., holding that § 337 was there inapplicable for failure to distribute all of the corporation's assets within the 12-month period and suggesting that the corporation could have complied with the requisites of § 337 by making a timely distribution to an escrow agent.
386 Rev. Rul. 65-257, 1965-2 C.B. 89.

II

Corporate Transfers:
Tax Impact on
Corporations

Generally, distributions to shareholders with respect to their stock or in redemption of their stock will not cause recognition of income to the distributing corporation.[1] The distributing corporation will never recognize income when the distribution to its shareholders is made in cash; but when the distribution is made in kind, there are several circumstances in which it will recognize income. The reason for taxing gain to the distributing corporation may be: (i) an express exception included in the statutory provisions providing generally for nonrecognition of gain for such distributions; or (ii) a judicially constructed exception; or (iii) a specific recognition provision in the Code which takes precedence over other sections of the Code.

The provisions for nonrecognition of gain or loss to a distributing corporation apply only when the distribution is made to a shareholder *qua* shareholder. The corporation will recognize gain or loss when it distributes appreciated or depreciated property to a shareholder in his capacity as a creditor or employee.[2] However, a subsidiary corporation liquidated under § 332 will not recognize gain

---

[1] *See* General Utilities & Operating Co. v. Helvering, 296 U.S. 200 (1935). Since 1954, there are statutory provisions requiring non-recognition of gain or loss on many corporate distributions. I.R.C. §§ 311 and 336.

[2] Treas. Reg. § 1.311-1(e); and S. Rept. No. 1622, 83 Cong., 2d Sess., p. 247. *See also* Northern Coal & Dock Co., 12 T.C. 42 (1949), Acq. 1949-1 C.B. 3.

or loss on account of distributions made to its parent corporation in satisfaction of debts, unless the subsidiary is insolvent.[3]

A. STATUTORY PROVISION FOR NONRECOGNITION OF INCOME TO DISTRIBUTING CORPORATION

Section 336 provides that the corporation shall not recognize any gain or loss on a distribution to its shareholders in partial[4] or complete liquidation except that a distribution of an installment obligation will cause the distributing corporation to recognize any income realized under § 453(d). As noted below, there are several other circumstances where gain will be recognized.

Section 311(a) provides that, with certain exceptions,[5] a corporation will not recognize gain or loss on distributions made with respect to its stock (i.e., dividends and other distributions made to shareholders which are not made in partial or complete liquidation of the corporation).

Section 311(c) requires a distributing corporation to recognize gain on a distribution to its shareholders of property subject to a liability (or where the shareholders assume a corporate liability) to the extent that the liability exceeds the adjusted basis of the distributed property in the hands of the distributing corporation. Unless the shareholder assumes the transferred liability, the amount of gain recognized to the corporation can be no greater than the difference between the fair market value of the distributed property and its adjusted basis in the hands of the corporation. The characterization of the gain to the corporation (i.e., whether as ordinary income, or as long or short-term capital gain) is made by treating the distributed property as if it were sold on the date of distribution.[6]

> **Ex.** The X Corporation owned unimproved Blackacre with an adjusted basis of $20,000 and a fair market value of $45,000. Blackacre was subject to a mortgage of $35,000, but X had no *personal liability* to repay the debt secured

---

3 I.R.C. § 332(c). *See* p. 67 *supra.*
4 Partial liquidations are defined in I.R.C. § 346. *See* pp. 23-26 *supra.*
5 The exceptions listed in § 311 include gain or loss recognized under § 453(d) on distribution of an installment obligation and the exceptions provided in § 311(b) and (c).
6 Treas. Reg. § 1.311-1(d).

by the mortgage. *X* distributed Blackacre to *A*, an individual who is the sole shareholder of *X*, as a dividend, and *A* took the property subject to the $35,000 mortgage. Under § 311(c), *X* recognized a gain of $15,000 on the distribution ($35,000 mortgage — $20,000 basis). If Blackacre were a capital asset in *X*'s hands and if *X* had held Blackacre for more than six months, this $15,000 income to *X* will be a long-term capital gain.

Section 311(b) provides that where a corporation which uses the last-in, first-out (LIFO) method for reporting income from sales of its inventory makes a distribution of its inventory to its shareholders on account of their stock holdings, the corporation will recognize income to the extent (if any) that the value of the distributed inventory (as determined under the LIFO method) exceeds the value that such distributed inventory would have had, if the value were determined under a first-in, first-out (FIFO) method (or in some instances some other method exclusive of LIFO). Both §§ 311(b) and 311(c) are applicable only to distributions made in redemption of stock or made on account of stock, and do not apply to distributions made in partial or complete liquidation.[7]

As previously noted, where a corporation makes a distribution of an installment obligation to its shareholders, irrespective of whether or not such distribution is made in liquidation, the corporation will recognize gain or loss to the extent of the difference between the corporation's basis in such obligation and the fair market value of the obligation at the date of distribution.[8] There are two exceptions to this recognition rule. One exception is the distribution of an installment obligation by a subsidiary corporation to its parent pursuant to a complete liquidation of the subsidiary under § 332;[9] however, where the basis of the distributed obligation in the hands of the parent corporation is determined under § 334(b)(2),[10] gain will be recognized to the distributing

---

7 Treas. Reg. § 1.311-1(a).

8 I.R.C. §§ 453(d), 336, and 311(a).

9 I.R.C. § 453(d)(4).

10 The codification of the Kimbell-Diamond rule. *See* pp. 68-70, *supra*.

corporation, but only to the extent that such gain is attributable to § 1245 gain or § 1250 gain.[11]

A second exception is that where a corporation is completely liquidated in compliance with I.R.C. § 337, the distribution in liquidation of an installment obligation will cause the recognition of income to the distributing corporation only to the extent that the corporation would have recognized income from the sale of such obligation.[12] The extent to which gain is recognized under § 337 on the sale of an installment obligation is discussed in Chapter I.

B. JUDICIAL DOCTRINES IMPOSING THE RECOGNITION OF INCOME ON THE DISTRIBUTING CORPORATION

It is unclear to what extent a corporation may be required to recognize income from distributions to its shareholders under an "assignment of income" concept or pursuant to a utilization of § 446(b) by the Commissioner to require the distributing corporation to recognize earned but previously unrecognized income which the corporation transferred to its shareholders. In *Commissioner v. First State Bank of Stratford*,[13] after a bank had written off notes held by it as worthless and had deducted them as bad debts, the notes became collectible. The bank then declared a dividend in kind of the notes and assigned the notes to a bank employee who proceeded to collect the amounts due and turn the proceeds over to an account held on behalf of the shareholders of the bank. In collecting the notes, the bank's employee "did nothing that he did not do in collecting notes owed to the bank." The Fifth Circuit held that the bank recognized income on the collection of the notes. The rationale of the decision is not clear, but it appears to rest on an assignment of income concept. While the express terms of § 311 would appear to negate the applicability of an assignment of income or similiar doctrines to corporate distributions, the Senate Report[14] on § 311 stated that there was no intention "to change existing law with re-

---

11 Treas. Reg. §§ 1.453-9(c)(1)(i); and 1.1245-6(d). While the regulations refer only to § 1245, presumably the same rule will apply to § 1250 gain. For a discussion of "§ 1245 gain" and "§ 1250 gain" see pp. 84-85 *supra*.
12 Treas. Reg. § 1.453-9(c)(1)(ii).
13 168 F.2d 1004 (C.A. 5 1948), *cert. denied*, 335 U.S. 867 (1948).
14 S. Rept. No. 1622, 83d Cong., 2d Sess., p. 247.

spect to attribution of income of shareholders to their corporation as exemplified, for example, in the case of *Commissioner v. First State Bank of Stratford.*" The presence of peculiar facts in the *Stratford* case (*i.e.*, the collection of the notes by an employee of the bank in the normal conduct of his employment) together with the uncertainty as to the basis of the court's decision in that case, have complicated the question of just what "existing law" Congress intended to leave unimpaired. Moreover, it is not certain that the above single statement in the Senate Report is sufficient to negate the explicit language of § 311 and § 336.

Thus, the status of the assignment of income doctrine, and related doctrines, to corporate distributions is unresolved. Examples of other concepts which might apply to corporate distributions are: change of accounting methods;[15] and the "Court Holding" doctrine.[16]

C. RECOGNITION OF INCOME REQUIRED BY SPECIFIC CODE SECTIONS HAVING PRIORITY OVER THE GENERAL NON-RECOGNITION PROVISIONS FOR CORPORATE DISTRIBUTIONS

Several sections of the Code provide for recognition of income notwithstanding the existence of contrary provisions elsewhere in the Code, and those sections take priority over §§ 311 and 336 even though they are not explicitly mentioned therein.

1. Sections 1245 and 1250

Sections 1245 and 1250 of the Code[17] (the recapture of depreciation provisions) frequently require recognition of gain on the disposition of section 1245 property or section 1250 property notwithstanding that gain would not otherwise be recognized from such disposition.[18] While §§ 1245 and 1250 expressly exempt certain transactions from their coverage,[19] no exception is made for corporate distributions to a shareholder, other than distributions

---

15 I.R.C. § 446(b). *See* Idaho First National Bank v. United States, 265 F.2d 6 (C.A. 9 1959).
16 *See* United States v. Lynch, 192 F.2d 718 (C.A. 9 1951), *cert. denied,* 343 U.S. 934 (1952); and Waltham Netoco Theatres, Inc., 49 T.C. 399 (1968).
17 For a brief discussion of those two sections, *see* pp. 84-85 *supra*.
18 Treas. Reg. § 1.1245-6.
19 I.R.C. §§ 1245(b) and 1250(d).

under § 332 in liquidation of a subsidiary. Indeed, the Regulations expressly provide that § 1245 overrides both § 311(a) and § 336.[20]

Distributions in liquidation of a subsidiary corporation are excluded[21] from § 1245 and §1250 where the liquidation is covered by § 332 unless[22] the basis of the assets in the hands of the acquiring corporation is determined under § 334(b)(2).[23] Thus where § 334(b)(2) is applicable in determining the basis of property received by the parent corporation in a liquidation under § 332, then § 1245 and § 1250 will apply to the distributions made in liquidation.

The imposition of income recognition on a distributing corporation in a liquidation where basis is determined under § 334 (b)(2) is somewhat inconsistent with the underlying premise that motivated the adoption of that section. Section 334(b)(2) codified the Kimbell-Diamond rule[24] presumably because Congress accepted the rationale of that rule, *viz.*, that the purchase of a controlling interest in a corporation followed promptly by a liquidation of the corporation is in substance an acquisition of the assets of the corporation rather than its stock. If the purchase of a corporation's stock is actually a purchase of assets, it would be reasonable to impose ordinary income treatment on the seller of the stock rather than indirectly imposing it on the purchaser, since it is the seller who actually recaptured the corporate assets' depreciation. There are several reasons why the seller is not so treated. First, there is not necessarily an identity of purpose between the buyer and the seller. The seller may not have had the sale of assets as his purpose; however, a difference of purpose is likely to exist only where the purchaser acquired a controlling interest in the corporation by purchasing the stock of several shareholders. Second, historically there has been a judicial reluctance to impugn the separate existence of a corporate entity for tax purposes, and consequently neither Con-

---

20 Treas. Reg. § 1.1245-6(b). At this date, no regulations have been promulgated under § 1250, but it is clear that § 1250 also overrides §§ 311 and 336.
21 I.R.C. §§ 1245(b)(3) and 1250(d)(3); and Treas. Reg. § 1.1245-4(c).
22 Treas. Reg. § 1.1245-4(c)(3).
23 Section 334(b)(2) is the codification of the Kimbell-Diamond rule. For a discussion of the Kimbell-Diamond rule and § 334(b)(2), *see* pp. 59-60, 68-70 *supra*.
24 H. Rept. No. 1337, 83d Cong., 2d Sess., p. A109; S. Rept. No. 1622, 83d Cong., 2d Sess., p. 257.

gress nor the courts have been willing to treat a shareholder's stock interest (even where he is a sole shareholder) as merely representative of his aggregate interests in the various corporate assets.[25] Since the seller could not be taxed under § 1245 or § 1250, the alternatives were either to waive collection of a tax on the recapture of depreciation or to tax the corporation (and indirectly thereby the purchaser) when the assets are distributed in liquidation. The first alternative would have created a loophole, and Congress properly chose the latter course. As a practical matter, it makes little difference (except to the unwary) whether the tax is imposed on the purchaser or the seller, since knowledgeable parties will take this liability into account in negotiating the purchase price of the corporate stock.

2. Section 47

Section 47 provides for the recapture of an investment credit previously allowed under § 38 *et seq.* where the taxpayer disposes of section 38 property prior to the minimum holding period required to qualify for the credit previously taken by the taxpayer.[26] The recapture of credit provision imposes a tax liability on the taxpayer equal to the tax credit previously allowed to the extent that the credit would have been reduced if the property had been deemed to have a useful life equal to the period of time that the taxpayer actually held it. Section 47 will impose tax liability on a corporation for making an untimely disposal of a section 38 asset whether the distribution of that asset was made on account of a shareholder's stock, or in redemption thereof, or in partial or complete liquidation. However, § 47 will not cause any tax consequences where a subsidiary corporation distributes section 38 property to its parent pursuant to a complete liquidation under § 332 unless § 334(b)(2) is applicable in determining the basis of such property.[27]

---

25 Congress has not been deterred from piercing the entity existence of a partnership, at least as to specific categories of partnership assets. I.R.C. § 751. However, the entity existence of a partnership is a more amorphous concept than is the corporate entity concept.

26 For a brief discussion of the recapture of tax credit provisions, *see* p. 85.

27 I.R.C. § 47(b) excludes transactions covered by § 381(a), and the latter section covers transfers to a parent corporation under § 332, except where § 334(b)(2) applies.

3. Section 341(f)

Where a shareholder sold stock of a collapsible corporation, and an election under § 341(f) was made so that certain assets of the distributing corporation are "subsection (f) assets,"[28] then the corporation's distribution of such assets may cause it to recognize income.[29] Section 341(f) will not apply to a liquidation of a subsidiary under § 332, unless § 334(b)(2) is applicable in determining basis, if the parent corporation is not a tax-exempt organization and if the parent consents to having the subsection (f) assets received by it deemed subsection (f) assets in the hand of the parent also.[30]

---

28 I.R.C. § 341(f)(4).
29 For a discussion of § 341(f), *see* Hall, *The Consenting Collapsible Corporation—Section 341(f) of the Internal Revenue Code of 1954,* 12 U.C.L.A. L. REV. 1365 (1965), and p. 44 *supra.*
30 I.R.C. § 341(f)(3). The requisites for complying with § 341(f)(3) are set forth in Rev. Rul. 69-33; I.R.B. 1969-5, p. 17.

III

Reorganizations and Corporate Divisions

A. CORPORATE DIVISIONS

A corporate division is a separation of two or more business activities that previously were conducted by a single corporation, or by an affiliated group of corporations having one common parent, into two or more nonaffiliated corporations each of which is controlled by one or more persons who, immediately prior to the division, were shareholders of the single corporation, or of the parent corporation of the affiliated group. The separated business activities may or may not have been functionally integrated prior to the division, and in some instances, a single business may be divided into two business activities. The provisions concerning the recognition of income from a corporate division are contained in I.R.C. §§ 355 and 356. Section 355 establishes that no gain or loss will be recognized if a corporate division complies with the conditions established in that section. Section 356 establishes the tax consequences if a corporate division complies with every condition of § 355, except for the payment of boot to shareholders.[1]

1. The alternative forms of corporate divisions

Three basic forms are utilized in effecting a corporate division.

---

1 In tax parlance, where there is an exchange of properties in compliance with a Code provision granting nonrecognition of gain or loss for exchanges of such properties, and where as part of the same transaction, one party receives additional property (or "other property") which is not protected by a nonrecognition provision, the additional or other property received is called "boot"; *i.e.*, the party received a tax-free exchange and other property "to boot." The usual rule is that the receipt of boot will cause recognition of income to the recipient to the extent of the boot; but in some transactions (*i.e.*, in "B" reorganizations) the receipt of boot may characterize the entire transaction as a taxable exchange.

These forms are frequently referred to as a "spin-off," a "split-off" and a "split-up," respectively. Prior to 1954, the form of effecting a division frequently determined whether gain or loss was recognized. Since 1954, nonrecognition does not turn upon the form utilized; nevertheless, there may be a significant difference in the tax consequences of using one form rather than another.[2]

(a) The spin-off. In a "spin-off," a parent corporation distributes stock representing a controlling interest in its subsidiary corporation to one or more of the shareholders of the parent corporation, and the shareholders do not surrender any of their stock of the parent corporation in exchange.

> **Ex.** X Corporation operates a hardware business. X owns all 200 shares of the outstanding stock of the Y Corporation which operates a grocery business. X has 100 shares of common stock outstanding, 50 shares of which are owned by A and 50 shares of which are owned by B. X distributes 100 shares of Y stock to A and 100 shares of Y stock to B. Neither A nor B gave X anything in exchange for the Y stock. Those distributions would constitute a spin-off.
>
> If the hardware and grocery business had both been conducted by the X Corporation, and if immediately prior to the spin-off, X had created the Y Corporation and distributed the grocery business to it, the transaction would nevertheless be classified as a spin-off. Similarly, although it would be unusual, the transaction would also constitute a spin-off even though all of the Y stock were distributed to A and none were distributed to B.

The question of whether gain will be recognized because of a spin-off or other corporate division is discussed below.

(b) The split-off. The "split-off" is identical to a spin-off except that the parent's shareholders who receive distributions of the subsidiary's stock surrender some or all of their stock of the parent corporation in exchange therefor.

> **Ex.** X Corporation has 100 shares of common stock outstanding, 50 shares of which are owned by A and 50

---

2 The tax differences arise where gain is recognized either because boot was received (§ 356) or because the transaction failed to qualify for nonrecognition treatment under §§ 355 and 356.

shares of which are owned by *B*. *X* owns all 200 shares of the outstanding stock of the *Y* Corporation. *X* operates a hardware business and *Y* operates a grocery business.

(1) *X* distributes 100 shares of *Y* stock to *A*, and in exchange *A* surrenders 25 shares of *X* stock to *X*. *X* also distributes 100 shares of *Y* stock to *B*, and in exchange *B* surrenders 25 shares of *X* stock to *X*.[3]

(2) *X* distributes all 200 shares of *Y*'s stock to *A* in exchange for the 50 shares of *X* stock held by *A*.

Both transactions in examples (1) and (2) are split-offs. However, the result reached in (2) is quite different from that obtained in (1)—*i.e.*, in Ex. (2), *A* acquired complete control of the grocery business and *B* acquired complete control of the hardware business, and *A* and *B* were divorced from each other as co-investors; in Ex. (1), *A* and *B* retain their status as co-investors and only the number of corporate entities held by them was changed.

(c) **The split-up.** In the "split-up," the parent corporation distributes to its shareholders, in complete liquidation of the parent corporation, the stock of two or more subsidiary corporations. Thus, unlike the other two forms of division, the split-up causes the termination of the existence of the parent corporation.

Ex. *X* has 100 shares of common stock outstanding, 50 shares of which are owned by *A* and 50 shares of which are owned by *B*. *X* operates two separate businesses: a hardware business and a grocery business. *X* causes the formation of two corporations, the *Y* Corporation and the *Z* Corporation. *X* transfers the hardware business to *Y* in exchange for 200 shares of *Y*'s stock, and transfers the grocery business to *Z* in exchange for 200 shares of *Z*'s stock.[4]

(1) *X* then distributes 100 shares of *Y* stock plus 100

---

3 The net effect of this split-off is identical to the effect of a proportionate spin-off; *i.e.*, the two shareholders, *A* and *B*, obtain joint control of two separate corporations, each of which conducts a separate business.

4 *X*'s transfers of properties to *Y* and *Z* do not cause any tax consequences to *X* because of I.R.C. § 351.

shares of Z stock to A and a like amount to B in complete liquidation of X.[5]

(2) Instead, X distributes all 200 shares of Y stock to A and all 200 shares of Z stock to B in complete liquidation.

Both examples (1) and (2) are split-ups. Moreover, it would not matter whether Y and Z were recently created subsidiaries or whether X had held them for some time prior to the split-up.

2. The qualification of a corporate division for nonrecognition of gain or loss

The end result of a corporate division is that the shareholders of one corporation cause the assets controlled by that corporation to be divided into two or more corporations directly controlled by the shareholders. Thus the shareholders are in a position to liquidate one of the resulting corporations and thereby to acquire its assets in a taxable exchange which produces capital gains for the shareholders.[6] On the other hand, if, in lieu of the division and liquidation, the assets obtained from the liquidated corporation had been distributed directly from the parent corporation pursuant to a proportionate redemption of the parent's stock, the distribution might have constituted a dividend taxable to the shareholders as ordinary income.[7] The risk that a corporate division might be utilized to escape dividend consequences led Congress to impose stringent requisites for nonrecognition treatment and the Internal Revenue Service to scrutinize corporate divisions with great care.

The risk of tax avoidance is greater if the corporate division is effected by making proportionate distributions among the shareholders than if the shareholders are divorced from each other so that the several resulting corporations are not owned by the same persons. The Service has indicated that it will be more liberal in

---

5 The net result of this split-up is identical to a proportionate spin-off or a proportionate split-up, except that the corporate shell Z is substituted for the corporate shell X.

6 I.R.C. § 331(a)(1).

7 If the assets of the liquidated corporation constituted a complete business activity, it is possible that had such assets been distributed by the original corporation in redemption of its stock, the redemption would have qualified as a partial liquidation under § 346. See pp. 23-26 *supra*.

determining the applicability of nonrecognition rules to divisions when the distributions to shareholders are disproportionate than it will be when the distributions are proportionate.[8] In any event, whether or not the distributions to the shareholders are made pro rata, and irrespective of whether the division was effected for bona fide business purposes, the corporate division must comply with each of several specific statutory requisites[9] to obtain nonrecognition treatment. These requisites are listed below and thereafter discussed in greater detail.

Under § 355, gain or loss will not be recognized by a shareholder for the receipt of corporate distributions if the following requisites are satisfied:

(i) The distribution made to the shareholder consists exclusively of stocks or securities of a corporation or corporations controlled by the distributing corporation immediately prior to the distribution.[10] Where securities are distributed to a shareholder, he will recognize gain therefrom unless the distributing corporation receives from the shareholder its own securities in a principal amount at least as great as the principal amount of the securities distributed to that shareholder;[11]

(ii) The transaction must not have been used principally as a device for the distribution of the earnings and profits of any of the involved corporations;

(iii) Unless certain conditions are satisfied, the corporation must distribute all of the stock and securities of the controlled corporation that it holds at the time of distribution; and in any event, without exception, the distributing corporation must distribute a sufficient amount of stock of the controlled corporation to consti-

---

8 *See* Rev. Rul 64-102, 1964-1 C.D. 136. *But see* Lloyd Boettger, 51 T.C. 324 (1968).

9 I.R.C. § 355. In Commissioner v. Gordon, 391 U.S. 83 (1968), the Supreme Court stated: "The requirements of [section 355] are detailed and specific, and must be applied with precision." The Court further stated: "Congress has abundant power to provide that a corporation wishing to spin off a subsidiary must, however bona fide its intentions, conform the details of a distribution to a particular set of rules." *See also* Lloyd Boettger, 51 T.C. 324 (1968).

10 I.R.C. § 355(a)(1)(A). For a definition of "control," see I.R.C. § 368(c).

11 I.R.C. § 355(a)(3). The tax consequences of having gain recognized because of the distribution of securities is discussed at pp. 134-138 *infra.*

tute control thereof.[12] This requisite refers to the total amount of stock and securities distributed to the shareholders rather than the amount distributed to any single shareholder;

(iv) The distributions must comply with the "active business" requisite, *i.e.*, generally, this test requires that immediately after the distribution, and as a result of the division, there be at least two corporations each of which is engaged in the active conduct of a trade or business, which trade or business had been actively conducted for at least five years prior to the date of distribution;[13]

(v) There must have been a business purpose for the corporate division.

The nonrecognition provisions of § 355 will apply whether or not: the distributions to the shareholders are made pro rata;[14] a shareholder surrenders stock in the distributing corporation;[15] the distribution is made in pursuance of a plan of reorganization.[16]

(a) Distribution of stock and securities of a controlled corporation. To qualify for nonrecognition, the property distributed to a shareholder must consist exclusively of stocks and securities of a corporation controlled by the distributing corporation immediately prior to the distribution.[17] The distributed stock of the subsidiary may consist of either common or preferred stock, but there is a risk that

---

12 I.R.C. § 355(a)(1)(D).
13 I.R.C. § 355(a)(1)(C).
14 I.R.C. § 355(a)(2)(A). This provision permits *inter alia* the separation of shareholders from a joint investment, which can be accomplished through a split-off or a split-up.
15 I.R.C. § 355(a)(2)(B). This provision includes spin-offs in the nonrecognition treatment by expressly permitting a distribution to a shareholder who surrenders nothing in exchange therefor.
16 I.R.C. § 355(a)(2)(C). This provision permits the distribution of the stock of a previously existing subsidiary corporation. Prior to the adoption of the 1954 Code, a corporate division had to qualify as a reorganization to obtain nonrecognition treatment. Consequently, where X Corporation owned all of the stock of Y Corporation and wished to split off Y to its shareholders, under prior law, X would have had to form a new corporation, Z, transfer the stock of Y to the Z Corporation, and then distribute the stock of the Z Corporation to its shareholders. See I.R.C. § 368(a)(1)(D) for a statement of the requisites of the "reorganization" provision that is applicable here. By removing the condition that the distribution be made pursuant to a reorganization, the 1954 Code eliminated the expense and time consumption of forming a new corporation.
17 I.R.C. § 355(a)(1)(A).

preferred stock may be deemed section 306 stock.[18]

The distributing corporation has "control" of a subsidiary corporation only where it owns stock possessing at least 80% of the total combined voting power of the voting stock of the subsidiary and owns at least 80% of the total number of shares of nonvoting stock of the subsidiary corporation.[19] The Service has ruled that the statutory reference to ownership of 80% of the total number of shares of nonvoting stock requires the ownership of 80% of the total number *of shares of each separate class* of nonvoting stock.[20]

It is unsettled whether the distribution of stock rights permitting the shareholders to purchase stock of a controlled subsidiary qualifies as a distribution of "solely stock or securities."[21]

Stock of a controlled corporation acquired by the distributing corporation in a taxable transaction which occurred within five years of the distribution of the controlled corporation's stock does not qualify as stock of the controlled corporation and is treated as boot.[22]

The distribution to a shareholder of securities of a controlled corporation will cause recognition of gain to the shareholder unless, in connection with the distribution, he surrendered to the distributing corporation securities of the latter having a principal amount which was at least as great as the principal amount of the

---

18 Treas. Reg. § 1.355-3(b); and I.R.C. § 306(c)(1)(B). *See* pp. 51-58 *supra* for a discussion of section 306 stock.

19 I.R.C. § 368(c).

20 Rev. Rul. 59-259, 1959-2 C.B. 115. It will be interesting to observe whether this interpretation will withstand litigation.

21 Treas. Reg. § 1.355-1(a) states that stock rights or warrants do not qualify, but *compare* Commissioner v. Gordon, 382 F.2d 499 (C.A. 2 1967) *with* Commissioner v. Baan, 382 F.2d 485 (C.A. 9 1967). Both *Gordon* and *Baan* were appeals from a tax court decision in a consolidated case (45 T.C. 71). The Tax Court held that stock rights to purchase a subsidiary's stock were covered by § 355 and the Second and Ninth Circuits split over this issue. The *Baan* and *Gordon* cases were ultimately resolved in favor of the Government by the Supreme Court's decision in Commissioner v. Gordon, 391 U.S. 83 (1968), but the Supreme Court rested its decision on another issue and never discussed the question of whether stock rights qualify under § 355. On remand, the Tax Court held *inter alia* that stock rights do not constitute stocks or securities for purposes of § 354 or § 355. Oscar E. Baan, 51 T.C. 1032 (1969). The taxpayers have appealed again.

22 I.R.C. § 355(a)(3). However, for purposes of determining whether the distributing corporation has complied with the requirement (§ 355(a)(1)(D)) to distribute all of the subsidiary's stock, such stock is deemed to be stock of the controlled corporation. I.R.C. § 355(a)(3); and Treas. Reg. § 1.355-2(f).

securities distributed to him.[23] If a distribution to a shareholder qualifies under § 355 except that boot is also distributed, whether the boot consists of securities of the controlled corporation or of other property, the boot does not disqualify the transaction from nonrecognition treatment; but in that event, the amount and characterization of the gain is determined under I.R.C. § 356, discussed below.[24]

(b) Use of the transaction as a device to distribute earnings and profits. If a corporate division is used principally as a device for the distribution of the earnings and profits of one or more of the involved corporations, gain realized by a shareholder from that transaction will be recognized.[25] The Code provides that the subsequent sale by a shareholder of the stock or securities of the corporations involved in the division will not mean that the transaction was a "device," unless the sale was negotiated or agreed upon prior to the corporate division.[26] However, the Regulations state that the sale of such stock will constitute *evidence* that the transaction was a device.[27] Also, if either surviving corporation is liquidated soon after the division, the Service is likely to contend that the transaction was a "device."

The "device" exception will not usually apply to a split-off or a split-up where the distributions are substantially disproportionate, so that if gain were recognized on the exchange, it would constitute capital gains to the shareholders because the transaction complies with the redemption provisions established in § 302(b)(3),[28] or possibly those established in § 302(b)(2).[29] If the distributions are not significantly disproportionate or the division is effected by a spin-off, the "device" question must be weighed carefully.

(c) Business purpose. In addition to the "device" test, a corporate

---

23 I.R.C. § 355(a)(3).
24 Treas. Reg. § 1.355-2(a).
25 I.R.C. § 355(a)(1)(B). This provision is similar to the judicial doctrine that a transaction which takes the form of a tax-free transfer, but which has no purpose other than to serve as a tax avoidance device, will not qualify for nonrecognition treatment. *See* Gregory v. Helvering, 293 U.S. 465 (1935).
26 I.R.C. § 355(a)(1)(B).
27 Treas. Reg. § 1.355-2(b)(1).
28 A complete termination of one or more shareholders' stock interests.
29 Rev. Rul. 64-102, 1964-1 C.B. (Part I) 136.

division must have been effected for a legitimate business purpose to qualify for nonrecognition.[30] The business purpose requisite is a judicially established test for determining whether a transaction qualifies as a tax-free reorganization.[31] While the 1954 Code has removed the condition that a corporate division qualify as a reorganization, the business purpose requisite remains applicable.[32]

The Regulations define the business purpose requisite as referring to purposes "germane to the business of the corporation."[33] However, in *Parshelsky's Estate*, the Second Circuit has held that the test is satisfied even where the distribution is germane to a valid business purpose of the *shareholders*, and the court further held that estate planning considerations of the shareholders constituted a valid business purpose.[34] While in this one respect the *Parshelsky's* decision gave a liberal construction to the meaning of "business purpose," another aspect of that decision could make it quite difficult to comply with the business purpose test. The court suggested that it is not sufficient to demonstrate a business purpose for a corporate distribution, but that the taxpayer must also demonstrate that there was not readily available an alternative means of satisfying those business purposes which did not require making corporate distributions.[35] If the *Parshelsky's* view is accepted,[36] purposes which once were regarded as adequate business reasons for a corporate division may no longer qualify. For example, in the *Parshelsky's* case, the court held that the desire to segregate a risk venture from a more stable venture in order to insulate the assets of the latter from the creditors of the former

---

30 Treas. Reg. § 1.355-2(c).
31 *See* Gregory v. Helvering, 293 U.S. 465 (1935).
32 Commissioner v. Wilson, 353 F.2d 184 (C.A. 9 1965).
33 Treas. Reg. § 1.355-2(c).
34 Parshelsky's Estate v. Commissioner, 303 F.2d 14, 21 (C.A. 2 1962). The *Parshelsky's* case involved the 1939 Code, but there is no reason to construe the business purpose doctrine differently for post-1954 years. *See also* Bonsall, Jr. v. Commissioner, 317 F.2d 61, 65 (C.A. 2 1963) (dictum).
35 Parshelsky's Estate v. Commissioner, *supra* at pp. 20-21.
36 In Howard P. Blount, 51 T.C. 1023 (1969), the Tax Court adopted a rationale similar to the one in question for purposes of determining whether a stock redemption had a business purpose that would qualify it as not essentially equivalent to a dividend within the meaning of § 302(b)(1). While the Court found a business purpose for the redemption, it held that § 302(b)(1) was not applicable because that purpose "could have been accomplished more directly" by other means.

was not a business justification for a corporate division, because the parties could have achieved that protection by shifting the risk venture to a subsidiary corporation without making any distribution to the shareholders.[37]

Some examples of valid business purposes for a corporate division are: the separation of dissident shareholders;[38] the spin-off of one business activity to insulate it from union organizational efforts aimed at the corporation's other business activity;[39] and the split-off of a business activity which competed with customers of the parent corporation.[40]

In addition to demanding a business purpose, the Regulations also require that there be a continuity of enterprise and a continuity of interest in the surviving corporations.[41]

(d) Distributions of subsidiary's stock and securities. Section 355(a)(1)(D) requires that the parent corporation distribute all of the subsidiary's stock and securities held by the parent immediately before the distribution unless it can be established to the satisfaction of the Commissioner that the retention of a part of the subsidiary's stock or securities was not done for tax avoidance purposes. The Regulations suggest that it will be very difficult to convince the Commissioner that the retention of any stocks or securities was valid.[42] In any event the parent must distribute sufficient stock of the subsidiary to constitute control,[43] irrespective of whether it has bona fide reasons for retaining some shares.[44]

The Supreme Court has held[45] that a distribution of a subsidiary's stock made in two separate distributions two years apart did not qualify under § 355. The Court stated that it may not be essential that all of the subsidiary's stock be distributed in one taxable year,

---

37 This holding is somewhat inconsistent with Rev. Rul. 56-554, 1956-2 C.B. 198, which permitted a bank to spin-off speculative land holdings the bank did not wish to hold.
38 Rev. Rul. 69-460, I.R.B. 1969-35, p. 11; Rev. Rul. 55-655, 1956-2 C.B. 214; Albert W. Badanes, 39 T.C. 410 (1962).
39 Sidney L. Olson, 48 T.C. 855 (1967).
40 Rev. Rul. 59-197, 1959-1 C.B. 77.
41 Treas. Reg. § 1.355-2(c). The continuity of enterprise and interest doctrines are discussed at pp. 145-147 infra.
42 Treas. Reg. § 1.355-2(d).
43 "Control' is defined in § 368(c).
44 I.R.C. § 355(a)(1)(D).
45 Commissioner v. Gordon, 391 U.S. 83 (1968).

but that several steps could not be collapsed and treated as an integrated transaction unless when the first step was taken there was "a binding commitment to take the later steps." This is an unusual construction of the step transaction doctrine in that it imposes stricter standards for its implementation than have customarily been applied.[46]

(e) The five-year active business requisite. The one condition of § 355 that has caused the greatest amount of litigation is the five-year active business test.[47] The active business test requires that immediately after the distribution to the shareholders:

(i) Each of the surviving corporations[48] must be engaged in the active conduct of a trade or business or its assets must consist of stock and securities of a controlled subsidiary that is so engaged;

(ii) Each such trade or business must have been actively and continuously conducted throughout the five-year period preceding the date of distribution;

(iii) None of such trades or business was acquired, directly or indirectly, during the five-year period preceding the distribution in a taxable exchange; and

(iv) Control of a corporation which at the time of acquisition was conducting such trade or business was not acquired directly or indirectly during the said five-year period in a taxable exchange.

> **Ex. (1)** The X Corporation has 100 shares of common stock outstanding, 50 shares of which are owned by A and 50 shares by B. The X Corporation has owned and operated a sweater factory in Cleveland and a retail jewelry store in Cleveland since 1955 and 1960 respectively. In 1966, X causes the Y Corporation to be formed, and X distributes the jewelry store to Y in exchange for all 200 shares of Y's common stock. X then distributes 100 shares of Y to A and 100 shares of Y to B. This divi-

---

46 *See* Jacobs, *Supreme Court further restricts the step transaction doctrine,* 29 J. OF TAXATION 2 (July 1968).

47 I.R.C. § 355(a)(1)(C) requires that the conditions of subsection (b), the active business test, be satisfied.

48 In a spin-off or split-off the surviving corporations will be the parent corporation and the controlled subsidiary corporation (§ 355(b)(1) (A)), but in a split-up, the parent corporation is terminated, and the surviving corporations are the controlled subsidiary corporations (§ 355(b)(1)(B)).

sion complies with the active business test, and if other conditions of § 355 are satisfied (*e.g.*, the business purpose requisite), neither *A* nor *B* will recognize any income from the distribution.

Ex. (2) The *X* Corporation has owned and operated a sweater factory in Cleveland since 1955. The *Y* Corporation has owned and operated a jewelry store in Cleveland since 1958. In 1960, *X* purchased all 200 shares of outstanding stock of *Y* for cash plus promissory notes. In 1966, *X* distributed all 200 shares of *Y* stock to *A* in exchange for *A*'s 50 shares of *X*'s stock. The active business test is satisfied, and *A* will not recognize any gain or loss on the exchange.

Ex. (3) Assume the same facts as in Example (2), except that *X* purchased the *Y* stock in 1963. The active business test is not satisfied, and *A* will recognize gain or loss on the 1966 exchange. The *Y* Corporation was actively engaged in a business immediately after the distribution to *A*, and that business had been conducted for more than 5 years prior thereto, but *X* acquired control of the *Y* Corporation during the 5-year period in a taxable transaction, and regardless of the bona fide purposes of the division, the distribution of *Y* stock will not qualify for nonrecognition treatment.

Ex. (4) Assume the same facts as in Example (1), except that when *X* transferred the jewelry store to *Y*, *X* received in exchange 200 shares of common stock of *Y* and 100 shares of nonvoting preferred stock of *Y*. *X* then distributed the common and preferred stock of *Y* to *A* and *B* proportionately. The active business test is satisfied, and if there is compliance with the business purpose rule and other conditions of § 355, *A* and *B* will not recognize any gain on the distribution; but the preferred stock of *Y* will likely be section 306 stock.[49]

The determination of what constitutes the active conduct of a trade or business is a complex question, and the failure to anticipate correctly the resolution of that question has brought grief to many taxpayers.[50] Wherever feasible, the taxpayer should consider

---

49 I.R.C. § 306(c)(1)(B).
50 *E.g.*, Theodore F. Appleby, 35 T.C. 755 (1961), *affirmed per curiam*, 296 F.2d 925 (C.A. 3 1962), *cert. denied*, 370 U.S. 910.

seeking a letter ruling before embarking on a corporate division, particularly when the plan contemplates a spin-off.[51]

(i) *Division of a single business.* The Regulations construed the active business requirement narrowly and stated that § 355 would not apply to a division of a single business into two viable business activities. However, the Service has conceded the invalidity of that provision of the Regulations.

> **Ex.** *A* and *B* were equal stockholders of the *X* Corporation, which corporation had operated a construction business for more than 5 years. *X* formed the *Y* Corporation and then transferred ½ of its contracts, equipment, etc., to the *Y* Corporation for *Y* stock. *X* then transferred *Y* stock to *A* for all of *A*'s stock in *X*. The *Y* Corporation and the *X* Corporation were actively engaged in the construction business after the distribution, and that business had been conducted for more than 5 years prior to the distribution. The Service, initially adhering to its Regulations, determined that gain would be recognized on a transaction of this kind because it constituted a vertical division of a single business. In the *Coady* decision,[52] the majority of the Tax Court held that the Regulations were invalid and that this transaction does qualify under § 355. After two courts of appeals[53] repudiated the Regulations, the Service conceded that the Regulation was invalid to the extent that it prohibited vertical divisions of a single business.[54]

The Service's repudiation of its position that § 355 would never apply to a division of a single business into two viable business activities has sometimes caused a reversal of roles between the taxpayer and the Commissioner. Prior to this time, the taxpayer argued that the businesses existing after the division had previously been two separate businesses so as not to lose § 355 status

---

51 The spin-off closely resembles a dividend, and consequently the Service frequently will scrutinize spin-off transactions carefully. Moreover, where gain is recognized on a spin-off, the usual consequence is dividend treatment.

52 Edmund P. Coady, 33 T.C. 771 (1960), *affirmed,* 289 F.2d 490 (C.A. 6 1961).

53 Commissioner v. Coady, *supra;* and United States v. Marett, 325 F.2d 28 (C.A. 5 1963).

54 Rev. Rul. 64-147, 1964-1 C.B. (Part I) 136. This ruling also announced that modification of the Regulations was under consideration.

because of the Commissioner's prohibition against divisions of a single business; the Commissioner, of course, argued that the post-division businesses had previously been part of a single business. Now, the taxpayer often argues that the post-division businesses had previously been separate parts of a single business; and hence, both post-division businesses will not need separate five-year active business histories. Of course, in such cases the Commissioner takes the opposite view.

To date, the courts have permitted this combining of business histories even though one of the post-division businesses was inaugurated by the original corporation less than five years before the § 355 division occurred;[55] but the Tax Court has denied nonrecognition of income under § 355 when one of the post-division businesses was purchased in a taxable transaction less than five years before the division was effected. In the *Boettger* case,[56] the taxpayers owned stock in a corporation that operated a hospital in Stockton, California. In 1961, in a taxable transaction, the corporation purchased the assets of a hospital in Los Angeles, California; and thereafter operated both hospitals. In 1964, in order to satisfy dissident shareholders, the original corporation was split up into two separate corporations, the stocks of which were distributed to the shareholders of the original corporation in liquidation. Four of the shareholders acquired one of the new corporations, and the remaining three shareholders acquired the other new corporation. Thus, the two groups of shareholders of the original corporation were thereby divorced from each other. Each of the two post-division corporations owned and operated one of the hospitals. The Tax Court held that irrespective of whether the original corporation's operation of the two hospitals constituted a single business, the division did not qualify for nonrecognition treatment because § 355(b)(2)(C) specifically precludes the coverage of that section where a post-division trade or business was acquired in a taxable transaction within the five-year period ending on the date of distribution.

If *Boettger* is followed, it may be difficult to determine whether an existing business has merely expanded its activities or has pur-

---

55 Lockwood's Estate v. Commissioner, 350 F.2d 712 (C.A. 8 1965); Patricia W. Burke, 42 T.C. 1021 (1964).
56 Lloyd Boettger, 51 T.C. 324 (1968).

chased such a substantial quantity of new assets as to constitute the purchase of a trade or business. The decision in *Boettger* is not entirely reconcilable with the results reached in *Lockwood* and *Burke,* and indeed appears inconsistent with *Coady* itself. The decision in *Boettger* treats the Los Angeles hospital as a separate trade or business which was purchased by the original corporation; and despite the court's protestations, there is no apparent reason for resolving the separate business issue differently for purposes of § 355(b)(2)(C) than for § 355(b)(2)(B) since the relevant language in those subsections is identical.

(ii) *Division of vertically integrated activities.* The fact that a single business may be divided under § 355 does not necessarily protect the separation of vertically integrated activities where one of the separated activities did not itself constitute an actively conducted profit venture prior to the separation. The Regulations construe an active trade or business as "a specific existing group of activities being carried on for the purpose of earning income or profit from only such group of activities, and the activities included in such group must include every operation which forms a part of, or a step in, the process of earning income or profit from such group."[57]

Some examples of divisions of corporate activities that will not qualify for nonrecognition treatment under the Regulations are: the separation of a sales division from a manufacturing process;[58] the separation of a coal mining activity whose sole function was to supply coal to a steel manufacturing activity conducted by the same corporation that owned and operated the mine;[59] the separation of an executive dining room which was operated by a corporation to provide meals for the executives of its automobile manufacturing and sales business;[60] and the separation of a research department from the manufacturing division.[61] While the *Coady* and

---

57 Treas. Reg. § 1.355-1(c). The Regulations further provide (§ 1.355-1(c)(3)) that an active trade or business does not include a group of activities which are part of a business operated for a profit, but which do not themselves produce income.
58 Treas. Reg. § 1.355-1(d) Ex. (11).
59 Treas. Reg. § 1.355-1(d) Ex. (12).
60 Treas. Reg. § 1.355-1(d) Ex. (16).
61 Treas. Reg. § 1.355-1(d) Ex. (5).

Marett decisions cast some doubt on the validity of the above Regulations concerning vertically integrated activities, the Service has not repudiated those Regulations and consequently cautious skepticism is appropriate here.[62] The Tax Court permitted the division of vertically integrated activities in *Marne S. Wilson*,[63] but in that case both activities had earned income from outside sources.

> **Ex.** *X* Corporation owned and operated wholesale and retail divisions of a drug business for more than 5 years. Approximately 80% of the sales of *X*'s wholesale division were made to *X*'s retail division, but the sales to outside purchasers produced substantial income. Each division had its own employees. *X* transferred its wholesale division to a newly created corporation, the stock of which was promptly distributed to *X*'s shareholders pursuant to a plan for a pro rata spin-off. The Service has ruled that the spin-off qualified for nonrecognition treatment under § 355.[64]

(iii) *Passive assets and property used in a trade or business.* Investment or passive assets of a corporation do not constitute an active trade or business, *e.g.*, the holding for investment purposes of stocks, securities or unimproved land does not qualify.[65] The ownership of land and buildings substantially

---

62 As previously noted, if left unchecked, a corporate division can be used as a device for withdrawing corporate earnings from a corporation. The "device" test is one obstacle to a shareholder's abusing the nonrecognition provisions for such a purpose, but Congress adopted the active business test as additional protection that § 355 would not be so used. If passive assets could be segregated into a separate corporation, there would be little to deter the shareholders from liquidating that corporation. However, where each of the separated business activities was actively conducted for at least five years prior to the distribution, there is evidence that the corporation did not acquire the activity as a means of disguising a distribution of its profits, and there will frequently be a profit incentive to continue the operation of that activity after the distribution has been completed. While in some instances an integrated activity may be too inconsequential to satisfy the active business test, there is little justification for disqualifying all vertically integrated activities merely because they are integrated.

63 42 T.C. 914 (1964), *reversed on another issue*, 353 F.2d 184 (C.A. 9 1965).

64 Rev. Rul. 68-407, I.R.B. 1968-31, p. 20.

65 Treas. Reg. § 1.355-1(c), and 1(d) Ex. (1), (6) and (7). However, where a bank owned 1,800 acres of farmland which it leased to eleven different farms, the land rental business of the bank was deemed to be actively conducted. Rev. Rul. 56-555, 1956-2 C.B. 210.

all of which are occupied and used by the corporation in the conduct of its trade or business will not qualify, even where a portion of the building is leased to unrelated tenants.[66] Where part of a corporation's building is leased to third parties and part is occupied and used by the corporation, the determination of whether the corporation occupies and uses a sufficient percentage of the building to render it a passive investment turns on a difficult factual issue.[67] The Regulations give two examples: where an owner corporation occupied and used 75% of the space of a two-story building, the building was deemed a passive asset;[68] but where an owner corporation operated only one floor of an eleven-story building and leased the remaining ten floors, the rental activity was deemed a separate business activity.[69] In addition to the percentage of space occupied, other factors might be considered in determining whether the building rental constituted an active business, such as the relative rental values of the leased and occupied spaces; and whether the corporation conducts its rental activities as a separate business, maintaining separate books and employees.

(iv) *Division of horizontally integrated activities.* The Regulations under § 355 permit the division of several activities where the separated business activities were each independently producing income:

> (aa) Corporation H manufactures and sells ice cream at a plant in State X and at a plant in State Y. Each plant is a separate business.[70]

> (bb) Corporation J has manufactured and sold ice cream in State X for ten years. In 1965, J purchased land and constructed a new plant in State Y. In 1967, J proposed to spin off the plant operated in State X to its shareholders. The Regulations state that the plant in

---

66 Treas. Reg. § 1.355-1(c)(2); Bonsall, Jr. v. Commissioner, 317 F.2d 61 (C.A. 2 1963); and Theodore F. Appleby, 35 T.C. 755 (1961), *affirmed per curiam,* 296 F.2d 925 (C.A. 3 1962), *cert. denied,* 370 U.S. 910.
67 *Id.*
68 Treas. Reg. § 1.355-1(d) Ex. (4).
69 Treas. Reg. § 1.355-1(d) Ex. (3).
70 Treas. Reg. § 1.355-1(d) Ex. (8).

State Y will not satisfy the five-year test, because it was conducted for only two years.[71]

(cc) Corporation K owns and operates two men's retail clothing stores — one in the downtown area of the City of R and one in the suburban area of the City of R. Each store is operated independently, and they do not share a common warehouse. Each store is a separate business.[72]

(dd) Corporation M had owned and operated a hotel business and a rental real estate business since 1956. In 1965, M spun off the rental real estate business to its shareholders. During the five-year period preceding the distribution, M had purchased additional rental properties. The Service has ruled that unless M can demonstrate that the rental property acquired during that five-year period was substantially financed from the earnings of the rental business (rather than from the earnings of the hotel business), the spin-off will not comply with the active business test.[73]

With the exception of the intrusion of the *Coady* doctrine, the Service's construction of the active business test has created complex and frequently arbitrary rules which may ensnare innocent taxpayers seeking nonrecognition for legitimate corporate divisions.[74] The test has been subjected to criticism for this reason.[75]

(v) *The consequences of a reorganization or corporate acquisition effected shortly after the corporate division.* If shortly after a corporate division was effected, or if pursuant to a prearranged plan, one of the corporations involved in the division is a party to a reorganization or is acquired by an unrelated party, the corporate division may fail to qualify for nonrecognition treatment if the transaction contravenes the

---

71 Treas. Reg. § 1.355-1(d) Ex. (9). *But see* pp. 127-129 *supra.*
72 Treas. Reg. § 1.355-1(d) Ex. (10).
73 Rev. Rul. 59-400, 1959-2 C.B. 114. The ruling is questionable, but it would be foolhardy to ignore it.
74 *E.g.,* Theodore F. Appleby, 35 T.C. 755 (1961), *affirmed,* 296 F.2d 925 (C.A. 3 1962), *cert. denied,* 370 U.S. 910.
75 *See* Whitman, *Draining the Serbonian Bog: A New Approach to Separations Under the 1954 Code,* 81 HARV. L. REV. 1194 (1968).

active business requirement or the continuity of proprietary interest requirement.

> **Ex.** (1) The *A* Corporation, which owns and operates a hardware business and a grocery business, wishes to merge with the *B* Corporation. The *B* Corporation is willing to join with *A*'s hardware business, but it wants no part of the grocery business. To resolve this situation, *A* transfers the grocery business to a newly created *C* Corporation and spins off the *C* Corporation to its shareholders. The *A* Corporation then merges into *B* pursuant to local statutory merger laws. After a mixed success in litigating the question of whether § 355 is applicable to transactions of this kind, the Commissioner has conceded that this transaction complies with the active business test, even where *B* is the surviving corporation of the merger of *A* and *B*.[76] While the Commissioner has apparently conceded that a statutory merger immediately following a corporate division will not disqualify the division for nonrecognition treatment, no statement has been made as to the tax consequence of an acquisition of an involved corporation's assets through some means other than a statutory merger. If an involved corporation's assets are acquired by an unrelated corporation in a tax-free "C" reorganization[77] there is no apparent reason why a preceding corporate division should be accorded different tax treatment than would have been the case if the subsequent reorganization had been a statutory merger. However, the Service has not ruled on this question, and consequently caution is warranted; moreover, in such transactions there is some risk that the acquisition of the involved corporation's assets will not qualify for tax-free treatment as a "C" reorganization for failure to comply with the requisite that substantially all of the acquired corporation's assets be transferred to the acquiring corporation — *i.e.*, the cor-

---

76 *Compare* Curtis v. United States, 336 F.2d 714 (C.A. 6 1964) *with* Commissioner v. Morris Trust, 367 F.2d 794 (C.A. 4 1966), *affirming* 42 T.C. 779 (1964). In *Morris Trust,* the Tax Court and the Fourth Circuit granted nonrecognition treatment under § 355 to a transaction of the kind described in the above example. The Service has announced that it accepts the decision in *Morris Trust* insofar *inter alia* as that case holds that a merger after the corporate division does not prevent satisfaction of the "active business" test. Rev. Rul. 68-603, I.R.B. 1968-47, p. 10.

77 A "C" reorganization (*i.e.*, the exchange of voting stock of one corporation for substantially all of the assets of another corporation) is discussed at pp. 168-173 *infra.*

porate division may be treated as a step transaction for the purpose of finessing the "substantially all" requirement.

If the assets of a corporation involved in a corporate division or the capital stock of that corporation is acquired in a taxable exchange shortly after the division was effected, it is extremely likely that the division will not qualify for nonrecognition treatment. Moreover, if the proprietary interests in an involved corporation are significantly changed after this division, § 355 will not apply.

> **Ex. (2)** X Corporation was engaged in the active conduct of a liberal arts college for more than 5 years. All of the stock of the X Corporation is owned equally by two individuals. For more than 5 years, X owned all of the stock of the Y Corporation which owns and operates a technical and trade school. Both X and Y were operated for profit. For valid business reasons, X distributed all of the Y stock to X's two shareholders equally. In order to qualify for governmental financial aid, the charter of X was amended to convert it into a nonprofit, membership corporation. The Service ruled[78] that this conversion constituted a change of the proprietary interests in X, and consequently it ruled that the corporate division did not comply with the continuity of interest requirements of § 355. The Y stock distributed to X's two shareholders was treated as a taxable dividend to the extent of X's earnings and profits.

3. Tax consequences to shareholder of receiving boot

Where a shareholder receives a corporate distribution in compliance with § 355, the shareholder will not recognize gain or loss. As previously noted, one of § 355's conditions is that the distribution to the shareholder consist solely of stock or securities of a controlled corporation;[79] and in some circumstances even distributions of stock or securities may not qualify.[80] However, where a corporate distribution to a shareholder complies with every condition of § 355, except that in addition to distributing property which qualifies under § 355, other property ("boot") is also distributed,

---

78 Rev. Rul. 69-293, I.R.B. 1969-23, p. 9.
79 I.R.C. § 355(a)(1)(A).
80 I.R.C. § 355(a)(3).

the tax consequences of the exchange are determined under I.R.C. § 356, discussed below.

(a) Determination of the amount of boot. The following corporate distributions constitute boot in the amounts indicated:

(i) Cash;

(ii) The fair market value of property[81] other than stocks or securities of the controlled corporation;[82]

(iii) The fair market value of stock of the controlled corporation which had been acquired by the distributing corporation in a taxable transaction which occurred within five years of the distribution;[83]

(iv) Where securities of a controlled corporation are distributed to a shareholder, and where in connection with the distribution the shareholder either did not surrender any securities of the distributing corporation or surrendered securities of the distributing corporation having a lesser total principal amount than the total principal amount of the securities distributed to him, then the *fair market value* of the difference between the principal amount of the securities distributed to the shareholder and the principal amount of the securities (if any) surrendered by the shareholder is boot.[84]

> **Ex. (1)** Pursuant to a corporate division, the X Corporation made the following exchange with its shareholder A. A exchanged 100 shares of X stock for 100 shares of Y stock and a security of Y in the principal amount of $1,000 and having a fair market value of $990. If § 355 otherwise applies, A received boot of $990.[85]

> **Ex. (2)** Pursuant to a corporate division, the X Corporation made the following exchanges with its shareholder B. B exchanged 100 shares of X stock and a security of

---

81 The amount of boot is determined according to the fair market value of the property irrespective of whether the shareholder is a corporation. Treas. Reg. § 1.356-1(d).

82 The validity of the regulatory provision (Treas. Reg. § 1.355-1(a)) that stock rights or warrants to purchase stock of the controlled corporation are boot is unsettled. *See* note 21 *supra* for a discussion of this question.

83 I.R.C. § 355(a)(3).

84 I.R.C. § 356(d); and Treas. Reg. § 1.356-3.

85 Treas. Reg. § 1.356-3(b) Ex. (1).

X in the principal amount of \$1,000 for 300 shares of Y stock and securities of Y in the principal amount of \$1,500 having a fair market value of \$1,575. If § 355 otherwise applies, B received boot of \$525, computed as follows: The difference in principal amount of the securities (\$500) constituted ⅓ of the principal amount of securities distributed to B, and consequently the fair market value of that difference is ⅓ × \$1,575 = \$525.[86]

(b) Recognition of gain or loss. Where § 355 would be applicable to a corporate distribution were it not for the distribution of boot, no loss will be recognized to the shareholder from that transaction[87]— *i.e.*, if the corporate division were a split-off in which the shareholder surrendered stock of the parent corporation which had depreciated in value, the shareholder would not recognize a loss on the exchange. The Service has ruled (Rev. Rul. 68-23, 1968-1 C.B. 144) that when a shareholder exchanges several blocks of stock for properties of the corporation in an exchange covered by § 356, the shareholder's gain or loss on each block of stock must be computed separately, any realized loss disallowed, and any realized gain recognized in the manner and amounts described below.

The amount and characterization of gain recognized by a shareholder on account of receiving boot in a corporate division depend upon the form of corporate division utilized: spin-off, split-off or split-up.

Where a shareholder receives boot in a spin-off,[88] the fair market value of the boot is treated as a distribution of property under § 301, and consequently will constitute ordinary dividend income to the extent of earnings and profits.[89]

> **Ex.** The X Corporation has two equal shareholders, A and B. X owns all 100 shares of the outstanding stock of the Y Corporation plus a \$100 bond of Y having a fair market value of \$105. Pursuant to a spin-off, X distributes 50 shares of Y plus \$105 cash to A, and X distributes 50 shares of Y plus the \$100 bond of Y to B. The \$105 cash distributed to A and the \$105 fair market value of

---

86 Treas. Reg. § 1.356-3(b) Ex. (2).
87 I.R.C. § 356(c). Treas. Reg. § 1.356-1(a)(2).
88 In a spin-off, the shareholder does not exchange any of the parent's stock or securities for the corporate distribution received by him.
89 I.R.C. § 356(b); and Treas. Reg. § 1.356-2.

the bond distributed to *B* are treated as distributions under § 301.

Where a shareholder receives boot from a split-off or split-up, and where the shareholder realized a gain on the exchange (*i.e.*, the aggregate value of the properties distributed to the shareholder exceeds his basis in the stock[90] and securities surrendered by him), then the gain realized by the shareholder will be recognized, but the amount of gain recognized by the shareholder will not exceed the amount of boot received by him.[91] If the exchange had "the effect of the distribution of a dividend," then the gain recognized by the shareholder will be treated as a dividend to the extent of the shareholder's ratable portion of the corporation's earnings and profits accumulated since March 1, 1913, and the balance of the gain, if any, will usually be capital gains.[92] For some reason, § 356 does not employ the bifurcated dividend test (*i.e.*, for the purpose of determining what amount of a corporate distribution is a dividend, § 316 refers distributions first to current earnings and profits and then the excess, if any, is referred to accumulated earnings and profits), but instead, § 356 uses accumulated earnings and profits as the sole test. Section 356 does not define the phrase "has the effect of the distribution of a dividend"; and while a reasonable construction thereof would permit the shareholder to use the standards established in §§ 302 and 346 for determining dividend equivalence, there is support for the position, asserted by the Service in several cases, that those standards are inapplicable and that dividend equivalence under § 356 means only that the distributing corporation has earnings and profits available.[93] This position of the Service, sometimes called "the Bedford doctrine" because it was apparently adopted by Justice Frankfurter in his opinion in the *Bedford* case,[94] has little to commend it.

Where a shareholder exchanged section 306 stock in a split-up or split-off, the amount of boot received by the shareholder for

---

90 If the stock surrendered by the shareholder is section 306 stock, the recognized gain is determined differently as noted in the discussion below.

91 I.R.C. § 356(a)(1).

92 I.R.C. § 356(a)(2).

93 *Compare* Commissioner v. Estate of Bedford, 325 U.S. 283 (1945), *with* Hawkinson v. Commissioner, 235 F.2d 747 (C.A. 2 1956); and Idaho Power Co. v. United States, 161 F. Supp. 807 (Ct. Cl. 1958).

94 Commissioner v. Estate of Bedford, *supra.*

the section 306 stock is treated as a distribution of property under
§ 301.[95] Where the shareholder exchanged both section 306 stock
and other stock, the boot received by him is first allocated to the
section 306 stock and only the balance, if any, is allocated to the
other stock.[96]

> **Ex.** A received boot of $110 from the X Corporation pur-
> suant to a split-off in which A surrendered to X one share
> of X's common stock having a basis of $80 and a fair
> market value of $100 and one share of section 306 stock
> having a fair market value of $100. X has a large amount
> of accumulated earnings and profits. $100 of boot is allo-
> cated to the section 306 stock and is treated as a divi-
> dend. The remaining $10 of boot is allocated to the com-
> mon stock, and consequently A also recognized $10 of
> the $20 gain he realized from the exchange of that share
> of stock. If the distribution had the effect of a dividend,
> the $10 gain recognized on the common stock will be
> treated as a distribution under § 301; but if the distribu-
> tion did not have the effect of a dividend, the $10 gain
> is a capital gain.

It should be emphasized that where a shareholder receives stock
and boot pursuant to a split-off or a split-up which qualifies under § 356, and where no section 306 stock is involved in the exchange, the amount of gain recognized by the shareholder is equal
to *either* the amount of his realized gain *or* the amount of boot
distributed to him, whichever is less. But, where section 306
stock is exchanged, the entire amount of boot allocated to that
stock is treated as a distribution of property under § 301 and will
frequently constitute ordinary income to the shareholder.

4. Tax consequences of corporate division to distributing cor-
poration

(a) **Recognition of gain or loss.** Where a corporation makes distributions pursuant to a corporate division in which the corporation
either receives nothing from the shareholder (a spin-off) or receives only its own stock in exchange, the corporation will not recognize gain or loss,[97] except that the corporation's distribution of
boot may cause tax consequences where the boot is depreciable

---

95 I.R.C. § 356(e).
96 Treas. Reg. § 1.356-4.
97 I.R.C. § 311(a).

property[98] or section 341(f) assets, or inventory[99] or property subject to a mortgage or other liability.[100] However, where pursuant to a division, the corporation receives its own securities from its shareholders, the amount distributed in exchange for those securities may cause the corporation to recognize gain or loss depending upon whether the distributed property was appreciated or depreciated. If the corporate division constituted a reorganization,[101] and it need not do so,[102] it is arguable that the corporation would not recognize gain or loss, but it requires a very liberal reading of the Code to provide nonrecognition.[103] Additionally, the distributing corporation may recognize gain or loss if the value of property distributed to a shareholder in exchange for a security of the distributing corporation is greater or less than the corporation's debt obligation under such security, after an appropriate adjustment has been made for unrecaptured premium or discount.[104] In the event that the corporation realizes a gain by cancelling its debt obligation under the security, the corporation could utilize §§ 108 and 1017 to elect nonrecognition.

(b) **Earnings and profits.** Where a corporate division qualifies for non-

---

98 I.R.C. §§ 1245, 1250 and 47.
99 I.R.C. § 311(b). This provision does not apply to liquidating distributions.
100 I.R.C. § 311(c). Income is recognized to the extent that the amount of the said liabilities exceeds the basis of the transferred property. This provision does not apply to liquidating distributions.
101 I.R.C. § 368(a)(1)(D).
102 I.R.C. § 355(a)(2)(C).
103 I.R.C. § 361 provides nonrecognition where a corporation transfers property in exchange for stock and securities of "another corporation a party to the reorganization," but in a corporate division, the distributing corporation receives *its own stock and securities* Also, while the nonrecognition provisions of § 354 appear applicable on their face, that section is included in Subpart B which applies only to shareholders. It is a reasonable contention that § 361 is intended as the corporate counterpart to § 354, and therefore that it should be deemed applicable to the distribution, even though the literal language of that section does not encompass such exchanges.
   If § 361 were deemed applicable, in addition to not recognizing gain on the exchange, the distributing corporation also would not recognize gain for distributing boot which consists of depreciable property (I.R.C. §§ 47(b)(2), 1245(b)(3), and 1250(d)(3)) or inventory; but the corporation could recognize gain from the distribution of § 341(f) assets; and in certain circumstances the corporation will recognize gain from distributing property subject to liabilities (§ 357(b) and (c)).
104 Treas. Reg. § 1.61-12. *See* United States v. Kirby Lumber Co., 284 U.S. 1 (1931).

recognition treatment under § 355 or under that portion of § 356 that pertains to corporate divisions, the Secretary has been granted broad discretion to promulgate Regulations defining the re-allocation of the earnings and profits of the distributing corporation among the distributing and controlled corporations.[105]

The Regulations provide that in no event will any part of a deficit earnings and profits of the distributing corporation be allocated to a controlled corporation.[106]

The Regulations further provide that where a corporate division constituted a "D" reorganization,[107] and where the controlled corporation was newly created, the earnings and profits of the distributing corporation will usually be allocated between the distributing and controlled corporations according to the proportion of the fair market value of the properties in each corporation immediately after the transaction; but in appropriate cases, the allocation may be made according to the net basis of such assets.[108]

The Regulations also provide a means of allocating earnings and profits where the corporate division does not qualify as a reorganization.[109]

Where corporate distributions include boot, the earnings and profits of the distributed corporation may be affected thereby. Appropriate adjustments should be made in the earnings and profits of a distributing corporation where: (i) the distributing corporation recognized a gain or loss on the distribution (as indicated in paragraph (a) above); (ii) the distribution of boot is treated as a distribution under § 301; (iii) the distribution of boot caused the recipient shareholder to recognize capital gain on his surrender of *stock* of the distributing corporation (*i.e.*, to the extent that the distribution of boot is deemed to be given in exchange for stock of the distributing corporation, it is a distribution in redemption of stock and thereby reduces earnings and profits to the extent that it is not properly chargeable to capital account).[110]

---

105 I.R.C. § 312(i).
106 Treas. Reg. § 1.312-10(c).
107 I.R.C. § 368(a)(1)(D).
108 Treas. Reg. § 1.312-10(a). As used therein, the term "net basis" means the basis of the assets less liabilities assumed or to which the assets are subject.
109 Treas. Reg. § 1.312-10(b).
110 I.R.C. § 312(e), *and see* pp. 26-27 *supra*.

5. Basis of assets distributed to shareholder

Where a distribution of stocks and securities of a controlled corporation is made to a shareholder under § 355, the shareholder's basis[111] in the stock and securities of the distributing corporation held by him immediately prior to the distribution is allocated among the stocks and securities of the distributing corporation and of the controlled corporation held by him immediately after the distribution, such allocation to be made according to the respective fair market values of the stocks and securities. This method of allocation applies to all forms of corporate divisions including spin-offs.[112] Where boot is distributed, the basis of the boot in the hands of the shareholder is equal to the fair market value of the boot,[113] irrespective of whether the shareholder is an individual or a corporation.[114]

Where prior to the distribution, the shareholder held both stock and securities, or held more than one class of stock, or held more than one class of securities, then a factual determination must be made as to which stocks and securities of the controlled corporation were distributed on account of stock (and of which class) and which were distributed on account of the securities (and of which class). The shareholder's basis in each class of the stock of the distributing corporation and in each class of the securities of the distributing corporation is allocated separately.[115]

> **Ex.** A owned 100 shares of common stock of X having a basis of $15,000, and a fair market value of $30,000. X distributed to A 50 shares of Y stock having a fair market value of $10,000 and securities having a principal amount and a fair market value of $5,000. In exchange, A surrendered 50 shares of his stock of X. Assuming that § 356 is applicable, A realized a gain of $7,500 of which $5,000 is recognized. A's basis in the Y security is equal to its fair market value — $5,000. A's basis in his common stock ($15,000) is reduced by the

---

111 The basis of the shareholder's stock and securities is first adjusted by reducing it by the total amount of boot received and increasing it by the amount of dividend or gain recognized on the transaction. I.R.C. § 358.
112 I.R.C. § 358(b).
113 I.R.C. § 358(a)(2).
114 *See* Treas. Reg. § 1.356-1(d).
115 Treas. Reg. § 1.358-2(a)(4).

boot he received ($5,000) and increased by the gain he recognized ($5,000) so that the "adjusted" basis equals $15,000. This $15,000 adjusted basis is allocated pro rata between the X and Y stock as follows:

$$\frac{\$10,000 \quad (\text{fmv of } Y)}{\$10,000(\text{fmv of } Y) + \$15,000(\text{fmv of } X)} \times \$15,000 = \$6,000 \text{ basis}$$
for the 50 shares of Y stock;

$$\frac{\$15,000 \quad (\text{fmv of } X)}{\$15,000(\text{fmv of } X) + \$10,000(\text{fmv of } Y)} \times \$15,000 = \$9,000 \text{ basis}$$
for the 50 shares of X stock retained by A.

B. REORGANIZATIONS

1. Nature and definition of a reorganization

The word "reorganization" is a term of art for tax law purposes, and its tax meaning should not be confused with the ordinary use of that term or its use in the bankruptcy area. The Regulations state that the purpose of the reorganization provisions of the Code is to provide nonrecognition for "certain specifically described exchanges incident to such readjustments of corporate structures made in one of the particular ways specified in the Code, as are required by business exigencies and which effect only a readjustment of continuing interest in property under modified corporate forms."[116] The term "reorganization" is strictly limited to those transactions described in I.R.C. § 368.[117] Section 368(a)(1) lists six categories of transactions which qualify as reorganizations, and each separate category constitutes a subheading of that section which is given a capital letter as a prefix. The capital letters that constitute the organizational subheadings for the six forms of reorganizations have become the shorthand nomenclature for each form. Thus § 368(a)(1)(A) designates a statutory merger or consolidation as a reorganization, and that form is frequently referred to as an "A" reorganization. Similarly, a stock acquisition (§ 368(a)(1)(B)) is called a "B" reorganization, and so forth. The "A," "B" and "C" reorganizations are corporate acquisitions. "D" reorganizations are primarily corporate divisions. An "E" reorganization is a recapitalization; and an "F" reorganization is a mere change in identity, form or place of organization,

116 Treas. Reg. § 1.368-1(b). *See also* Treas. Reg. § 1.1002-1(c) for a statement of the purpose of granting nonrecognition to certain exchanges made pursuant to a reorganization.
117 Treas. Reg. § 1.368-2(a).

albeit the scope of the F reorganization may be in the process of growing.[118]

The different types of reorganizations may be classified in three general categories.

(i) *Divisive reorganizations.* As noted above, a corporate division may qualify as a reorganization, but need not do so. When a corporate division constitutes a reorganization, it is sometimes referred to as a divisive reorganization. A divisive reorganization will usually be a D reorganization, but in a recent Tax Court case, the taxpayers contended unsuccessfully that a corporate division could qualify as an F reorganization,[119] and the taxpayers have appealed from their adverse judgment in that case.

(ii) *Nonacquisitive reorganizations.* Certain changes in the identity, form or place of organization of a corporation and certain changes in the capital structure of a corporation are sometimes referred to as nonacquisitive reorganizations. These changes may be effected on a single existing corporation or, in some circumstances, they may be effected on several corporations. The typical nonacquisitive reorganization is an E or F reorganization, discussed below in this chapter.

(iii) *Acquisitive reorganizations.* If a corporation (hereinafter called the "acquiring corporation") acquires the assets of a second corporation, or acquires a controlling stock interest in the second corporation, in exchange for voting stock of the acquiring corporation, the exchange may qualify as a reorganization. Typically, this type of reorganization will be either an A, B or C reorganization, all three of which are discussed below in this chapter, and is sometimes classified as an acquisitive reorganization. In some circumstances, an acquisitive reorganization may be a D reorganization.

2. Significance of qualifying as a reorganization

One consequence of classifying a transaction as a reorganization is that certain exchanges of stock or securities or assets of a cor-

---

118 *See* Pugh, *The F Reorganization: Reveille for a Sleeping Giant?*, 24 TAX L. REV. 437 (1969).
119 Oscar E. Baan, 51 T.C. 1032 (1969), decided on remand from the Supreme Court. The position urged by the taxpayers in *Baan* was criticized by Pugh in his excellent article *The F Reorganization: Reveille for a Sleeping Giant?*, 24 TAX L. REV. 437, 465-467 (1969).

poration that is a party to a reorganization[120] are given nonrecognition treatment in whole or in part. Section 354 provides nonrecognition for shareholders who exchange stock or securities in a corporation that is a party to a reorganization solely for stock or securities in that corporation or in another corporation which is a party to the reorganization. If a shareholder's exchange of stock and securities would qualify under § 354 except that the shareholder also received boot (*i.e.*, property other than stock or securities of a party to a reorganization, and even securities will constitute boot to the extent of the fair market value of the difference between the principal amount of securities received and the principal amount of securities surrendered),[121] then § 356 provides that the shareholder will recognize gain in an amount equal to the lesser of either the amount of gain realized by him or the amount of boot he received. Section 356 operates in conjunction with § 354 in the same manner that it operates in conjunction with § 355, the corporate division provision.[122]

Section 361 provides nonrecognition where, pursuant to a plan of reorganization, a corporation which is a party to the reorganization exchanges property solely for stock or securities of another corporation which is a party to the reorganization. Section 361(b) deals with an exchange in which the distributing corporation receives boot.[123]

A corporation which distributes its own stock in exchange for property will not recognize gain or loss thereon irrespective of whether the transaction is made pursuant to a reorganization.[124]

A second consequence of reorganization treatment is that the surviving corporation *may* succeed to the tax attributes of the transferor corporation including such useful tax attributes as carry-

---

120 The phrase "party to a reorganization" is also a term of art and is defined in I.R.C. § 368(b).
121 I.R.C. §§ 354(a) and 356(d).
122 *See* pp, 134-138 *supra,* for a discussion of the operation of § 356.
123 Where a distributing corporation transfers assets subject to liabilities, the *total amount* of transferred liabilities will be treated as boot to the distributing corporation if the purpose of the transfer of *any* of the liabilities was federal income tax avoidance. I.R.C. § 357(b); and Treas. Reg. §§ 1.357-1(c). Where a transfer of liabilities is made pursuant to a D reorganization, the distributing corporation will recognize income to the extent that the total amount of liabilities exceeds the adjusted basis of the distributed property. I.R.C. § 357(c).
124 I.R.C. § 1032.

forward net operating losses.[125] Of course, not all tax attributes are desirable, *e.g.*, accumulated earnings and profits.

The nonrecognition provisions for corporate exchanges and the limitations on acquisitions of tax attributes present extraordinarily complex issues, and the above paragraphs merely sketch the skeleton of those issues.[126]

In an exchange of stocks and securities qualifying for nonrecognition under § 354 or § 356, the shareholder's basis in boot received by him is equal to the fair market value of the boot at the date of exchange, and the shareholder's basis in the stocks and securities he received which were not boot is equal to the basis of the stocks and securities he transferred decreased by the sum of the amount of boot he received plus the amount of loss he recognized, and increased by the amount of income (gain or dividends) he recognized on the exchange.[127]

3. Judicially imposed restrictions on reorganization treatment

Over the years since the tax reorganization concept was born, the courts have enunciated a number of judicial doctrines imposing limitations and conditions on qualifying for reorganization treatment. If construed literally, the reorganization provisions would be highly susceptible to utilization for tax avoidance purposes, and the judicially imposed conditions were designed to restrict reorganization treatment to those transactions that conform with the spirit and purpose of the legislation. These judicially imposed requisites are now accepted as basic elements of a reorganization, and several of those listed below are set forth in the current Regulations.

(a) Continuity of proprietary interest. The rationale for providing nonrecognition treatment to certain exchanges made pursuant to a reorganization is that the reorganization constitutes a mere change in the form in which the business is operated, and that the tax laws should not hamper the rearrangement of a corporate form

---

125 *See* I.R.C. §§ 381 and 382. In some circumstances, the net operating losses of a party to a reorganization may be disallowed in whole or in part as carry-over deductions. *See* §§ 382, 269 and 482.
126 For a more extensive discussion, *See* BITTKER AND EUSTICE, FEDERAL INCOME TAXATION OF CORPORATIONS AND SHAREHOLDERS (2d ed., 1966), chapters 12 and 13, pp. 497-708.
127 I.R.C. § 358.

where there are legitimate business purposes for the change. Taxpayers are given great latitude in making such changes, and many reorganizations involve considerable alteration of ownership interests. However, a minimum requirement established by the judiciary,[128] and reflected in the Regulations,[129] is that the transferor have a proprietary interest in the acquiring corporation after the transfer is completed. If there is no continuing proprietary interest, the transaction resembles a sale more than it does a mere change of the corporate form in which business is conducted, and it is treated accordingly.

The determination whether a transaction complies with the continuity of proprietary interest requirement turns on several factual issues: *i.e.*, whether the transferor retained a substantial proprietary interest in the enterprise; and whether such retained proprietary interest constituted a substantial part of the value of the property transferred.[130] Thus, the transferors, or shareholders of a corporate transferor, must not only have retained a significant interest in the enterprise, but that interest must constitute a substantial portion of the consideration they received in the exchange.

When the transferors or shareholders of the corporate transferor receive only securities or other debt instruments of the acquiring corporation, there is no continuity of proprietary interest since the transferor's interest is that of a creditor rather than an equity owner.[131] However, the transferors' receipt of nonvoting preferred stock would provide them with equity ownership in compliance with the continuity of interest requirements.[132]

To qualify as a reorganization, it is not necessary that the transferors receive only preferred or common stock of the acquiring corporation; it is sufficient if the aggregate amount of stock received by all of the transferors is substantial.[133] The Service has

---

128 *E.g.*, Pinellas Ice & Cold Storage Co. v. Commissioner, 287 U.S. 462 (1933); and Helvering v. Minnesota Tea Co., 296 U.S. 378 (1935).
129 Treas. Reg. § 1.368-1(b).
130 Southwest Natural Gas Co. v. Commissioner, 189 F.2d 332 (C.A. 5 1951), *cert. denied,* 342 U.S. 860.
131 LeTulle v. Scofield, 308 U.S. 415 (1940). The fact that the securities received by the transferor in LeTulle v. Scofield were long-term bonds did not change the status of the transferors from creditors to equity owners.
132 John A. Nelson Co. v. Helvering, 296 U.S. 374 (1935).
133 In John A. Nelson Co. v. Helvering, *supra,* even though the transferors received $2,000,000 in cash in addition to preferred stock, the transaction nevertheless qualified as a reorganization.

ruled that the requirement of continuity of interest is satisfied where the shareholders of the acquired corporation receive stock of the acquiring corporation having an aggregate value, at the effective date of the reorganization, of no less than 50% of the aggregate value of the outstanding stock of the acquired corporation, valued at the date of reorganization.[134] It is sufficient if one or more of the shareholders of the acquired corporation receives stock of the acquiring corporation having the value indicated above; it is not necessary that all of the shareholders of the acquired corporation receive such stock.[135]

(b) **Continuity of business enterprise.** Continuity of business enterprise under a modified form is a requisite to qualifying as a reorganization.[136] While the Service initially contended that the transferred business itself must be continued,[137] the Second Circuit held that it was sufficient if the acquiring corporation conducted a business activity of any nature, and such business activity need not be the business that was conducted by its predecessors.[138] The Service ultimately accepted the Second Circuit's construction and revoked Rev. Rul. 56-330.[139]

(c) **Business purpose doctrine.** A transaction will be classified as a reorganization only where it has a legitimate business purpose.[140] The business purpose doctrine is discussed in the material above dealing with corporate divisions.[141]

(d) **Step transactions.** The opinions promulgated in tax cases frequently articulate the superannuated principle of substance over form; *viz.*, that tax consequences turn upon the substance of a

---

134 Rev. Proc. 66-34 (Sec. 3.02), 1966-2 C.B. 1232, 1233. Of course, the receipt of boot may cause the recognition of gain to the extent of the boot. I.R.C. §§ 356 and 361(b).

135 *Id.*

136 Treas. Reg. § 1.368-1(b). Standard Realization Co., 10 T.C. 708 (1948); and Pridemark, Inc. v. Commissioner, 345 F.2d 35 (C.A. 4 1965).

137 Rev. Rul. 56-330, 1956-2 C.B. 204.

138 Becher v. Commissioner, 221 F.2d 252 (C.A. 2 1955).

139 Rev. Rul. 63-29, 1963-1 C.B. 77.

140 Gregory v. Helvering, 293 U.S. 465 (1935). Treas. Reg. § 1.368-1(b) and (c), and § 1.368-2(g).

141 Pp. 122-124 *supra.*

transaction rather than on the form in which it is clothed.[142] The step transaction doctrine is a specific application of the substance over form principle. Under the step transaction principle, a circuitous route taken by a taxpayer to achieve a result is ignored where the only purpose for the detour was tax avoidance.[143] The following example illustrates the step transaction principle.

> **Ex.** X Corporation wishes to acquire the assets of Y Corporation in a reorganization. If X were to issue its own voting stock to Y in exchange for all of Y's assets, that would be a "C" reorganization. If X were to issue its own voting stock to the shareholders of Y in exchange for all of Y's outstanding stock, that would be a "B" reorganization. If immediately after the "B" reorganization, X were to liquidate Y under § 332, the net effect of the two transactions (the acquisition of Y's stock and the liquidation of Y) is identical to a "C" reorganization (the direct acquisition of Y's assets for stock). A difference in tax consequences is that § 382 imposes restrictions on acquisition of tax attributes through a "C" reorganization that are not applicable to a "B" reorganization or a § 332 liquidation. Accordingly, the Service has ruled[144] that a "B" reorganization followed promptly by a liquidation of the subsidiary is a step transaction if the two steps were executed pursuant to a predetermined plan and therefore is treated as a "C" reorganization which is subject to the restrictions of § 382(b).

C. NONACQUISITIVE REORGANIZATIONS

1. Changes in corporate identity, form, or place of organization ("F" reorganizations)

A typical F reorganization[145] is a transfer of all of the assets of

---

142 *E.g.*, Gregory v. Helvering, 293 U.S. 465 (1935). The application of the substance over form rule to specific circumstances is far more difficult than the statement of the rule suggests. For a discussion of the rule, *see* United States v. General Geophysical Co., 296 F.2d 86 (C.A. 5 1961).

143 *See* Minnesota Tea Co. v. Helvering, 302 U.S. 609 (1938); Helvering v. Alabama Asphaltic Limestone Co., 315 U.S. 179 (1942); and Commissioner v. Court Holding Co., 324 U.S. 331 (1945). In *Minnesota Tea,* the Court said (p. 613): "A given result at the end of a straight path is not made a different result because reached by following a devious path." *See also* Mintz and Plumb, *Step Transactions in Corporate Reorganizations,* 12 N.Y.U. TAX INST. 247 (1954).

144 Rev. Rul. 67-274, 1967-2 C.B. 141.

145 I.R.C. § 368(a)(1)(F). The F reorganization first appeared in § 202(c)(2) of the Revenue Act of 1921.

one corporate entity to a newly created corporate shell. A common reason for such a transfer is to change the state of incorporation of a business enterprise. However, in recent years, there are signs that the F reorganization will be deemed applicable to a broader range of transactions than was true prior to the adoption of the 1954 Code.[146]

In many instances, a transaction will qualify as both an F reorganization and as another type of reorganization. For example, the X Corporation in State A forms the Y Corporation in State B, and then X merges into Y. The "merger" qualifies as both an A reorganization and an F reorganization. The Service has ruled that in such cases the transaction shall be treated as an F reorganization[147] which takes precedence.

(a) Characteristics of an F reorganization. Neither the Code nor the Regulations shed light on the minimum qualifications of an F reorganization; however, several requirements have emerged from the administrative and judicial decisions that have dealt with that provision. These requirements are:

(i) The prereorganization business of the transferor must be continued by the transferee, and virtually all of the transferor's assets, other than liquid assets, must be distributed to the transferee.[148]

(ii) The shareholders of the transferee corporation must be substantially the same persons as were shareholders of the transferor corporation, and there must be no significant change in proprietary interests.[149] However, the Service has ruled that an inconsequential change in shareholders' interests will not disqualify a

---

146 *See, e.g.,* Reef Corporation v. Commissioner, 368 F.2d 125 (C.A. 5 1966), *cert. denied,* 386 U.S. 1018 (1967); Davant v. Commissioner, 366 F.2d 874 (C.A. 5 1966); and Pridemark, Inc., 42 T.C. 510 (1964), *reversed,* 345 F.2d 35 (C.A. 4 1965). *See* also Pugh, *The F Reorganization: Reveille for a Sleeping Giant?*, 24 TAX L. REV. 437 (1969).

147 Rev. Rul. 57-276, 1957-1 C.B. 126. *See also* Reef Corporation v. Commissioner, 368 F.2d 125 (C.A. 5 1966) in which the court stated that where a reorganization qualifies under both "F" and "D," then "F" takes precedence unless there is a substantial change in the corporate operation.

148 *See* Pridemark, Inc. v. Commissioner, 345 F.2d 35 (C.A. 4 1965); and Rev. Rul. 58-422, 1958-2 C.B. 145.

149 Davant v. Commissioner, 366 F.2d 874 (C.A. 5 1966); and Rev. Rul. 58-422, 1958-2 C.B. 145.

transaction;[150] and in a split decision, the Fifth Circuit permitted a significant shift of ownership.[151]

The Service's position is that there is a third requirement for F reorganization. The F reorganization provision only applies to a transfer of assets from one single corporate entity to another; and consequently the merger of corporations X and Y (both wholly owned by I) into a newly formed corporate entity Z will not qualify as an F reorganization.[152] While the Tax Court has adopted the Service's position, the Ninth Circuit has rejected it.[153] The position of the Ninth Circuit was criticized by Pugh in an excellent article which examined the logical consequences of applying F reorganizations in these circumstances.[154]

(b) Tax consequences of an F reorganization to shareholders. Normally, where an F reorganization is effected, a transferor's exchange of stock and securities in the old corporate entity for stock and securities in the new corporate entity will not cause recognition of gain

---

150 Rev. Rul. 66-284, 1966-2 C.B. 115. In that ruling, dissenting shareholders owning less than 1% of the transferor corporation did not participate in the reorganization.

151 Reef Corporation v. Commissioner, 368 F.2d 125 (C.A. 5 1966). *See also* Dunlap & Associates, Inc., 47 T.C. 542 (1967). In *Reef,* shareholders owning 48% of the stock of the transferor corporation received no proprietary interest in the acquiring corporation. The majority of the court held that the stock of the 48% shareholders was redeemed by the transferor corporation in a separate transaction from the reorganization, even though both transactions occurred simultaneously. The majority of the court deemed the two transactions to be "functionally unrelated." This "functionally unrelated" test conforms with the position taken by the Service in Rev. Rul. 61-156, 1961-2 C.B. 62. The liberality of the *Reef* decision may be partly attributable to the fact that the Government, rather than the taxpayer, was urging that the transaction be classified as an F reorganization, and to the fact that the taxpayer in *Reef* had effected a complex sham arrangement to avoid adverse tax consequences. *Cf.* Casco Products Corp., 49 T.C. 32 (1967), pending on appeal in the Second Circuit; and Griswold v. Commissioner, 400 F.2d 427 (C.A. 5 1968).

152 Rev. Rul. 69-185; I.R.B. 1969-16, p. 11. For a thorough discussion of this issue, *compare* Pugh, *The F Reorganization: Reveille for a Sleeping Giant?*, 24 TAX L. REV. 437, 458-467 (1969) *with* Comment, *(F) Reorganization and Proposed Alternate Routes for Post-Reorganization Net Operating Loss Carrybacks,* 66 MICH. L. REV. 498 (1968).

153 Stauffer v. Commissioner, 403 F.2d 611 (C.A. 9 1968), *reversing* 48 T.C. 277 (1967); and Associated Machine v. Commissioner, 403 F.2d 622 (C.A. 9 1968), *reversing* 48 T.C. 318 (1967). While the Government will not seek certiorari in *Stauffer* and *Associated Machine,* it has announced that it will not follow those decisions. Rev. Rul. 69-185, I.R.B. 1969-16, p. 11.

154 Pugh, *The F Reorganization: Reveille for a Sleeping Giant?*, 24 TAX L. REV. 437, 458-467 (1969).

or loss to the transferor.[155] However, where a transferor receives boot on the exchange, he will recognize the realized gain from the transaction to the extent of the boot received by him,[156] and such recognized gain will be treated as ordinary income if the distribution has the effect of the distribution of a dividend.[157] Since the shareholders of a corporation undergoing an F reorganization must retain their proportionate interests in the new corporate entity, the boot received by any such shareholder will usually constitute ordinary income unless there are insufficient earnings and profits available to classify the boot as a dividend.

(c) **Tax consequences of an F reorganization to the transferor corporation.** The transferor corporation will not usually recognize any gain or loss from the transaction.[158] The transfer of depreciable property will *not* cause it to recognize income under §§ 1245 and 1250 (recapture of depreciation provisions) or under § 47 (recapture of investment credit).[159] Nor will the transfer of an installment obligation to the new entity cause the recognition of gain.[160] However, the transferor corporation could recognize income on the transfer of section 341(f) assets unless the transferee consents to having the assets treated as section 341(f) assets in its hands.[161]

(d) **Tax consequences to a new corporate entity.** The new corporation will succeed to the tax attributes of the prior entity,[162] including such attributes as: earnings and profits, net operating loss carry-forwards, capital loss carry-overs, methods of accounting employed by the prior corporation, qualified deferred compensation plans, and basis of assets.[163] Since the shareholders in both corporations are virtually identical and have the same interests, there should be no limitation on the shifting of the tax attributes of the old cor-

---

155 I.R.C. § 354.
156 I.R.C. § 356. If a shareholder transferred section 306 stock, the boot allocated to that stock is treated as a distribution under § 301. I.R.C. § 356(e). *See* pp. 134-138 *supra* for a discussion of the treatment of boot under § 356.
157 I.R.C. § 356(a)(2). For a discussion of dividend equivalence under § 356, *see* pp. 137-138 *supra.*
158 I.R.C. § 361.
159 I.R.C. §§ 1245(b)(3), 1250(d)(3), and 47(b)(2).
160 Treas. Reg. § 1.453-9(c)(1)(i).
161 I.R.C. § 341(f)(3).
162 I.R.C. § 381.
163 The basis of assets is determined under I.R.C. § 362.

poration to the new one.[164] Moreover, where the acquiring corporation suffers a net operating loss in a year subsequent to the reorganization, that loss may be carried back to prereorganization years and deducted from income of the transferor corporation.[165]

(e) Applicability of "F" to a liquidation and reincorporation. A corporate liquidation followed by a reincorporation of the assets, or a sale, prior to liquidation, of corporate assets to a second corporation having shareholders with significant proprietary interests in both corporations is a prominent tax avoidance device. One defense against such devices is the contention that the transaction constitutes a reorganization rather than a liquidation, and that any assets not transferred to the second corporation constitute boot to the shareholders of the first corporation.[166] To that end, the Government has frequently contended that such transactions constitute a D reorganization. However, the requisites of a D reorganization are not always satisfied in these arrangements, and while the courts have generally been willing to stretch the D reorganization provisions to serve that purpose, they are not always willing to do so.[167]

The F reorganization provision may provide a solution to the above problem. In two cases, each involving a liquidation and subsequent reincorporation, the courts have found both a D reorganization and an F reorganization.[168] However, if the Service's position that the F reorganization provision does not apply to mergers of brother-sister corporations[169] is adopted, the F reorganization will be much less useful for solving the reincorporation problem. The applicability of the F reorganization provision to reincorporations also depends upon the liberality employed in construing the requis-

---

164 *See* I.R.C. § 382(b).
165 I.R.C. § 381(b). It was because of this provision that the Commissioner argued in the *Stauffer* and *Associated Machine* cases that the F reorganization provision does not apply to mergers of brother-sister corporations. *See* p. 150 *supra.*
166 *See* Chapter I, pp. 60-62 *supra. See also* Surkin, *Reincorporation Quandary,* 53 CORNELL L. REV. 575 (1968); and Lane, *The Reincorporation Game: Have the Ground Rules Really Changed?,* 77 HARV. L. REV. 1218 (1964).
167 *Id.*
168 Davant v. Commissioner, 366 F.2d 874 (C.A. 5 1966); Reef Corporation v. Commissioner, 368 F.2d 125 (C.A. 5 1966). *But see* Pridemark, Inc. v. Commissioner, 345 F.2d 35 (C.A. 4 1965) *reversing* 42 T.C. 510 (1964) for an illustration of an unsuccessful attempt by the Commissioner to employ the F reorganization provisions in the reincorporation situation.
169 *See* p. 150 *supra.*

ites that virtually all of the acquired corporation's assets (other than liquid assets) must be transferred and that no change in shareholder interests may result.[170]

If the reorganization provisions prove inadequate to resolve the reincorporation problem, the Commissioner may contend that the "liquidation" was never effected, because the corporation never terminated its business activities but merely transferred them to a different corporate shell.[171] In essence, the genius of this argument is that the corporation merely changed its outer clothing and perhaps redeemed some of its shares, but no significant change or termination occurred.

2. Recapitalization ("E" reorganization)

Since 1921, the Code has provided that a "recapitalization" qualifies as a reorganization[172] (commonly referred to as an "E" reorganization). Neither the Code nor the Regulations define a recapitalization, but the Regulations provide several illustrative examples. In a 1925 ruling, the Service stated that a recapitalization "signifies an arrangement whereby the stock and bonds of the corporation are readjusted as to amount, income, or priority, or an agreement of all stockholders and creditors to change and increase or decrease the capitalization or debts of the corporation, or both."[173] While in one instance, the Supreme Court stated[174] that a recapitalization was a "reshuffling of a capital structure, within the framework of an existing corporation," the Court subsequently held[175] that the meaning of "recapitalization" for federal tax purposes[176] is to be determined by examining the judicial application of that provision to a variety of concrete circumstances

---

170 See Pugh, op. cit., note 154 supra.
171 See Pugh, op. cit., note 154 supra; see Casco Products Corp., 49 T.C. 32 (1967), pending on appeal.
172 I.R.C. § 368(a)(1)(E). Recapitalizations were first included in the statutory definition of reorganizations by § 202(c)(2) of the Revenue Act of 1921.
173 S.M. 3710, IV-1 C.B. 4 (1925). This definition was derived from corporate law concepts.
174 Helvering v. Southwest Corp., 315 U.S. 194, 202 (1942).
175 Bazley v. Commissioner, 331 U.S. 737 (1947).
176 In Bazley, supra, the Court held that the definition of recapitalization for corporate law or accounting purposes is not dispositive. 340 U.S. at pp. 740-741. The Court said (p. 741): "But the form of transaction as reflected by correct corporate accounting opens questions as to the proper application of a taxing statute, it does not close them."

rather than by resort to an abstract definition. Thus, the applicability of the E reorganization provisions can best be determined by examining several different types of changes in a corporation's capital structure that either were or were not classified as recapitalizations.

Since a recapitalization is a change in the capital structure of a corporation, the transactions included are exchanges of stock and securities by the shareholders and creditors of the corporation, and usually no transfer of corporate assets is made. Several possible exchanges of stock and securities, and the consequences thereof, are discussed below. First, it should be noted that the exchange of stocks and securities pursuant to recapitalization will not cause the recognition of gain or loss to the transferor[177] except that the transferor will recognize realized gain to the extent that he received boot in the exchange.[178] Where the principal amount of securities received exceeds the principal amount of securities surrendered, the fair market value of the difference constitutes boot.[179]

(a) Purposes of a recapitalization. As noted above,[180] no transaction can qualify as a reorganization unless it was effected for a business purpose. A few examples of reasons for a recapitalization, without consideration of whether such reasons will qualify as a "business" purpose, are:

(i) A corporation overburdened with debt so that its interest obligations are adversely affecting the conduct of its business might exchange its stock for outstanding bonds.

(ii) A corporation with a high capital-debt ratio might exchange its bonds for outstanding stock to create a more favorable ratio because interest payments are deductible (and dividends are not) and repayment of loans does not usually cause tax consequences to the creditor.

(iii) A corporation might exchange preferred stock for outstanding common stock for the reasons suggested in Chapter VI *infra*.

---

177 I.R.C. § 354.
178 I.R.C. § 356. If the transferor exchanged section 306 stock, the amount of boot allocated to the stock will be treated as a distribution under § 301. I.R.C. § 356(e).
179 I.R.C. §§ 354(a)(2) and 356(d). *See* pp. 134-138 for a discussion of the treatment of boot under § 356.
180 *See* p. 147.

(iv) A corporation in some circumstances might remove § 306 taint on outstanding preferred stock by exchanging common stock for the preferred.[181]

(v) A corporation might wish to exchange its debentures or common stock for outstanding preferred stock in order to eliminate defaulted dividends.[182]

(vi) A recapitalization might be used to provide a parent corporation with 80% voting control of its subsidiary so that the parent could make a tax-free distribution of the subsidiary's stock to the parent's shareholders pursuant to § 355.

> **Ex.** Y Corporation had 1,000 shares of $100 par common voting stock outstanding, 700 of which shares were owned by X Corporation and the remaining 300 of which were owned by individuals A and B who had no proprietary interest in the X Corporation. The Y Corporation was recapitalized so that Y issued 200 shares of $150 par Class A voting stock to A and B in exchange for their 300 shares of $100 par stock; and Y issued 800 shares of $87.50 par Class B common voting stock in exchange for X's 700 shares of $100 par stock. Class A and B stocks had one vote each, and the value of the stocks issued to X, A and B was equal to the value of the stocks received in exchange therefor. Thus, the shareholders' proportionate interests in Y were not altered but the voting rights of the parties were shifted so that X had 80% of the votes. Both X and Y had been actively conducting business activities for over 10 years. The recapitalization was effected primarily for the purpose of permitting X to spin-off its Y stock to the shareholders of X for valid business reasons, and shortly after the recapitalization was completed, X did so. The Service ruled[183] that both the recapitalization and the subsequent spin-off qualified for nonrecognition treatment. However, if A and B had owned a proprietary interest in X, the shifting of voting control of Y might not have been deemed a significant change, and might therefore have been ignored in determining whether the spin-off qualified for tax-free treatment under § 355.[184]

---

181 I.R.C. § 306(e).
182 *See* Daisey Seide, 18 T.C. 502, 511 (1952).
183 Rev. Rul. 69-407, I.R.B. 1969-30, p. 7.
184 *Cf.* Rev. Rul. 63-260, 1963-2 C.B. 147.

The discussion below of the tax consequences of exchanges between a corporation and a shareholder or bondholder of that corporation are premised on the assumption that the transactions comply with the requisites of a reorganization (*e.g.*, business purpose) other than those which are specifically aimed at changes in the capital structure, *i.e.*, the continuity of interest doctrine.

(b) Exchange of stock for stock. Where pursuant to a plan of reorganization, a shareholder exchanges[185] common stock for common stock of the same corporation, the shareholder does not recognize gain or loss on the exchange.[186] Indeed, the exchange of common stock for common stock of the same corporation will usually qualify for nonrecognition treatment even where not made pursuant to a reorganization.[187]

Where pursuant to a plan of reorganization, preferred stock is exchanged for common stock of the same corporation, no gain or loss is recognized.[188] Where at the time of exchange dividends on the preferred stock were in arrears, and where the common stock received in exchange was given in respect of both the preferred stock and the defaulted dividends, the exchange will nevertheless qualify for nonrecognition; except that if the exchange were made *solely* for the purpose of paying the dividends owing on the preferred stock for the current and immediately preceding taxable years, then an amount equal to the dividends for those two years will be treated as distributions to which § 301 applies.[189]

---

185 All "exchanges" referred to in this Paragraph C2 of Chapter III are exchanges between a corporation and a shareholder or bondholder of that corporation; and the stocks and bonds exchanged are all issued by the transferee corporation.

186 I.R.C. § 354 (a)(1); and Rev. Rul. 54-482, 1954-2 C.B. 148. The exchange of common for common does not interrupt the continuity of proprietary interests in the corporation.

187 I.R.C. § 1036; and Treas. Reg. § 1.1036-1(a).

188 Treas. Reg. § 1.368-2(e)(2) and (4). The exchange of preferred and common does not affect the continuity of proprietary interests in the corporation. John A. Nelson Co. v. Helvering, 296 U.S. 374 (1935).

Section 1036 is applicable only where the exchange is common for common of the same corporation, or preferred for preferred of the same corporation.

189 Treas. Reg. § 1.368-2(e)(5). The provision in this Regulation for treatment of stock given in payment of dividends in arrears is analogous to the provisions in § 305(b)(1), for stock dividends, except that the latter provision imposes § 301 treatment on stock distributed in satisfaction of the current year's and immediately past year's preference dividend rights of the preferred stock irrespective of the subjective motives of the parties.

Where preferred stock contains a provision permitting the stockholder to convert the preferred stock to common stock, a shareholder's exercise of that privilege may not qualify for nonrecognition treatment under § 354, because it constitutes an isolated transaction rather than a "plan of reorganization.[190] Nevertheless, even if the exchange is not covered by § 354, it is likely that the Service will not permit gain or loss to be recognized therefrom. The Service has maintained that a bondholder's exercise of a conversion privilege (converting the bond to common stock in one case and to a different class of bond in another) did not cause recognition of gain or loss.[191] The Service reasoned that the conversion privilege was a basic element of the bond and that therefore the exercise of that privilege did not constitute a closed transaction. Since the transaction is deemed open, no gain or loss will be recognized prior to the sale or other disposition of the property received on account of exercising the conversion privilege. Presumably, the identical reasoning would preclude the recognition of gain or loss on exercising a conversion privilege contained in preferred stock.

Where pursuant to a plan of reorganization, preferred stock is exchanged for preferred stock of the same corporation, no gain or loss is recognized.[192] The preferred stock received in exchange will constitute section 306 stock to the extent that cash distributed in lieu of said stock would have constituted a distribution under § 301.[193]

Where a shareholder exchanges common stock for preferred stock, no gain or loss is recognized.[194] However, the preferred stock will be section 306 stock[195] to the extent that a distribution of cash in lieu of the preferred stock would have constituted a distribution under § 301.[196]

---

190 Rev. Rul. 54-65, 1954 1 C.B. 101. However, it is possible that a conversion privilege may be included as one aspect of a plan of reorganization, in which event the exercise of the privilege will qualify as a reorganization. *See* Rev. Rul. 56-179, 1956-1 C.B. 187.

191 G.C.M. 18436, 1937-1 C.B. 101; Rev. Rul. 57-535, 1957-2 C.B. 513. *See generally*, Fleischer and Cary, *Taxation of Convertible Bonds and Stock*, 74 HARV. L. REV. 473 (1961).

192 Rev. Rul. 56-586, 1956-2 C.B. 214. Moreover, § 1036 prevents recognition of gain or loss.

193 Rev. Rul. 56-586 *supra;* and I.R.C. § 306(c)(1)(B).

194 Treas. Reg. § 1.368-2(e)(3).

195 I.R.C. § 306(c)(1)(B).

196 *See* Rev. Rul. 56-586, 1956-2 C.B. 214.

(c) **Exchange of bonds for stock.** The exchange of bonds for preferred or common stock does not cause recognition of gain or loss.[197] The fact that accrued interest on the bonds was in default and was satisfied by the exchange does not make it taxable.[198]

(d) **Exchange of bonds for bonds.** The exchange of bonds for bonds will qualify for nonrecognition treatment as a recapitalization;[199] but if the principal amount of bonds received exceeds the principal amount of bonds surrendered, the fair market value of the difference constitutes boot and will cause the bondholder to recognize capital gain to the extent of whichever is less, the amount of gain realized on the exchange or the amount of boot.[200]

Where a bondholder exercises a conversion privilege to exchange his bonds for stock or bonds of a different class, the exchange will be deemed an open transaction, and consequently, no gain or loss will be recognized,[201] notwithstanding that the exchange may not qualify under § 354 because there was no plan of reorganization.

(e) **Exchange of stock for bonds.** In *Bazley v. Commissioner*,[202] the Supreme Court held that where stock of a family corporation was exchanged for stock and bonds of the same corporation, and where the shareholders' percentage interests in the corporation were not altered by the exchange, the transaction was not a reorganization, but rather was a disguised effort to withdraw earnings and profits from the corporation. Accordingly, the Court treated the bonds received as disguised dividends. In *Bazley*, the bonds and stocks were distributed to the shareholders pro rata. Because of considerable

---

197 Treas. Reg. § 1.368-2(e)(1); and Rev. Rul. 59-98, 1959-1 C.B. 76.
198 Commissioner v. Carman, 189 F.2d 363 (C.A. 2 1951) Acq., 1954-2 C.B. 3; and Rev. Rul. 59-98, 1959-1 C.B. 76. One commentator has raised a question as to whether the Service's acquiescence in *Carman* is limited to exchanges effected prior to the adoption of the 1954 Code. *See* Portfolio #52, "Corporate Recapitalizations" TAX MANAGEMENT (BNA) pp. 35-36.
199 Commissioner v. Neustadt's Trust, 131 F.2d 528 (C.A. 2 1942); and I.T. 4081, 1952-1 C.B. 65, which revoked earlier rulings to the contrary.
200 I.R.C. §§ 354(a)(2) and 356. The bond will usually be a capital asset in the hands of the bondholder; and the distribution will not be equivalent to a dividend.
201 G.C.M. 18436, 1937-1 C.B. 101; and Rev. Rul. 57-535, 1957-2 C.B. 513.
202 331 U.S. 737 (1947).

doubt as to the scope[203] of *Bazley*, there is an *in terrorem* restraint on similar transactions. Moreover, the provisions of § 354(a)(2) and § 356 greatly restrain the issuing of bonds for stock, since the fair market value of the bonds will be deemed boot, and may well be taxed to the recipient shareholder as ordinary income (*i.e.*, as a dividend). Indeed, under present law, the transaction effected in *Bazley* would have been caught by § 356, which would provide a result identical to that reached in *Bazley*.

(f) Continuity of proprietary interest. The Service has been reasonably liberal in its application of the continuity of proprietary interest doctrine to recapitalizations by permitting the elimination of the proprietary interests of some shareholders.[204] However, the Tax Court has gone much further and has held that the doctrine of continuity of proprietary interest is not applicable to a recapitalization.[205] While the Commissioner has nonacquiesced in *Hickok*, there is considerable merit to the Tax Court's position; particularly since under the 1954 Code, bonds may constitute taxable boot, and therefore there is little risk of tax avoidance.

(g) Carry-over of tax attributes. Since a recapitalization does not require a transfer of corporate assets, or a change of corporate entity, the tax attributes of the corporation will usually remain unimpaired. Section 382(a) will not usually cause difficulties since a recapitalization does not involve the purchase or redemption of a shareholder's stock, and normally the business of the corporation will be con-

---

203 Some unanswered questions are whether a disproportionate distribution would have been treated differently even though it was a family corporation; and if the allocation of the distribution is a crucial factor, how disproportionate must it be? In Daisey Seide, 18 T.C. 502 (1952), the Tax Court distinguished *Bazley* where an exchange of preferred stock for debentures was disproportionate, even though the corporation there involved was controlled by two family groups, and the exchanges were proportionate between the two groups, but were disproportionate within each group. However, one factor considered by the Tax Court in *Seide* was that while the debentures had value, they could not readily have been sold because they were unsecured and had a remote maturity date. *See also* Wolf Envelope Co., 17 T.C. 471 (1951), Non acq., 1952-1 C.B. 6.
204 Rev. Rul. 56-179, 1956-1 C.B. 187.
205 Alan O. Hickok, 32 T.C. 80 (1959), Non. acq., 1959-2 C.B. 8. In *Hickok*, the court reasoned that the continuity of interest doctrine was necessary to distinguish acquisitive reorganization from sales, but that recapitalizations usually involve changes in interests (such as stockholder to bondholder), and therefore that it would be inappropriate to apply the doctrine to recapitalizations.

tinued. There is a minor risk that in special circumstances § 269 (a)(1) might disallow the benefits of some of the corporation's tax attributes.

D. ACQUISITIVE REORGANIZATIONS

The reorganization provisions permit the tax-free acquisition by one corporation of either the assets of a second corporation or a controlling interest in the stock of a second corporation.[206] These acquisitive reorganizations will fall within the A, B, C or sometimes the D reorganization provisions. The nature of these different types of acquisitive reorganizations is described below. Of course, the judicial doctrines applicable to all reorganizations (e.g., the continuity of proprietary interest, the continuity of business enterprise, and the business purpose doctrines) described above in Part B must be considered when predicting the tax consequences of a proposed acquisition, and the following discussion rests on an assumption that the transactions in question comply with these judicially imposed requisites.

1. Statutory mergers or consolidations ("A" reorganizations)

Section 368(a)(1)(A) provides simply that "a statutory merger or consolidation" constitutes a reorganization, frequently described as an "A" reorganization. Since the statute does not require that the surviving corporation issue only voting stock or some specified percentage of voting stock pursuant to the merger or consolidation, particular care should be observed that the merger does not contravene the continuity of proprietary interest requisite.[207] The following simplified example illustrates the means of effecting an A reorganization and the tax consequences thereof.

The X Corporation has 100 shares of common stock outstanding, all of which are owned by Jones. Jones has a basis of $20,000 in his X stock. The X Corporation owns assets with a combined fair market value of $200,000 and a combined basis of $120,000. The X Corporation is merged into the Y Corporation under the local statutory merger provisions. Accordingly, Y becomes the owner of all the assets previously owned by X, and X ceases to

---

206 *See* Sapienza, *Tax Considerations in Corporate Reorganizations and Mergers*, 60 Nw. U. L. Rev. 765 (1966).
207 *See, e.g.*, LeTulle v. Scofield, 308 U.S. 415 (1940).

exist as an entity. Jones' stock in X is cancelled, and the Y Corporation issues to Jones 2,000 shares of Y common stock, having a fair market value of $200,000.

Jones realized a gain of $180,000 on the exchange of his X stock for Y stock; but under § 354, none of that gain is recognized.[208] However, if instead of Y's having issued 2,000 shares of its common stock to Jones, Y had issued 1,500 shares of its common stock plus its bonds in the principal amount of $50,000, then the $50,000 principal amount bonds would constitute boot and Jones would recognize $50,000 income under § 356.[209] If instead of the above transactions, Y had issued only 500 shares of its common stock and had issued bonds in the principal amount of $150,000, the merger probably would not comply with the continuity of proprietary interest requisite[210] and consequently would not qualify as a reorganization.[211]

Jones' basis in the 2,000 shares of Y stock he received from Y will be $20,000—the same as his basis in his cancelled X stock.[212]

The Y Corporation will not recognize any income by virtue of acquiring the assets of X.[213] Y's basis in the acquired assets will be $120,000—the same basis that X had in the property.[214]

The X Corporation will not recognize any income because of the provisions for recapture of depreciation and investment credit.[215]

Under a 1968 amendment[216] effective for statutory mergers occurring after October 22, 1968, where an acquired corporation is merged into an acquiring corporation, it is possible to distribute to the shareholders of the acquired corporation the stock of a

---

208 Section 354 provides nonrecognition of gain or loss for the exchange, pursuant to a plan of reorganization, of stock or securities of a party to a reorganization solely for stock or securities of that corporation or of another party to the reorganization.
209 §§ 354 and 356. *See* pp. 134-138 *supra* for a discussion of the operation of § 356. It is assumed in the above example that the fair market value of the Y bonds is equal to their principal amount.
210 Rev. Proc. 66-34 (Sec. 3.02), 1966-2 C.B. 1232, 1233.
211 *See* Treas. Reg. § 1.368-1(b).
212 § 358. *See* p. 145 *supra* for a discussion of the method of determining Jones' basis if he had received boot from Y.
213 § 1032. Indeed, Y will not recognize income from an exchange of its own stock for other assets, irrespective of whether the exchange was made pursuant to a reorganization.
214 § 362.
215 §§ 1245(b)(3), 1250(d)(3), 47(b)(2), and 361.
216 Sec. 1 of Public Law 90-621 (Oct. 22, 1968).

parent corporation of the acquiring corporation in lieu of the stock of the acquiring corporation itself.[217] One of the requisites for characterizing a transaction of this kind as a reorganization is that only stock of the parent corporation is transferred—*i.e.*, it is not possible to issue a mixture of the parent's stock and the stock of the acquiring corporation.

In some corporate acquisitions (whether an A, B or C reorganization), the parties may not be able to agree upon the amount of stock to be issued by the acquiring corporation, and they may therefore wish to defer the distribution of a specified number of shares to be distributed only upon the occurrence or nonoccurrence of some contingency (*e.g.*, increased earnings by the acquired business) within a specified time period. Alternatively, a specified number of shares may be held in escrow to be released to the distributees only upon the occurrence of some predetermined contingency. The determination of the tax consequences of such arrangements and their effect on the qualification of the acquisition as a reorganization raises complex issues. The reader should proceed cautiously in this area, and he might wish to consult Tillinghast's excellent article on the subject.[218]

2. Stock for stock exchanges ("B" reorganizations)

The B reorganization is a popular form of corporate acquisition. The B reorganization is an exchange by the acquiring corporation of its own voting stock (or the voting stock of a parent corporation which controls[219] the acquiring corporation) for the stock of another corporation if immediately after the acquisition, the acquiring corporation has control[220] of the acquired corporation, irrespective of whether the acquiring corporation had control prior to the acquisition.[221] The acquiring corporation (or its

---

217 § 368(a)(2)(D) and 368(b).
218 Tillinghast, *Contingent Stock Pay-Outs in Tax-Free Reorganizations,* 22 THE TAX LAWYER 467 (Spring, 1969).
219 For purposes of the reorganization provisions, the term "control" means the ownership of stock possessing at least 80% of the voting power of the corporation plus at least 80% of the total number of shares of all nonvoting classes of stock of the corporation. § 368(c). The Service has ruled that where a corporation has several classes of nonvoting stock outstanding, the controlling corporation must own at least 80% of the shares of each separate class. Rev. Rul. 59-259, 1959-2 C.B. 115.
220 *Id.*
221 § 368(a)(1)(B).

parent) can transfer only its voting stock; if the acquiring corporation transfers any nonvoting stock or any securities, cash or other boot, the transaction will not qualify as a reorganization, and all realized gain will be recognized.[222] Thus, the tax consequence of boot in a B reorganization is extraordinary; the typical consequence of including boot in what would otherwise be a tax-free exchange is to force recognition of gain only to the extent of the boot received;[223] but in a B reorganization, the transfer of boot disqualifies the entire transaction and the entire amount of realized gain or loss is recognized. Since only voting stock can be transferred by the acquiring corporation, a B reorganization will usually cause no difficulty with the continuity of interest requirement.

> **Ex. (1)** The Y Corporation has 1,000 shares of common stock outstanding—500 shares are owned by Goldsmith, 400 shares are owned by Katz, and 100 shares are owned by O'Neill. The X Corporation wishes to acquire Y, and accordingly X issues 250 shares of X common voting stock to Goldsmith in exchange for his 500 shares of Y stock, and X issues 200 shares of its common voting stock to Katz in exchange for his 400 shares of Y stock. O'Neill refused to participate in the exchange. The exchange qualifies as a B reorganization since X transferred nothing other than its own voting stock and immediately after the acquisition X controlled[224] the Y Corporation. Neither Katz nor Goldsmith will recognize any income on the exchange of their Y stock for X stock,[225] and they will have the same basis in their newly acquired X stock that they had in the Y stock exchanged by them.[226] The X Corporation will have the same basis in its ac-

---

222 Turnbow v. Commissioner, 368 U.S. 337 (1961). *See* Toll, *Transfers of Boot in Stock-for-Stock Acquisitions,* 15 U.C.L.A. L. Rev. 1347 (1968) for a criticism of the result reached in *Turnbow.*

223 *See, e.g.,* §§ 356, 351(b), and 361(b).

224 § 368(c) defines "control" for purposes of the reorganization provisions. *See* note 219 *supra.*

225 § 354.

226 § 358. For example, if Katz had had a basis of $20 per share in his 400 shares of Y stock, his total $8,000 basis would be allocated among the X stock received by him in the exchange in accordance with the fair market value of the X stock. Since Katz received only one class of X stock, the fair market values of the X shares are equal, and consequently, Katz will have a basis of $40 in each share of X stock held by him.

quired stock as Katz and Goldsmith had in that stock prior to the exchange.[227]

The Service has strictly enforced the requirement that only voting stock be issued by the acquiring corporation. One consequence of having an absolute prohibition against boot is that it permits taxpayers to elect to recognize gain or loss on a stock-for-stock exchange by having the acquiring corporation purchase some shares for cash. However, wherever tax treatment turns on fixed arbitrary standards, the parties have the opportunity of designing their transaction within or without those standards depending upon the tax consequences they desire; but the establishment of precise standards has the compensating advantage of permitting the parties to predict the tax consequences of proposed transactions with a fair degree of confidence.

The Regulations provide that stock rights or warrants do not constitute stock[228] and therefore are boot, the transfer of which precludes classification as a B reorganization. This is consistent with the position of the Service that the distribution of stock rights in a corporate division does not qualify as stock or securities for purposes of § 355.[229]

If an acquiring corporation acquired sufficient stock to constitute control of the acquired corporation solely in exchange for its voting stock, but the acquiring corporation used other property to purchase additional shares of the acquired corporation, the transaction will not qualify as a B reorganization.[230] Section 368(a)(1) (B) applies to stock exchanges where the acquiring corporation controlled the acquired corporation prior to the exchange as well as where the acquiring corporation obtained control by virtue of the

---

227 § 362(b). Thus, if Katz had had a basis of $20 per share in his 400 shares of Y stock and Goldsmith had had a basis of $30 per share in his 500 shares, X would have a basis of $20 per share in the 400 shares of Y stock it received from Katz and X would have a basis of $30 per share in the 500 shares it received from Goldsmith.

228 Treas. Reg. § 1.354-1(e). See Helvering v. Southwest Consolidated Corporation, 315 U.S. 194, 200 (1942); and Hobbet, *Using Stock Warrants in Corporate Acquisitions and Reorganizations*, 8 J. OF TAXATION 160 (1958).

229 *See* note 21 *supra*. Of course, the distribution of boot in a corporate division does not necessarily require the recognition of all realized gain. § 356.

230 Richard M. Mills, 39 T.C. 393 (1962), *reversed on a different issue*, 331 F.2d 321 (C.A. 5 1964).

exchange. In either case, the statute prohibits the acquiring corporation from transferring any property other than its voting stock (or the voting stock of a parent of the acquiring corporation). Thus, it is clear that the "solely voting stock" requirement is not limited to exchanges for the acquisition of control.

> **Ex. (2)** The same facts as in Example (1) above, except that in addition to acquiring the 900 shares of Y stock held by Katz and Goldsmith, the X Corporation purchased O'Neill's 100 shares for cash. The transaction will not qualify as a B reorganization, and both Katz and Goldsmith must recognize any gain they realized on the exchange.

One minor inconvenience in complying with the "only voting stock" rule is that the fair market value of the shares of the issuing corporation may be such that fractional shares must be issued in order to deliver the exact amount of the purchase price of the acquired shares of stock. In order to avoid issuing fractional shares, the acquiring corporation might wish to pay cash to each of the shareholders of the acquired corporation in an amount equal to the value of the fractional share of the acquiring corporation to which the shareholder would otherwise be entitled. In *Richard M. Mills*,[231] the majority of the Tax Court held that the cash payment of $82.08 for fractional shares disqualified a stock-for-stock exchange, involving stock of the acquiring corporation valued at almost $84,000, from treatment as a B reorganization. On appeal, the Fifth Circuit reversed.[232] The Fifth Circuit, however, declined to consider whether a *de minimis* rule could be invoked; and instead held that the cash payment for the fractional shares was not part of the bargained-for consideration of the deal but was merely a means of effecting a "mathematical rounding off" of the shares. The Service subsequently conceded that an acquiring corporation's rounding off of voting shares by paying cash for a fractional share does not exclude a transaction from classification as a B reorganization.[233]

Since 1954, it is possible for an acquiring corporation to obtain the stock of another corporation in a "creeping" acquisition that

---

231 39 T.C. 393 (1962).
232 331 F.2d 321 (C.A. 5 1964).
233 Rev. Rul. 66-365, 1966-2 C.B. 116.

will nevertheless qualify as a B reorganization—*i.e.*, the acquiring corporation need not acquire control in a single transaction or series of prearranged integrated transactions.

> **Ex.** The Y Corporation had 100 shares of common stock outstanding—40 of which were owned by Jones, 30 of which were owned by Smith, 20 of which were owned by Peters, and 10 of which were owned by King. In 1960, the X Corporation paid cash for Jones' 40 shares of Y and Smith's 30 shares. In 1965, X acquired the 20 shares of Y owned by Peters in exchange for X's voting stock; and in 1967, X acquired the 10 shares of Y owned by King in exchange for X's voting stock. The exchanges effected with Peters and King in 1965 and 1967 respectively will qualify as a B reorganization.[234] However, if X's cash purchase of the 70 shares of Jones and Smith had been effected in 1965, a few months prior to the exchange for Peters' 20 shares, the Service might regard the acquisition of those 90 shares as several steps in a prearranged plan, and accordingly treat the acquisition of those 90 shares as a single transaction which does not qualify as a B reorganization because some of the shares were acquired for property other than voting stock. Even in that event, the 1967 exchange for King's 10 shares would probably qualify as a B reorganization.

One advantage of a B reorganization over a statutory merger is that under corporate law an affirmative vote of a specified percentage of the shareholders of both corporations is a prerequisite to a merger, and dissenting shareholders will be granted appraisal rights; but in a stock-for-stock exchange, no vote is required[235] and no appraisal rights are granted. Of course, in a very real sense, the shareholders of the acquired corporation "vote" by either agreeing or refusing to exchange their stock for that of the acquiring corporation. If shareholders owning more than 20% of the voting power of the owning corporation (or possibly owning more than 20% of the outstanding shares of any class of non-voting stock) do not wish to participate in the exchange, the

---

234 Treas. Reg. § 1.368-2(c).
235 If the acquiring corporation is not authorized by its charter to issue a sufficient number of shares of voting stock to acquire the stock of the other corporation, the acquiring corporation will have to cause its charter to be amended, and that requires a shareholder vote.

transaction may be effectively blocked unless the other shareholders are willing to recognize gain on the exchange. Where the dissenting shareholders own less than the requisite 20%, they may nevertheless constitute an irritant to the acquiring corporation, which may prefer to purchase their shares rather than to live with them as frequent dissenters. However, a cash purchase within a short time after the stock-for-stock exchange was effected could endanger the qualification of the entire transaction. Several alternatives that have been employed successfully are: (i) to have the acquired corporation redeem the shares of the dissenting stockholders prior to effecting the stock-for-stock exchange,[236] and (ii) a shareholder of the acquiring corporation may purchase the stock of the dissenting shareholders.[237] In a recent ruling,[238] where a shareholder owning 90% of the outstanding stock of the acquiring corporation had purchased 50% of the stock of the acquired corporation two months before the stock-for-stock exchange was effected, the Service concluded that the transaction qualified as a B reorganization. The ruling stressed that the shareholder was not acting on behalf of the acquiring corporation in making the purchase, and no part of the payment he made was contributed by the corporation nor was he subsequently reimbursed. Any use of the acquiring corporation's funds to effect a redemption or purchase of the shares of dissenting shareholders would risk the loss of reorganization treatment.

Caution should be observed whenever cash or property (other than voting stock) of the acquiring corporation is to be employed in a transaction related to a stock-for-stock acquisition for purposes other than the satisfaction of debts or obligation of the acquiring corporation. For example, the following arrangements should be viewed skeptically: (i) the acquiring corporation pays the legal or accounting fees or commissions incurred by the shareholders of the acquired corporation in completing the exchange; (ii) the acquiring corporation assumes or guarantees the satisfaction of certain debts of the acquired corporation;[239] (iii) the acquiring corporation

263 *See* Bittker and Eustice, Federal Income Taxation of Corporations and Shareholders (2d ed., 1966) pp. 521-522.
237 Rev. Rul. 68-562, I.R.B. 1968-43, p. 11.
238 *Id.*
239 Bittker and Eustice, *supra,* p. 523 suggests that this transaction may be separable from the stock-for-stock exchange, but it does create some risk.

assumes debts of the shareholders of the acquired corporation; and (iv) the acquiring corporation loans cash to the acquired corporation, particularly if the borrowed funds are used to redeem stock of the acquired corporation or to satisfy outstanding debts owed to its shareholders.

3. Acquisition of assets for stock ("C" reorganizations)

An exchange by one corporation of its voting stock (or the voting stock of its parent corporation) for substantially all the assets of a second corporation may constitute a C reorganization.[240] If the charter of the acquiring corporation authorizes it to issue a sufficient number of shares to effect the exchange, there usually will be no requirement of obtaining a favorable vote of the shareholders of the acquiring corporation. State laws differ as to whether the shareholders of the acquired corporation must approve the transfer of substantially all its assets, and consequently local law must be examined before initiating such an exchange.

The following simplified example illustrates the C reorganization.

The X Corporation desires to acquire all the assets of the Y Corporation. The fair market value of Y's assets is $300,000; Y's assets are subject to liabilities amounting to $100,000; and Y has a basis of $150,000 in its assets. X transfers 10,000 shares of its common voting stock to Y in exchange for Y's assets which are transferred to X subject to the outstanding liabilities of $100,000. The fair market value of X's common stock is $20 per share; consequently Y received stock valued at $200,000, transferred liabilities of $100,000 and realized a gain of $150,000.

The exchange of solely voting stock for substantially all the properties of another corporation will qualify as a C reorganization. In the absence of a statutory exception, a transfer of properties subject to liabilities is usually treated as boot received by the transferor to the extent of those liabilities;[241] however, the liabilities transferred to X will not constitute boot so as to disqualify the exchange from reorganization treatment because a statutory exception does exist.[242]

---

240 I.R.C. § 368(a)(1)(C).
241 United States v. Hendler, 303 U.S. 564 (1938).
242 § 368(a)(1)(C). *Note also* § 357.

While Y realized a gain of $150,000 on the exchange of its assets, it will not recognize any part of that gain.[243] The existence of liabilities on the property transferred by Y does not constitute boot to Y for purposes of determining the income recognized by Y.[244] Even if Y had received boot from X, Y would recognize gain only to the extent of the value of boot received by it which is not distributed to Y's shareholders pursuant to the plan of re-organization.[245] Thus, an acquired corporation can avoid recognizing gain from boot by distributing it to its shareholders. In no event can a corporation recognize a loss on an exchange made pursuant to a C reorganization.[246]

X recognizes no gain on the exchange, irrespective of whether it qualifies as a reorganization.[247] X receives a basis in Y's assets equal to the basis Y had—*i.e.*, $150,000.[248] On the other hand, Y transfers the $150,000 basis it had in its assets to the X stock it received in the exchange and reduces that basis by the $100,000 liabilities to which the transferred assets were subject.[249] Thus, Y has a basis of $50,000 in its X stock.

After the exchange was completed in the above example, X owned all of Y's assets, and Y possessed a stock interest in X. The shareholders of Y could continue Y as a holding company[250] if they wish; or they could liquidate Y, and thereby hold X's voting stock in their individual capacities. If Y is liquidated shortly after the exchange is completed and pursuant to the plan of re-organization, the shareholders of Y will not recognize any gain or loss on the exchange of their Y stock for the shares of X

---

243 § 361. Also, Y will not recognize gain under the recapture of depreciation or the recapture of investment credit provisions. §§ 1245(b)(3), 1250(d)(3), and 47(b)(2).
244 § 357.
245 § 361(b)(1).
246 § 361(b)(2).
247 § 1032.
248 § 362(b). If Y had recognized any gain on the exchange by having received boot which it failed to distribute, X's basis in the assets would have been increased by the amount of the gain so recognized by Y.
249 § 358(a)(1), and § 358(d).
250 If Y is not liquidated, the shareholders of Y should make certain that it does not run afoul of the personal holding company provisions (§§ 541-547) or the accumulated earnings surtax (§§ 531-537) unless they are willing to accept the consequences imposed by those provisions.

stock held by Y.[251] If Y had retained assets other than the stock of X, then such other assets (including securities of X in some cases) will constitute boot to Y's shareholders upon Y's liquidation; and each of them will recognize gain to the extent of the boot received by him.[252] The shareholders of Y will have the identical basis in the X stock received by them in liquidation as they had in their Y stock.[253] If a shareholder had received boot from Y on the liquidation, his basis in the boot (other than cash) would equal the fair market value of such boot,[254] and his basis in the X stock would equal his basis in his Y stock reduced by any boot he received and increased by any gain recognized by him on the liquidation.[255]

It is noteworthy that if Y is liquidated, the net effect of the C reorganization is identical to a statutory merger—*i.e*, X acquires the assets of Y, and the former shareholders of Y become shareholders of X. Consequently, a C reorganization is sometimes referred to as a practical merger. Similarly, where a B reorganization is promptly followed by a liquidation of the newly acquired subsidiary corporation,[256] the transaction is identical to a C reorganization, and the Service has ruled that in such cases the two steps of the transaction (the acquisition of the stock of the controlled corporation followed by its liquidation) should be collapsed, and the transaction should therefore be treated as a C reorganization.[257]

The requirement of § 368(a)(1)(C) that only voting stock of the acquiring corporation (or its parent) be exchanged for the assets of the acquired corporation is relaxed by two statutory exceptions granted for C reorganizations. First, § 368(a)(1)(C) itself provides that the acquiring corporation's assumption of liabilities or its acceptance of properties subject to outstanding liabilities will not disqualify the transaction as a C reorganization. However, if the amount of liabilities accepted by the acquiring corporation con-

---

251 § 354.
252 §§ 354 and 356.
253 § 358.
254 § 358(a)(2).
255 § 358(a)(1).
256 The liquidation of the subsidiary will usually not cause the recognition of gain or loss to the parent corporation. § 332.
257 Rev. Rul. 67-274, 1967-2 C.B. 141. The classification of the transaction as a C reorganization rather than as a B reorganization followed by a liquidation can determine whether the limitations on the use of net operating loss carry-overs imposed under § 382(b) are applicable.

stitutes a substantial percentage of the value of the acquired assets, the transaction may resemble a sale more closely than a reorganization; and in such event, the transaction may fail to qualify as a reorganization for failure to comply with the continuity of proprietary interest requisite.[258]

> **Ex. (1)** The Y Corporation owns assets with a value of $400,000 and subject to liabilities of $100,000. Y has ac-Corporation has accounts payable in the amount of $30,000. The X Corporation exchanges its voting stock for the assets of Y, subject to their outstanding liabilities, and X assumes the debts evidenced by the accounts payable. The transaction qualifies as a C reorganization.

> **Ex. (2)** The Y Corporation owns assets with a value of $400,000 and subject to liabilities of $360,000. Y has accounts payable in the amount of $30,000. X exchanges its voting stock for Y's assets, subject to outstanding liabilities, and X assumes the accounts payable owing by Y. It is possible, but by no means certain, that the liabilities constitute such a high percentage of the value of the assets transferred that the exchange will be treated as a sale rather than as a reorganization. In valuing Y's assets, good will should be taken into account if the business of Y is to be continued.

A second exception to the solely voting stock requirement permits the acquiring corporation to transfer cash or other boot provided that at least 80% of the assets obtained by the acquiring corporation in the exchange are received in consideration of the transfer of voting stock.[259]

> **Ex. (1)** The Y Corporation has assets valued at $200,000 and no outstanding liabilities. X transfers $30,000 cash and common voting stock of X valued at $170,000 in exchange for Y's assets. Since X acquired 85% of Y's assets in exchange for its voting stock, the cash payment will not disqualify the exchange from classification as a C reorganization. Of course, the cash payment will constitute boot to Y and will cause it to recognize any realized gain to that extent, unless it distributes the cash

---

258 *See* Treas. Reg. § 1.368-2(d)(1).
259 § 368(a)(2)(B).

to its shareholders;[260] and in that latter event, Y's shareholders will recognize the gain realized by them on the
exchange to the extent that cash was distributed to
them.[261]

Ex. (2) The same facts as those given in Ex. (1) above,
except that X paid $50,000 cash and transferred voting
stock valued at $150,000 for Y's assets. Since in that
event X will have acquired only 75% of Y's assets in exchange for its voting stock, the exchange will not qualify
as a C reorganization.

It is noteworthy that where boot is transferred, the amount of
liabilities accepted by the acquiring corporation will affect the determination of whether the exchange qualifies as a C reorganization,
since the transfer of liabilities reduces the percentage of assets
acquired solely for voting stock.

Ex. (3) The Y Corporation owns assets with a value of
$200,000 and subject to liabilities of $20,000. The X
Corporation exchanges $30,000 cash plus X voting stock
valued at $150,000 for the assets of Y subject to their
outstanding liabilities. Since X received assets valued at
$200,000 and X transferred voting stock valued at
$150,000, X acquired only 75% of Y's assets in ex-
change for its voting stock, and consequently the transaction does not qualify as a C reorganization.

Section 368(a)(1)(C) requires that "substantially all" the properties of the acquired corporation be transferred to the acquiring
corporation in a C reorganization. The amount of assets that can
be retained by the acquired corporation is uncertain. The Service
has ruled that no specific percentage can be retained but that "the
nature of the properties retained by the transferor, the purpose of
retention, and the amount thereof" are relevant factors in determining whether the retained assets will cause the disqualification of
the transaction as a C reorganization.[262] The reader should not
rely on court decisions either permitting or rejecting the retention of
a specified percentage of assets as dispositive of the question of
the tax consequences of retaining a like percentage of assets under

---

260 § 361(b).
261 §§ 354 and 356.
262 Rev. Rul. 57-518, 1957-2 C.B. 253.

different circumstances.[263] However, the Service has apparently established a bench mark by ruling that a transfer by a corporation of assets representing at least 90% of the fair market value of the net assets *and* at least 70% of the fair market value of the gross assets held by the corporation immediately before the transfer constitutes "substantially all" its assets within the meaning of § 368(a)(1)(C). Rev. Proc. 66-34 (Sec. 3.01), 1966-2 C.B. 1232, 1233.

4. Exchanges of assets for the stock of a controlled corporation ("D" reorganizations)

As previously noted, a corporate division may sometimes constitute a D reorganization, but it need not do so.[264] A corporate acquisition may also constitute a D reorganization in certain circumstances. A D reorganization can occur in either of two types of transactions:

(i) A transfer by one corporation of substantially all its assets to another corporation which is controlled[265] immediately after the transfer by the transferor corporation or by one or more of its shareholders or by any combination thereof provided that pursuant to the plan of reorganization, the transferor corporation is liquidated shortly after the transfer;[266]

(ii) A transfer by one corporation of part of its assets to another corporation which the transferor corporation controls[267] immediately after the transfer provided that the controlled corporation's stock is then distributed to the shareholders of the transferor corporation as a qualified corporate division under § 355 or § 356.[268]

The following examples illustrate corporate acquisitions that qualify as D reorganizations.

> **Ex. (1)** Jones owned all 100 outstanding shares of stock of the X Corporation and all 450 shares of outstanding stock of the Y Corporation. X transferred all its assets to Y in exchange for 50 shares of Y stock. X was then liq-

---

263 *See* Bittker and Eustice, Federal Income Taxation of Corporations and Shareholders (2d ed., 1966) pp. 525-529.
264 § 355(a)(2)(C).
265 "Control" is defined in § 368(c). *See* note 219 *supra*.
266 §§ 368(a)(1)(D) and 354(b).
267 *See* note 219 *supra*.
268 § 368(a)(1)(D).

uidated. Since Y was controlled by X's shareholder, Jones, immediately after the transfer and X was promptly liquidated after transferring all its assets, the transaction constitutes a D reorganization. The transaction also qualifies as a C reorganization, but the provisions of the D reorganization are granted priority over the C reorganization provisions.[269]

Ex. (2) The Y Corporation had 100 shares of stock outstanding, 90 shares of which were owned by Clark and 10 shares of which were owned by Lewis. The X Corporation had 100 shares of stock outstanding all of which were owned by Abner. The X Corporation wished to acquire the assets of Y, but Lewis threatened to demand his appraisal rights if Y transferred its assets to X. In order to avoid that problem, X transferred all its assets to Y in exchange for 2,000 shares of Y's common voting stock. Thus, immediately after the transfer, X was in control of the Y Corporation. X was then liquidated, and X's shareholder, Abner, thereby obtained control of Y. This type of transaction is sometimes called a "reverse acquisition." The exchange falls within the definition of both a C reorganization and a D reorganization; but in that case, the D reorganization provisions are granted priority.[270]

5. Nontax considerations in corporate acquisitions

In planning a corporate acquisition, due regard must be given: (i) to the state and federal restrictions on the issuance and transfer of stock; (ii) to anti-trust laws; and (iii) to local corporate law requirements.[271] The examination of these important aspects of an acquisition is beyond the scope of this book.

E. RECORDING AND REPORTING REQUIREMENTS OF REORGANIZATION

The plan of reorganization must be adopted by each of the cor-

---

269 § 368(a)(2)(A). The purpose of granting priority to the D reorganization provisions is to preclude a taxpayer from using the C reorganization provisions as a means of avoiding the stringent requirements established in § 355 for corporate divisions.
270 *Id.*
271 For a thorough discussion of corporate law consideration in effecting a corporate division, *see* Siegel, *When Corporations Divide: A Statutory and Financial Analysis,* 79 HARV. L. REV. 534 (1966).

porations that is a party to the reorganization.[272] The Service requires that each corporation that is a party to the reorganization and each person who receives stock or securities from a party to a reorganization in an exchange that is at least partly tax-free shall maintain certain records and shall include certain information in its or his tax return for the year in which the reorganization or exchanged occurred. The records and information required to be maintained and filed are described in Treas. Reg. § 1.368-3.

272 Treas. Reg. § 1.368-3(a).

IV

Mandatory Buy-out of the Stock of a Deceased Shareholder

A buy-out of a shareholder's stock is a sale of the shareholder's stock holdings in a specific corporation pursuant to a pre-existing contract. The discussion of buy-outs in this chapter focuses on mandatory buy-out agreements to purchase the stock of a shareholder upon his demise. However, a buy-out agreement need not be mandatory if the parties choose otherwise; in lieu of a mandatory purchase, the decedent's executor may be given an option to sell; or the purchaser may be given an option to buy. Usually, the purposes of a buy-out plan are best served by a mandatory arrangement, but an option either to sell or to purchase may be more appropriate in special circumstances.[1] A buy-out agreement for purchasing a deceased shareholder's stock will frequently provide the purchaser with first refusal rights during the shareholder's life. A buy-out agreement may provide for the purchase of a shareholder's stock during his life where the shareholder retires or becomes disabled,[2] but the consideration of the merits of that type of buy-out is beyond the scope of this book.

---

1 For example, where a corporation has made an election under Subchapter S (I.R.C. § 1371 *et seq.*), the corporation may wish to have the option to purchase the stock of a deceased shareholder so that it can protect its election, but it may not wish to be compelled to make the purchase. *See* pp. 281-284 *infra. See also* Crumbley, *Buy and Sell Agreements for Subchapter S Corporations*, 108 TRUSTS AND ESTATES 17 (1969).

2 *See* Note, *A Closer Look at Disability "Buy-Outs" For the Close Corporation*, 52 MINN. L. REV. 483 (1967).

There are two popular categories of buy-out plans, which are distinguished by the identity of the purchaser. Where the prospective purchaser of a decedent's stock is the corporation that issued the stock, the plan is called either an "entity purchase" plan or a "stock retirement" plan or a "stock redemption agreement." Where the prospective purchasers of the decedent's stock are the surviving shareholders, the plan is called a "cross-purchase agreement." The relative merits and disadvantages of these two plans are discussed below. In some circumstances a buy-out agreement might combine an entity purchase and a cross-purchase plan, so that part of the deceased shareholder's stock is to be redeemed by the corporation and the remainder is to be purchased by the surviving shareholders. Normally, a buy-out agreement is used only for stock of closely held corporations.

A. CONSIDERATIONS FAVORING THE EXECUTION OF A BUY-OUT AGREEMENT

Buy-out agreements generally have two basic goals: to prevent the disposition of the decedent's stock to outside interests; and to convert the decedent's interest in a closely held business to liquid assets. The first of these goals is primarily of concern to the corporation itself and the continuing shareholders; the second satisfies a concern of the deceased shareholder and his beneficiaries. Following are several specific objectives that might be sought.

1. Liquidity for the decedent's estate

Where the amount of a decedent's gross estate[3] is substantial, but a major part of his estate is represented by stock holdings in a closely held corporation, his executor may have difficulty obtaining sufficient liquid assets to satisfy the decedent's outstanding debts and to pay the administrative expenses of the estate and the death taxes imposed by both federal and state governments. A buy-out plan can insure that the decedent's stock will be convertible into liquid assets when they are most needed, and this assurance of

---

3 As used herein, the term "gross estate" refers to a decedent's gross estate for federal estate tax purposes. This encompasses far more than decedent's probated estate. For example, insurance proceeds and jointly held property may be included in the decedent's gross estate even when they are excluded from his probated estate.

liquidity may be important to all the shareholders in their personal estate planning.

> **Ex.** *X*, a widower, and his brother, *Y*, each own 50% of the stock of Widgets, Inc. *X* dies leaving a taxable estate of $1,000,000. *X*'s 50% interest in Widgets is valued at $910,000; the proceeds of his life insurance are $120,000; the aggregate value of his other stocks and securities and bank accounts is $30,000. The remainder of his assets was used in satisfying his outstanding debts. The estate tax liability[4] owing on *X*'s death is $325,700 and the liquid assets available total only $150,000. The $175,700 balance must be obtained from the Widget stock, but the executor is likely to have some difficulty selling a minority interest in a closely held corporation. The executor might seek to have the corporation redeem part of *X*'s stock, but if *Y* refuses to cooperate with a redemption or if the parties cannot agree on the redemption price, the estate could be embarrassed. Had *X* and *Y* anticipated this problem and executed a mandatory buy-out agreement prior to *X*'s death, those difficulties would have been avoided. The parties are more likely to settle on a redemption plan and a valuation formula at a time when they are compatible co-investors and when neither knows which of the two will survive the other.

One obstacle to a redemption of a decedent's stock is the danger that the redemption will be deemed essentially equivalent to a dividend.[5] Even where the entirety of a decedent's stock is re-

---

4 For convenience, state death taxes and funeral expenses were ignored in the above Example.

5 I.R.C. § 302(d). The net effect of a redemption of a shareholder's stock may bear greater resemblance to a dividend than to a purchase of the stock, and if so, it is treated accordingly.

For example, *A* owns 60 of the 100 outstanding shares of stock of the *X* Corporation and *B* owns the other 40 shares. *X* has sizable earnings and profits. *X* redeems 30 shares of *A*'s stock for $30,000, and it redeems 20 shares of *B*'s stock for $15,000. Since both before and after the redemption *A* and *B* respectively owned 60% and 40% of the *X* Corporation, the only significant alteration made by the "redemption" was that $45,000 cash was withdrawn from the corporation. Thus, it is likely that the putative "redemption" will be treated as the distribution of a dividend.

The criteria for determining whether or not a stock redemption constitutes a dividend are intricate and should be studied carefully. For an analysis of this question, *see* pp. 11-26 *supra;* and Chapter 7 of BITTKER AND EUSTICE, FEDERAL INCOME TAXATION OF CORPORATIONS AND SHAREHOLDERS (2d ed., 1966).

deemed, there is a risk that attribution rules will cause the redemption to be characterized as a dividend.[6] However, to the extent that a redemption qualifies under I.R.C. § 303, the distributions to the shareholders will not constitute dividends, and the benefits of that provision often prove too valuable to decline.[7]

In planning a buy-out arrangement, the satisfaction of liquidity needs may be tempered in appropriate cases by the anticipated

---

6 I.R.C. § 318. It would be unrealistic to examine the net effect of a stock redemption solely from the viewpoint of the shareholders whose stocks were redeemed without accounting for the stockholdings of the natural persons and fictional entities who are closely related to them. Accordingly, in determining whether a stock redemption constitutes a dividend, the rules of attribution embodied in I.R.C. § 318 are usually applied. I.R.C. § 302(c).

For example, where C and D each own 50% of the outstanding stock of the Y Corporation and where the Y Corporation redeems all of C's stock, the redemption is completely disproportionate between the two shareholders and, therefore, will usually be treated as a purchase of C's stock rather than as a dividend distribution. However, if C and D are husband and wife, it might be more accurate to view their stockholdings as combined in a single family unit; and in that event, the redemption was not disproportionate to any extent. Under I.R.C. § 318(a)(1), a shareholder's stock will be attributed to his or her spouse and is treated as if the latter also owned it. Consequently, the redemption of C's stock will usually constitute a dividend, but it should be noted that in certain circumstances, defined in I.R.C. § 302(c)(2), attribution rules are disregarded.

For a discussion of the attribution rules established by § 318, see pp. 13-16 supra.

7 I.R.C. § 303 provides that where certain conditions (a few of which are described below) are satisfied, the redemption of stock which was included in the gross estate of a decedent will be treated as a purchase rather than as a dividend. The maximum value of stock redeemable under § 303 is an amount equal to the sum of the decedent's federal and local death taxes plus the administrative and funeral expenses that were allowable as federal estate tax deductions for the decedent's estate. To qualify, the estate tax valuation of the stock of the redeeming corporation that is included in the decedent's gross estate must exceed either 35% of the value of decedent's entire gross estate or 50% of decedent's taxable estate. Where the stocks of each of two or more corporations that are included in the decedent's gross estate exceed 75% in value of the outstanding stocks of such corporations, then the value of such included stocks may be totaled for purposes of determining whether the 35%-50% test has been satisfied. Only stock redeemed within a prescribed time period (often about 4½ years) following the decedent's death will qualify. See pp. 31-36 supra.

For a discussion of the requisites of § 303 and planning techniques for using it, see Barrett, How to Handle Distributions in Redemption of Stock to Pay Death Taxes—§ 303, 2 P-H TAX IDEAS. ¶ 26,004 (June 2, 1965).

availability of a deferral for payment of federal estate tax liability.[8]

2. Risks of continuing the business

Once the projected liquidity problems of the estate have been resolved, there remains the question whether the balance of the decedent's interest in the corporation should be liquidated. A shareholder may prefer that the investment portfolio for his beneficiaries concentrate on security rather than on yield, and an investment in the corporation's business may not conform with that desire. For the same reason, the shareholder may wish to have his holdings diversified after his death, and thus he will wish his executor to disengage his estate from the corporate business. The disadvantages of retaining a major portion of the decedent's estate in an investment in a closely held business are aggravated where this interest constitutes a minority share of the corporation. In such event there is a risk that the majority shareholders may engage in oppressive tactics such as increasing their salaries as corporate employees and reducing or eliminating dividends. Thus, the decedent's widow or surviving children may be "starved out" of the corporation and forced to sell at a sacrifice.[9] The development of a deadlock between the decedent's widow and the other shareholders may also prove unfortunate, and this prospect should be viewed skeptically.[10]

In some circumstances a shareholder may desire that his interest in the closely held corporation be retained after his death. The earnings of the corporation may provide a substantially higher yield than the shareholder's widow would otherwise obtain, and the shareholder may have confidence in the stability of the business of the corporation. If the corporation is owned by one family, the shareholder may be confident that his widow will be treated equitably by the other shareholders. However, even close family members have been known to become enemies, and if a deceased shareholder's interest is not to be purchased, it may prove desirable

---

8 I.R.C. § 6166. If the estate does not comply with the objective standards for deferral provided by § 6166, there is a possibility of obtaining a deferral under § 6161(a)(2) where the executor can demonstrate that immediate payment would impose an undue hardship.

9 For a comprehensive treatment of the many techniques available to majority shareholders for squeezing out a minority shareholder, see O'NEAL AND DERWIN, EXPULSION OR OPPRESSION OF BUSINESS ASSOCIATES: "SQUEEZE-OUTS" IN SMALL ENTERPRISES (1961).

10 See O'NEAL, CLOSE CORPORATIONS, § 8.06 (1958).

to provide for its conversion on death into an investment form that will maximize the widow's security, *e.g.*, preferred stock or debentures which provide the holder with substantial or even exclusive voting rights in the event of a default in dividends or interest.[11]

3. Estate tax valuations

Where the shareholders have executed a mandatory buy-out agreement to purchase the stock of a shareholder upon his death, the purchase price set in the buy-out agreement, either as a fixed dollar amount or under a formula, will establish the value of the stock for estate tax purposes if all of the following conditions are satisfied:[12] (a) the decedent's estate must be obligated to sell;[13] (b) the agreement must prohibit the shareholder from disposing of the stock during his life without first offering it to the prospective purchaser(s) at the contract price;[14] and (c) the purchase

---

11 The above arrangement alone may not be sufficient to prevent a squeeze-out. For example, the majority shareholders might cause a merger or recapitalization of the corporation resulting in the elimination or dilution of the widow's protection. *See* O'NEAL AND DERWIN, EXPULSION OR OPPRESSION OF BUSINESS ASSOCIATES: "SQUEEZE-OUTS" IN SMALL ENTERPRISES (1961) for a discussion of the means of protecting minority shareholders. *See also* O'Neal, *Arrangements Which Protect Minority Shareholders Against "Squeeze-Outs,"* 45 MINN. L. REV. 537 (1961).

12 Treas. Reg. § 20.2031-2(h); and Rev. Rul. 59-60 (Sec. 8), 1959-1 C.B. 237, 243-244. *Cf.* Helvering v. Salvage, 297 U.S. 106 (1936).

13 *E.g.,* Estate of Orville B. Littick, 31 T.C. 181 (1958), Acq. 1959-2 C.B. 5; and United States v. Land, 303 F.2d 170 (C.A. 5 1962). Where the decedent's executor is required to sell only upon the corporation's exercise of an option to buy, the purchase price established in the option agreement will control the estate tax valuation if the other tests are satisfied. Commissioner v. Bensel, 100 F.2d 639 (C.A. 3 1938); and Wilson v. Bowers, 57 F.2d 682 (C.A. 2 1932). However, a mandatory buy-out is a safer arrangement, particularly where the shareholders are members of the same family. If the decedent's estate has an option to sell, but before selling to a third party, the executor must first offer the stock to the corporation at a set price, the agreement does not impose sufficient restrictions on the sale of the stock to fix the valuation thereof, since the executor need not sell at all; however, the obligation to offer the stock to the corporation at a given price before making a sale may depress the market value of the stock somewhat. Worcester County Trust Co. v. Commissioner, 134 F.2d 578 (C.A. 1 1943). *See* LOWNDES AND KRAMER, FEDERAL ESTATE AND GIFT TAXES (2d ed., 1962), pp. 484-491 for an excellent discussion of restrictive agreements.

14 Treas. Reg. § 20.2031-2(h); Rev. Rul. 59-60 (Sec. 8) *supra;* Estate of Robert R. Gannon, 21 T.C. 1073, 1080 (1954) (holding that the value of a partnership interest was not determined by a purchase agreement which did not restrict sales during the partner's life). If the agreement provides the purchasers with first refusal rights during the shareholder's life at the contract price, that should be suf-

price must have been established through an arms-length business bargain; and particularly for family corporations, this test may require that the purchase price have been reasonable at the date the buy-out agreement was executed, viewing the potential growth of the business as of that date.[15] One advantage of establishing the stock's estate tax valuation is that it avoids the "horse-trading" negotiations which frequently attend a dispute with the Service over the value of closely held stock.

If the purchase price fixed in the buy-out agreement is not treated as determinative of the value of the stock, there may be serious adverse consequences. If the amount distributed by the corporation in payment of the stock is deemed greater than the stock's value, the amount of the difference would not constitute a distribution in redemption of the stock and consequently will not be protected by I.R.C. § 303 or § 302(a). Thus, the amount of the difference might be characterized as a dividend distribution; or, alternatively, it might be treated as a gift from the surviving

---

ficient. Brodrick v. Gore, 224 F.2d 892 (C.A. 10 1955); and May v. McGowan, 194 F.2d 396 (C.A. 2 1952).

An agreement which is binding *only* during the shareholder's life and not at death does not fix the value of the stock. United States v. Land, 303 F.2d 170 (C.A. 5 1962); and Mathews v. United States, 226 F. Supp. 1003 (E.D.N.Y. 1964).

15 Treas. Reg. § 20.2031-2(h); and Rev. Rul. 59-60 (Sec. 8) *supra*. The requirement of an arms-length bargain creates uncertainties since the test is somewhat subjective; and where the agreement is made among compatible family members, the best evidence that will usually be available to demonstrate an arms-length dealing is the fact that the purchase price established in the agreement was reasonable. *See* Slocum v. United States, 256 F. Supp. 753 (S.D.N.Y. 1966), holding that where there was a business justification for an agreement at the date of execution, the parties' failure to amend the agreement to reflect a subsequent rise in value of the shares (from $100 per share to more than $1,100 per share) was not apposite. In Estate of Orville B. Littick, 31 T.C. 181 (1958), Acq. 1959-2 C.B. 5, the court sustained an agreement among shareholders who were members of the same family where there was a business purpose for the agreement, *viz.,* to maintain present management in control. A surprising taxpayer success on this issue is May v. McGowan, 194 F.2d 396 (C.A. 2 1952) where the formula in the buy-out agreement resulted in a payment of zero for the decedent's stock and the court held that the estate tax value of the stock was therefore zero. In *May,* the decedent was the father of the purchaser, but the court found valid business consideration for the agreement in that the son had guaranteed repayment of a large debt of the decedent. While *May v. McGowan* is a significant case, for planning purposes, it would be prudent to establish a fair price for the stock which is subject to the purchase agreement. *See* Polasky, *Planning for the Disposition of a Substantial Interest in a Closely Held Business (Part III),* 46 IOWA L.R. 516, 567-69, 572 (1961).

shareholders giving rise to gift tax consequences. On the other hand, if the amount distributed by the corporation in payment of the stock is less than the stock's value, the shareholder will be required to pay estate taxes based on a value in excess of that which he realized, and this could cause considerable hardship. Indeed, it is conceivable that where the payment in redemption is substantially less than the stock's value, the estate tax liability incurred on account of the stock may actually exceed the amount realized on its redemption. Consequently, care should be taken that the agreement does fix the estate tax value of the stock, and in any event the established price should be reasonable so that a failure to comply with the above-mentioned requisites will not have disastrous consequences.

4. Prevent disruption of corporate business

The three objectives discussed above concerned advantages to the estate of the deceased shareholder. A buy-out arrangement may also be desirable to the corporation and the surviving shareholders. The buy-out can prevent a deadlock or harassment by dissident shareholders who inherited stock from the decedent. Moreover, the decedent's widow and the surviving shareholders often have conflicting goals for the corporation and that can complicate the management of the company. The question of whether corporate earnings should be distributed as dividends or reinvested in the business and the question of the amount of risk that the business should undertake in entering new ventures are examples of potential areas of conflict. A buy-out will eliminate that problem.

If the corporation has made an election under Subchapter S,[16] a buy-out agreement may be useful to prevent a shareholder from bequeathing his stock to a trust or to a party who will refuse to consent to the Subchapter S election, since in either case the Subchapter S election would be terminated.[17]

---

16 Subchapter S (I.R.C. § 1371 *et seq.*) is an election permitted a corporation which complies with certain requisites. Under that election, the corporation pays no income tax (other than a capital gains tax in certain circumstances (§ 1378)), and the earnings of the corporation are included in the income of shareholders. *See* pp. 267-284 *infra.*

17 I.R.C. § 1372(e)(1) (new shareholders), and §§ 1371(a)(2) and 1372(e)(3) (trust).

Buy-out arrangements for the redemption or purchase of stock of a Subchapter S corporation raise problems and considerations pecu-

It is noteworthy that, except for fixing the estate tax valuation of the stock, the purposes of the deceased shareholder's estate can be satisfied by requiring the prospective purchaser to purchase the stock if the estate elects to sell; but for the purposes of the continuing shareholders and the corporation, and for the purpose of fixing estate tax values, the decedent's estate must be obligated to sell if the prospective purchaser elects to buy. Consequently, in most circumstances a mandatory buy-out will be the more desirable arrangement since it will satisfy the needs of both parties.

B. POTENTIAL PURCHASERS

In preparing a buy-out plan, the first consideration is the selection of the party who will purchase a shareholder's stock upon his death. As indicated above, the choice is usually made between an entity purchase plan (a stock redemption by the corporation) and a cross-purchase plan; and in some instances a combination of those two plans will be employed. However, there are other alternatives, the most significant of which is to have part of the deceased shareholder's stock purchased by a trust held under a qualified deferred compensation plan established by the corporation for its employees.[18] The Service prohibits a qualified trust fund from acquiring the employer's stock unless it is purchased for the "exclusive benefit of the employees or their beneficiaries" and local law permits such investments.[19] The requisites of the exclusive benefit test are:[20] the stocks must be purchased at no more than their fair market value; the stocks must provide a fair return commensurate with the prevailing rate; sufficient liquidity must be maintained in the trust fund to permit distributions according to the terms of the plan; and the safeguards and diversity that a prudent investor would adopt must be present. The common stock of most closely held corporations will not satisfy the "exclusive benefit" test be-

---

liar to Subchapter S corporations. *See* Crumbley, *Buy and Sell Agreements for Subchapter S Corporations,* 108 TRUSTS AND ESTATES 17 (1969). I have not attempted to deal with those problems in this book.

18 There are many advantages to using the trust funds for that purpose. It provides the employees of the corporation with an equity interest in the business, and it serves as a convenient source of liquid assets. Moreover, in some circumstances there are tax advantages to the employees who receive distribution of such stock on retirement. I.R.C. § 402(a)(1); and Treas. Reg. § 1.402(a)-1(b).

19 Rev. Rul. 65-178, 1965-2 C.B. 94, 104.

20 *Id.*

cause such stock usually has no available market and frequently little or no dividends will have been paid on the stock (fair return). However, the Service has held in a Technical Advice Memo from the National Office to the District Director, San Francisco, November 27, 1961, that the "exclusive benefit" test is satisfied by a trust which maintains separate accounts for each employee if (a) the plan permits each employee at his option to direct that part of his trust account be invested in his employer's stock and (b) where the employee elects to have part of his account so invested, the trustees are required to make that investment.[21] The Memo of the National Office is buttressed by a subsequently published ruling concerning profit-sharing trusts;[22] and it is likely that while this arrangement may be useful for profit-sharing plans, it will not be feasible for most pension plans.[23]

In some circumstances it may be feasible to recapitalize the corporation so that the deceased shareholder's estate receives preferred stock in exchange for common, and the preferred shares may then be sold to the trust if they comply with the "exclusive benefit" test. However, if the recapitalization is effected after the shareholder's death, the planner must give due regard to § 306.[24]

Where trust funds of a qualified trust are invested in the stock or securities of the employer, the trustee is required to give notice to the Service of such investment and to disclose the reasons for the investment and the circumstances under which it was made.[25]

The use of trust funds for stock purchase purposes can be a highly valuable device, but the path to this modern-day Valhalla is no less perilous than the journey to the original, and the planner should proceed with both caution and private rulings.

---

21 P-H Pens & Profits Sharing Serv. ¶ 11,983. For a discussion of this issue, *see* ROTHMAN, ESTABLISHING & ADMINISTERING PENSION & PROFIT SHARING PLANS & TRUST FUNDS, (ALI/ABA, 1967), pp. 160-163.
22 Rev. Rul. 65-178, Part 5(r), 1965-2 CUM. BULL. 94, 125.
23 "Money-purchase" pension plans might adopt separate investment accounts for each employee's share, but most pension trusts could not readily adopt separate accounts.
24 Stock sold to the trust will not qualify under I.R.C. § 303 since it is not redeemed by the corporation. Consequently, the priority of § 303 over § 306 is of no assistance in this case.
  Preferred stock issued after the decedent's death will likely be tainted by I.R.C. § 306. One significance of this "taint" is that all or part of the amount received as consideration for the sale of such stock may be characterized as ordinary income, irrespective of the vendor's basis in the stock. § 306(a)(1). *See* pp. 51-58 *supra*.
25 Treas. Reg. § 1.401-1(b)(5)(ii).

C. ENTITY PURCHASE PLANS

The entity purchase plan is the most popular form of buy-out arrangement. Since the principal competition to the entity purchase is the cross-purchase agreement, the following discussion will occasionally contrast the two types of plans.

1. Net cost of the redemption

One of the attractive features of the entity purchase is that the use of corporate funds to redeem a deceased shareholder's stock usually imposes a smaller net cost on the corporation and the surviving shareholders than does the cross-purchase agreement.

Despite some initial doubts, it is now clear that a corporation's redemption of a deceased shareholder's stock will not constitute a constructive dividend to the surviving shareholders where the plan conforms to the guidelines established by the Service's rulings.[26] Basically, these guidelines require that the agreement to buy must be made by the corporation, rather than by the other shareholders, and that the corporation must not supply the compensation for a purchase which in fact is being made by the surviving shareholders.

Since the amount paid to redeem a shareholder's stock is not deductible, a determination of the actual cost of the purchase of the decedent's stock should reflect the amount that the corporation must earn before taxes to make that payment. For example, where the X Corporation is in a 48% income tax bracket, and where X agrees to redeem the stock held by A for $52,000, X must earn $100,000 to have sufficient funds after taxes to redeem A's stock. Of course, the corporation need not necessarily draw on its earnings to redeem a shareholder's stock, but instead may contract its capital investments and distribute previously contributed capital; but in the usual buy-out arrangement a contraction of the corporation's business investments will not be desirable and may not even be feasible. Moreover, the shareholder's stock will often be valued at an amount greatly in excess of his capital contributions, and the earnings of the corporation are the best available source for the funds needed to acquire the stock.

In a cross-purchase plan the surviving shareholders will usually

---

26 Rev. Rul. 59-286, 1959-2 C.B. 103; and Rev. Rul. 58-614, 1958-2 C.B. 920.

obtain the funds to purchase the decedent's stock from the corporation.[27] If the funds must be withdrawn as dividends, the additional cost to the corporation and the shareholders can be severe. Compare the above illustrative example of the cost of an entity purchase with the following example of a cross-purchase arrangement.

> **Ex. (1)** The X Corporation is in a 48% tax bracket and has three equal shareholders, A, B and C. A, B and C have agreed that the X stock of the first to die will be purchased by the two survivors for $52,000. A, B and C are each in the 60% tax bracket.[28] When A dies, B and C wish to withdraw sufficient funds from X to pay $52,000 to A's estate. Since B and C will retain only 40% of the dividends paid to them after taxes, they must withdraw $130,000 to obtain the $52,000 needed. Moreover, the corporation must earn $250,000 to have $130,000 available after taxes to distribute to B and C. Thus, the net cost of obtaining $52,000 from the corporation for a cross-purchase is $250,000 as compared with a cost of $100,000 under the entity purchase.

Where the amounts distributed to the surviving shareholders can be made in a deductible form[29] (*e.g.*, as salary or interest or

---

27 Where the cross-purchase agreement is funded by life insurance, the premiums for that insurance will usually be paid from funds withdrawn from the corporation, and consequently, the comparison of relative costs of a direct purchase of the stock will be equally applicable to the payment of insurance premiums.

In some circumstances, the net cost of purchasing life insurance for shareholders who are also employees of the corporation may be reduced by utilizing a split dollar insurance plan, the relative merits and disadvantages of which are discussed in Part D of this chapter. *See also* Note, *Estate Planning for the Disposition of Control of a Family Corporation,* 52 MINN. L. REV. 1019, 1030, n.46 (1968). For the reasons stated in Part D, I do not believe that split dollar insurance should be employed to fund a buy-out agreement.

28 The withdrawal of a large sum from the corporation, which will be included in the shareholder's gross income, would be taxed in a higher bracket than 60%; but for convenience, we shall treat the effective tax rate on amounts withdrawn as remaining stable at 60%. If the higher tax rates were used in making the computations, the expense of withdrawing funds from the corporation would be increased, and therefore the comparison of the costs of the two buy-out methods would be even more dramatic.

29 This is sometimes possible where the corporate funds are withdrawn annually for the purpose of paying life insurance premiums, if the annual distribution does not exceed a reasonable salary and the funds are paid as such.

rent), the difference in net cost is less dramatic; but the entity purchase is still the cheaper method, unless the shareholders are in an income tax bracket that is lower than the corporation's.[30]

> **Ex. (2)** Assume the same facts as in Example (1) above except that B and C are able to withdraw funds from X as deductible expenses, such as salary. In order to obtain the needed $52,000 after taxes, B and C must withdraw $130,000 from X; but since the amounts paid to B and C are deductible, X need earn only $130,000 to provide B and C with after-tax dollars of that amount. Thus, the net cost of the cross-purchase plan ($130,000) will be $30,000 greater than the cost of the entity plan even though the payments to the shareholders were deductible.

The means by which a corporation may fund its obligation to redeem stock under an entity purchase agreement and the obstacles the corporation may encounter are discussed below.

It should not be assumed that the entity purchase will be superior to a cross-purchase plan in every case. Both plans have their distinctive merits and disadvantages, and both should be considered carefully in the context of the specific factual circumstances and goals that exist in each individual case.

2. Basis of redeemed stock

One disadvantage of the entity purchase is that the corporation derives no tax benefit from the acquisition of the decedent's stock irrespective of whether it cancels the redeemed shares or carries them as treasury stock. The corporation cannot recognize a gain or loss on the sale of its stock, including treasury stock,[31] and consequently its basis in the redeemed shares is meaningless. In contrast, where a surviving shareholder acquires stock under a cross-purchase agreement, his basis in the acquired stock will be meaningful if he disposes of the stock prior to his death.

3. Corporation's funding of the redemption price

Upon the death of a shareholder who is a party to an entity

---

30 Where the shareholders are in a lower tax bracket than the corporation and funds can be withdrawn from the corporation in a deductible form, the cross-purchase plan will be a less expensive arrangement; but that is an atypical situation.

31 I.R.C. § 1032.

purchase agreement, the corporation must have sufficient assets to redeem the shareholder's stock. Several alternative means for the corporation to raise the necessary funds are discussed below.[32]

(a) **Establishment of a reserve.** The corporation may seek to raise the necessary funds by investing a portion of each year's corporate earnings in liquid assets that will constitute a funded reserve. A major failing of a self-funding plan is that a shareholder might die soon after the plan is executed, and the corporation will not have had time to accumulate a sufficient surplus in its reserve fund to redeem his stock. Moreover, even where the shareholders obligingly live long after the plan is established, the accumulation of a sizable surplus may have adverse tax consequences—*i.e.*, the corporation may be subjected to the imposition of an accumulated earnings tax[33] on its income.

(i) *The accumulated earnings tax.* The accumulated earnings tax is a surtax of either $27\frac{1}{2}\%$ or $38\frac{1}{2}\%$ imposed on accumulated taxable income[34] in addition to the normal corporate tax and surtax imposed under I.R.C. § 11. The accumulated earnings tax applies to corporations "formed or availed of for the purpose of avoiding the income tax with respect to its shareholders or the shareholders of any other corporation by permitting earnings and profits to accumulate instead of being divided or distributed."[35] If the earnings and profits of the corporation are accumulated beyond the rea-

---

32 For a discussion of the use of a third party as an interim financing intermediary for the corporation in an arrangement similar to the "ABC" transactions employed in the oil and gas field, *see* Sexton, *Providing Security for the Outgoing Stockholder and Avoiding Tax Disadvantages to Selling and Remaining Stockholders,* 24 N.Y.U. TAX INST. 555, 584-585 (1966).

    In some circumstances the corporation may be able to borrow the needed funds directly from a third party and repay the loan from subsequent earnings. *Cf.* Murphy Logging Co. v. United States, 378 F.2d 222 (C.A. 9 1967).

33 I.R.C. §§ 531-537.

34 "Accumulated taxable income" refers to the corporation's taxable income modified in accordance with I.R.C. § 535. One important modification is a deduction for dividends paid, but many other adjustments are also applicable.

    It is noteworthy that the temporary surtax (I.R.C. § 51) imposed by Section 102 of Public Law 90-364 (June 28, 1968) also serves to increase the amount of the accumulated earnings surtax.

35 I.R.C. § 532(a).

sonable needs of the business,[36] the corporation is presumed to be availed of for the proscribed purpose unless it proves the contrary.[37]

The accumulated taxable income of a corporation is reduced by the sum of dividends paid plus an accumulated earnings credit.[38] Generally, the accumulated earnings credit is equal to that part of the earnings and profits for the taxable year that is retained for the reasonable needs of the business.[39] In no event will the accumulated earnings credit be less than the amount by which $100,000 exceeds the corporation's accumulated earnings and profits determined as of the end of the preceding taxable year.[40]

The discussion above merely sketches the nature of the accumulated earnings tax, and the reader may wish to peruse one or more of the many articles written on the subject.[41]

While in the great majority of cases litigated under § 531, the parties have treated the question of whether the corporation accumulated earnings and profits beyond the reasonable needs of the business as dispositive,[42] that question is only evidentiary of the crucial issue, viz., whether the corporation's accumulation was for the purpose of avoiding a shareholder's income tax. The question

---

36 The phrase "reasonable needs of the business" includes the reasonably anticipated needs of the business. I.R.C. § 537.
37 I.R.C. § 533.
38 I.R.C. § 535(a).
39 I.R.C. § 535(c). The credit is reduced by the excess of the corporation's net long term capital gains over net short term capital losses for the taxable year minus the corporation's income taxes attributable to such excess. The reason for that reduction is that in determining accumulated taxable income, the taxable income is reduced by that amount (§ 535(b)) which is therefore made available for the reasonable needs of the business; and if no reduction were made in the credit, the capital gains would, in effect, net a double deduction.
40 I.R.C. § 535(c)(2).
41 See Faber, *Practitioner's Guide to Defending a 531 Case: Theory and Practice,* 27 J. OF TAXATION 274 (November, 1967); and BITTKER AND EUSTICE, FEDERAL INCOME TAXATION OF CORPORATIONS AND SHAREHOLDERS (2d ed., 1966), pp. 209-238.
42 Because of the presumption in § 533(a) that accumulations beyond the reasonable needs of the business demonstrate that the corporation had the proscribed purpose, the parties have usually litigated only the business purpose question, and there have been few attempts to rebut the presumption.
For a thorough discussion of the application of the "reasonable needs of the business" test to corporate accumulations related to a stock redemption, see Herwitz, *Stock Redemptions and the Accumulated Earnings Tax,* 74 HARV. L. REV. 866 (1961).

of whether the accumulated earnings tax applies whenever the proscribed purpose was present, or whether it applies only when the proscribed purpose was the *dominant* motive, was settled by a recent decision of the Supreme Court.[43] The Court held in *Donruss* that if any one purpose of the corporation for accumulating its earnings was the proscribed purpose, the tax is applicable even though the proscribed purpose was not dominant. In all likelihood there will be precious few instances where a taxpayer can successfully negate the inference that tax avoidance was at least one of the purposes for the accumulation of earnings by a closely held corporation. Of course, as a result of the aforementioned statutory credit, to the extent that a corporation's accumulations do not exceed the reasonable needs of the business, the accumulated earnings surtax will not be imposed irrespective of the motive for the accumulation.[44] Despite the statutory restriction of the credit to the accumulation of such earnings and profits "as are retained for the reasonable needs of the business,"[45] it appears that the credit will be granted for accumulations that are not in excess of the reasonable needs of the business without regard to the actual purpose of the accumulations; and to date, the Commissioner has not contended otherwise. In sum, *Donruss* may have virtually eliminated a contention that a corporate accumulation was not made for a proscribed purpose, and has thereby elevated the significance of the "reasonable needs of the business" test.[46]

(ii) *Application of the accumulated earnings tax to a buy-out reserve.* The accumulation of a reserve for redemption of a shareholder's stock may cause the imposition of an accumulated earnings tax where the accumulated earnings and profits of the corporation exceed the minimum $100,000 credit.[47] There are two separate issues here: (1) whether accumulations in anticipation of a stock redemption are within the

---

43 United States v. Donruss Co., 393 U.S. 297 (1969). *See also* Commissioner v. Shaw-Walker Co., 393 U.S. 478 (1969), vacating the judgment of the Sixth Circuit in that case (390 F.2d 205 (1968)).

44 I.R.C. § 535(c)(1) grants a credit for amounts accumulated for the reasonable needs of the business. *See* Magic Mart, Inc., 51 T.C. 775 (1969), *acq. in result,* I.R.B. 1969-33, p. 7.

45 I.R.C. § 535(c)(1).

46 *See* Altman and Muchin, *Supreme Court's Donruss decision calls for a shift in tactics in 531 area,* 30 J. OF TAXATION 202 (April, 1969).

47 I.R.C. § 535(c)(2). *See* Herwitz, *Stock Redemptions and the Accumulated Earnings Tax,* 74 HARV. L. REV. 866 (1961).

reasonable needs of the business; and (2) even if not, whether the accumulations are exempt from the surtax because not made for the proscribed purpose.[48]

(aa) *Reasonable needs of the business.* The business needs test refers only to the business needs of the *corporation.*[49] In *Pelton Steel Casting Co.,*[50] the accumulated earnings tax was imposed where income of the corporation was accumulated in order to redeem the stock of two shareholders who owned 80% of the corporation's outstanding stock. However, a number of courts have held that accumulations for the purpose of redeeming a shareholder's stock *may* qualify as a reasonable need of the business.[51] In *Emeloid Co., Inc. v. Commissioner,*[52] the court held that the purchase of single premium life insurance on the life of each of the corporation's two 50% shareholders for the purpose of funding a mandatory buy-out agreement was a business purpose in that it provided for the continuity of harmonious management after the death of one shareholder and established a reimbursement to the corporation for the loss of a key man.[53] While the *Emeloid* case did not involve the accumulated earnings tax,[54] courts and commentators alike have treated *Emeloid* as establishing that a stock re-

48 *See* Polasky, *Planning for the Disposition of a Substantial Interest in a Closely Held Business (Part III),* 46 IOWA L. REV. 516, 541-546 (1961).
49 Youngs Rubber Corporation, ¶ 62,300 P-H Memo T.C., *affirmed per curiam,* 331 F.2d 12 (C.A. 2 1964).
50 28 T.C. 153 (1957), *affirmed,* 251 F.2d 278 (C.A. 7 1958), *cert. denied,* 356 U.S. 958.
51 Dill Manufacturing Co., 39 B.T.A. 1023 (1939), Non acq. 1939-2 C.B. 47; Gazette Publishing Co. v. Self, 103 F. Supp. 779 (E.D. Ark 1952); Mountain State Steel Foundries, Inc. v. Commissioner, 284 F.2d 737 (C.A. 4 1960), *reversing,* ¶ 59,059 P-H Memo T.C.; and Ted Bates & Company, Inc., ¶ 65,251 P-H Memo T.C. *Mountain State Steel* involved accumulations after the redemption for the purpose of paying notes given in exchange for redeemed stock.
52 189 F.2d 230 (C.A. 3 1951).
53 Accumulations for the purpose of providing self-insurance against the loss of key personnel, including shareholder employees, were sustained in Bradford-Robinson Printing Co. v. United States, 1 A.F.T.R.2d 1278 (D. Colo. 1957).
54 *Emeloid* involved a claim for an excess profits tax credit for borrowed investment capital. The question was whether a loan made for the purpose of paying an insurance premium was made for a business purpose so that it qualified as borrowed investment capital.

demption agreement may serve the needs of the corporate business for purposes of the accumulated earnings tax as well.[55]

Thus, notwithstanding the broad language employed in *Pelton Steel*, it is reasonably certain that a stock redemption does serve business needs in certain circumstances. The test is whether the redemption is for the purpose of continuing the harmonious management of the business by eliminating the stock of potentially dissident shareholders or whether the redemption is merely for the benefit of a shareholder. Where the shareholders have adverse interests as to the manner in which the corporate business should be conducted, the business purpose of the redemption is evident. The redemption of stock of a minority shareholder is more likely to withstand attack than the redemption of the stock of a majority shareholder, but there are circumstances where a redemption of a majority shareholder's stock serves the needs of the corporation.[56]

The subjectivity of the tests for determining whether a stock redemption is a reasonable need of the business creates uncertainties. The risk of imposition of a surtax should be neither ignored nor exaggerated: in some circumstances a buy-out plan will be advantageous even if the surtax is imposed.[57]

---

55 Herwitz, *Stock Redemptions and the Accumulated Earnings Tax,* 74 HARV. L. REV. 866 (1961); Polasky, *Planning for the Disposition of a Substantial Interest in a Closely Held Business (Part III),* 46 IOWA L. REV. 516 (1961).
  Mountain State Steel Foundries, Inc. v. Commissioner, 284 F.2d 737, 745 (C.A. 4 1960); Ted Bates & Company, Inc., ¶ 65,251 P-H Memo T.C., n. 9.
  Additional cases, which did not involve an accumulated earnings tax, suggesting that a stock redemption may serve business needs are: Prunier v. Commissioner, 248 F.2d 818 (C.A. 1 1957); and Sanders v. Fox, 253 F.2d 855 (C.A. 10 1958).
56 *See* Herwitz, *Stock Redemptions and the Accumulated Earnings Tax,* 74 HARV. L. REV. 866, 909-919 (1961).
57 Where the shareholders are in high income tax brackets and funds can be withdrawn from the corporation only as dividends, the surtax on accumulations plus the ultimate cost of withdrawing funds either at capital gains rates on liquidation, or perhaps at no tax cost if withdrawn after a shareholder's death, may be substantially less than the cost of withdrawing the funds as dividends.

(bb) *Purpose to avoid shareholder's income tax.* Even
where an accumulation in anticipation of a stock redemption does not satisfy the business needs test, the
surtax may not be applicable because the accumulation
was not made for the purpose of avoiding the income
tax of a shareholder.[58] Where a projected redemption
will likely qualify under I.R.C. § 303 for exclusion from
dividend treatment, it is arguable[59] that accumulations
for the purpose of effecting that redemption are not for
the proscribed purpose, but rather are pursuant to a con-
gressionally approved policy to permit and even encourage the use of corporate assets to satisfy a deceased
shareholder's tax liabilities and other death costs. It
would be anomalous to encourage a corporation to redeem the stock of a deceased shareholder on the one
hand, and to deter it from accumulating the funds needed
for the redemption on the other. Three cases[60] have held
that an accumulation in anticipation of a section 303
redemption is not a reasonable need of the business. The
opinions in those cases do not attempt to reconcile their
holdings with the rationale of § 303, nor do they discuss
whether the corporation was availed of for the proscribed purpose. There is language in *Mountain State
Steel*[61] suggesting that the surtax should not be imposed where § 303 is applicable; the court said (284
F.2d at p. 745): "Among other things, [Congress] specifically provided that a partial redemption of the shares
held by an estate would be treated as a sale, not as a
distribution of earnings, if the amount of the distribution did not exceed the estate's liabilities for estate and
inheritance taxes, interest and funeral and administra-

---

58 As previously noted, it is the existence or absence of this proscribed
purpose that is crucial to determining whether the accumulated earnings surtax is applicable. I.R.C. § 532(a).

59 This argument was suggested to the author by Mr. Lawrence Robin-
son in a research paper prepared by the latter.

60 Youngs Rubber Corporation, ¶ 62,300 P-H Memo T.C., *affirmed per
curiam,* 331 F.2d 12 (C.A. 2 1964); The Kirlin Co., ¶ 64,260 P-H
Memo T.C., *affirmed per curiam,* 361 F.2d 818 (C.A. 6 1966); and
Dickman Lumber Co. v. United States, 15 A.F.T.R.2d 27 (W.D. Wash.
1964), *affirmed,* 355 F.2d 670 (C.A. 9 1966).

61 284 F.2d 737 (C.A. 4 1960).

tive expenses. When Congress specifically provided favorable tax treatment for such transactions and sought to encourage them to facilitate the administration of estates, it hardly could have intended to penalize the corporation for doing the favored act."

While there is little precedent to comfort the taxpayer at this date, the issue has not yet been adequately discussed by the courts, and if attention were focused on the *purpose* of the accumulation rather than on the business needs, it is possible that the present trend would be reversed. However, the recent Supreme Court decision in *United States v. Donruss*[62] may well foreclose this contention, and consequently taxpayers may be forced to rely exclusively on the credit granted to accumulations for the reasonable needs of the business.

The arguments in support of permitting corporate accumulations for the purpose of redeeming the stock of its shareholders are vulnerable to the response that such accumulations will frustrate the congressional policy for eliminating the so-called "incorporated pocketbook." Where a corporation accumulates assets to redeem its stock, the net worth of the corporation will increase and consequently the value of its stock and the cost of redeeming its stock will rise proportionately. The resulting increase in the amount of the corporation's liability to redeem its stock will justify additional accumulations which in turn will further increase the redemption price and thereby justify even greater accumulations. The potential spiraling effect of such accumulations weighs against permitting any accumulations for the purpose of redemption. However, in the usual case, the accumulations will not rise in this manner, because the corporation will establish a reserve only for a portion of the purchase price. A reasonable solution to this dilemma is to permit accumulations for redemption purposes where that fulfills corporate objectives, but to preclude

---

62 393 U.S. 297 (1969). *Donruss* held that if any single purpose for accumulating the funds was to avoid a shareholder's income tax, that is sufficient to trigger the imposition of an accumulated earnings tax.

accumulations for that part of the redemption value of the stock that is attributable to the corporation's funded reserve. This issue is unresolved at this date.

(b) Funding with life insurance. A common means of funding an entity buy-out plan is to have the corporation purchase life insurance policies on the lives of its shareholders.[63] The proceeds of the policies may be made payable to the corporation upon the death of a shareholder, and the corporation may then use the proceeds to redeem the decedent's shares of stock. Or, preferably, the policies may be held by a trustee who will collect the proceeds on the death of the insured, purchase the decedent's shares of stock and turn over the purchased shares to the corporation and the insurance proceeds to the decedent's estate or beneficiary. A third alternative is to make the insurance proceeds payable directly to a person or fiduciary appointed by the insured subject to the conditions that the insured's stock is surrendered to the corporation and that the insurance proceeds will be credited against the purchase price of the surrendered stock; the advantage of this third alternative, which is rarely employed, is to permit the recipients of the insurance proceeds to elect among the settlement options provided by the policy.

Life insurance funding is available only where the shareholders are insurable; if one or more insurable shareholders are given a high risk rating, the insurance costs may be prohibitive. This difficulty can be overcome if the uninsurable or high risk shareholder already owns life insurance policies which he is willing to sell to the corporation for their cash surrender value,[64] but that situation is atypical.

---

63 *See* Note, *The Use of Life Insurance to Fund Agreements Providing for Disposition of a Business Interest at Death,* 71 HARV. L. REV. 687 (1958).

64 If the shareholder sells the policy to the corporation for an amount greater than his net premium cost (*i.e.,* total aggregate premiums paid less dividends), the difference will constitute income to the shareholder, and may well be characterized as ordinary income. Edwin A. Gallan, ¶ 63,167 P-H Memo T.C.; and Bolling Jones, Jr., 39 T.C. 404 (1962). *Cf.* Roff v. Commissioner, 304 F.2d 450 (C.A. 3 1962), *affirming* 36 T.C. 818 (1961).

The sale to the corporation will *not* cause the proceeds of the insurance to be included in the corporation's gross income when the policy matures. I.R.C. § 101 (a) (2) (B).

(i) *Nondeductibility of payment of premiums.* Section 264(a)(1) disallows any income tax deduction for payment of premiums on a life insurance policy covering the life of a person financially interested in the trade or business conducted by the corporation, where the corporation is directly or indirectly a beneficiary of the policy. Since the proceeds of the insurance acquired under a buy-out plan are used as consideration for the corporation's redemption of its stock, the corporation is at least an indirect beneficiary; and consequently no income tax deduction is allowed for its payment of the insurance premiums.

(ii) *Income tax consequences to shareholders of corporation's payment of premiums.* While there was once some reason for doubt, it is now settled that a corporation's payment of premiums on policies insuring the life of its shareholder will not be included in the gross income of the shareholder where the corporation has substantial ownership rights in the policy, if either (1) the corporation is the beneficiary of the policy, or (2) a trustee or other party is the beneficiary, and the distribution of the proceeds is conditioned upon the surrender of the insured's stock.[65]

(iii) *Effect of payment of premiums on corporation's earnings and profits.* "Earnings and profits" is a term of art which is employed in corporate taxation. The earnings and profits of a corporation are the measuring rod for determining whether corporate distributions to shareholders constitute dividends and therefore are taxed as ordinary income.[66] Also, as indicated above, the earnings and profits of a corporation may be a factor in determining whether the accumulated earnings surtax will be imposed; and the amount of earnings and profits may be significant in determining the effect of some liquidations.[67] Earnings and profits reflect the assets of the corporation that are available for distribution to shareholders without impairing capital. While the term "earnings and pro-

---

65 Prunier v. Commissioner, 248 F.2d 818 (C.A. 1 1957); Sanders v. Fox, 253 F.2d 855 (C.A. 10 1958); Casale v. Commissioner, 247 F.2d 440 (C.A. 2 1957); and Rev. Rul. 59-184, 1959-1 C.B. 65.
66 I.R.C. §§ 316(a) and 301(c)(1). *See* pp. 4-6 *supra.*
67 I.R.C. § 333(e) and (f).

fits" is not defined in the Internal Revenue Code, § 312 and the Regulations thereunder give many examples of how earnings and profits are determined.[68] While the earnings and profits concept is analogous to the earned surplus concept employed in corporate law and the amount of a corporation's earnings and profits is often virtually identical to its earned surplus, it could be a disastrous mistake to assume that a corporation's earned surplus is necessarily identical to its earnings and profits. There are adjustments made to one that are not made to the other. For example, the distribution of stock dividends will reduce earned surplus but, except in the unusual circumstance where a stock dividend is taxable,[69] they will have no effect on the corporation's earnings and profits. Similarly, the capitalization of earned surplus by other means will not reduce earnings and profits.

Since so many corporate tax consequences turn upon the amount of the corporation's earnings and profits, an analysis of the merits of redemption plans must consider the effect on earnings and profits of the corporation's purchasing insurance, receipt of insurance proceeds and the redemption of its stock. The first of these items is discussed immediately below and the other two are discussed subsequently in this chapter.

The corporation's earnings and profits are reduced by the excess of the amount of premiums paid over the increase in the policy's cash surrender value.[70] It is unsettled whether the

---

68 For a discussion of the determination of earnings and profits, *see* pp. 7-10 *supra. See also* Zarky and Biblin, *The Role of Earnings and Profits in the Tax Law,* 18 U.S.C. Tax Inst. 145 (1966).

69 I.R.C. § 305 provides that stock dividends are usually not taxable and describes the two circumstances where they are taxed. Recently promulgated regulations have sought to expand the taxation of stock dividends. *See* pp. 45-49 *supra.*

70 One author has written that he knows of a private ruling that so held. Katcher, *What is Meant by Earnings and Profits,* 18 N.Y.U.Tax Inst. 235, 236, n. 10 (1960). Zarky and Biblin, *The Role of Earnings and Profits in the Tax Law,* 18 U.S.C. Tax Inst. 145, 152 (1966) state that earnings and profits are reduced by the total amount of the premiums paid and are increased by the total annual increment in cash surrender value; they rely on a stipulation between the Service and a taxpayer permitting the reduction (Shellabarger Grain Products Co., 2 T.C. 75, 81 (1943)) and a ruling (Rev. Rul. 55-257, 1955-1 C.B. 428) that increments in cash surrender value may be added to accumulated earnings and profits for the purpose of computing equity invested capital under the excess profits tax provisions.

entire increase in value is taken into account or only the increase caused by the payment of such premiums. The rationale for this rule is that the portion of a premium payment which increases the policy's cash surrender value has not been expended by the corporation but has merely been exchanged for an asset of equal value.

(iv) *Accumulated earnings tax considerations.* Since the portion of the premium that is reflected in the policy's cash value is treated as an investment, if the corporation has a substantial equity in the policy, the presence of that equity and the failure to reduce earnings and profits by the full amount of the premium payments may cause the corporation's earnings and profits to accumulate beyond the reasonable needs of the business.[71] The corporation's defenses to an attempted imposition of the surtax for accumulations in anticipation of a stock redemption are equally applicable where life insurance is employed as the means of funding. Thus, the corporation must demonstrate that the stock redemption plan serves the needs of the business; or that the insurance protects the corporation from the loss of a key man; or possibly that because of the interplay of I.R.C. §§ 303 and 531, the accumulations reflected in the insurance policies are not for the proscribed purpose.

If the corporation were to use term life insurance[72] to fund the redemption plan, it would avoid accumulated earnings problems insofar as the insurance policy is concerned. Since term insurance policies have no cash surrender value, the full amount of the premiums paid reduces the corporation's earnings and profits; and consequently the corporation's purchase of term insurance will not contribute to its accumulations. However, in most circumstances term insurance will not solve the corporation's surtax problems. Term insurance is useful to

---

71 I.R.C. § 533(a) creates a presumption that the corporation possessed the proscribed purpose where earnings and profits are accumulated beyond reasonable business needs.

72 "Term life insurance" is pure risk insurance, *i.e.*, the owner purchases insurance against the risk that the insured will die during the period of coverage, and no part of the premiums constitutes an equity of investment. As the insured ages, the risk of his death in any period of coverage becomes greater and the insurance premium for $1,000 of coverage increases correspondingly.

provide a level amount of insurance for a short period of time or a declining amount of insurance for a longer period, but the cost of maintaining a level amount of term insurance for a substantial period of time normally will be prohibitive.[73] Where the corporation purchases declining term insurance,[74] the dollar amount of insurance proceeds payable on the insured's death will be reduced each year, but the corporation's dollar obligation under its stock redemption agreement will not usually decline, and, indeed, the purchase price of the stock will often increase if the corporation's business is successful. Therefore, it is customary to complement declining term insurance funding with an investment program which establishes a funded reserve, so that the value and amount of the investments will increase as the insurance declines. Of course, an investment reserve fund creates a risk that an accumulated earnings surtax will be imposed; and consequently, insofar as the surtax is concerned, term insurance does not offer any advantages over ordinary life insurance. Nevertheless, for reasons discussed hereafter, term insurance is often the best available funding method.

Receipt of the proceeds of a life insurance policy will increase the corporation's earnings and profits,[75] but there should be no surtax problems if the proceeds are paid out in redemption of the decedent's stock in the same taxable year. Even where the proceeds cannot be distributed that promptly, there should be no surtax problems in view of the corporation's contractual obligation to distribute the proceeds in redemption of the decedent's stock within a reasonably short period of time.[76] However, as noted below, there may be an adverse consequence in that after receiving the insurance pro-

---

73 For a defense of using pure term insurance for a substantial period of coverage, *see* Pawlick, HOW TO AVOID BEING OVERCHARGED BY YOUR LIFE INSURANCE SALESMAN (New Salem Press 1968).

74 "Declining term insurance" is term insurance where the annual premium payments remain level or nearly so and the amount of proceeds payable on the insured's death is reduced annually or at other stated periods. Thus, while the insurance premium "rate" increases, the coverage is reduced so that the amount of premium payable for the policy remains constant.

75 *See* pp. 207-208 *infra*.

76 *Cf.* Mountain State Steel Foundries, Inc. v. Commissioner, 284 F.2d 737 (C.A. 4 1960).

ceeds and redeeming the stock, the corporation could realize
a net increase in earnings and profits; but in most instances
this will not be a serious risk and will involve small amounts.

(v) *Income tax consequences of collecting the proceeds of the
life insurance.* The proceeds of life insurance are ordinarily
excluded from the gross income of the recipient.[77] An important exception to this exclusion is the so-called "transfer
for value" rule — *i.e.*, where a life insurance policy is transferred for consideration prior to maturity, the transferee will
recognize as gross income the excess of the proceeds of such
insurance over the consideration paid by the transferee plus
premiums subsequently paid by him.[78] However, there are several exceptions to the "transfer for value" rule, one of which
excludes from income insurance proceeds payable to a corporate transferee where the insured had been either a shareholder or an officer of the corporation.[79] Thus, where prior
to the death of an insured shareholder, the corporation purchased a policy from the insured for valuable consideration,[80]
the insurance proceeds received by the corporation on maturity will nevertheless be excluded from the corporation's
gross income. As noted subsequently, the "transfer for value"
rule may create difficulties for insurance funding of a cross-
purchase agreement, and therefore one of the advantages of
the entity purchase is the avoidance of that rule.

(vi) *Estate tax consequences.* Where a corporation is the
beneficiary of an insurance policy, the receipt of the proceeds
of that policy increases the net worth of the corporation,
and accordingly the value of the outstanding shares of the
corporation's stock is increased proportionately. Consequently,
unless there is a buy-out agreement which establishes a price
for the decedent's stock according to a formula or figure that
does not include the increment in value caused by the collection of the insurance proceeds, and unless the redemption

---

77 I.R.C. § 101(a)(1).
78 I.R.C. § 101(a)(2).
79 I.R.C. § 101(a)(2)(B). *See* note 197 *infra.*
80 The corporation might have purchased the policy from its shareholder because the shareholder was uninsurable at the time the redemption plan was adopted or simply because the annual premium
on an older policy is smaller.

price of the stock qualifies as determinative of the estate tax value of the stock,[81] the resulting increase in the value of the decedent's stock will be reflected in the stock's estate tax valuation.[82] Of course, if a buy-out agreement did fix the value of decedent's stock for estate tax purposes and the established value was determined exclusive of the insurance proceeds, the insurance will not be reflected in the value of decedent's stock. While apparently the Service has not yet raised the issue, it is arguable that where the price established in the buy-out agreement expressly excludes life insurance proceeds, the established price is not bona fide and therefore is not determinative. However, in most circumstances the exclusion of insurance proceeds should not render the redemption price unreasonable.

Where an insured died possessing incidents of ownership in a policy on his life, whether such incidents were exercisable alone or in conjunction with any other person, the full amount of the insurance proceeds are included in the insured's gross estate for estate tax purposes.[83] "Incidents of ownership" include *inter alia* the right to change the beneficiary of the policy, the right to borrow from the insurer against the cash surrender value of the policy, and the power to surrender or cancel the policy.[84] The Regulations provide that incidents of ownership possessed by an insured in a solely fiduciary capacity—*e.g.*, as a trustee—will nevertheless cause inclusion of the insurance proceeds in his estate even though the insured had no beneficial interest in the trust.[85] If a deceased

---

81 Treas. Reg. § 20.2031-2(h); and Rev. Rul. 59-60 (Sec. 8), 1959-1 C.B. 237, 243-244 state the position of the Government as to when the price established in the buy-out agreement is determinative of the stocks estate tax value. *See* pp. 184-185 *supra*.

82 Annie S. Kennedy *et al.*, Executors, 4 B.T.A. 330 (1926). *See also* Newell v. Commissioner, 66 F.2d 103 (C.A. 7 1933). Thus, in net effect, a portion of the insurance proceeds is reflected in decedent's gross estate for estate tax purposes.

83 I.R.C. § 2042(2).

84 Treas. Reg. § 20.2042-1(c)(2).

85 Treas. Reg. § 20.2042-1(c)(4). In Estate of Harry R. Fruehauf, 50 T.C. 915 (1968) (appeal pending), the majority of the Tax Court held that incidents of ownership held by an insured in a fiduciary capacity were sufficient to trigger § 2042 and thereby cause inclusion of the proceeds in the insured's estate. However, four Tax Court judges concurred with the result in *Fruehauf*, but stated that the rule of the case should be restricted to narrower grounds in con-

shareholder died possessing incidents of ownership in policies on his life held by the corporation, the full proceeds of those policies are included in his gross estate.[86] Where an insured shareholder is an officer or director of the corporation, it is arguable that in that capacity he, in conjunction with other officers or directors, possesses incidents of ownership (*e.g.*, the power to change beneficiaries or borrow against the policy). The possession of such powers, even where exercisable only with the consent of others, could cause the proceeds to be included in the decedent's gross estate.[87] The Regulations[88] provide that where a corporation is solely owned by one shareholder, the corporation's power to change the beneficiary of a policy on the shareholder's life is deemed an incident of ownership belonging to the shareholder. It is possible that this "attribution" of incidents of ownership may apply to shareholders who own less than 100% of the corporation,[89] particularly where they serve as an officer and director of the company. The author knows of no case that found incidents of ownership in an insured because of his position as a director or officer of the corporation which owns the policy, but there is a danger that the Service will raise this issue in future cases,[90] and therefore care should be taken that the insured is excluded from participating in any decisions concerning the insurance on his life, regardless of the capacity in which he would otherwise participate.

The insurance proceeds are also included in the insured's gross estate where the policy is payable to the insured's executor in that capacity.[91]

---

formity with the facts—*e.g.*, that the insured was not only the trustee of the insurance trust, but he was also an income beneficiary and his power to surrender the policies and to reinvest the proceeds could affect his income interest.

86 Estate of Grant H. Piggott, ¶ 63,061 P-H Memo T.C.; and Hall v. Wheeler, 174 F. Supp. 418 (D. Maine, 1959).

87 *See* Treas. Reg. § 20.2042-1(c)(2) and (4).

88 Treas. Reg. § 20.2042-1(c)(2). *See also* Cockrill v. O'Hara, 24 A.F.T.R.2d__ (M.D. Tenn. 1969).

89 The mention in the Regulations only of sole stockholders does raise a negative inference that the principle is limited to that class, but it is a very weak inference.

90 *Cf.* Estate of Bert L. Fuchs, 47 T.C. 199 (1966); and Landorf v. United States, 408 F.2d 461 (Ct. Cl. 1969).

91 I.R.C. § 2042(1).

Where the decedent's estate is obligated to apply the proceeds of life insurance held by the corporation against the redemption price of the decedent's stock, and where the decedent died possessing incidents of ownership in the life insurance, the insurance proceeds are nevertheless includible in decedent's gross estate; but in that event, to avoid double taxation, the value of the decedent's stock for estate tax purposes is reduced by the amount of insurance proceeds to be applied against the redemption price.[92] Where a buy-out agreement establishes the estate tax value of decedent's stock, and where insurance proceeds, which are included in the decedent's gross estate because of retained incidents of ownership, are not accounted for in that valuation,[93] the Service might well contend that there would not be a double inclusion if the full value of both the stock and the insurance proceeds were included in the decedent's gross estate and, accordingly, that both should be so included.

Also note that where a corporation uses life insurance proceeds to redeem a decedent's stock, but the corporation was not obligated to use them for that purpose, there is some danger that the estate tax value of the stock will not be reduced by the insurance proceeds, even where the latter is also included in the decedent's gross estate because of retained incidents of ownership. While that would constitute a double inclusion which the judiciary may well abhor, it would be prudent to avoid the risk.

(vii) *Effect of receipt of insurance proceeds on a corporation's earnings and profits.* The Service has ruled[94] that a corporation's earnings and profits are increased by the excess of life insurance proceeds received by it over the aggregate amount of premiums previously paid. Presumably, the ruling is ground-

---

92 *E.g.,* Estate of John T. H. Mitchell, 37 B.T.A. 1 (1938), Acq., 1938-1 C.B. 20; and Estate of Ray E. Tompkins, 13 T.C. 1054 (1949), Acq., 1950-1 C.B. 5. While *Mitchell* involved a cross-purchase agreement and *Tompkins* involved a cross-purchase of a partnership interest, the rationale of those cases is clearly applicable to the entity purchase as well.

93 The purpose of excluding the insurance proceeds in valuing the decedent's stock is to prevent an escalation of value where insurance is used in funding. See the discussion below.

94 Rev. Rul. 54-230, 1954-1 C.B. 114. *See also* Cummings v. Commissioner, 73 F.2d 477 (C.A. 1 1934).

ed on the premise that to the extent of premiums paid, the insurance proceeds are a return of the corporation's capital, and normally a return of capital does not affect earnings and profits. However, at the time of payment, a portion of the premiums did reduce earnings and profits;[95] and consequently the recapture of that portion of the premium payments should be restored to the corporation's earnings and profits. Moreover, the difference between an annual premium payment and the increment in cash surrender value caused by that payment is largely attributable to the pure insurance risk that the insured may die within that policy year,[96] and the consideration for that portion of the premium is consumed in the year for which the premium is paid (*i.e.*, one year's risk coverage), and in no sense is that portion of the premium returned to the corporation's capital by its collection of the proceeds. However, until the Service's ruling is revoked, a taxpayer is surely entitled to follow it.

(viii) *Effect of redemption of stock on the corporation's earnings and profits.* Where a redemption of stock constitutes a § 301 distribution (*i.e.*, the redemption is essentially equivalent to a dividend), the effect of the distribution on the corporation's earnings and profits is determined in the same manner as a distribution to a shareholder which is not in redemption of stock.[97] Where a redemption constitutes a purchase of a shareholder's stock under § 302(a), or a partial liquidation under § 331(a)(2), the distribution in redemption will reduce earning and profits to the extent that the distribution is not properly chargeable to capital account.[98] The cor-

---

95 *See* pp. 200-202 *supra.*
96 Part of the premium is attributable to costs (including commissions), but costs constitute a small portion of the premium, except for the first few annual payments.
97 The earnings and profits of the corporation are reduced by the amount of cash distributed plus the adjusted basis to the corporation of property distributed in kind. I.R.C. § 312(a). This reduction is subject to modification where property is transferred to the shareholders subject to liabilities or where the corporation recognizes gain on the distribution. I.R.C. § 312(c). *See* pp. 9-10 *supra.*
98 I.R.C. § 312(e). Note that a redemption may appear to qualify as a purchase under the auspices of an agreement filed pursuant to § 302(c) and may subsequently be treated as a dividend because the distributee acquired an interest in the corporation within the 10-year period. Query, whether the change in earnings and profits caused by the loss of § 302(c) treatment will be prospective from the date the distributee acquired the prohibited interest?

rect method for computing the amount of distribution which is properly chargeable to capital account is unsettled. A few of the unresolved questions are: (i) whether the corporation's capital account is to be determined by the fair market value of property and services given the corporation in payment for its stock, or is only the tax basis of the property given the corporation to be taken into account; (ii) what is the effect of the corporation's having several classes of stock with different rights; (iii) whether the amount of distribution which reduces earnings and profits is limited to the distributee's ratable share of the corporation's earnings and profits,[99] or instead is an amount equal to the difference between the amount received by the distributee and the distributee's ratable share of the corporation's capital account?[100]

> **Ex.** *A* and *B* formed the *X* Corporation and each contributed $10,000 cash for 100 shares of the stock of *X*. After 2 years of operation, *X* had accumulated earnings and profits of $15,000, and the fair market value of *X* was $50,000. *X* then redeemed *A*'s 100 shares of stock for $25,000. If the reduction in earnings and profits of *X* were limited to *A*'s ratable share of the earnings and profits, then the amount of reduction would be $7,500 (50% × $15,000). However, if the reduction in earnings and profits is determined by the difference between the amount distributed to *A* ($25,000) and *A*'s ratable share of the capital account (50% × $20,000 = $10,000), then the $15,000 earnings and profits would be reduced to zero.[101]

It is noteworthy that the amount of reduction in earnings and profits caused by a stock redemption will almost always be a different figure than the amount of increment to earnings and profits caused by the receipt of life insurance proceeds, since the two figures are derived from unrelated sources. Where the increment to earnings and profits from

---

99 *See* Woodward Investment Co., 46 B.T.A. 648 (1942), Acq., 1942-2 C.B. 20.
100 *See* Helvering v. Jarvis, 123 F.2d 742 (C.A. 4 1941). *Note* G.C.M. 23460, 1942-2 C.B. 190 in which the Service contends that *Woodward* and *Jarvis* are reconcilable.
101 *See* BITTKER AND EUSTICE, FEDERAL INCOME TAXATION OF CORPORATIONS AND SHAREHOLDERS, (2d ed., 1966), § 7.85, pp. 323-325.

the insurance exceeds the reduction caused by the redemption, a net effect of the entity purchase (*i.e.*, viewing the collection of the insurance and the redemption of the stock as a single integrated transaction) is to increase the corporation's earnings and profits.[102] However, a corporation is permitted to reduce its earnings and profits by a portion of the premiums paid for the insurance; and since the reduction to earnings and profits previously enjoyed by the corporation is not restored when the corporation collects the insurance proceeds,[103] the total impact on the corporation's earnings and profits usually will not be significant. Indeed, in some cases the total reduction to earnings and profits caused by the payment of premiums and the stock redemption may exceed the increment caused by receipt of the insurance proceeds, and the resulting net reduction is something of a windfall.

(ix) *Settlement options.* Where life insurance is used as a means of funding a stock purchase plan, the parties should consider the benefits of the several settlement options[104] permitted under the policy, *e.g.*, an interest only or deposit option,[105] a fixed period option,[106] a fixed amount option,[107] an

---

102 A net increase in earnings and profits could cause adverse tax consequences under the accumulated earnings tax provisions, or by characterizing subsequent corporate distributions to shareholders as dividends.

103 Rev. Rul. 54-230, 1954-1 C.B. 114.

104 See Dillon, *Settlement Options—Their Benefits and Limitations,* 57 ILL. BAR JOUR. 306 (Dec. 1968) for a helpful discussion of available options.

105 Under an "interest only" or deposit option, the insurance proceeds are left with the insurer and the beneficiary receives interest thereon at a guaranteed *minimum* rate. Customarily, but not inevitably, an interest only option will permit the beneficiary to withdraw all or part of the insurance proceeds on demand, and frequently the beneficiary has the right to elect other settlement options, although the latter right may be limited to a specific time period after the insured's death (usually one or two years).

106 Under a fixed period option, the insurance proceeds are paid out in installments over a fixed period of time. Since the policy provides a guaranteed *minimum* interest, the minimum amount of each payment is certain; and if the policy earns more than the minimum interest, the payment for that period is larger, but the number of payments is not increased.

107 In a fixed amount option, the amount of each periodic payment is fixed, and the minimum number of such payments is established according to the guaranteed minimum interest; and if the policy earns more than the minimum interest, the number of payments is increased, but the dollar amount of each payment is not affected.

annuity option,[108] a self and survivor annuity option,[109] a joint
and survivor annuity option,[110] an annuity option with refund
features,[111] an annuity option with guaranteed payments[112]
and combinations of the foregoing.[113] The minimum rate guaranteed by most policies written in the past two decades ranges
from 2 to $2\frac{1}{2}\%$, and some present policies guarantee as much
as 3%. However, at this time the actual interest paid by in-
surers is greater than the guaranteed minimum; most policies
are returning 4% to $4\frac{1}{2}\%$ interest.

Where the shareholder desires to elect one of the settlement
options available under the policy or wishes to permit such an
election to be made after his death, the insurance proceeds
can be made payable to a trustee; or in peculiar circumstances
the proceeds can be made payable directly to persons named
by the shareholder. In such event the insurance payment
must be conditioned on the surrender of the deceased shareholder's stock. Where the recipient of the insurance proceeds
is a trustee, there will usually be no difficulty in imposing

---

108 A straight annuity is a fixed dollar amount payable periodically for
the life of the beneficiary. A "variable" annuity is also paid for the
life of the beneficiary, but the dollar amount of the periodic payments will vary according to the success of the investments. Insurance
policies do not now offer *variable* annuities, but there are indications
that they may begin offering that option at some future date.

109 A self and survivor annuity refers to a fixed dollar amount payable
periodically to a beneficiary during his life followed by the periodic
payment of a fixed dollar amount (which may be a smaller amount
than that paid to the first beneficiary, but need not be) to a second
beneficiary during his life.

110 A joint and survivor annuity refers to a fixed dollar amount payable
periodically to two beneficiaries for their joint lives, and to the survivor of the two beneficiaries for his life. The phrase "joint and survivor annuity" is often used to describe an option that is actually a
"self and survivor annuity."

111 An annuity with a refund feature is an annuity which provides that
if the beneficiary dies before receiving a certain dollar amount, the
difference shall be paid to the beneficiary's estate or to a third party.

112 Where an annuity contains a provision for guaranteed payments, the
insurer guarantees that if the annuitant should die within a stated
period of time (*e.g.*, 5, 10 or 15 years), the insurer will continue
to make payments for the guaranteed period of the same amount
that would have been payable were the annuitant still living. These
guaranteed payments can be made payable to a contingent beneficiary. Of course, if the annuitant survives the guaranteed period,
the annuity payments will be made for the duration of his life.

113 These options do provide some flexibility. For example, it is possible
to have a fixed period option where a larger periodic payment is
made during the period of a child's minority and the payments are
reduced when the child attains his majority.

that condition, *i.e.*, the trust instrument will instruct the trustee not to distribute the proceeds to the insured's estate or legatees until the stock is surrendered; or the shareholder's stock may even be held by the trustee in escrow during the shareholders' lives.[114] Where a trustee is the beneficiary of the policy and the election of a settlement option is desired, it may be necessary to obtain the prior consent of the insurance company to the trustee's election of an option, since the terms of many insurance policies do not permit a fiduciary to receive proceeds under a settlement option. When requested, many insurance companies will amend the policy's provisions to permit such an election, and this amendment should be obtained before the shareholder's death. Also, the trust instrument should expressly authorize the trustee to utilize the settlement options.

Where the insurance proceeds are made payable to an individual beneficiary, in contrast to a trustee, and where the distribution to the individual beneficiary is conditioned on a surrender of the shareholder's stock, it would be prudent to incorporate that restriction in the designation of beneficiary. For example, the designation of beneficiary clause might read: "to *A* if he survives the insured and if the insurer receives written notice from the president of the *X* Corporation, a Delaware corporation, within one year after the insured's death that all of the insured's stock of *X* has been surrendered to *X*; and if *A* fails to survive the insured, or if the insurer does not receive such written notice from the president of *X* within one year after the insured's death, the proceeds shall be distributed to the *X* Corporation."

In most circumstances it will be preferable to name a trustee as beneficiary, but if the insurer will not permit a trustee

---

114 If the corporation has made an election under Subchapter S (§ 1371 *et seq.*), the trustee should not hold a shareholder's stock since that entails some risk that the Subchapter S election will be terminated. *See* Treas. Reg. § 1.1371-1(e); and § 1.1371-4(b)(3). *But see contra,* A & N Furniture & Appliance Co. v. United States, 19 A.F.T.R.2d 1487 (S.D. Ohio 1967). While one writer has suggested that stock may be held in escrow without violating the prohibition against trustees holding Subchapter S stock (Crumbley, *Buy and Sell Agreements for Subchapter S Corporations,* 108 TRUSTS AND ESTATES 17 (1969)), the *in terrorem* aspect of the risk of terminating an election will likely deter all but the bravest from using escrow arrangements.

to elect among the policy's settlement options, the arrangement suggested above may be employed if the insurer agrees to accept the restrictions on distribution.

While settlement options are useful in some circumstances, they are not always the most desirable alternative, and careful consideration should be given to other available choices. Depending upon the desired goals, a lump sum distribution of the insurance proceeds to a trustee either for immediate distribution to a named beneficiary or to be held in trust under the terms of a trust instrument will frequently be more beneficial. The choice between using a trust arrangement or a settlement option should rest on an evaluation of the parties' goals and the relative merits and disadvantages of each alternative in light of those goals.[115] Some sample considerations are:

Trust arrangements are far more flexible than settlement options; and if the trust assets are invested wisely, the trust should produce a much higher yield than that obtained from insurance options which provide a relatively low rate of return. The trust provides better protection against the present inflationary spiral; and where beneficiaries are minor children, the flexibility of distribution provided by a trust may be needed. However, the trust vehicle usually involves costs not associated with insurance—e.g., legal fees for creating the trust and trustee fees for administering it. If the proceeds are relatively small ($25,000 is frequently named as a rule-of-thumb amount of demarcation), the costs of the trust arrangement may outweigh its advantages. In this regard it should be noted that the fees of a professional fiduciary are determined by the size of the trust estate and the annual trust income, but there is usually a minimum fee charge which makes small trust funds uneconomical. However, trustee fees, and perhaps some of the legal fees incurred in creating the trust, will usually be deductible for income tax purposes under I.R.C. § 212; and in weighing costs, only the net expenses

---

115 For a slightly biased but nevertheless relevant discussion of the circumstances where settlement options may be useful, see Snitzer, *Investment Growth Through Settlement Options*, 108 TRUSTS AND ESTATES 204 (1969).

of the trust arrangement—*i.e.*, the fees less the tax savings enjoyed by deducting them—should be considered.

The insurance options provide greater security. There is virtually no risk of loss, and a recession in the economy will have less effect on insurance than on almost any other investment. There are no direct costs for managing the insurance proceeds, and where small amounts are involved, costs can be a substantial factor. Where the beneficiary of the insurance is the surviving spouse of the insured, there may be a small tax advantage to using insurance options—*i.e.*, if the proceeds are payable to the surviving spouse in installments over a period of years (*e.g.*, an annuity option), the interest portion of the installment payments to the spouse may be exempt from federal income tax; however, the exemption for interest is limited to $1,000 per year.[116] While this exemption is advantageous, particularly where the surviving spouse is in a high income tax bracket, its usefulness has been exaggerated by some commentators. For example, if the spouse is in a 30% income tax bracket, the maximum benefit of the exemption is $300 per year. There is no reason to scorn that amount, but its enjoyment does not warrant distorting an entire estate plan.

In some instances it might be desirable to split the insurance proceeds between a trusteed arrangement and payments under a settlement option. In that manner the beneficiary is provided with a hedge against inflation but retains a minimum floor of security.

Insurance companies are making considerable efforts to make settlement options more flexible; and as more insurance companies enter the mutual fund business, it is likely that in the not-too-distant future companies will offer variable annuities[117] (*i.e.*, the amount payable under the annuity

---

116 I.R.C. § 101(d).
117 One of the difficulties encountered by insurance companies who wish to adopt a variable annuity is that such plans will usually constitute a security and will therefore be subject to regulations and restrictions imposed by the federal government on the sale of securities, some of which restrictions may not be compatible with insurance goals. *See* S.E.C. v. Variable Annuity Co., 359 U.S. 65 (1959); and S.E.C. v. United Benefit Life Ins. Co., 387 U.S. 202 (1967).

each year varies with current market conditions). Consequently, the available options must be scrutinized carefully in each case, since favorable changes may have occurred since the last inquiry was made.

A word of warning where the widow of the deceased shareholder is the ultimate recipient of the insurance proceeds. If, in such case, a settlement option is selected prior to the shareholder's death, the method of settlement should be one that will qualify for the marital deduction allowance.[118] There will be no marital deduction allowed for insurance proceeds which are made payable in a manner which contravenes the terminable interest rule.[119] An important exception to this rule is that a terminable interest in the insurance proceeds will qualify for the marital deduction if the surviving spouse has the power to appoint the property to herself or to her estate and if the other conditions of I.R.C. § 2056(b)(6) are satisfied.[120]

An additional warning concerning the use of I.R.C. § 303 is warranted. While § 303 is not limited exclusively to redemptions of stock from the estate of a decedent,[121] according to the Regulations, it does not apply to redemptions of stock acquired from the decedent's estate in satisfaction of a specific pecuniary bequest.[122] Consequently, if the decedent's

---

118 I.R.C. § 2056. Where the insurance proceeds are paid to the widow in exchange for the decedent's stock, and where the redemption of the stock is mandatory, the property transferred from the decedent to the widow will likely be deemed the insurance proceeds rather than the stock, and the qualifications for deductibility will almost certainly be measured against those proceeds.

119 I.R.C. § 2056(b)(1) disallows a deduction for the transfer of property to a surviving spouse which will terminate on the lapse of time or on the occurrence or failure to occur of an event or contingency if by reason of such termination, an interest in the property will pass to a third party who received his interest in the property from the decedent for less than full and adequate consideration in money or money's worth. Thus, insurance proceeds payable to the widow under a joint and survivor annuity option with the widow and her daughter as beneficiaries will not qualify; and an annuity with a refund feature will not qualify unless the provisions of § 2056(b)(6) are satisfied, or unless the refund is payable to the estate of the surviving spouse.

120 The conditions of I.R.C. § 2056(b)(6) are discussed in Treas. Reg. § 20.2056(b)-6.

121 Treas. Reg. § 1.303-2(f).

122 Treas. Reg. § 1.303-2(f). The validity of this Regulation has been questioned. Meyer, *Redemption of Stock in the Close Corporation to*

stock is to be distributed to his widow or to a marital trust, in satisfaction of a pecuniary bequest, including a bequest defined in terms of a marital deduction pecuniary formula, and if a redemption under § 303 is contemplated, the stock should be redeemed from the decedent's estate and then the proceeds of redemption can be distributed to the widow or marital trust.

(x) *Merits and disadvantages of insurance funding.* Where life insurance is acquired by a corporation to fund a stock purchase agreement, the receipt of the proceeds of the insurance will increase the value of the deceased shareholder's stock proportionately; and if the stock is to be redeemed at fair market value, the corporation will need sufficient liquid assets to cover the increment in value caused by the insurance. Of course, the corporation could acquire additional insurance to fund that obligation, but such additional insurance would further raise the value of the decedent's stock, and thus the corporation's dollar obligation will pyramid upward.

> **Ex. (1)** The outstanding shares of the *X* Corporation were owned equally by *A* and *B*. *X* had a net worth of $400,000; and consequently the value of each shareholder's stock was $200,000. *X* purchased life insurance in the amount of $200,000 on *A* and a like amount on *B*, in order to fund a stock redemption plan. *X* was the beneficiary of the policies. *A* died shortly after the insurance was acquired. After *A*'s death the net worth of *X* was $600,000; and the value of each shareholder's stock was $300,000. Consequently, *X* needed $100,000 liquid assets in addition to the insurance proceeds to redeem *A*'s stock. If, in anticipation of that obligation, *X* had purchased an additional $100,000 insurance on *A*'s life, its net worth on *A*'s death would be $700,000; and the value of *A*'s stock would then be $350,000. The corporation could have funded its additional $50,000 obligation by purchasing life insurance in that amount, but that would raise its obligation to *A* another $25,000. Obviously, this arrangement is self-defeating, and the principal beneficiaries are the insurance company and its agents.

Pay Death Taxes, 27 N.Y.U. TAX INST. 401, 403-405 (1969). *Cf.* United States v. Lake, 406 F.2d 941 (C.A. 5 1969) which construed the Regulation narrowly.

The escalation of insurance coverage can be finessed by establishing a price for the shareholder's stock in a stock redemption agreement in such manner that the insurance proceeds are omitted from the valuation formula. Of course, the agreement should be so designed that the redemption price will fix the value of the stock for estate tax purposes,[123] and the deceased shareholder must not possess any incidents of ownership in the policy at his death.[124] The principal failing in this arrangement is that the deceased shareholder will not receive payment for the true value of his stock, and consequently the transaction favors the surviving shareholders.

> **Ex. (2)** The X Corporation had two equal shareholders, A and B. The corporation and the shareholders executed a stock redemption agreement under which X agreed to redeem the stock of the first shareholder to die at a price equal to 50% of the net worth of the corporation exclusive of insurance proceeds. X acquired insurance of $200,-000 on the life of A and a like amount on B. When A died, the net worth of the corporation exclusive of insurance proceeds was $400,000, and consequently X redeemed A's shares for $200,000. However, the actual worth of the corporation was $600,000, and A was shortchanged $100,000.

The exclusion of the insurance proceeds from the redemption price may be somewhat justifiable where A dies shortly after the insurance is purchased, since in that event the proceeds are a product of A's death rather than the corporate earnings. But even there it might be questioned why B should derive a windfall from the death of his fellow shareholder. If ordinary life insurance is used and if A's death occurs many years after the insurance is purchased, a significant portion of the insurance proceeds payable on A's death represents the corporation's equity in the policy, which equity was derived from premiums paid from corporate earnings; and a redemption agreement's forfeiture of A's interest in that equity is harsh. This can be resolved by limiting the exclusion of insurance proceeds from the purchase price to the excess of the

---

123 *See* pp. 184-186 *supra.*
124 I.R.C. § 2042. *See* pp. 205-207 *supra.*

proceeds over the cash surrender value of the policy.

This is not to say that a deceased shareholder derives no benefit from a plan of this kind, or that such a plan should not be adopted. The decedent's estate does obtain a market for liquidating the stock promptly. However, the primary advantage of the arrangement is that it permits a surviving shareholder to continue a business which otherwise would have to be liquidated. It might be suggested that few investors are so unselfishly devoted to the continuity of their business that they would wish to forfeit large sums in furtherance of that end. But, at the time that the redemption agreement is executed, the identity of the surviving shareholder is a mystery; and where the forfeiture of a significant sum by the first to die is necessary to the continuance of the business, the parties may wish to gamble on that question. It should be made clear to the parties that they are gambling and that the first to die is a financial loser and that the survivor takes home the kitty. The gamble is often desirable from a business viewpoint, but the parties should make their agreement with open eyes and not delude themselves with a myth that a deceased shareholder will be paid the full value of his stock.

Of course, the liquidation value of a business will usually be substantially less than its value as a going concern, and consequently, in some cases, the amount paid to a deceased shareholder's estate may reflect in part the loss that would be suffered if the business were liquidated.

An important decision to be made with respect to insurance funding is the selection of the kind of insurance. In the author's view, the choice[125] will usually lie between ordinary life and declining term insurance. Ordinary life insurance comprises two separate property interests: one is a reserve (or equity) in the policy which reflects the policyholder's in-

---

125 Occasionally, group term life insurance may be used for funding. *See* Walker, *Life Insurance From the Standpoint of the Federal Corporate and Personal Income Tax, Gift Tax and Estate Tax,* 18 U.S.C. Tax Inst. 543, 588-593 (1966). For a recent statement of the Service's position on the effectiveness of an assignment of group term life insurance for estate tax purposes, *see* Rev. Rul. 69-54, 1969-6 I.R.B. p. 20. *See also* Landorf v. United States, 408 F.2d 461 (Ct. Cl. 1969).

vestment plus interest earned thereon, and the second is pure risk coverage, *i.e.*, the risk that the insured will die during the policy period. As the equity grows larger over the years, the amount of insurance risk (the difference between the face value of the policy and the equity therein) declines.

Declining term[126] is pure insurance; the policyholder has no equity in the policy. The amount of insurance coverage under declining term is reduced periodically. Thus, if liquid assets are to be available when a shareholder dies, it is necessary to complement declining term with a periodic investment program; the amount invested periodically could, for example, be the difference between an ordinary life premium and a declining term premium.

It is noteworthy that there are sophisticated plans for purchasing what amounts to declining term life insurance at a smaller cost than that charged for the outright purchase of such a policy. The most common technique is to purchase ordinary life insurance and each year to "borrow" from the insurer an amount equal to the policy's cash surrender value and to use the "borrowed" funds as partial payment for the policy's premium plus the interest accrued on prior loans. This type of insurance plan is frequently referred to as "minimum deposit insurance." Since the amount loaned will increase each year and since the owner maintains little equity in the policy, and since the insurer will collect the loans from the insurance proceeds on maturity, the net effect of the minimum deposit insurance plan is to acquire a declining term policy—*i.e.*, the amount payable to the insured's beneficiary decreases each year when an additional loan is made. Minimum deposit insurance is used primarily by persons in high income tax brackets. The cash surrender value (a rough estimate of the owner's equity in the policy) increases each year, but the rate of increase will be lower than the rate of interest payable on funds borrowed from the insurance company by the owner—*e.g.*, the rate of increase may be 2.5% and the loan may bear interest at 5%. Thus, the owner pays a greater

---

126 For definitions of "term insurance" and "declining term insurance," *see* notes 72 and 74 *supra*.

amount of interest on his loans than he earns on his investment in the policy made with those borrowed funds. However, the increments in cash value of the policy do not constitute taxable income to the owner,[127] nor will they be taxed to the beneficiaries of the policy on maturity.[128] If the owner is permitted to take an income tax deduction for his interest payments, the net cost of the loans may be less than the increments in the policy's value. I.R.C. § 264 prohibits the deduction of interest paid on loans incurred pursuant to a systematic borrowing plan for the purchase of life insurance, endowment or annuity contracts unless one of several explicit exceptions is applicable. The most useful exception permits deduction of the interest if no part of any four of the annual premiums due during the first seven years of the policy is paid with borrowed funds. To use this exception, not only must those four-years' premiums be paid by the policy owner, but also the amount of loans made to the policy owner in subsequent years must not exceed the amount of premiums paid to the insurer for years subsequent to those said four years.[129] Thus, in effect, the premiums paid for those four years must be left with the insurer and not withdrawn as loans at some subsequent date, particularly not within the first seven-year period of the policy.

If a corporation (or an individual) owns a policy insuring a shareholder's life and desires to purchase additional life insurance coverage through a minimum deposit insurance plan, it may exchange its existing policy for a new policy of a greater principal sum, and its reserve in the existing policy will constitute premium payments for the new policy. Any unpaid balance of the premiums due for the first four years of the new policy can be paid in cash. Since I.R.C. § 1035 will usually preclude the recognition of any income realized on such exchanges, this arrangement can be a relatively painless means of acquiring minimum deposit insurance coverage while complying with the requisites of § 264 for the deduction of interest on subsequent loans borrowed against the policy's reserve value.

---

127 Theodore H. Cohen, 39 T.C. 1055 (1963).
128 I.R.C. § 101.
129 Treas. Reg. § 1.264-4(d)(1).

The minimum deposit insurance plan can be advantageous even where no interest deduction is allowed. Where a policy owner has a liquidity shortage, systematic borrowing permits him to maintain a high level of insurance coverage; and when his liquidity problems are resolved, he can pay subsequent premiums outright and perhaps repay the outstanding loans.

While the cost of declining term may be slightly higher than the pure insurance cost factor in ordinary life, the primary basis for choosing between the two kinds of insurance is the policyholder's evaluation of the comparative merits of an investment in an insurance policy as contrasted to investments in other markets.[130]

Insurance provides security of both income and capital, but the rate of return is small. However, as previously noted, the interest earned on equity in an insurance policy, reflected in increments in cash surrender value, is not included in the policyholder's gross income for income tax purposes.[131] This income tax exclusion may be an important consideration in selecting an investment.

On the other hand, investments in stocks, securities or real estate may yield a substantially greater return than insurance provides, and the appreciation of those assets will not be taxed until the corporation disposes of them. Moreover, a funded reserve may be utilized by the corporation in furtherance of its business interests. For example, the corporation might use the funded reserve to construct a building which the corporation would occupy; and on the death of a shareholder, the building could be sold or distributed in kind to the decedent's estate as part of the redemption price.

---

130 For an unabashed polemic against the use of ordinary life insurance rather than term insurance, *see* PAWLICK, HOW TO AVOID BEING OVERCHARGED BY YOUR LIFE INSURANCE SALESMAN (New Salem Press 1968).

131 Theodore H. Cohen, 39 T.C. 1055 (1963); and Abram Nesbitt, 2d, 43 T.C. 629 (1965). Dividends received by a policyholder from a mutual insurance company constitute a partial refund of the premium paid by the policyholder and therefore are excluded from the policyholder's gross income. *See* I.R.C. § 316(b)(1); and S.M. 5680, V-1 C.B. 32 (1926). However, interest earned on dividends received from a mutual insurance policy, where the policyholder left the dividends with the insurer to earn interest, is included in the policyholder's gross income. Theodore H. Cohen, *supra*.

(c) Establishing the redemption price. There are a variety of means available to fix the redemption price of stock under a buy-sell agreement.[132] The parties could agree on a dollar figure, and that is frequently done. However, provision should be made for periodic review of that figure by requiring the parties to set a new figure every one or two years,[133] and if they fail to set a figure within one or two years prior to a shareholder's death, the figure set by the parties is unreliable and should be disregarded,[134] and an alternative method of pricing should then be made applicable. Other methods which might be employed, but by no means an exclusive list, are: a capitalization of earnings[135] formula; book value; an appraisal of the corporation's tangible assets by a selected appraiser or members of a selected group of appraisers;[136] a provision for arbitration; and a weighted combination of two or more of these alternatives.

There is considerable literature on the subject of valuation, and the reader may well locate writings discussing the appropriate methods of valuing the very kind of business in which his corporation is engaged.

Where the shareholders are members of the same family unit, they should resist the temptation to establish a low value for a deceased shareholder's stock; and for reasons previously stated, they should attempt to make a realistic valuation. Moreover, a low valuation may deprive the shareholder's estate of the use of I.R.C. § 303 where the established value of decedent's stock is less than

---

132 Corneel, *Valuation Techniques in Buy-Sell Agreements: Effect on Gift and Estate Taxes,* 24 N.Y.U. TAX INST. 631 (1966).

133 The stock redemption agreement should include a page for inserting the established figure, the signatures of the parties and the date of execution of that page.

134 The agreement should state that the figure is effective only if established within a given period prior to the shareholder's death.

135 The capitalization rate should be agreed upon by the parties and stated in the agreement. The rate may be determined by considering the price earnings ratio of comparable companies whose stock is sold on the open market and therefore easily valued. The annual earnings to be capitalized may be determined under a formula where appropriate. For example, if the corporation's earnings are erratic, the parties may wish to average the last five years' earnings and capitalize that amount; or in some circumstances they may wish to average the three years of the last five that had the highest (or the lowest) earnings.

136 An appraisal of assets may be appropriate where the corporation is a real estate holding company.

both 35% of the decedent's gross estate and 50% of his taxable estate.[137]

(d) Payment of redemption price with the corporation's promissory notes.
Where the corporation lacks sufficient liquid assets to redeem a shareholder's stock within a few years after his death, the corporation can use its own personal notes as partial or full payment for the redeemed stock. Where such notes are given within the time period permitted under I.R.C. § 303, the tax relief accorded by that section is available, even though the payments on the note will extend beyond the statutory period.[138] However, care should be taken that the corporation's notes do not constitute an equity interest in the corporation. If the notes are treated as hybrid stock, the "interest" paid on the notes cannot be deducted by the corporation on its income tax returns, and the payments made on those notes will be treated as a redemption of stock which may well cause ordinary dividend income to the recipient. Section 303 is not applicable to corporate distributions made after the statutory period.[139] Thus, if the notes represent equity interests in the corporation, payments made on the notes after the statutory period will not lie within the protective umbrella of § 303.

The normal precautions in avoiding the characterization of notes as equity interests are: the debt-capital ratio should not be overbalanced in favor of debt; the maturity dates of the notes should not be far removed from the date of issue,[140] preferably no more than five years if that is feasible;[141] the notes should not be subordi-

---

137 *See* note 7 *supra*.
138 Rev. Rul. 65-289, 1965-2 C.B. 86; and Rev. Rul. 67-425, 1967-2 C.B. 134.
139 The statutory period referred to above extends approximately 4½ years after the deceased shareholder's death, but the period may be extended if an estate tax deficiency is litigated in a Tax Court proceeding. I.R.C. § 303(b)(1).
140 The Service has announced that it will not issue rulings on the applicability of § 302(b) to a redemption where the corporation makes payment in its notes which are to be paid over "a long future period." Rev. Proc. 64-31 (Sec. 3.01-5(b)), 1962-2 C.B. 947, 949. Presumably, that announcement will also apply to section 303 redemptions.
141 If it is necessary, and the parties are willing to undertake the risk, the notes can be made payable for a longer period of time. In one instance, a seventeen-year payment was approved. BULLETIN OF THE SECTION OF TAXATION (ABA), p. 134 (Fall, 1967). However, subsequent to that date, the Service has announced that *ordinarily* it will not rule on the tax effect of a stock redemption when payment is made in notes which are payable over a period in excess of fifteen years. Rev. Proc. 69-6 (Sec. 4.01-3), I.R.B. 1969-1, p. 31.

nated to the claims of creditors; and the notes should bear a reasonable rate of interest. Of course, business considerations may not permit the parties to take all of those precautions.

The use of promissory notes to redeem stock can be helpful whether or not § 303 is applicable. For example, the corporation may issue its notes in redemption of all of a shareholder's stock, and if there are no attribution problems and the corporate notes are not treated as hybrid stock, the redemption should qualify under I.R.C. § 302(b)(3). Even where there are stock attribution problems because of stock owned by the members of the shareholder's family, the family attribution rule can be avoided in some circumstances by utilizing the relief afforded by I.R.C. § 302(c). In any event, irrespective of whether § 303 is applicable, where the corporation purchases stock with its own notes, the parties must determine the interest rate for the notes and what security should be provided. In addition to the obvious business reasons for doing so, unsecured corporate notes, bearing little or no interest, are more susceptible to being characterized as hybrid stock than are secured interest bearing notes.

(i) *Imputed interest.* For federal income tax purposes, if the notes of the corporation do not bear interest of at least 4%,[142] interest will be imputed at a 5% rate.[143]

(ii) *Security of payment.* Where payment is made by distribution of a corporate note or other evidence of obligation, the deceased shareholder's estate or legatees are subject to the risk of collection. The net asset value of the corporation may be of such magnitude as to render the risk inconsequential; or the risk may have to be undertaken because no other means of payment is feasible. In any event, if the distributees of the note desire security, it would be preferable for the corporation to secure the note with assets other than the redeemed stock, since a pledge of the redeemed stock may prevent the transfer

---

142 Treas. Reg. § 1.483-1(d)(2).
143 I.R.C. § 483; and Treas. Reg. § 1.483-1(c)(2). While a redemption does not constitute an *actual* sale or exchange, § 483 applies to transactions that are "treated as a sale or exchange for purposes of the Code." Treas. Reg. § 1.483-1(c)(2).

    If the note is payable within one year after redemption, § 483 is not applicable (I.R.C. § 483(c)(1)(B)), but few notes will be payable in such a brief period.

of the corporation's note from qualifying as a payment,[144] *i.e.*, the transaction may not be deemed closed when the stock is surrendered because there is a possibility that the shareholder will reacquire it on default. Whether or not that contention is sound, the Service's refusal to rule on the question justifies the avoidance of this arrangement, if it is feasible to do so. If the transaction is not deemed closed when the note is issued, payments made after the statutory period will not come within § 303 and the shareholder's interest in the pledged stock may render inoperative the exclusions contained in § 302(b) to dividend treatment on redemption. Moreover, a pledge of the redeemed stock is not a valuable security device. If the corporation is unable to pay its debts, the defaulted stock is not likely to be of greater value than the defaulted notes. An additional consideration is that if the pledge of the stock constitutes a secured transaction within the coverage of Article 9 of the Uniform Commercial Code, the secured party *may* be required to hold a public sale of the stock in order to foreclose on his lien; and where such a public offering is required, it may be necessary to comply with federal and state security regulations which can be costly. *See* Mitchell, *Corporate Buy-Sell Agreements and the Uniform Commercial Code*, 46 MICH. ST. B.J. (May, 1967), p. 12.

The selling shareholder may desire security for tax reasons as well as for financial protection, *i.e.*, a secured note is less likely to be characterized as an equity interest in the corporation.

One means of insuring payment is to have the corporation's notes personally guaranteed by the surviving shareholders. The corporation's subsequent payments on the notes will not constitute constructive income to the surviving shareholders, even though it reduces their potential secondary liability, since the corporation is the primary obligor, and the shareholders

---

144 Rev. Proc. 69-6 (Sec. 3.01-5), I.R.B. 1969-1, p. 29, states that the Service will not rule on whether a redemption qualifies under § 302(b) where the redeemed stock is held as security, or in escrow, for the payment of corporate notes, if there is a possibility that the stock may be returned to the shareholder on default.

For a discussion of this issue, *see* Sexton, *Providing Security for the Outgoing Stockholder and Avoiding Tax Disadvantages to Selling and Remaining Stockholders*, 24 N.Y.U. TAX INST. 555 (1966).

are merely incidental beneficiaries of the corporation's satisfaction of its debts.[145] However, if the corporation's capacity to satisfy the obligations is extremely doubtful, the corporation's liability may be deemed a sham, and the payments made by the corporation may constitute dividend income to the shareholder-guarantors.

(iii) *Limitations on corporation's payment of its notes.* The financial and equitable limitations on a corporation's redemption of its own stock are discussed in Paragraph (f) below. A common financial limitation on redemptions is that the corporation's payments must be made from its surplus.[146] The question whether the corporation must satisfy the applicable financial requirements when it distributes its promissory note or when it makes payment on the note or at both times is unsettled.[147] Under one view the financial limitations are applicable only when the corporation makes payment on its note and only to the extent of such payments, since the mere transfer of a corporate note does not prejudice the corporation's creditors or other stockholders.[148] Under that approach, the transferee of the note must accept the risk that financial restrictions will prohibit the corporation from making payment thereon. An alternative view would treat the transaction as closed when the note is given. Unless the issue is settled in the controlling jurisdiction, the planner should attempt to provide for the corporation's compliance with the financial requisites at all relevant dates.

(e) Income tax consequences to holders of the decedent's stock. A potential tax problem on the redemption of stock is whether the redemption will be deemed essentially equivalent to a dividend and taxed accordingly. The applicable principles in this area are

---

145 *See* Murphy Logging Co. v. United States, 378 F.2d 222 (C.A. 9 1967); Arthur J. Kobacker, 37 T.C. 882, 895 (1962), Acq., 1964-2 C.B. 6; Princess Coals, Inc. v. United States, 239 F. Supp. 401, 411-412 (S.D. W. Va. 1965); Rev. Rul. 59-286, 1959-2 C.B. 103.
146 The definition of "surplus" is not uniform among the several states. It may refer to earned surplus or to both earned and capital surplus or to any surplus, depending upon state law.
147 *See* BULLETIN OF THE SECTION OF TAXATION (ABA), p. 134 (Fall, 1967).
148 *See, e.g.,* Mountain State Steel Foundries, Inc. v. Commissioner, 284 F.2d 737 (C.A. 4 1960).

highly technical, and caution should be observed; but guideposts have been established, and if he plots carefully, the planner can steer a safe course in avoidance of dividend treatment.[149]

A revocable trust can be employed in some instances to avoid the operation of attribution rules.

> **Ex.** *A* owns 50 shares of the outstanding stock of the *X* Corporation, and *A*'s brother, *B*, owns the remaining 50 shares. *A* wishes to make a testamentary bequest to *B* and to leave his residuary estate to his wife, *W.* Upon *A*'s death, if the *X* Corporation redeems his 50 shares of stock from *A*'s estate, the redemption will not be deemed substantially disproportionate or a termination of interest because *A*'s estate will have attributed to it the 50 shares of stock owned by *B* who is a beneficiary of the estate.[150]

Proper tax planning prior to *A*'s death could prevent difficulties on redemption. One possible plan would be to eliminate mention of *B* from *A*'s will and to utilize an inter vivos revocable trust as a vehicle for transferring *B*'s interest to him. Alternatively, *A*'s stock in *X* could be placed in a revocable trust[151] which is insulated from attribution of *B*'s stock, since *B* will not be a beneficiary of the trust.

---

149 *See* note 5-7 *supra.*
150 It is theoretically possible to avoid attribution in the above example by first distributing *B*'s bequest to him, and then subsequently effecting the redemption of the stock, since in that event *B* will not be a beneficiary of the estate at the time of redemption if certain conditions are satisfied. Treas. Reg. § 1.318-3(a). One of the conditions is that there must be no more than a remote possibility that the estate will seek contribution from the beneficiary for payment of claims against the estate or expenses of administration. This is a dangerous planning device, and the author does not recommend it. *See, e.g.,* Estate of Webber v. United States, 263 F. Supp. 703 (E.D. Ky. 1967), *affirmed* 404 F.2d 411 (C.A. 6 1968), for an indication of the seriousness of that danger. In *Webber,* the beneficiary of several specific bequests had received distribution of all his bequests prior to a stock redemption but was nevertheless deemed a beneficiary of the estate at the date of redemption because there was a possibility that he would have to contribute to the estate or to other beneficiaries a pro rata portion of the estate's tax liabilities.
    A residuary legatee of an estate does not cease to be a beneficiary until the estate is closed. Rev. Rul. 60-18, 1960-1 C.B. 145.
151 This second alternative should not be employed if the *X* Corporation has made an election under Subchapter S, since the transfer to the revocable trust may terminate the election. Treas. Reg. §§ 1.1371-1(e) and 1.1372-4(b)(3).

Where the stock is included in the deceased shareholder's gross estate, the dividend question can be avoided to the extent that § 303 is applicable. It does not matter for purposes of § 303 whether the decedent's stock was held in a revocable trust at the decedent's death so long as the stock is included in the decedent's gross estate.

Where the redeemed stock was included in the decedent's gross estate and the dividend problem is solved (by § 303,or by § 302 (b), or even by §§ 331 (a)(2) and § 346), there will usually be no tax consequence on the redemption. Under I.R.C. § 1014, the basis of the stock is equal to its fair market value at decedent's death[152] so there will likely be no gain realized on the redemption of the stock. If the stock included in the decedent's estate were section 306 stock,[153] it loses that taint on the decedent's death.[154] Thus, there should be no problem with § 306 unless there is a corporate reorganization or stock dividend paid after the decedent's death and before the redemption, and the newly issued stock constitutes section 306 stock. A redemption of the newly issued section 306 stock will not have adverse tax consequences if the redemption qualifies under § 303.[155]

(f) Corporate law considerations in an entity buy-out plan. The corporate laws dealing with the transfer and redemption of stock differ from state to state. Several of the underlying considerations which are uniformly applicable are discussed below, but the preparation of a specific entity buy-out plan must include a careful examination of the corporate laws of the appropriate jurisdiction.

(i) *Restrictions on transfer of stock.* As previously noted, one purpose of a mandatory buy-out is to prevent a decedent's stock from falling into the hands of persons who will disrupt managerial harmony.[156] For that reason, where a mandatory

---

152 Unless the estate elects the alternate valuation date (I.R.C. § 2032), in which event the date on which the stock is valued for estate tax purposes controls. I.R.C. § 1014(a). As used in § 1014, the phrase "fair market value" refers to the value determined under the estate tax laws (Treas. Reg. § 1.1014-1(a)), and in most cases, the estate tax value will equal the purchase price of the stock.
153 *See* pp. 51-58 *supra.*
154 I.R.C. § 306(c).
155 Treas. Reg. § 1.303-2(d) provides that § 303 takes precedence over § 306.
156 A mandatory buy-out agreement constitutes a restraint on transfer after the death of the shareholder.

buy-out is contemplated, restrictions should be imposed on a shareholder's transfer of his stock during his life.[157] Moreover, a buy-out agreement will not establish a value of the decedent's stock for estate tax purposes unless there are adequate restrictions on the shareholder's right to sell the stock during his life.[158] The most popular form of restriction on lifetime transfers is to grant the corporation a right of first refusal.

The extent to which restrictions can be imposed upon the transfer of stock depends upon local law. Generally, an absolute restraint on alienation, unlimited in time, is invalid,[159] but reasonable restraints on transfers have been sustained.[160] A right of first refusal will usually constitute a reasonable restraint.[161] Mandatory stock purchase agreements to be implemented on death will likely be valid in all jurisdictions today.[162] While a 1928 New York Court of Appeals decision[163] (the *Topken* case) held a stock purchase agreement to be invalid as lacking mutuality because the corporation might not have sufficient surplus to make the purchase when the time came to acquire the stock, it is highly unlikely under present law that a court, in New York or in any other jurisdiction, would hold a stock redemption agreement invalid for that reason.[164] Indeed, the remote possibility that

---

157 These restrictions may take many forms; *e.g.,* absolute prohibition against a transfer; requirement of obtaining prior consent to transfer from other shareholders or directors or a percentage of them; "first-option" provisions granting the corporation or its directors or shareholders a right of first refusal to purchase stock a shareholder wishes to sell. O'NEAL, 2 CLOSE CORPORATIONS § 7.05 (1958) provides a list of types of restrictions that have been imposed.

158 *See* note 14 *supra.*

159 O'Neal, *Restrictions on Transfer of Stock in Closely Held Corporations: Planning and Drafting,* 65 HARV. L. REV. 773, 777-778 (1952).

160 FLETCHER, CYCLOPEDIA CORPORATIONS § 5453 (1957 Rev. Ed.); and BALLANTINE ON CORPORATIONS § 336 (1946 ed.).

161 O'NEAL, 2 CLOSE CORPORATIONS § 7.09 (1958).

162 O'NEAL, 2 CLOSE CORPORATIONS § 7.10 (1958). If the provisions of the agreement are too severe, *e.g.,* where the buy-out price is extremely low, there is a risk that the agreement will be invalid (Greene v. E. H. Rollins & Sons, Inc., 22 Del. Ch. 394, 2 A.2d 249 (1938)), but otherwise there is little danger of invalidity. This is an additional reason for establishing a reasonable price for the stock.

163 Topken, Loring & Schwartz, Inc. v. Schwartz, 249 N.Y. 206, 163 N.E. 735 (1928).

164 O'NEAL, 2 CLOSE CORPORATIONS § 7.10 (1958). *See* Greater New York Carpet House, Inc. v. Herschmann, 258 App. Div. 649, 17 N.Y.S.2d

Topken might have a continuing influence on New York corporate law was terminated by statutory enactment.[165]

The extent to which restrictions on stock transfers are valid depends in part upon the means by which they are imposed. The restrictions on transfer should be included in the *articles of incorporation*, and should also be included in a separate contractual agreement among the corporation and the shareholders.[166] As an alternative in some states, the provision might be included in the bylaws.[167] In any event, under both the Uniform Stock Transfer Act and the Uniform Commercial Code, the restriction must be stated on the face of the share certificates.[168]

A restriction against all inter vivos transfers could prevent the shareholders from donating part of their stockholdings to members of their family for estate planning purposes. It may be desirable to exempt gifts to a limited class of close family members (*e.g.*, spouse, children and grandchildren) provided that the restrictions on stock transfers are also made applicable to the donee and that the transferred stock is subject to a mandatory redemption at the donor's death.[169]

---

483 (1940) enforcing a stock purchase agreement and distinguishing *Topken* on the ground that the corporation's purchase of life insurance policies to fund the agreement constituted sufficient consideration.

The *Topken* decision has been expressly repudiated by several courts; *e.g.*, Cutter Laboratories, Inc. v. Twining, 221 C.A.2d 202, 313-314, 34 Cal. Rptr. 317 (1963).

165 Section 514(b) of the NEW YORK BUSINESS CORPORATION LAW, adopted in 1961 (effective September 1, 1963).

166 FLETCHER, CYCLOPEDIA CORPORATIONS § 5453 (1957). O'NEAL, 2 CLOSE CORPORATIONS § 7.14 (1958) provides an excellent discussion of the advantages of including the restrictive provision in both the charter and a shareholder agreement.

167 The placing of a restrictive provision in the bylaws is sufficient in some states (O'NEAL, 2 CLOSE CORPORATIONS § 7.07 (1958)), but it is safer to use the articles of incorporation.

168 UNIFORM STOCK TRANSFER ACT, § 15; UNIFORM COMMERCIAL CODE, § 8-204. *See* O'NEAL, 2 CLOSE CORPORATIONS § 7.16 (1958) for a discussion of the amount of information concerning the restriction which must be noted on the certificate. O'Neal states (p. 26, note 78) that in Michigan, the restrictions imposed on *all* classes of stock must be stated on each share certificate, irrespective of which class of stock it represents.

169 This exemption should not affect the estate tax valuation of the stock, since neither the shareholder nor the donee can dispose of the stock for a greater price than that which is payable on the shareholder's death. *Cf.* Lomb v. Sugden, 82 F.2d 166 (C.A. 2 1936).

(ii) *Limitations on a corporation's power to purchase its own stock.* With a few exceptions, the American jurisdictions rejected the English rule[170] that a corporation cannot purchase its own shares.[171] Most states, including some whose courts had accepted the English rule, have adopted statutes expressly permitting a corporation to do so.[172] A leading commentator on corporate law states that probably no jurisdiction in America would hold that a corporation lacked the power *per se* to purchase its own stock.[173] Nevertheless, it may be prudent to include in the corporation's charter a grant of the power to purchase its own stock.

In at least one state (California), the parties may be required to obtain a permit from the appropriate state official to (i) enter into an effective redemption or buy-sell agreement, and (ii) to transfer shares of stock of certain closely held corporations.[174] Usually, such permits are not difficult to acquire.

A corporation's power to purchase its own shares is subject to both financial and equitable limitations. The equitable limitations bar a corporation from acquiring its own shares where there is a showing of fraud, misrepresentation, breach of fiduciary duty or similar misconduct.[175] The equitable restrictions will not constitute a significant problem where the buy-out agreement is made in good faith.

The financial limitations on stock purchases vary greatly from state to state. These requirements are designed to protect creditors and the other shareholders. The limitations can be divided into three broad categories:[176]

---

170 Levy, *Purchase by an English Company of Its Own Shares,* 79 U. OF PA. L. REV. 45 (1930) discusses the English rule in depth.
171 BALLANTINE ON CORPORATIONS § 256(a) (1946); and FLETCHER, CYCLOPEDIA CORPORATIONS § 2847 (1950).
172 *Id. See, e.g.,* MICH. COMP. LAWS § 450.10(h) (1948). The statutory citations for each state are set forth in 7 CAVITCH, BUSINESS ORGANIZATIONS § 147.03, note 3.
173 CAVITCH, BUSINESS ORGANIZATIONS § 147.03. A few specific types of corporations are prohibited from acquiring their own shares. *See* 12 U.S.C. § 83 (1964) for restrictions imposed on national banks.
174 Walker, *Life Insurance from the Standpoint of the Federal Corporate and Personal Income Tax, Gift Tax, and Estate Tax,* 18 U.S.C. TAX INST. 543, 548-551 (1966).
175 7 CAVITCH, BUSINESS ORGANIZATIONS § 147.04(2).
176 7 CAVITCH, BUSINESS ORGANIZATIONS § 147.04(1).

(aa) *Shares must be purchased from surplus.* Surplus is variously defined as earned surplus, or as capital surplus plus earned surplus, or simply as any surplus, depending upon state law. A number of states prohibit the impairment of capital, which is essentially the same as requiring that the purchase be made from any surplus. Some state laws permit the use of capital surplus only if a requisite number of shareholders approve, or if the articles permit it. Virtually all of the states have some form of surplus requirement.

(bb) *Solvency.* The corporation is prohibited from purchasing its own shares if it is insolvent or if the purchase would result in its insolvency.[177]

(cc) *Net assets must exceed preferential rights of shareholders on liquidation.* This provision has not been widely adopted.

The financial limitations imposed by a given jurisdiction may demand compliance with only one of the above tests or with several of them in combination.

The word "redemption" or "redeem" has been used in this chapter in the tax sense, *i.e.*, a redemption for tax purposes is a corporation's acquisition of its own stock in exchange for property.[178] However, for corporate law purposes, the term "redemption" has a special meaning which is distinct from an ordinary purchase of its stock by a corporation. For corporate law purposes, a redemption is a specific form of a corporation's purchase "of its own shares exercised pursuant to pre-existing redemption provisions in the articles or certificate of incorporation."[179] The difference between redeemable stock and ordinary stock subject to a mandatory entity purchase agreement rests on a subtle concept; nevertheless, the

---

177 "Insolvent" in the bankruptcy sense is where the corporation's liabilities exceed its assets. This test adds little to a surplus test. However, some statutes have adopted the equity test of insolvency, *i.e.*, the corporation is insolvent when it is unable to pay its debts when they become due in the normal course of business. Some states employ both the bankruptcy and the equity test of insolvency; *e.g.*, MD. ANN. CODE, Art. 23, § 32(c).
178 I.R.C. § 317(b).
179 7 CAVITCH, BUSINESS ORGANIZATIONS § 147.05(2).

financial restrictions imposed on stock redemptions are less stringent than those imposed on stock purchases.[180] Generally, redeemable stock differs from stock subject to an entity purchase agreement in that the purchase provisions for redeemable stock are an attribute of the stock itself whereas the purchase provisions of nonredeemable stock are the product of contractual agreements. Redeemable stock is usually preferred stock; indeed, there is some doubt as to whether common stock can be made redeemable.

(iii) *Security of payment.* Since there is some risk that financial limitations will prohibit a corporation from purchasing a decedent's stock on the latter's death, the stock purchase agreement should obligate the surviving shareholders to use all available surplus to purchase the stock, and the corporation and the shareholders should agree to take all necessary steps (perhaps short of capital contributions) to provide the corporation with sufficient surplus to purchase the stock. In some jurisdictions, state law may permit the corporation to use capital surplus only if authorized in the articles of incorporation, and, where applicable, the articles should so provide. Where the corporation has appreciated assets, it is possible in some jurisdictions to "write up" the appreciation on the corporation's books and create an appraisal surplus.

The agreement should require that if the corporation does not purchase the deceased shareholder's stock after a given period of time, either the surviving shareholders shall make the payments on behalf of the corporation (*i.e.*, the surviving shareholders shall guarantee the corporation's obligation to

---

180 7 CAVITCH, BUSINESS ORGANIZATIONS § 147.05(1). The same equitable limitations are applicable to redemptions as to stock purchases, but the financial limitations are liberalized. For example, the corporation may be permitted to use the stated capital of the redeemed stock for its redemption.

In addition to the treatment of redemptions, there are other special exceptions to the requirement that purchases be made out of surplus, *e.g.,* elimination of fractional shares, and payment of appraisal rights to dissenting shareholders. 7 CAVITCH, BUSINESS ORGANIZATIONS § 147.04(1)(a). Those special exceptions have little significance to buy-out plans.

purchase)[181] or alternatively the surviving shareholders shall purchase the stock on their own behalf.

In some circumstances it may be possible to recapitalize the corporation so that the deceased shareholder's stock is exchanged for redeemable preferred stock, taking advantage of the more liberal provisions for purchasing redeemable stock. It is uncertain whether a recapitalization after the decedent's death will be effective for this purpose;[182] and the preferred stock received after decedent's death will likely be characterized as section 306 stock.[183]

D. CROSS-PURCHASE OF DECEDENT'S SHARES BY SURVIVING SHAREHOLDERS

Under the cross-purchase plan, the surviving shareholders purchase the stock of the deceased shareholder rather than having the corporation redeem the stock. The usual cross-purchase is a mandatory buy-out plan.

> **Ex.** The *X* Corporation has three equal shareholders, *A*, *B* and *C*. The three shareholders execute a written agreement that upon the death of one, the other two will purchase the decedent's stock, and upon the death of the second shareholder, the sole survivor will purchase his stock.

1. Advantages of the cross-purchase plan

Where the stock of a corporation is held by several family groups, the cross-purchase arrangement is a useful device for providing for the purchase of a decedent's stock without disturbing the balance of power for control of the corporation. For example, the *X* Corporation has 100 shares of common stock outstanding— 30 shares are owned by Joseph Smith, 30 shares are owned by Joseph's brother, Robert Smith, 20 shares are owned by Paul Rand

---

181 As noted in note 145 *supra,* and accompanying text, the secondary liability of the surviving shareholders will not cause payments made by the corporation as primary obligor to be treated as dividends to them.

182 The success of this arrangement may depend upon whether all of the shareholders either consent to the recapitalization or had consented to it in a prior shareholder's agreement.

183 Of course, where the redemption qualifies under I.R.C. § 303, it will not matter that the redeemed shares were section 306 stock. Treas. Reg. § 1.303-2(d).

and 20 shares are owned by Paul's sister, Rose Rand. The Smiths want a buy-out agreement for their stock, but if the stock of either Smith brother were redeemed by the corporation pursuant to an entity purchase plan, control of the corporation would pass to the Rand family, who would then possess over 57% of the corporation's common stock. The Smiths could execute a cross-purchase agreement between themselves so that on the death of one Smith, his brother would purchase his stock, thus retaining control of X in the Smith family.

The dilemma of the Smith family in the above hypothetical situation could be resolved by other means which permit the use of an entity purchase plan. For example, it may be possible to recapitalize the X Corporation so that the outstanding common stock of X is exchanged for common and preferred stock of X.[184] The X Corporation could then execute a buy-out agreement to purchase the preferred stock of a shareholder upon his demise. Since only preferred stock will be purchased under the agreement, there will be no shift of control. If the preferred stock is owned by the decedent at the time of his death, it will not constitute section 306 stock.[185] However, the amount distributed by X in redemption of the decedent's preferred stock may be treated as essentially equivalent to a dividend and consequently taxed as ordinary income unless the distribution is protected by § 303 or unless the redemption is deemed to be not essentially equivalent to a dividend under § 302(b)(1) or possibly even § 346. While there is support for the exclusion of such a redemption from dividend treatment under § 302(b)(1),[186] the uncertainty as to the applicability of that exception might deter the parties from adopting a plan of this nature unless they were reasonably certain that the mechanical and there-

---

184 A recapitalization of this nature will usually cause no recognition of income to the shareholders. I.R.C. §§ 368(a)(1)(E) and 354(a).

185 Since the basis of stock included in a decedent's gross estate will not be a substituted or transferred basis (§ 1014), preferred stock so held by a decedent at his death does not fall within the definition of section 306 stock. I.R.C. § 306(c). Even if the recapitalization of X were effected after the decedent's demise, the decedent's preferred stock could be redeemed without adverse consequences under § 306 to the extent that the amount received for the stock is within the protection of § 303. I.R.C. § 303(c) and Treas. Reg. § 1.303-2(d). See note 7 supra.

186 See Commissioner v. Estate of Antrim, 395 F.2d 430 (C.A. 4 1968), affirming ¶ 67,060 P-H Memo T.C.

fore more readily ascertainable requisites for protection under § 303 would be satisfied. Moreover, even if the potential dividend problem can be resolved, the Rands may refuse to permit a recapitalization of X or the execution of an entity purchase agreement. In that event a cross-purchase plan may be the only viable alternative.

Thus, while the cross-purchase plan is by no means the only route for effecting a mandatory purchase at death without disrupting the lines of corporate control, it is a useful device for that purpose, and in some cases will be the only available route. In some circumstances control can be maintained by combining an entity purchase plan for part of a decedent's stock with a cross-purchase plan to acquire the remainder of his stock.

As previously demonstrated, the net cost of effecting a cross-purchase plan will usually be greater than the cost of effecting an entity purchase plan. However, in the rare circumstances where the shareholders are in a lower income tax bracket than the corporation and the funds needed for the purchase can be withdrawn from the corporation in gradual stages and in a deductible form, then the net cost of a cross-purchase will be lower. As demonstrated below, split dollar insurance is not a desirable method of reducing the cost of a cross-purchase plan.

As previously noted, a corporation's accumulation of earnings as a reserve for redemption of stock increases the net asset value of the corporation and causes the value of the corporation's stock to rise in value. If a deceased shareholder's estate is to receive the actual value of its stock, the effect of the accumulation is to drive the redemption price of the stock upwards. This spiraling effect does not occur in a cross-purchase agreement.

The cross-purchase plan does not raise some of the tax problems attendant to an entity purchase plan—*e.g.*, accumulated earnings tax problems and the risk that payments in redemption of stock will be characterized as dividend income. However, as noted below, the cross-purchase plan creates other tax problems which may be equally as serious in some cases.

2. Restrictions on transfer of stock

Unless there are restrictions on the shareholders' transfer of stock, the buy-out agreement will not prevent a third party from purchasing a shareholder's stock before his death. The considerations applicable to the restriction of the transfer of stock subject to an entity purchase agreement discussed above are equally applicable to stock subject to a cross-purchase agreement. Consequently, restrictions on stock transfers should be included in the corporation's charter as well as in the shareholder's agreement, and such restrictions should be noted on the face of the certificates of shares of stock.[187]

3. Basis of stock acquired by shareholders

The surviving shareholders will acquire a basis in the decedent's stock equal to the purchase price. The significance of obtaining that basis depends upon whether they subsequently sell the stock or cause the complete or partial liquidation of the corporation or receive distributions from the corporation in excess of its earnings and profits.

The acquisition of a useful basis for the purchased stock is one small advantage that a cross-purchase enjoys over the entity purchase plan.

4. Income and estate tax consequences to the deceased shareholder's estate

The question whether the price established in a cross-purchase agreement will fix the estate tax valuation of the decedent's stock depends upon the identical considerations applicable to entity purchase agreements. Thus, the agreement must be a bona fide, arms-length bargain; the price should be reasonable; the decedent's estate must be obligated to sell; and the decedent must not have been permitted to sell during his life for a price greater than that established in the agreement.

The proceeds of a life insurance policy will not be included in the insured's gross estate for estate tax purposes unless either the insured died possessing incidents of ownership[188] in the policy or the proceeds of the policy were payable to the insured's executor.[189] Where an insured dies possessing incidents of ownership in a policy or the proceeds are payable to his executor, the proceeds are included in the decedent's gross estate; however, if the distribution

---

187 *See* notes 166-168 *supra,* and accompanying text, for a discussion of the requirements for imposing effective restrictions on stock transfers.
188 The term "incidents of ownership" is defined in Treas. Reg. § 20.2042-1(c)(2).
189 I.R.C. § 2042.

of the proceeds is conditioned on the surrender of the insured's stock in the corporation, the estate tax value of the insured's stock will be reduced by an amount equal to the insurance proceeds.[190] Thus, in the interests of caution, the insured should avoid possessing incidents of ownership in an insurance policy held by a fellow shareholder to fund a purchase agreement.

Where the purchased stock is included in the decedent's gross estate for estate tax purposes, the decedent's estate should have no adverse income tax consequences from the sale. Under I.R.C. § 1014, the estate's basis in the stock is equal to its fair market value at the date of decedent's death, and since the estate will usually sell the stock for a price equal to its value at the date of death,[191] there should be no gain or loss. Moreover, where the stock was included in the decedent's gross estate and there was no reorganization or stock dividend effected after the decedent's death, there will be no problems with § 306.[192]

5. Net cost of purchase

Frequently, the surviving shareholders will obtain the funds to purchase the decedent's stock from the corporation or from the proceeds of insurance, the premiums for which were paid from funds withdrawn from the corporation. In either case, as previously demonstrated, the net cost of the cross-purchase is usually higher than the equity purchase plan. The one exception is where the shareholders are in a lower income tax bracket than the corporation and the needed funds can be withdrawn from the corporation in some tax deductible form (*e.g.*, as rent or salary) over a period of years. If a large sum were distributed to a shareholder in one year, the tax imposed on that distribution would usually be greater than the tax payable by the corporation, and consequently it is not sufficient to make the distributions deductible but they must also be spread over a number of years.

In addition, the shareholders must face financial and equitable

---

190 *E.g.,* Estate of John T. H. Mitchell, 37 B.T.A. 1 (1938), Acq. 1938-1 C.B. 20. *See* note 92 *supra,* and accompanying text.
191 Of course, where elected, the alternate valuation date (§ 2032) controls. In any event, where the buy-sell agreement establishes the estate tax value of the stock, the stock's basis will be identical to the amount of the purchase price.
192 I.R.C. § 306(c)(1).

limitations imposed by state corporate law on the corporation's power to make distributions to shareholders *qua* shareholders where it is not possible to withdraw the needed funds as a business expense of the corporation.

6. Establishing the purchase price

The various formulas available for fixing the value of stock in a buy-sell agreement were discussed above in the material on entity purchase agreements.

7. Life insurance funding

Life insurance is commonly used to fund cross-purchase agreements, and often the premiums for the insurance are derived from corporate distributions to the shareholders.

> **Ex.** The *X* Corporation has two equal shareholders, *A* and *B*. *A* agrees to purchase *B*'s stock if he predeceases *A*, and *B* makes a reciprocal commitment. *A* purchases insurance on the life of *B*, and *B* acquires insurance on *A*'s life.

(a) Nondeductibility of premiums. The premiums paid by one shareholder on the life of another shareholder are not necessarily business expenditures;[193] but, even if the insurance premiums are deemed to be incidental to the shareholder's business, they will *not* be deductible.[194]

(b) Multiplicity of insurance policies and income tax consequences of collecting insurance proceeds. One disadvantage of cross-purchase plans which are funded with life insurance is that the complexity of having multiple insurance policies held by the shareholders can become burdensome where the corporation has more than two shareholders.

> **Ex. (1)** The *X* Corporation has three equal shareholders, *A*, *B* and *C*. The agreed net worth of *X* is $300,000. The three shareholders execute a cross-purchase agreement

---

193 If it is not a business expense, no deduction is allowed. I.R.C. § 262.
194 I.R.C. § 264 denies an income tax deduction for premiums paid for insuring the life of a person financially interested in any of the taxpayer's trades or businesses if the taxpayer is directly or indirectly a beneficiary of the policy. *See also* I.R.C. § 265.

under which the surviving two shareholders will purchase the stock of the first to die for $100,000; and the last surviving shareholder will purchase the stock of the second to die for $150,000. Accordingly, *A* purchases two $50,000 life insurance policies, one on the life of *B* and one on *C*; *B* purchases $50,000 insurance on the life of both *A* and *C*; and *C* purchases $50,000 life insurance on the life of both *A* and *B*. The plan requires the purchase of six policies, and if there had been four shareholders, they would have needed twelve policies.[195]

The difficulties of *A*, *B* and *C* have just begun. When one of the shareholders dies, the buy-out arrangement between the two survivors creates additional problems.

Ex. (2) Continuing the facts established in Ex. (1), *A* dies and *B* and *C* each collect $50,000 insurance proceeds which they use to purchase *A*'s stock. The insurance proceeds received by *B* and *C* are not included in their gross income for income tax purposes.[196] After purchasing *A*'s stock, *B* and *C* each have an obligation to pay $150,000 for the other's stock if the other dies next. However, *B* has only $50,000 insurance on *C*'s life, and vice versa. *B* and *C* could increase their insurance funding by purchasing new policies, but it would be less expensive to acquire an existing policy. Consequently, *B* will want to purchase from *A*'s estate the policy *A* owned on *C*'s life, and *C* would like to purchase the policy *A* held on *B*'s life. That will still leave *B* and *C* $50,000 short in their funding, and they face a serious problem in the "transfer for value" rule.[197] Thus, when *B* dies and *C* collects $100,000 insurance proceeds, *C* is not taxed

---

195 The use of a trust arrangement to avoid this plethora of policies is discussed below.

196 I.R.C. § 101(a)(1).

197 Where an insurance policy is transferred to a party for valuable consideration, the exemption from income provided for insurance proceeds under § 101 is not applicable (I.R.C. § 101(a)(2)), *i.e.*, the recipient of the proceeds may exclude from his income only that portion of the amount of proceeds which is equal to the consideration paid for the policy plus premiums paid by the transferee. Certain classes of persons are exempted from the transfer for value rule, *e.g.*, a transfer for value to a partner of the insured or to a corporation in which the insured is a shareholder or officer does not cause the insurance proceeds to be included in the transferee's gross income. I.R.C. § 101(a)(2)(B). However, there is no exception for transfers to a fellow shareholder of a corporation in which the insured is a shareholder.

on the $50,000 proceeds from the policy he originally acquired from the insurer. But C is taxed on the proceeds from the insurance policy he purchased from A's estate to the extent that those proceeds exceed the consideration paid by C plus the premiums subsequently paid by him.[198]

One method of avoiding a multiplicity of policies and perhaps avoiding the transfer for value rule is to utilize a trust arrangement for the cross-purchase plan.

> **Ex. (3)** Returning to the facts of Ex. (1), the three shareholders establish a trust, and the trust acquires a $100,000 life insurance policy on the life of each shareholder. On the death of A, the trustee collects the proceeds and purchases A's stock. Thus, only three insurance policies are needed instead of six. When B subsequently dies, there is a possibility that the transfer for value rule will cause the proceeds of B's insurance to be taxed in part;[199] but the applicability of that rule to trust arrangements is unsettled. Of course, even this method provides only $100,000 insurance for the $150,000 obligation of the two surviving shareholders.

At this juncture, the financial utility of life insurance funding for cross-purchase plans should be examined.

> **Ex.** A and B are equal shareholders of the X Corporation which has a net worth of $100,000. A and B execute a cross-purchase agreement establishing the price of each other's stock at $50,000. A purchases a $50,000 life insurance policy on B's life, and B reciprocates. A and B are the same age, and the premiums for their policies are identical. A and B each pay premiums of $1,600 per year for the policy they hold on each other's life. After three years (and three premium payments) A dies, and B collects the $50,000 insurance and purchases A's stock

---

198 I.R.C. § 101(a)(2).
199 Polasky points out that upon the death of A there was a shifting of the equitable interests of B and C in the policy insuring B's life, and this shift may constitute a transfer of an interest in the policy. Polasky suggests that since the transfer of equitable interests is made for mutual consideration, it may trigger the transfer for value rule. Polasky, *Planning for the Disposition of a Substantial Interest in a Closely Held Business (Part III)*, 46 IOWA L. REV. 516, 526 (n. 38) (1961).

with the proceeds. The cash surrender value of *B*'s policy
at the time of *A*'s death is $500.

The most significant aspect of the above example is that in substance *A* received only $500 for his $50,000 interest in the *X*
Corporation. If the parties had not executed a buy-sell agreement,
A could have used the money he paid for premiums on *B*'s life to
purchase a $50,000 insurance policy on *A*'s own life, and upon his
death his estate would then have had the $50,000 proceeds plus
a half-interest in the corporation. Under the buy-out plan. *A*'s estate received $50,000 from *B*, and *A* retained the insurance policy
on *B*'s life which was valued at approximately $500 at *A*'s death.
In effect, *A* exchanged his share of the business for the $500
value in the policy on *B*'s life.

Where the ages of the shareholders differ significantly, the
problem is ameliorated, since the older shareholder will pay a smaller premium for insurance on the younger man's life than he would
pay for insurance on his own life, and the converse is true for
the younger man. Since the likelihood is that the younger man
will survive and reap the rewards of the buy-out arrangement, it
is fair to impose the greater burden on him. Thus, in that case
there are some differences between funding the purchase and having the shareholders buy their own insurance, but the differences
may be far less significant than the parties have imagined (particularly the older shareholder). In most cases these arrangements
greatly favor the survivors, and the parties should be informed
of that fact beforehand.

However, even where the parties do not wish to provide a deceased shareholder with a significant sum for his stock, there can
be estate tax advantages to effecting that through a buy-out arrangement. If, instead, *A* and *B* agreed that when either died, his
estate would receive only $500 for his stock, and if each party
acquired his own insurance protection, the insurance proceeds will
be included in the deceased shareholder's gross estate, and the
corporate stock will be included at a valuation that may well be
far in excess of the $500 payment.[200] Thus, if the decedent had

---

200 A $500 purchase price for the decedent's stock might not be regarded
as bona fide and if so, it would not fix the estate tax value of the
decedent's stock.

purchased a $50,000 life insurance policy, the $50,000 insurance proceeds plus the $50,000 value of the decedent's stock could both be included in the decedent's gross estate.[201] However, if a cross-purchase buy-out arrangement were employed, only the $50,000 value of the decedent's stock plus the $500 value of the survivor's policy is included, resulting in a reduction of $49,500 in the decedent's gross estate for tax purposes.

(c) Settlement options. Where life insurance is used as a means of funding a cross-purchase plan, the parties should consider the benefits of the several settlement options available under the policy. The considerations in using such options in a cross-purchase plan are essentially the same as those discussed above for entity purchase plans.

(d) Split dollar insurance. Split dollar insurance is a technique by which an employer may provide life insurance benefits for its employees at a minimum tax cost to them. Under a "split dollar" arrangement, an ordinary life insurance policy is issued on the life of an employee. The employer provides the funds for that part of the premium for the policy that is equal to the increase in the policy's cash surrender value for the year of such payment, and the employee provides the funds for the payment of the balance of the premium. Upon the employee's demise or upon a surrender of the insurance policy, that amount of the proceeds of the insurance policy which is equal to the total funds provided by the employer will be paid to the employer, and the remainder of the proceeds are payable to the beneficiary named by the employee. Thus, in the initial years of the policy, when there is little or no cash surrender value, virtually all of the premiums are paid by the employee. As the policy's cash value builds, the annual premium payable by the employee is reduced; and after a number of years the employee may not be required to make any payment at all. However, since the amount provided by the employer is a charge against the proceeds of the policy, each additional contribution of the employer diminishes the amount of proceeds payable to the employee's beneficiary, and consequently the net effect of

---

201 Of course, a shareholder might remove the insurance proceeds from his estate by assigning it during his life to a beneficiary or to an insurance trust. The advantages and pitfalls of assigning insurance and employing an insurance trust are beyond the scope of this book.

the plan to the employee is essentially the same as providing him with declining term life insurance—*i.e.*, the employee has no equity in the policy and his insurance coverage is reduced each year.

In 1964, the Commissioner revoked an earlier ruling[202] which had determined that a split dollar arrangement did not cause the employee to recognize gross income for income tax purposes. In his 1964 ruling[203] the Commissioner determined that the employee recognizes gross income each year to the extent that the value of the insurance provided him for such year (*i.e.*, the cost of term insurance coverage) exceeds the amount of premium paid by the employee for such year. The value of the insurance provided the employee is usually ascertained by determining the cost per $1,000 of term insurance as established in tables promulgated in the Service's rulings;[204] but if the employee's insurer has published rates for term insurance which are lower than the rates set forth in the Service's rulings, and if the insurer's lower published rates are available to all standard risk applicants, then the insurance cost can be determined by using the insurer's rates.[205]

Under a split dollar arrangement the employee will not recognize any taxable income in the initial years of the policy, but he will recognize an increasingly greater amount of income each subsequent year. The employee will recognize income as indicated above irrespective of whether the policy is held by the employer or the employee since that goes only to the form of the transaction.[206] Moreover, even though the employee must recognize income, the Commissioner maintains that the employer is not permitted any tax deduction for its payment of premiums because it is a direct or indirect beneficiary of the policy within the meaning of I.R.C. § 264 which bars deductions in such cases.[207]

It has been suggested[208] that a split dollar arrangement might be employed in conjunction with a cross-purchase plan in order to minimize the cost of funding. This arrangement could only be

202 Rev. Rul. 55-713, 1955-2 C.B. 23.
203 Rev. Rul. 64-328, 1964-2 C.B. 11.
204 Rev. Rul. 55-747, 1955-2 C.B. 228; and Rev. Rul. 66-110, 1966-1 C.B. 12.
205 Rev. Rul. 66-110, 1966-1 C.B. 12; and Rev. Rul. 67-154, 1967-1 C.B. 11.
206 Rev. Rul. 64-328, 1964-2 C.B. 11.
207 *Id.*
208 *E.g.*, Note, *Estate Planning for the Disposition of a Family Corporation*, 52 MINN. L. R. 1019, 1030, n. 46 (1968).

used where the shareholders are also employees of the corporation, but in the typical closely held corporation, the shareholders are employed by it.

> **Ex.** The X Corporation, with a net worth of $100,000, has two equal shareholders, A and B. A and B execute a cross-purchase agreement for the mandatory purchase of the stock of whoever dies first. The purchase price of $50,000 is to be funded by life insurance, the premiums for which will be paid under a split dollar plan. Thus, the X Corporation will take out a policy insuring A's life for $50,000, and X will pay the premiums for the policy up to its cash surrender value, and B will pay the balance of the premiums. Upon A's death the proceeds of the policy, less its cash value which is payable to X, will be paid to A's estate on behalf of B and as part or all of the purchase price payable by B on account of the buy-out agreement. X will provide a reciprocal arrangement for B, and A will share in the premium payments for the policy on B's life.

In the writer's opinion, the split dollar plan should *not* be employed to fund a cross-purchase agreement. Referring to the example immediately above, the amount of insurance coverage under a split dollar plan declines each year as the cash value increases, and consequently A and B will have to establish an additional reserve fund to supplement their declining insurance coverage. Secondly, A and B will recognize an increasing amount of gross income each year, and yet the Service apparently will not permit the X Corporation any tax deduction. That could be a far more expensive method of funding than withdrawing sufficient funds from X to purchase a declining term policy if those funds could be withdrawn in a deductible form. Even if those two objections were not sufficient to deter the use of a split dollar plan, there is an additional and sufficient reason for avoiding it. Under the split dollar plan A and B receive term insurance coverage of their fellow shareholder as compensation for services rendered (or arguably in some cases as a dividend). Consequently, A and B may be deemed transferees for value of the insurance—*i.e.*, to the extent that they recognized income, they purchased that portion of the insurance coverage from the X Corporation rather than directly from the insurer; and this is true, in substance, irrespective of whether the policies are held by the X Corporation or by A and B individually. But the policy acquired by or on behalf of A provides insurance on the life of B, and vice versa. Thus, neither A nor B qualifies for any of the exceptions[209] to the transfer for value rule, and therefore it is quite possible that upon receiving the proceeds of the policy, A or B will be required to include in his gross income the amount of such proceeds, reduced by the amount of premiums paid by him plus the sum of income previously recognized by the said employee-shareholder.[210] The tax consequences of such treatment are likely to be so severe that the risk cannot be assumed.

8. Use of long-term personal notes to purchase decedent's stock

If the surviving shareholders do not have sufficient assets to purchase decedent's stock for cash, they may give his estate their personal interest bearing notes. This has several disadvantages. First, the shareholders may want liquid assets made available for their estates shortly after their demise and therefore will not agree to a long-term note; second, the surviving shareholders may not be able to provide sufficient security that payment will be made on the note when due; and third, the surviving shareholders must obtain the funds needed to satisfy the note, and usually these funds must be withdrawn from the corporation with all of the tax problems attendant to corporate withdrawals. However, an advantage of using notes is that it permits the shareholders to withdraw funds from the corporation gradually over a period of years, so that there is greater prospect of casting the corporate distributions in some deductible form. If a long-term note is given, interest will be imputed at a 5% rate[211] unless the note bears interest of at least 4%.[212]

9. Default of purchaser

Where three or more shareholders execute a cross-purchase agreement, the parties should decide in advance whether on the default of one of the surviving shareholders, the other surviving shareholder(s) will have an option to purchase the decedent's stock which was to be sold to the defaulting shareholder; and if so, on

---

209 I.R.C. § 101(a)(2)(A) and (B).
210 I.R.C. § 101(a)(2).
211 I.R.C. § 483. Treas. Reg. § 1.483-1(c)(2).
212 Treas. Reg. § 1.483-1(d)(2).

what terms. The terms of this option, if any, should be enunciated in the buy-out agreement.

CONCLUSION

Buy-out agreements are an extremely useful planning device, and a virtually endless variety of alternative arrangements are available. Each plan has its own peculiar merits and disadvantages. There is no single universally correct plan; the plan must be selected and tailored to comply with the specific aims of the parties involved and to create only such business and tax risks as the parties are willing to assume.

Buy-out plans may create tax pitfalls and risks which are to be avoided and minimized to the extent that it is feasible to do so. For the entity purchase, the principal tax problems are the accumulated earnings surtax, the danger that redemptions of a decedent's stock may be treated as essentially equivalent to a dividend, and in some cases the taint carried by section 306 stock may cause difficulties. The cross-purchase arrangement does not usually create accumulated earnings or dividend problems, and the principal tax difficulties there are the "transfer for value" rule where insurance funding is employed and section 306 stock where the corporation is recapitalized after the shareholder's death. The net cost of the cross-purchase arrangement is usually higher than the entity purchase, and the shareholders may have difficulty withdrawing sufficient funds from the corporation in a deductible form to fund the purchase agreement. In both types of buy-out arrangements, care must be taken to protect against adverse estate tax consequences caused by inclusion of insurance proceeds in a decedent's estate or by failing to make the redemption price determinative of the estate tax value of the stock.

While tax considerations are important in determining which type of buy-out plan to employ, the choice will usually turn on a comparison of the net costs of funding and of the relative difficulty in obtaining funding and on both estate and business planning considerations, all of which, in truth, rest partially on tax consequences. Thus, while tax minimization should not be the exclusive goal of a buy-out plan, tax consequences are a significant consideration in drafting the plan and will often constitute the greatest single factor.

Many buy-out plans, particularly those funded with life insurance, greatly favor the surviving shareholders. While there are usually business and personal reasons for adopting such plans— *viz.*, the continuation of the business after the decedent's death and the creation of a ready market for the sale of the decedent's stock —the parties should be fully appraised of the actual consequences of the plan so that they can make an informed, intelligent decision concerning its adoption.

V

Organization of a Corporation

Upon the organization of a corporation, either for the purpose of commencing the ownership and operation of a new business or for the purpose of assuming the ownership and operation of an existing business, the transferors' interests in the corporation can take many different forms. For example, the transferors may receive: common stock of one class; common stock of several classes; common and preferred stock; common stock and debt; or common stock, preferred stock and debt. The form employed will have both business and tax consequences, and considerable planning efforts are often necessary at that early date.

Consideration of the form in which interests in a corporation should be held is of continuing concern during the life of the corporation. Where changes in the capital structure are desired, an existing corporation may be recapitalized. Changes in the capital structure may also arise from the distribution of stock dividends, corporate acquisitions or divisions, and transfers made to an established corporation.

A. TRANSFERS TO A CONTROLLED CORPORATION

Unless a specific provision of the Code provides otherwise, the exchange of one item of property for another is a taxable exchange, and each party recognizes gain or loss to the extent that the fair market value of the property received exceeds or is less than the adjusted basis of the property exchanged therefor.[1] Section

---

1 I.R.C. §§ 1001 and 1002.

351 of the Code provides nonrecognition of gain or loss for certain transfers made to a controlled corporation in exchange for its stock and securities. Were it not for the specific nonrecognition provisions of § 351, transfers to a corporation in exchange for its stock would constitute a taxable exchange;[2] it follows that if such exchange should fail to qualify under § 351, or under some other specific nonrecognition provision, the gain or loss will be recognized. The requisites for qualifying under § 351 are that property be transferred to a corporation in exchange solely for stock and securities of the corporation, and that immediately after the exchange, the persons who made the transfer be in control of the corporation. If a transferor receives other property from the corporation in addition to its stock and securities, but the other requisites of § 351 are satisfied, no loss will be recognized on the exchange; and if the transferor realized a gain, part of the gain may not be recognized.

1. Control of the corporation

Section 351 requires that the persons who transferred property to the corporation in exchange for stock and securities be in "control" of the corporation immediately after the exchange.[3] Control is defined as the ownership of stock possessing at least 80% of the total combined voting power of all classes of outstanding voting stock, and at least 80% of the total number of shares of outstanding nonvoting stock.[4]

The control need not be held by one person; it is sufficient that control be held by the aggregate stock interests of a group of persons who transferred property to the corporation pursuant to a plan.[5] The exchanges of several persons with the corporation need not be made simultaneously so long as there was a pre-existing plan to make the transfers.[6] Moreover, control of the corporation need not be acquired as a result of the exchange; it is sufficient if the transferors have control after the exchange irrespective of how or when they acquired their stock.[7]

---

2 Jefferson Livingston, 18 B.T.A. 1184 (1930), Acq., IX-2 C.B. 36.
3 I.R.C. § 351(a).
4 I.R.C. §§ 351(a) and 368(c). The Service has ruled that control requires that the transferors own 80% *of each separate class* of outstanding nonvoting stock. Rev. Rul. 59-259, 1959-2 C.B. 115.
5 Treas. Reg. § 1.351-1(a)(1) and (2) Ex. (1).
6 Treas. Reg. § 1.351-1(a)(1).
7 *See* Treas. Reg. § 1.351-1(a)(2) Ex. (3).

Ex. (1) The X Corporation has 100 shares of common stock outstanding of which A owns 50 shares and B owns the other 50 shares. A owns a valuable patent in his individual capacity which he wishes to exploit. A and C agree that C will transfer a manufacturing business to X for 100 shares of X common stock and A will assign his patent to X in exchange for 50 shares of X common stock. C makes his exchange on July 10, 1965, and A makes his exchange on August 2, 1965. C and A together hold 200 shares (80%) of the 250 outstanding shares of X stock, and consequently, no gain or loss is recognized on the exchange.

Ex. (2) D owns all 60 shares of outstanding stock of X. E, the son of D, exchanges Blackacre for 190 shares of X stock. Since E did not acquire control of X (he holds less than 80% of the then outstanding 250 shares of X stock), gain or loss is recognized on E's exchange.[8]

Section 351 does not require that the transferors receive stock and securities in proportion to the value of their contributions.[9] However, if the distribution to the transferors is disproportionate, the transaction may be treated as a gift from one shareholder to the other, and therefore subject to gift tax consequences; or, depending upon the factual circumstances, the transaction may be treated as compensation received from the corporation or compensation received from one or more of the shareholders.[10]

Stock or securities issued for property of a relatively small value in comparison to the value of the stocks and securities already owned by the transferor (or in comparison to the value of stocks and securities to be issued to the transferor as compensation for services rendered or to be rendered by him) are not treated as issued in exchange for property if the primary purpose of the transfer of such property was to qualify exchanges of other parties under § 351.[11]

Ex. A, B, C and D each own 1,000 shares of common stock of the X Corporation having a value of $100 per share.

---

8 There is no attribution of stock ownership under § 351, and, consequently, E is not treated as an owner of D's stock.
9 Treas. Reg. § 1.351-1(b).
10 *Id.*
11 Treas. Reg. § 1.351-1(a)(1)(ii).

B, C and D own Blackacre which has a fair market value of $50,000. Their basis in Blackacre is $30,000. B, C and D wish to exchange Blackacre for 500 shares of X stock, but that exchange would not qualify under § 351 since they would hold less than 80% of the stock after the exchange. Therefore, A, B, C and D adopt a plan under which the latter three exchange Blackacre for 500 shares of X stock and A simultaneously gives $500 cash for five shares of X stock. A transferred property having a value equal to 0.5% of the value of his stock in X, and the probable purpose was to qualify the transfers of B, C and D under § 351. Consequently, if the Regulation[12] is valid, it is likely that A will not be treated as a transferor of property, and that the $20,000 gain realized by B, C and D will be recognized.

The question of nonrecognition under § 351 is aimed at the shareholders since the corporation does not recognize gain or loss on the sale of its stock.[13]

The problems concerned with the use of § 351 to diversify investments by exchanging stocks and securities for the stock of a holding company of substantial size having numerous unrelated shareholders (a so-called "swap-fund" exchange plan or "Centennial Fund") is beyond the scope of this book, but it should be noted that a 1966 amendment to § 351 was directed at eliminating that tax windfall at least as to transfers made after June 30, 1967.

One question frequently encountered under § 351 is the determination of the length of time after the exchange that the transferors must retain control. Where the transferors distribute stock promptly after the exchange to either purchasers or donees, it has frequently been contended that momentary control is inadequate and that the transaction fails to qualify under § 351.[14] A corporate transferor is authorized by statute to distribute stock it received to its shareholders,[15] but other transferors are not so pro-

---

12 *Id.*

13 I.R.C. § 1032.

14 In a number of instances, the above contention has been made by the transferee corporation for the purpose of characterizing the exchange as a sale and thereby increasing the corporation's basis in assets transferred to it.

15 I.R.C. § 351(c).

tected. The result of litigation on this issue is inconclusive.[16]

2. Transfer of property

The nonrecognition provisions of § 351 apply only to transfers of property.

Money is treated as property under § 351.[17] Of course, no gain or loss is ever recognized by the transfer of money; but the significance of treating money as property is that the contributor of cash can be included as a member of a group of transferors for purposes of determining whether the 80% control exists.

A contribution of services is not a transfer of property, and the stocks or securities received in exchange for the services are taxable.[18] It is often difficult to determine whether a contribution is one of property or services,[19] e.g., a party locates a tract of land, obtains an option to purchase, causes the zoning to be changed, and then obtains a favorable loan commitment; query, is the transfer of the option to purchase and the loan commitment a transfer of property or of the transferor's services?

The stock of a transferor who contributes nothing but services to the corporation cannot be considered in determining whether a group of transferors of property had control; but where a transferor contributes both property and services, all of the stock received by him in exchange can be taken into account.[20]

> **Ex. (1)** *A* owns all 50 outstanding shares of the *X* Corporation. Pursuant to a plan, *B* transferred Blackacre to *X* in exchange for 150 shares of *X* stock, and *C* received 50 shares of *X* stock in exchange for services. The transaction does not qualify under § 351 since only *B* is a transferor of property, and *B* lacked control.

---

16 *Compare* Fahs v. Florida Machine & Foundry Co., 168 F.2d 957 (C.A. 5 1948) *with* Wilgard Realty Co., Inc. v. Commissioner, 127 F.2d 514 (C.A. 2 1942), *cert. denied,* 317 U.S. 655. *See* the discussion of this issue in BITTKER AND EUSTICE, FEDERAL INCOME TAXATION OF CORPORATIONS AND SHAREHOLDERS (2d ed., 1966), Sec. 3.09, pp. 89-94.

17 Halliburton v. Commissioner, 78 F.2d 265 (C.A. 9 1935); and Rev. Rul. 69-357, I.R.B. 1969-26, p. 11.

18 Treas. Reg. § 1.351-1(a)(1)(i) and 1(a)(2) Ex. (3).

19 For an illustrative case, *see* United States v. Frazell, 335 F.2d 487 (C.A. 5 1964).

20 Treas. Reg. § 1.351-1(a)(2) Ex. (3).

Ex. (2) *A* owns all 50 outstanding shares of the *X* Corporation. Pursuant to a plan, *B* transferred Blackacre for 155 shares of *X* stock and *C* transferred Whiteacre for 20 shares of *X* stock and *C* also contributed services in exchange for an additional 25 shares of *X* stock. *C* is taxed on the 25 shares he received for his services. However, *C* did transfer property, and, consequently, the transferors of property (*B* and *C*) control the corporation immediately after this exchange and, therefore, § 351 is applicable.

3. Assignment of income and tax benefit rule

The assignment of income principle is a judicially constructed doctrine that the person who earns income cannot escape taxation by assigning the income to a third party.[21] The difference between assigning property with the income rights attached, which is not usually taxable to the assignor, and assigning only the income itself, is not always obvious.[22] While it is clear that the assignment of income doctrine is applicable to transfers to a controlled corporation, and consequently that the transferor will be taxed on such income when it is received by the corporation,[23] the extent of the doctrine's applicability is unclear.

Since a major purpose of § 351 was to remove tax impediments which would otherwise inhibit a taxpayer from changing the form in which his business is conducted, the transfer of an existing business to a corporation should not constitute an assignment of income as to any item that is an element of the business and which would normally be transferred with the business. A contrary result would thwart this purpose. Thus, where an existing business, including accounts receivable, is transferred to a corporation, the transferor should not be taxed on the collection of his receivables even though the receivables were not included in the transferor's income prior to the exchange because the transferor was on the

---

21 Lucas v. Earl, 281 U.S. 111 (1930); and Helvering v. Horst, 311 U.S. 112 (1940) are two of the landmark cases in this area.

22 *Compare* Strauss v. Commissioner, 168 F.2d 441 (C.A. 2 1948), *cert. denied,* 335 U.S. 858, *with* Heim v. Fitzpatrick, 262 F.2d 887 (C.A. 2 1959) for an illustration of how thin that line of demarcation can be.

23 *See* Clinton Davidson, 43 B.T.A. 576 (1941), holding that an assignment of insurance commissions to a controlled corporation was an assignment of income, and accordingly that the commissions were taxed to the transferor when paid to the corporation.

cash and disbursements method of accounting.[24] However, this question is unresolved, and a transferor might be prudent to retain the unrealized accounts receivable of a business which is to be transferred to a controlled corporation.

Where the income of a taxpayer's business is reported on the accrual method of accounting, and where the taxpayer had established a bad debt reserve for his accounts receivable and deducted the reserve from his gross income, the transfer of that business, including the receivables, to a controlled corporation may cause the taxpayer to recognize income in the amount of the bad debt reserve.[25] Relying on the "tax benefit rule," the Service contends[26] that the bad debt reserve causes income to the transferor to the extent that the reserve was a tax benefit when deducted, and the Service further contends that the value of the receivables has no bearing on the amount of income recognized, *i.e.*, the reserves constitute income even where they reflect an accurate estimate of the amount which will be collected on the receivables. The courts are divided on this issue. The Tax Court and the Fifth Circuit have adopted the Service's position,[27] but the Ninth Circuit[28] and three district courts[29] have held that the bad debt reserve will not cause income to the transferor to the extent that the reserve properly reflects the value of the receivables.

Ex. The *ABC* partnership operated a television supply

---

24 *Cf.* P. A. Birren & Son v. Commissioner, 116 F.2d 718 (C.A. 7 1940).
25 *See* Chapter I, pp. 86-89 for a discussion of the Service's position on bad debt reserves where the receivables are sold under § 337. The questions involved under both § 351 and § 337 are virtually identical, and the decisions concerning the treatment of bad debt reserves under those two provisions are usually interchangeable. One exception to this interchangeable attribute is the Tax Court's decision in Coast Coil Co., 50 T.C. 528 (1968) which rests on specific statutory language in § 337.
26 Rev. Rul. 62-128, 1962-2 C.B. 139.
27 Nash v. United States, 24 A.F.T.R.2d 69-5272 (C.A. 5 1969); Max Schuster, 50 T.C. 98 (1968) (three judges dissenting). The taxpayer has filed an appeal in *Schuster. Cf.* Bird Management, Inc., 48 T.C. 586 (1967) involving § 337.
28 Estate of Schmidt v. Commissioner, 355 F.2d 111 (C.A. 9 1966).
29 Scofield v. United States, 23 A.F.T.R.2d 69-1447 (C.D. Cal. 1969); Birmingham Trust National Bank v. United States, 22 A.F.T.R.2d 5202 (N.D. Ala. 1968), *reversed sub nom.* Nash v. United States, 24 A.F.T.R.2d 69-5272 (C.A. 5 1969); and Mountain States Mixed Feed Co. v. United States, 245 F. Supp. 369 (D. Colo., 1965) *affirmed without consideration of this issue,* 365 F.2d 244 (C.A. 10 1966). The Government has announced that it will appeal in *Scofield.*

and service business for several years. The partnership reported its income on the accrual method of accounting. The partners formed the *XYZ* Corporation and transferred the assets of the *ABC* partnership to the corporation in exchange for all of the corporation's common stock. Among the assets transferred were accounts receivable in the face amount of $30,000. The partnership had established a $2,000 bad debt reserve for the receivables and that amount had been deducted from partnership income. The fair market value of the receivables at the date of exchange was $28,000, and stock equal to that value was given in exchange therefor. Under the Service's position, the partners of the *ABC* partnership will recognize $2,000 income on the exchange, and under the Ninth Circuit's view, they will not recognize any income.

4. Transfer for stocks and securities—receipt of boot

With a few exceptions,[30] the transferor of property to a controlled corporation under § 351 will not recognize either gain or loss on the exchange.[31] The transfer of §§ 1245 and 1250 property will not cause the recognition of gain to the transferor;[32] nor will the transfer of an installment obligation.[33] Moreover, in most cases, § 47(b) will prevent tax consequences from the premature disposition of property for which an investment credit had been allowed.

If in addition to receiving stock and securities of the controlled corporation, the transferor also receives boot (in this context, the term "boot" refers to cash and property other than the stock and securities of the controlled corporation), the gain realized by the transferor from the exchange will be recognized to the extent of the boot.[34] The receipt of boot will not permit the recognition of a loss realized on the exchange.[35]

> **Ex. (1)** *B* is the sole shareholder of the *X* Corporation. *B* owns unimproved Blackacre in which he has a basis of

---

30 *See* pp. 261-262 *infra* and 256-257 *supra*.
31 I.R.C. § 351.
32 I.R.C. § 1245(b)(3) and § 1250(d)(3). However, if gain is otherwise recognized, the characterization of that gain (as capital gain or ordinary income) is influenced by §§ 1245 and 1250. Treas. Reg. § 1.1245-4(c)(1) and (c)(4) Ex. (1).
33 Treas. Reg. § 1.453-9(c)(2).
34 I.R.C. § 351(b).
35 I.R.C. § 351(b)(2).

$30,000. The fair market value of Blackacre is $55,000. B transfers Blackacre to X in exchange for: preferred stock of X valued at $35,000, five 10-year bonds of X having a combined value of $5,000, cash of $3,000 and common stock of the Z Corporation valued at $12,000. Thus, B realized a gain of $25,000 on the exchange. However, the amount of gain recognized by B is limited to the amount of boot he received. The cash ($3,000) and the Z stock ($12,000) are boot, but the X preferred stock and the X securities are not. The amount of gain recognized by B is $15,000.

Ex. (2) Assume the same facts as in Ex. (1) except that B's basis in Blackacre was $45,000. Accordingly, B realized a gain of $10,000 on the exchange, and he received $15,000 in boot. B recognized a $10,000 gain on the exchange.

Ex. (3) Assume the same facts as in Ex. (1) except that B's basis in Blackacre was $65,000. B realized a loss of $10,000 on the exchange, none of which is recognized.

When a shareholder transfers several assets to a corporation in exchange for the corporation's stock plus boot, the Service has ruled that the gain or loss on each transferred asset must be computed separately and that the boot is then allocated among the several assets according to their fair market value to determine the amount of gain that will be recognized.[36]

Ex. (4) A is the sole shareholder of the Z Corporation. A transferred unimproved Blackacre and common stock of the Y Corporation to Z in exchange for 150 shares of Z's common stock plus $9,000 cash. A's basis in Blackacre was $14,000 and its fair market value at the date of exchange was $8,000. A's basis in the Y stock was $6,000 and its fair market value was $16,000. The fair market value of Z's common stock was $100 per share or $15,000 for the 150 shares distributed to A. A realized a gain of $10,000 on the exchange of his Y stock and he realized a loss of ($6,000) on the exchange of Blackacre. Since A

---

36 Rev. Rul. 68-55, 1968-1 C.B. 140. For a thorough discussion of the Service's position and of alternative methods of allocation excluded by the Service's ruling, *see* Rabinovitz, *Allocating Boot in Section 351 Exchanges*, 24 Tax L. Rev. 337 (1969). *See* pp. 262-263 *infra*.

cannot recognize the loss realized on Blackacre,[37] the Service contends[38] that the gain and loss realized by *A cannot* be netted so as to limit the recognition of income to $4,000. However, because the Service ruled that the $9,000 cash boot is allocated between the two transferred assets according to their fair market value,[39] the transfer of Blackacre prevents *A*'s recognition of the full $9,000 boot even though *A* realized a gain of more than that amount on the *Y* stock. *A* will recognize a gain of only $6,000 as the following tabular chart demonstrates.

	A's basis	FMV	Gain or loss	*Z* stock allocation	Boot allocation	Gain recognized
Blackacre	$14,000	$8,000	($6,000)	50 shares valued at $5,000	$3,000	
Y stock	$6,000	$16,000	$10,000	100 shares valued at $10,000	$6,000	$6,000

Blackacre's fair market value constitutes one-third of the fair market value of the transferred assets, and consequently one-third of the distributed *Z* stock and one-third of the boot is allocated to the transfer of Blackacre. Thus, even though *A*'s gain on the exchange of *Y* stock was $10,000, only $6,000 of boot was allocated thereto, and so the gain recognized by *A* is limited to $6,000.

The Code does not define the term "stock or securities." The word "stock" refers to an equity interest in the corporation. It includes common and preferred stock, whether voting or nonvoting. It also includes hybrid stock. The Regulations state[40] that stock rights and stock warrants do not qualify as stock. This is consistent with the position taken by the Service as to the qualification of a distribution of stock rights or warrants pursuant to a corporate division,[41] and as previously noted, the validity of that regulatory provision is unsettled.[42]

The meaning of "securities" has been the subject of considerable

---

37 I.R.C. § 351(b)(2).
38 Rev. Rul. 68-55, 1968-1 C.B. 140.
39 *Id.*
40 Treas. Reg. § 1.351-1(a)(1).
41 *See* Chapter III, p. 121 *supra.*
42 *Id.*

litigation. A security is an instrument representing a corporate obligation, but not all such instruments are classified as securities.[43] The standards for distinguishing between securities and debt were described in the *Camp Wolters Enterprises* case[44] where the Fifth Circuit stated (230 F.2d at p. 560) that the test of whether a note should be classified as a security is not determined solely by the time period of the note, although that is an important factor, but instead the test is "an overall evaluation of the nature of the debt, degree of participation and continuing interest in the business, the extent of proprietary interest compared with the similarity of the note to a cash payment." Notwithstanding the Fifth Circuit's suggestion of a comprehensive flexible standard and its application of that standard in *Mills*, in most cases the distinction between debt and a security will rest on the time period of the obligation. Notes or bonds which mature in ten years or longer will usually be classified as securities; while notes or bonds which mature in five years or less will usually not be treated as securities. The characterization of notes or bonds which mature between five and ten years after issuance is unresolved. While these time periods are useful guidelines, they should not be regarded as absolute and considerable caution should be exercised in relying upon them.

5. Transfer of liabilities to the controlled corporation

With two exceptions, where pursuant to an exchange under § 351 a corporation assumes a liability or accepts property subject to a liability, the corporation's assumption or acceptance of the liability will not constitute boot to the transferor.[45] The two exceptions are:

---

43 *Compare* L & E Stirn, Inc. v. Commissioner, 107 F.2d 390 (C.A. 2 1939) holding that corporate bonds which had an average maturity of two and one-half years were not securities, *with* Camp Wolters Enterprises, Inc. v. Commissioner, 230 F.2d 555 (C.A. 5 1956) holding that non-negotiable unsecured installment notes which became due between the fifth and ninth years after issuance were securities. *See also* United States v. Mills, 399 F.2d 944 (C.A. 5 1968) affirming a jury verdict that a one-year promissory note of a corporation constituted a security.

44 Camp Wolters Enterprises, Inc. v. Commissioner, 230 F.2d 555 (C.A. 5 1956), *affirming* 22 T.C. 737. *See also* United States v. Mills, 399 F.2d 944 (C.A. 5 1968).

45 I.R.C. § 357(a). In an ordinary exchange between *A* and *B*, if *B* accepts property from *A* subject to a liability (such as a mortgage), the amount of the liability is treated as consideration paid to *A*. Crane v. Commissioner, 331 U.S. 1 (1947). This type of considera-

(i) Where the sum of liabilities assumed plus the amount of liabilities to which transferred property was subject exceed the aggregate basis of the property transferred by one transferor, the difference constitutes gain to the transferor.[46] The "gain" is allocated among the assets transferred by that transferor according to their respective fair market values,[47] and the gain is characterized accordingly, *i.e.*, as long-term or short-term capital gain or as ordinary income. Section 357(c) is applied to each transferor separately.

> **Ex**. In a § 351 exchange, *B* transfers two assets having a total basis of $20,000 in his hands. One of the assets has a basis of $10,000 and is subject to a mortgage of $30,000. The $10,000 difference between the mortgage and the aggregate basis of the transferred assets is gain recognized by *B*. The gain is allocated between the two transferred assets according to their respective fair market values and characterized accordingly.[48]

(ii) Where *any* liability transferred to the controlled corporation was transferred for the principal purpose of avoiding federal income taxes or for a purpose which was not a bona fide business purpose, then *all the liabilities* transferred by that transferor (including those transferred for a bona fide business purpose) are treated as boot.[49]

Where § 357(b) and § 357(c) are both apposite, § 357(b) takes precedence.[50]

6. Characterization of gain recognized because of receipt of boot

In order to determine the character of gain recognized in a § 351 exchange because of boot, it is necessary to allocate the gain to the assets transferred by that transferor. Since it is unusual to have boot in a § 351 exchange, there has been no dispositive judicial state-

---

tion was treated as boot in United States v. Hendler, 303 U.S. 564 (1938), but *Hendler* was overruled by the antecedent to § 357(a).
    However, as noted below, the transfer of liabilities will influence the basis of the transferor in the stocks and securities he receives in exchange.

46 I.R.C. § 357(c). The transferor cannot avoid recognition of income by giving a note to the corporation in the amount of this difference. Rev. Rul. 68-629; I.R.B. 1968-50, p. 12.

47 Treas. Reg. § 1.357-2(b).

48 Treas. Reg. § 1.357-2.

49 I.R.C. § 357(b); and Treas. Reg. § 1.357-1(c).

50 I.R.C. § 357(c)(2)(A).

ment or Regulatory provision as to the manner in which this allocation should be made.[51] Several viable alternatives are: to allocate
the recognized gain among the transferred assets according to their
respective fair market values; or to allocate the recognized gain only
among those transferred assets that have a value greater than the
transferor's basis therein and to allocate the gain among those assets proportionately according to the difference between value and
basis of each such asset. The Service has rejected both of those alternatives. The Service has ruled that the amount of gain recognized under § 351(b) on a transfer of several assets to a corporation
is determined on an asset-by-asset computation—i.e., the consideration, including boot, is allocated to each asset separately according
to its respective fair market value, and the gain realized on each
asset is recognized to the extent of the boot allocated to that asset,
and the loss realized on any asset is not recognized.[52] The character
of the gain recognized on each asset is determined by the nature of
the asset itself.[53] Thus, gain recognized on account of the transfer of
a capital asset will be characterized as long-term or short-term capital gains depending upon the transferor's holding period. Gain recognized on account of the transfer of depreciable property will be
characterized as ordinary income to the extent that § 1245 or
§ 1250 is applicable, and the balance of such gain (if any) will be
characterized as § 1231 gain (which is frequently treated as long-
term capital gain) unless § 1239 (discussed below) is applicable.

Under § 1239, where an individual sells to a corporation property which is depreciable *in the hands of the corporation*, the transferor's entire gain from the sale or exchange of such property
is treated as ordinary income if more than 80% of the *value* of
the outstanding stock of the corporation is owned by the transferor, his spouse, and his minor children, and minor grandchildren.
While the Regulations state that the 80% ownership requisite
includes beneficial ownership,[54] two Courts of Appeals have ex-

---

51 However, as noted above, the Regulations provide that where gain is
    caused by the transfer of liabilities in excess of basis (§ 357(c)), the
    gain is allocated among the transferred assets according to their re-
    spective fair market values. Treas. Reg. § 1.357-2.
52 Rev. Rul. 68-55, 1968-1 C.B. 140. *See* Rabinovitz, *Allocating Boot in
    Section 351 Exchanges,* 24 TAX L. REV. 337 (1969). *See* pp. 259-260
    supra.
53 *Id.*
54 Treas. Reg. § 1.1239-1.

cluded stock which is only beneficially owned by the persons named in the statute.[55]

The "more than 80%" requirement in § 1239 refers to the value of the outstanding stock, and consequently, it is possible for a transferor to own 80% or less of the number of shares of outstanding stock, but own over 80% of the value of the outstanding stock because of restrictions on the minority shares[56] or possibly because the possession of control adds to the value of the majority stockholder's shares.

Section 1239 is triggered by actual sales to the corporation and also by gain recognized on section 351 exchanges because of boot or because of transferred liabilities in excess of basis.

In a recent ruling (Rev. Rul. 69-109, I.R.B. 1969-10, p. 38), the Service relied on the reference in § 1239 to sales or exchanges "directly or indirectly" to a corporation for its determination that a sale of depreciable property from one corporation to a second corporation, both of which had more than 80% in value of their stock owned by the same individual, was an indirect sale from the individual to the transferee corporation and was therefore covered by § 1239. The meaning of "indirectly" is unresolved, and this issue may be litigated at some future date.

7. Transferor's basis in stock and securities and boot received in the exchange

The basis of a transferor in boot (other than money) received by him in a section 351 exchange is equal to the fair market value of the boot.[57]

The transferor's basis in the stocks and securities received by him in the section 351 exchange is equal to the transferor's basis in the property transferred to the corporation, increased by the amount of income recognized by the transferor on the exchange and decreased by the sum of (i) the amount of boot received, and (ii) the amount

---

55 United States v. Rothenberg, 350 F.2d 319 (C.A. 10 1965); and Mitchell v. Commissioner, 300 F.2d 533 (C.A. 4 1962).

56 United States v. Parker, 376 F.2d 402 (C.A. 5 1967) held that a transfer by a taxpayer who owned exactly 80% of the number of outstanding shares was covered by § 1239 because the value of the taxpayer's shares exceeded 80% of the value of the total outstanding stock. *See also* Rev. Rul. 69-339, I.R.B. 1969-25, p. 14; and Henry Trotz, P-H T.C. Memo ¶ 67-139, *on remand from* 361 F.2d 927 (C.A. 10 1966).

57 I.R.C. ¶ 358(a)(2).

of liabilities assumed or accepted by the corporation.[58] The basis would be further reduced by any loss recognized by the transferor on the exchange, but it is not possible for a transferor to recognize a loss in an exchange under § 351, so that provision is inapposite.

The basis of the stocks and securities is allocated among each class of stock and securities separately.[59] The percentage of total basis for the stocks and securities that is allocated to each separate class is determined in accordance with the ratio of the fair market value of the stocks or securities of that separate class to the fair market value of all the stocks and securities received in the exchange.[60]

> **Ex. (1)** *B* is the sole shareholder of the *X* Corporation. *B* transferred property having a basis of $40,000 to *X* in exchange for $20,000 of common stock, $10,000 of preferred stock, $20,000 of securities and a $10,000 note maturing in two years.[61] *B* realized a gain of $20,000 on the exchange, but his recognized gain is only $10,000 (the boot he received in the form of a short-term note). *B*'s basis in the two-year note is $10,000. *B*'s basis in the stocks and securities is $40,000 ($40,000 basis in property transferred to the corporation plus $10,000 recognized gain minus $10,000 boot received). The $40,000 basis is allocated among the stocks and securities as follows:
>
> (1) The basis of the common stock is $16,000
> $$(40,000 \times \frac{20,000}{50,000} = 16,000).$$
>
> (2) The basis of the preferred stock is $8,000
> $$(40,000 \times \frac{10,000}{50,000} = 8,000).$$
>
> (3) The basis of the securities is $16,000
> $$(40,000 \times \frac{20,000}{50,000} = 16,000).$$
>
> **Ex. (2)** *B* is the sole shareholder of the *X* Corporation. *B* exchanges Blackacre for 100 shares of *X* stock. *B*'s basis in Blackacre was $40,000, and Blackacre was subject to

---

58 I.R.C. § 358.
59 Treas. Reg. § 1.358-2(b)(2).
60 *Id.*
61 All of the amounts given for the properties transferred from the corporation to *B* represent the fair market value of such properties.

a mortgage of $10,000. *B* has a basis of $30,000 in the 100 shares of *X* stock.

8. Corporation's basis of assets received in the exchange

The basis of assets received by the corporation in a section 351 exchange is equal to the basis the assets had in the hands of the transferor increased by any gain recognized by the transferor on the exchange.[62] The Code and Regulations do not state how the increment in basis caused by the transferor's recognition of gain will be allocated among the several assets received by the corporation. Presumably, the increment in basis will be allocated in the same manner that the recognized gain is allocated for purposes of its characterization. If the Service's asset-by-asset method of computing and characterizing the amount of recognized gain is sustained,[63] the gain would surely be allocated accordingly for the purpose of determining the corporation's basis in the transferred assets.

9. Intentional avoidance of section 351

A transferor of property to a corporation may wish to avoid the application of § 351 so that the transferred property will have a higher basis in the hands of the corporation. Avoidance of § 351 is most likely to be advantageous in cases in which the transferor will realize capital gains upon transfer of the property and the corporation will realize ordinary gain when it subsequently disposes of the transferred property. For example, the transferor of a large tract of land to a corporation may realize capital gain if he avoids § 351; however, if the corporation subdivides the land it will most likely realize ordinary income on the sale of the subdivided parts and thus the stepped-up basis to the corporation results in a savings of ordinary income at a cost of an equivalent amount of capital gains.

One way of avoiding § 351 would be to simply sell the property to the controlled corporation for cash and notes. However, the

---

62 I.R.C. § 362(a).

63 *See* pp. 259-260 *supra* for the method of allocation of gain recognized because of the receipt of boot; and *see* p. 262 *supra* for the method of allocation of gain recognized because the liabilities transferred exceeded the basis of transferred assets. *See also* Rabinovitz, *Allocating Boot in Section 351 Exchanges,* 24 TAX L. REV. 337, 356-365 (1969) for a discussion of the possible methods of determining basis if the Service's asset-by-asset method is ultimately repudiated.

Service may contend that such a sale is in reality a contribution to equity and the courts have examined these transactions to determine whether the sale was in substance actually an equity contribution.[64] Other ways of avoiding § 351 are: to have the corporation give boot to the transferor so that the transferor will recognize gain up to the amount of boot; for the transferor to transfer property subject to liabilities in excess of the basis of the property;[65] or to intentionally avoid the control requirements set out in § 368(c).

B. SUBCHAPTER S

1. General statement

The following discussion of Subchapter S (I.R.C. §§ 1371-1378) is not intended to be exhaustive;[66] its purpose is to sketch the mechanics and effects of the provisions of Subchapter S so that the reader can gain some perspective as to the merits and disadvantages of electing Subchapter S treatment. The provisions of Subchapter S are applicable only by election. They permit, in very strictly defined circumstances, the taxation of corporate income directly to shareholders. It would be an oversimplification, however, to say that these provisions permit corporations to be taxed as partnerships.

2. Eligibility requirements of Subchapter S

To qualify for Subchapter S treatment, a corporation must satisfy the following requirements:[67] (1) it must be a domestic corporation; (2) it must not be a member of an affiliated group;[68] (3) it must not have more than ten shareholders;[69] (4) it must not have a nonresident alien as a shareholder; (5) it must not have shareholders who are neither individuals nor estates; and (6) it must not have more than one class of stock.

---

64 See Fisher, *The Conversion of Ordinary Income to Capital Gain by Intentionally Avoiding Section 351 of the Internal Revenue Code of 1954,* 32 Mo. L. Rev. 421 (1967).

65 I.R.C. § 357(c).

66 For additional discussion of Subchapter S, *see* BITTKER AND EUSTICE, FEDERAL INCOME TAXATION OF CORPORATIONS AND SHAREHOLDERS (2d ed., 1966) Chapter 14; and Portfolio #60-3rd, "Subchapter S—Elections and Operations," TAX MANAGEMENT (BNA).

67 I.R.C. § 1371.

68 "Affiliated group" is defined in I.R.C. § 1504.

69 Stock which is community property of a husband and wife or which is held by them as joint tenants, tenants by entireties, or tenants in common is treated as owned by one shareholder. I.R.C. § 1371(c).

In connection with the latter two requirements, two problems merit special attention: (1) the possibility that a voting trust arrangement might not satisfy either of those requirements; (2) the possibility that the indebtedness of a corporation might be treated as a second class of stock. The Regulations assert that a voting trust runs afoul of the requirement that shareholders must be individuals or estates.[70] However, the *A & N Furniture* case[71] challenged the validity of this Regulation. The court argued persuasively that the purpose of the requirement is to protect the integrity of the ten shareholders limitation by preventing corporations and trusts, which may have any number of shareholders or beneficiaries, from holding shares in a Subchapter S corporation, and that a voting trust does not involve the danger of increasing the number of shareholders since all the beneficiaries already hold shares.[72] The court further held that voting trusts do not violate the one class of stock requirement, despite language in the Regulations that "a difference as to voting rights . . . of outstanding stock will disqualify a corporation."[73] The court said that this language "is directed toward the issuance of two classes of stock and accounting difficulties resulting therefrom, rather than voting powers per se."

Corporate debt may be treated as stock for tax purposes when a debt instrument bears too many of the characteristics of an equity investment (hybrid stock).[74] A major factor in determining whether debt is to be treated as hybrid stock is whether the corporate entity is a "thin corporation," *i.e.*, the outstanding indebtedness of the corporation is disproportionately high in relation to its capital.[75] If debt is treated as hybrid stock, the Regulations provide that it "will generally constitute a second class of stock" for Subchapter S purposes;[76] but hybrid stock does not constitute a per se

---

70 Treas. Reg. § 1.1371-1(e).
71 The A & N Furniture & Appliance Co. v. United States, 271 F. Supp. 40 (S.D. Ohio, 1967). *But see* Fulk & Needham, Inc. v. United States, 288 F. Supp. 39, 47-48 (M.D.N.C. 1968).
72 *See contra,* Fulk & Needham, Inc. v. United States, 288 F. Supp. 39, 47-48 (M.D.N.C. 1968).
73 Treas. Reg. § 1.1371-1(g). Pollack v. Commissioner, 392 F.2d 409 (C.A. 5 1968), exemplifies a harsh and strict application of the regulatory injunction against having classes of stock with different voting rights.
74 *See* Chapter VI, pp. 294-295 *infra.*
75 *See e.g.,* Berkowitz v. United States, 23 A.F.T.R.2d 69-1582 (C.A. 5 1969).
76 Treas. Reg. § 1.1371-1(g).

disqualification from electing Subchapter S. The Regulations further provide that "if such purported debt obligations are owned solely by the owners of the nominal stock of the corporation in substantially the same proportion as they own such nominal stock, such purported debt obligations will be treated as contributions to capital rather than a second class of stock."[77] It is important to note that such proportionality may be destroyed by a subsequent issuance, redemption, sale, or other transfer of either the nominal stock or the purported debt; in such event, the Regulations call for a new determination of whether the corporation has more than one class of stock.[78]

The provisions of Subchapter S apply only to corporations that have made a valid election to be covered thereunder.[79] The election must be made by the corporation within the first month of a taxable year of the corporation or within the last month of its taxable year.[80] For an election to be valid, each shareholder of the corporation determined (i) as of the first day of the taxable year for which the election is effective or (ii) as of the date the election was made, whichever occurs later, must consent to the election.[81] When a valid election is made in the first month of the corporation's taxable year, it is effective for that taxable year and for each succeeding taxable year until the election is terminated; if a valid election is made in the last month of the corporation's taxable year, it is effective for the following taxable year and each taxable year thereafter until terminated.[82]

3. Effect of a Subchapter S election

An effective Subchapter S election virtually eliminates the corporation as an independent taxpaying entity. An electing corpora-

---

77 *Id. See also* W. C. Gamman, 46 T.C. 1 (1966) (appeal to Ninth Circuit dismissed).

78 *Id.*

79 I.R.C. § 1371(b).

80 I.R.C. § 1372(c)(1).

81 I.R.C. § 1372(a). In Harold C. Kean, 51 T.C. 337 (1968), two brothers had contributed equally to the purchase of stock of a closely held corporation. The stock was issued in the name of only one of the brothers. The corporation elected Subchapter S treatment, and the brother who was a shareholder of record consented to the election, but the other brother failed to file his consent. The court held that the shareholder of record held one-half of the shares titled in his name on behalf of his brother, and since the latter failed to consent, the election for Subchapter S treatment was invalid.

82 I.R.C. § 1372(d).

tion is not subject to federal income taxes of any type,[83] except for a capital gains tax in the very limited situation where long-term capital gains constitute an excessive proportion of its income (the tax the corporation pays on such capital gains is sometimes referred to as "the tax imposed by § 1378(a)").[84] Instead, the income which would otherwise be taxed to the corporation is taxed directly to the shareholders.

(a) Constructive dividends. At the outset, it should be noted that distributions to shareholders out of earnings and profits, as in the case of non-Subchapter S corporations, are treated as ordinary income to the shareholders and taxed directly to them. In addition, Subchapter S provides that each person who is a shareholder on the last day of an electing corporation's taxable year shall include in his gross income (for his taxable year in which the corporation's taxable year ends) the amount he would have received as a dividend had the corporation on the last day of its taxable year distributed pro rata to its shareholders an amount equal to its "undistributed taxable income" for its taxable year.[85] "Undistributed taxable income" is defined as the corporation's taxable income[86] minus the sum of (i) the *cash* dividends[87] actually distributed out of *current* earnings and profits during the taxable year plus (ii) the tax imposed on certain net long-term capital gains by § 1378(a).[88] Thus, each person who is a shareholder on the last day of the corporation's taxable year is treated as having received a constructive distribution from the corporation on that date in an amount equal to his pro rata share of the undistributed taxable income of the corporation. This constructive distribution is treated as a dividend to the shareholder to the extent that earnings and profits are available.

---

83 I.R.C. § 1372(b).
84 I.R.C. § 1378.
85 I.R.C. § 1373(b).
86 "Taxable income" is defined in I.R.C. § 63, but for purposes of Subchapter S, it is subject to the modifications provided in I.R.C. § 1373(d).
87 Distributions of property in kind do not affect the amount of undistributed taxable income, but they do complicate the computation of the shareholder's income. *See* Treas. Reg. § 1.1373-1.
88 I.R.C. § 1373(c). For purposes of Subchapter S, a corporation's current earnings and profits are not reduced by any item which is not allowable as a deduction, but this restriction does not apply to accumulated earnings and profits. § 1377(b). Moreover, earnings and profits will not be reduced by net operating losses incurred during an election year. § 1377(c).

The current year's earnings and profits are allocated first to the cash distributions made during the year, and the remaining balance of current earnings and profits is allocated pro rata between the constructive distributions (§ 1373 (b)) and distributions of property in kind (if any) taken into account at fair market value made during that year.[89] If the current earnings and profits are less than the amount of actual and constructive distributions, then the accumulated earnings and profits of the corporation are applied to both the actual and constructive distributions in the order of time made.[90] If the constructive distributions exceed the current and accumulated earnings and profits allocable thereto, the difference causes no tax consequences at all.

> **Ex. (1)** Corporation X, a Subchapter S corporation, has a taxable year commencing on June 1 and terminating on May 31. On May 31, 1960, it had four equal shareholders, A, B, C and E. E had purchased his stock from D on May 29, 1960. X had taxable income for the year June 1, 1959 to May 31, 1960 of $100,000, and X's earnings and profits for that year were also $100,000. As of May 31, 1959, X had no accumulated earnings and profits. X distributed a cash dividend of $40,000 to its four shareholders on March 10, 1960. A, B, C and D each should report his share ($10,000 each) of the cash dividend paid on March 10. In addition, X's undistributed taxable income was $60,000 ($100,000 minus $40,000), and thus A, B, C and E should each report a constructive dividend of $15,000, since they were the shareholders on the last day of the corporation's taxable year. For this same reason, D, who was not a shareholder on the last day of the corporation's taxable year, does not have to report a constructive dividend, even though he owned shares for all but two days of the corporation's taxable year.[91] Thus, A, B and C should report a total of $25,000 in actual and constructive dividends; E should report the $15,000 constructive dividend; and D should report the $10,000 actual cash dividend.
>
> **Ex. (2)** The facts are the same as in Ex. (1) with the following exceptions: the taxable income and current earn-

89 Treas. Reg. § 1373-1(e) and (g) Ex. (3).
90 Treas. Reg. §§ 1.1373-1(g) Ex. (4); and 1.316-2(c) Ex.
91 *See* Treas. Reg. § 1.1373-1(a)(2), which provides that if the transfer from D to E was not bona fide, D would have to report the constructive dividend.

ings and profits of X for the fiscal year were $60,000, and the distributions made by X among A, B, C and D on March 10, 1960, was unimproved Blackacre having a fair market value of $40,000, and a basis of like amount. No cash distributions were made during the fiscal year. A, B, C and D each received a distribution of $10,000 on March 10, as that is their respective share of Blackacre's value. X's undistributed taxable income (UTI) for the fiscal year was $60,000, since the UTI is *not* reduced by distributions of property in kind. Accordingly, A, B, C and E each received a constructive distribution of $15,000 on May 31, 1960. The current earnings and profits for the year ($60,000) are allocated pro rata between the distribution of Blackacre and the constructive distribution of UTI.

Thus, $$\frac{40,000}{40,000 + 60,000} \times 60,000 \text{ (e \& p)} = \$24,000,$$

the earnings and profits allocated to the distribution of Blackacre. A, B, C and D should each report dividend income of $6,000 from the March 10 distribution (*i.e.*, $\frac{1}{4}$ of the 24,000 e & p allocated to that distribution); and the remaining $4,000 of the distribution to each will reduce the basis of his X stock, and will be treated as gain from the sale of such stock to the extent that it exceeds the stock's basis. The remaining $36,000 of current earnings and profits are allocated to the constructive distribution of UTI, and thus A, B, C and E each received constructive dividend income of $9,000 on May 31. The balance of the constructive distribution of UTI to each shareholder ($6,000) has no tax consequences at all. Thus A, B and C should each report a total of $15,000 in actual and constructive dividends from X; D should report an actual dividend of $6,000; and E should report a constructive dividend of $9,000.

Ex. (3) The facts are the same as in Ex. (2) except that on May 31, 1959, X had accumulated earnings and profits of $24,000. As in Ex. (2), the current earnings and profits ($60,000) are allocated $24,000 to the March 10 distribution of Blackacre, and $36,000 to the constructive distribution of undistributed taxable income (UTI) on May 31, 1960. Thus, $16,000 (40,000 value—24,000 current e & p) of value of the March 10 distribution is not made from current earnings and profits. Since the March 10 actual distribution is earlier in time than the May 31 constructive distribution, X's accumulated earnings and profits are first allocated to the former and the balance is allocated to the constructive distribution of UTI. Accordingly, $16,000 of X's accumulated earnings and profits are allocated to the March 10 distribution, and therefore A, B, C and D each received an actual dividend of $10,000 on that date. The remaining $8,000 of X's accumulated earnings and profits are allocated to the constructive distribution of UTI. Thus, the total earnings and profits allocated to the constructive distribution is $44,000 (36,000 current e & p plus 8,000 accumulated e & p); and accordingly, A, B, C and E should each report a constructive dividend of $11,000. The remaining $16,000 portion of the UTI ($60,000 UTI—44,000 current and accumulated e & p allocated thereto) has no tax consequences. A, B and C should each report a total of $21,000 in actual and constructive dividends; D should report an actual dividend of $10,000; and E should report a constructive dividend of $11,000.

It should be kept in mind that the District Director has authority to allocate dividends of a Subchapter S corporation (including dividends from constructive distributions) among shareholders who are members of the same family if he determines that this is necessary to reflect the value of services rendered to the corporation by such shareholders.[92]

> **Ex. (4)** A husband (H) and wife (W) each own 50% of the outstanding stock of Corporation X, a Subchapter S corporation. X has taxable income for the year 1964 of $100,000 and earnings and profits of a like amount. H performed services worth $20,000 for the corporation, but he did not withdraw any amount as salary. Under the general rules of Subchapter S, H and W would each report a constructive dividend of $50,000. H would thus have shifted $10,000 of his income to W. However, the District Director may, in his discretion, allocate $10,000 of income from W to H so that H will be charged with $60,000 and W with $40,000 of income, thus reflecting the value of services performed by H.

---

92 I.R.C. § 1375(c). *See* Walter J. Roob, 50 T.C. 891 (1968). *Cf.* Michael F. Beirne, 52 T.C. 210 (1969) where a parent's transfer of stock to a minor under a custodial statute was deemed to lack any economic substance, and accordingly the parent was deemed taxable on the income of the electing corporation as the true shareholder.

It is clear from the above discussion that the constructive distribution concept may result in the shareholders of an electing corporation having to report income that they have not yet received. Subchapter S provides that the basis of a shareholder's stock in the corporation be increased by the amount of each constructive dividend;[93] in effect, this treats the shareholder as if he had actually received the constructive dividend and then returned it to the corporation as a contribution to capital. Under the normal rules of corporate taxation, if a shareholder should later wish to withdraw from the corporation the income which was previously taxed to him without being taxed again, he could do so only after the corporation's earnings and profits, both current and accumulated, were distributed; and any distribution made before earnings and profits were exhausted would be treated as a taxable dividend. Subchapter S mitigates the harshness of these general rules by expanding the circumstances under which the shareholders of electing corporations can make tax-free withdrawals, *i.e.*, an actual distribution of *cash* is nontaxable to the extent of the recipient shareholder's net share of previously taxed income, if the distribution would otherwise have been considered a dividend from *accumulated* earnings and profits.[94] This exception for withdrawal of previously taxed income (PTI) does not apply to distributions of property in kind, or to constructive distributions, or to any distribution made out of *current* earnings and profits. If the conditions of the PTI provisions are met, the distribution is not considered a dividend and is treated as a return of capital. Thus, it reduces the basis of the shareholder's stock and does not reduce the corporation's earnings and profits. It should be stressed that such a distribution can only be made after *current* earnings and profits are exhausted; otherwise it would not satisfy the requirement that it be a dividend from *accumulated* earnings. For purposes of this calculation a shareholder's net share of PTI is determined by the following formula: the total amount included in the gross income of the shareholder as constructive dividends for all prior taxable years (assuming there has been no termination of a previous Subchapter S election) minus the sum of (i) amounts previously distributed

93 I.R.C. § 1376(a). Also, the corporation's earnings and profits are reduced by the amount of a shareholder's constructive dividend. I.R.C. § 1377(a).
94 Treas. Reg. § 1.1375-(4)(a) and (b). I.R.C. § 1375(d).

to the shareholder as tax-free distributions of previously taxed income plus (ii) amounts allowable to the shareholder as net operating loss deductions (discussed below) for all prior taxable years.[95]

> **Ex.** Corporation Z, a Subchapter S corporation, had two equal shareholders, A and B, during its taxable year ended December 31, 1960. As of the beginning of 1960, Z had $20,000 of accumulated earnings and profits. For the taxable year 1960, Z had current earnings and profits and taxable income of $8,000. In June 1960, it made cash distributions of $5,000 to A and $5,000 to B, and in November 1960, it distributed the same amount in cash to each. Immediately before the June distributions, A's net share of previously taxed income was $6,000 and B's net share was $4,000. Current earnings and profits are allocated ratably to each of the four distributions; therefore, each distribution to A and B was a dividend from current earnings and profits to the extent of $2,000. As to the June distribution, the $3,000 distributions to both A and B which were not paid out of current earnings and profits were distributions of PTI and therefore were not dividends, since immediately before the distribution each had a net share of PTI in excess of $3,000. As to the November distribution, the $3,000 distributed to A which was not paid out of current earnings and profits was also a nondividend distribution since A's net share of PTI at that date was $3,000 ($6,000 minus the $3,000 absorbed by the June distribution); however, the $3,000 distribution to B which was not paid out of current earnings and profits was a nondividend distribution only to the extent of $1,000 and was a dividend from accumulated earnings and profits to the extent of $2,000, since B's net share of PTI at that date was $1,000 ($4,000 minus the $3,000 absorbed by the June distribution).[96]

Still, a shareholder may be reluctant to rely on the PTI provisions as a justification for the Subchapter S corporation's failure to distribute income to the shareholders, and such reluctance is well-founded. The right to withdraw PTI is personal to the shareholder, and thus if he should die or otherwise have to transfer his stock, the right would lapse unless (after a transfer) he again became a shareholder in the corporation while it was subject to the same

---

95 I.R.C. § 1375(d)(2).
96 This example is a paraphrase of Treas. Reg. § 1.1375-4(g), Ex. (3).

election. Moreover, when a Subchapter S election is terminated, an event which as we shall see below can occur inadvertently, the right to withdraw previously taxed income under the special rules of Subchapter S is lost irrevocably, and the regular corporate distribution rules will apply. This problem can be avoided by causing the electing corporation to distribute cash distributions equal to its taxable income before the end of the taxable year, so that there will be no constructive dividends. However, this is not easily accomplished. It may be difficult to determine the corporation's taxable income before the end of the taxable year so that the amount which should be distributed to shareholders can be ascertained. This aspect of the problem has been alleviated by the recently enacted provision that all distributions of money during the first $2\frac{1}{2}$ months of a taxable year to persons who were shareholders on the last day of the preceding taxable year shall be treated as distributions of the corporation's undistributed taxable income for the preceding year (to the extent, of course, that the distribution to any given shareholder does not exceed his share of the undistributed taxable income for the previous year).[97] This provision permits a corporation to balance its cash distributions to shareholders with the income previously taxed to them by providing a grace period during which the corporation can determine its exact income for the preceding year. Moreover, the provision applies even if the corporation loses its Subchapter S status during the grace period.

A more serious obstacle to keeping distributions in current balance with taxable income is that the corporation may not be able to finance its operations without retaining at least some of its earnings. A shareholder who has received distributions might of course turn around and put the money back into the corporation by loan or reinvestment. However, if he should reinvest the funds, his position would be worse than it would have been if no distribution had been made to him, since he would not have a right to withdraw the reinvested funds as income previously taxed to him (PTI). If instead, he should make a loan to the corporation, he runs the risk that it will be treated as a reinvestment under a theory that the debt constitutes hybrid stock. If the loan is treated as a reinvestment, then, as above, the shareholder will not have the right to withdraw the

---

97 I.R.C. § 1375(f). This provision was added to the Code on April 14, 1966, by Sec. 1 of Public Law 89-389.

contributed amount as previously taxed income; moreover, the corporation might well lose its Subchapter S status under the "one class of stock" requirement. Even if the loan is not deemed to constitute a reinvestment, the Internal Revenue Service might choose to ignore the whole arrangement as a "step-transaction," thus leaving the shareholder in the same position he had prior to the distribution.

(b) Pass-through of long-term capital gain. As a general rule, taxable income of a Subchapter S corporation, unlike that of a partnership, does not retain its character when taxed to the shareholders; rather, it passes to the shareholders as dividends taxable as ordinary income. However, if for any taxable year, there is an excess of net long-term capital gain over net short-term capital loss, all shareholders who receive dividends, either actual or constructive, out of *current* earnings and profits during the taxable year can treat a pro rata portion of such dividends as long-term capital gain rather than as ordinary income.[98] This capital gain pass-through cannot exceed the corporation's taxable income for the year.[99]

> **Ex. (1)** *Y* Corporation, a Subchapter S corporation, had $10,000 in long-term capital gains and had $4,000 in net losses from business activities in the year 1962. As of January 1, 1962, *Y* Corporation had $15,000 accumulated earnings and profits. *Y*'s current earnings and profits for the year 1962 was $6,000. *A* was the sole shareholder of *Y*. The year 1962 was the first year in which *Y*'s Subchapter S election became effective. In 1962, *Y* distributed $10,000 to *A*. *Y*'s taxable income for the year was $6,000 ($10,000 minus $4,000); therefore, of the $10,000 distributed to *A* only $6,000 is treated as capital gain, and the remaining $4,000 is treated as ordinary income dividends from accumulated earnings and profits.

> **Ex. (2)** *X* Corporation, a Subchapter S corporation, reports on a fiscal year basis commencing on June 1 and terminating on May 31. *A* is the sole shareholder of *X*, and he reports his income on a calendar year basis. In fiscal year 1967-68, *X* has current earnings and profits

---

98 I.R.C. § 1375(a). The pro rata portion is determined by the shareholder's percentage of the total actual and constructive dividends made during the corporation's taxable year.

99 I.R.C. § 1375(a)(1). Taxable income is modified in accordance with § 1373(d).

and taxable income of $10,000, $2,000 of which is long-term capital gain. On December 30, 1967, X distributed $5,000 in cash to A. X made no other actual distributions during that fiscal year. At the time A filed his return for 1967, he thus had insufficient information to determine what portion of the distribution to him could be treated as capital gains. In such a situation, a taxpayer has two options: (1) he can ask for an extension of time for filing his return and pay the interest accruing during the delay; (2) he can attempt to estimate the portion of his distribution which can properly be treated as capital gain, file the return, and later file an amendment to the return if this should become necessary in the light of full information. Ultimately, A should allocate ratably the $2,000 in long-term capital gain to the distributions to him of both constructive and actual dividends during the corporation's taxable year.[100] Thus, in his 1967 return, A should report the $5,000 in cash actually distributed to him, of which $1,000 is treated as capital gain. In his 1968 return, A should report his $5,000 constructive dividend, of which $1,000 is treated as capital gain.

(c) **Pass-through of corporate net operating losses.** If a corporation has net operating losses[101] incurred in years prior to its electing Subchapter S status, it may not carry these losses forward to an election year, although it may carry them forward to a subsequent nonelection year within the five-year carry-over period (intervening election years are counted in determining the length of the period).[102]

> **Ex.** X Corporation was formed on January 1, 1958. On December 31, 1958, X was not a Subchapter S corporation. X had a net operating loss of $40,000 for 1958. X elected Subchapter S status for 1050, but this election was terminated in 1961. X could not carry its 1958 net operating loss over to the years 1959 and 1960, since those were election years. However, the loss could be carried forward to 1961, a nonelection year coming within the five-year carry-over period.

If a Subchapter S corporation has a net operating loss in an election year, it cannot carry the loss forward or backward;[103]

---

100 Treas. Reg. § 1.1375-1(c).
101 For a definition of "net operating losses" see I.R.C. § 172.
102 I.R.C. § 1373(d)(1).
103 I.R.C. § 172(h).

rather, a net operating loss incurred by a Subchapter S corporation is passed through to its shareholders, who can deduct the loss as a trade or business expense and apply the deduction against their other income.[104] It should be noted that only net operating losses are passed through; capital losses incurred by an electing corporation are not passed through but are applicable against the corporation's capital gains. Shareholders may resort to the general carry-back and carry-over provisions of the Code with regard to any unused excess of net operating loss over the shareholder's income in a given year.

For each shareholder, however, this pass-through of an electing corporation's net operating loss is limited to the adjusted basis of the corporation's stock held by him during the taxable year plus his basis in any indebtedness of the corporation to him.[105] Moreover, just as in the case of constructive dividends, the basis of a shareholder's investment in a Subchapter S corporation is affected by the net operating loss pass-through provisions. The basis of a shareholder's stock in an electing corporation is reduced by his share of any net operating loss incurred by the corporation in any taxable year, regardless of whether he derives any tax benefit from the loss.[106] If a shareholder's portion of the loss exceeds the basis of his stock, the loss is applied to reduce the basis of any of the corporation's indebtedness held by him.[107] In no event is the basis of stock or indebtedness reduced below zero. If a shareholder has no basis in stock or indebtedness against which to allocate any part of his portion of the corporation's net operating loss, then such part is lost to him forever.

> **Ex.** X, a Subchapter S Corporation, had a net operating loss in 1968 of $40,000. A, its sole shareholder, had a basis of $10,000 in X's stock. A loaned X $10,000 on December 20, 1968. A can utilize the net operating loss only to the extent of the basis of his investment in and loans to the corporation, here $20,000; he can never take advantage of the remainder of the loss. A's basis in both the stock and the indebtedness is reduced to zero. Notice

---

104 I.R.C. § 1374. Since net operating losses pass through the corporation to its shareholders, such losses do not reduce the corporation's earnings and profits. § 1377(c).
105 I.R.C. § 1374(c)(2).
106 I.R.C. § 1376(b)(1).
107 I.R.C. § 1376(b)(2).

that he can take advantage of the basis of the indebtedness even though he made the loan only eleven days before the close of the taxable year. This result suggests that a shareholder may be able to circumvent the basis limitation by increasing his investment in or loans to the corporation so as to give himself added basis against which he can take advantage of the corporation's net operating losses. However, if he should make additional contributions of capital to the corporation, he will have committed those funds to the corporate enterprise, and this may not be desirable, particularly if the corporation is in financial difficulty. If he should increase his loans to the corporation, the new debt may constitute hybrid stock with all the undesirable consequences attendant thereto. Moreover, even if a shareholder's loans to a corporation should not be considered a reinvestment, the advantage of the loan is mitigated by the fact that when the loan is repaid by the corporation, the shareholder will realize a gain, since his basis in the indebtedness is reduced by his share of the corporation's net operating loss.[108]

It is important to recognize that the net operating loss pass-through is not allocated solely among those who are shareholders on the last day of the corporation's taxable year, as is the case with constructive dividends; rather, it is apportioned among all persons who owned stock *at any time* during the taxable year.[109] This is done by computing the corporation's "daily net operating loss" (the total net operating loss for the year divided by the number of days in the taxable year), which is then assigned pro rata to the persons owning stock on each given day.

> Ex. *X*, a Subchapter S Corporation, had a net operating loss of \$36,500 and a capital loss of \$10,000 in 1967. *A* and *B* were the equal and only shareholders of *X* from January 1 to January 16, 1967. On January 16, *A* sold all of his stock to *B* for \$40,000. At the time of the sale, *A* and *B* each had a basis of \$40,000 in their stock of the

---

108 If the loan to the corporation is evidenced by a written instrument, the gain recognized by the shareholder will usually qualify as a capital gain under I.R.C. § 1232; but if the loan to the corporation is made on an open account, the Service has ruled that the shareholder's gain constitutes ordinary income to him. Rev. Rul. 68-537, I.R.B. 1968-41, p. 33; and *see* Rev. Rul. 64-162, 1964-1 C.B. (Part 1) 304.

109 I.R.C. § 1374(b) and (c)(1).

corporation. Here, the daily net operating loss was $100 ($36,500 divided by 365 days). Thus, for the first fifteen days (on the day of sale, stock is regarded as being held by the transferee) of the year, A and B will be assigned $50 loss per day for a total of $750 each. The remainder of the loss is allocated to B, who was the sole shareholder for the rest of the year. A's benefit from the $750 deductions is offset by the fact that his basis in his stock is reduced by his pro rata share of the net operating loss, thus giving him a taxable capital gain of $750 on the sale to B. The capital loss of $10,000 is not passed through to the shareholders, but can be carried forward to be applied against the corporation's capital gains for the succeeding five years.[110]

4. Termination of a Subchapter S election

An election under Subchapter S is effective for the taxable year of the corporation for which it is made and for all succeeding years of the corporation, unless it is terminated in one of the following ways:[111]

(a) **Revocation.** After the first taxable year for which an election is effective, it may be revoked with the consent of all who are shareholders on the day the revocation is filed.[112] If the revocation is made within the first month of a taxable year of the corporation, it will be effective for that year and for all subsequent years. If the revocation is not made within the first month of the taxable year, the earliest date at which it may be effective is the beginning of the following year. If revocation by consent is not feasible in a given year, for timing reasons or otherwise, a corporation wishing to terminate should not despair; for as shown below, there are other, less formal, ways to accomplish the same result.

(b) **Failure of new shareholder to consent.** Termination will result if a new shareholder fails to make a timely consent to the election.[113] It is unclear, however, whether termination will be effected by the transfer of an insignificant amount of stock for the sole purpose of

---

110 I.R.C. § 1212.
111 I.R.C. § 1372(d).
112 I.R.C. § 1372(e)(2).
113 I.R.C. § 1372(e)(1). The manner of making this consent and the time for filing are established in Treas. Reg. § 1.1372-3.

introducing a nonconsenting new shareholder.[114] A corporation might be able to minimize the risk of termination under this rule by buy-out agreements imposing restraints on transfers of stock.[115]

(c) The corporation ceases to satisfy the eligibility requirements of Subchapter S. An election will be terminated if a corporation ceases to meet the requisites of Subchapter S qualification discussed earlier.[116] The ease with which a corporation can be disqualified under this rule seems to undermine the requirement of unanimous consent for a voluntary revocation, *e.g.*, the election can be terminated by transferring shares of stock to a trust, or to a corporation.

(d) Foreign income. An election will be terminated if for any taxable year the electing corporation derives more than 80% of its gross receipts from outside the United States.[117]

(e) Passive investment income. An election will be terminated if for any taxable year more than 20% of a corporation's gross receipts constitute "passive investment income."[118] "Passive investment income" is defined to include "gross receipts derived from royalties, rents, dividends, interest, annuities, and sales and exchanges of stock or securities."[119] This rule does not apply to an electing corporation in its first or second year of active conduct of a trade or business if its passive income is less than $3,000.[120] The Service has ruled[121] that a corporation's gross receipts include liabilities of the corporation which are assumed or accepted by another party pursuant to a sale made by the corporation to the other party.

Special mention should be made of the definition of "rents" for the purposes of Subchapter S. The Regulations provide that "rents" does not include "payments for the use or occupancy of rooms or other space where significant services are also rendered to the oc-

---

114 *See* BITTKER AND EUSTICE, FEDERAL INCOME TAXATION OF CORPORATIONS AND SHAREHOLDERS (2d ed., 1966), 717.
115 *See* Chapter IV *supra.*
116 I.R.C. § 1372(e)(3).
117 I.R.C. § 1372(e)(4).
118 I.R.C. § 1372(e)(5)(A).
119 I.R.C. § 1372(e)(5)(C). Gross receipts from the sale or exchange of stocks or securities are taken into account only to the extent of gains therefrom.
120 I.R.C. § 1372(e)(5)(B).
121 Rev. Rul. 68-364, I.R.B. 1968-28, p. 19.

cupant."[122] The supplying of maid service, for example, constitutes a significant service; whereas the furnishing of heat and light and the cleaning of public entrances does not.[123]

5. Effect of terminating a Subchapter S election

An unfortunate corollary to the ease with which shareholders may terminate a Subchapter S election is that the election can be lost inadvertently.[124] A rise in passive income, the death of a shareholder whose legatees will not consent, a shareholder's transfer of stock to his wife or to a trust for his wife pursuant to a separation or divorce, a shareholder's transfer of stock to a revocable trust created by a form agreement the shareholder acquired in a book for laymen; all of these and many others may cause the termination of the election. The consequences of a termination can be significant. A corporation which has had its Subchapter S election terminated is not eligible to make another election for five years, unless the Commissioner consents to a new election at an earlier date.[125] And, even if the Commissioner should so consent, the right of the shareholders to withdraw previously taxed income (PTI) under the special provisions of Subchapter S is lost irrevocably as a result of the termination and cannot be restored by a subsequent election. Consequently, income which was taxed to the shareholders may be effectively "frozen" in a corporation which has sizable earnings and profits.

---

122 Treas. Reg. § 1.1372-4(b)(5)(iv). *See also* Rev. Rul. 64-232, 1964-2 C.B. 334; Rev. Rul. 65-40, 1965-1 C.B. 429; Rev. Rul. 65-83, 1965-1 C.B. 430; Rev. Rul. 65-91, 1965-1 C.B. 431.

123 Treas. Reg. § 1.1372-4(b)(5)(iv). *See* Bramlette Building Corporation, Inc., 52 T.C. 200 (1969) holding that income from the lease of an office building with the usual services provided constituted rental income.

124 *See, e.g.,* Old Virginia Brick Co., 44 T.C. 724 (1965), where an election was lost when an estate of a deceased shareholder was kept open for an unreasonably long period and was therefore treated as terminated and the stock deemed to have passed to a trust, which automatically terminated the Subchapter S election; *and* Lansing Broadcasting Co., 52 T.C. 299 (1969) where an electing corporation's receipt of a liquidating distribution from a subsidiary was treated as gross receipts from the sale of the stock of the liquidating corporation, the gain from which is characterized as passive investment income under § 1372(e)(5)(C), and consequently resulted in the electing corporation's exceeding the 20% limitation for passive investment income so that its Subchapter S election was terminated. There has been some speculation that Congress might eliminate the passive investment income limitation; but to date, no action has been taken.

125 I.R.C. § 1372(f).

The Subchapter S election is laden with many pitfalls, and an electing corporation should be carefully overseen by its attorney and accountant; but they cannot be present at every transaction each shareholder contemplates; and even if they were, there are circumstances which will terminate the election which are beyond the control of the parties. Thus, a shareholder of a Subchapter S corporation is at the mercy of each of his fellow shareholders' whims, domestic quarrels, and mortality. One means of protection that may be employed is to utilize a buy-out agreement with restrictions on the shareholder's rights to transfer his stock,[126] but that will not entirely eliminate the risk of termination.

C. LOSSES ON SMALL BUSINESS STOCK (§ 1244)

Normally, a loss recognized on the sale of corporate stock and securities, or upon the date that stock and securities become worthless,[127] is treated as a capital loss. A limited exception to this rule is provided for losses on stock or securities that were purchased for purposes that were appropriate and helpful to the conduct of taxpayer's business.[128] For example, losses recognized on stock or securities which the taxpayer acquired to insure a source of inventory for his business are deductible as ordinary business expenses or losses.[129] However, in the usual case, losses on stocks and securities are capital losses.

Loans made by a shareholder to his corporation which become bad debts will usually be treated as short-term losses.[130] If the

---

126 *See* Chapter IV *supra*.

127 When stocks and securities become worthless, they are treated as having been sold for zero on the last day of the taxable year in which they became worthless. I.R.C. § 165(g).

128 Commissioner v. Bagley & Sewall Co., 221 F.2d 944 (C.A. 2 1955). *Cf.* Corn Products Refining Co. v. Commissioner, 350 U.S. 46 (1955).

129 *E.g.,* Electrical Fittings Corporation, 33 T.C. 1026 (1960); Western Wine & Liquor Co., 18 T.C. 1090 (1952); and Tulane Hardwood Lumber Co., 24 T.C. 1146 (1955).

The losses recognized by an attorney on stock he purchased in a corporation for which the attorney served as secretary and general counsel were allowed as an ordinary loss deduction; the court found that the purpose of the stock acquisition was to protect the attorney's position as secretary and general counsel. Charles W. Steadman, 50 T.C. 369 (1968).

130 I.R.C. § 166(d). Most loans which become worthless and were made by a shareholder to a corporation will constitute a nonbusiness bad debt. United States v. Whipple, 373 U.S. 193 (1963). *But see* Trent v. Commissioner, 291 F.2d 669 (C.A. 2 1961) where the loan was incidental to the taxpayer's business and the loss was treated as a business bad debt and therefore deductible as an ordinary loss.

shareholder guarantees a corporate loan, his payment of that loan upon the corporation's default is usually a capital loss.[131]

If several persons were to form a partnership and to conduct business in that form, the operating losses of the partnership would pass through to the individual partners, who would treat them as ordinary loss deductions.[132] Prior to 1958, if those same persons were to form a corporation and to conduct their business in a corporate form, the operating losses of the corporation would not pass through to the individual shareholders; and any loss suffered by the shareholders in their stock would be a capital loss. In 1958, Congress sought to "encourage the flow of new funds into small business" and to minimize the differences in tax treatment of shareholders of small corporations and partners.[133] To this end, Congress made two major changes in the Code; one was the addition of Subchapter S,[134] and the second was the addition of § 1244, allowing an ordinary loss deduction for losses recognized by an individual in "section 1244 stock," subject to maximum dollar limitations.

1. Operation of § 1244

Where an individual recognizes a loss on section 1244 stock[135] which would otherwise be treated as a sale or exchange of a capital asset, the loss will be treated as a deduction from ordinary income.[136] The maximum amount of ordinary loss allowed an individual under § 1244 in any single taxable year is $25,000, unless the individual files a joint income tax return with his spouse for that taxable year, in which event the limitation is increased to $50,000.[137]

Section 1244 is applicable only to losses recognized by individuals; it does not apply to losses on section 1244 stock held by cor-

---

131 *See* Putnam v. Commissioner, 352 U.S. 82 (1956).
132 I.R.C. § 702.
133 H. Rept. No. 2198, 85th Cong., 1st Sess. (June 16, 1958).
134 *See* pp. 267-284 *supra.*
135 "Section 1244 stock" is defined below.
136 § 1244(a).
137 § 1244(b). Moreover, § 1244(d) imposes additional limitations. If the section 1244 stock was acquired by the transfer of depreciated assets (*i.e.,* an asset whose basis exceeded its value), and if the shareholder's basis in his section 1244 stock reflects the excess basis over value of the assets, then the amount of loss on such stock that is attributable to that excess basis does not qualify for § 1244 treatment. Also, any increase in basis of the section 1244 stock from subsequent contributions to capital or otherwise does not qualify for § 1244 treatment.

porations, estates and trusts.[138] A loss on section 1244 stock which is held by a partnership may be taken as an ordinary loss deduction by those individual partners who were also partners when the stock was acquired by the partnership to the extent of each such partner's distributive share of the loss and subject to maximum dollar limitations.[139]

Since § 1244 was intended to encourage investments in small corporations, the relief accorded by that section is limited to losses recognized on section 1244 stock held by the individual who acquired the stock on its issuance and who held it continuously since that date.[140] Thus, section 1244 stock acquired by purchase, gift or devise does not qualify for § 1244 treatment.[141] Where section 1244 stock held by a partnership is distributed to a partner, the partner will not be permitted to use § 1244 for that stock since he was not its original owner.[142] The Regulations provide § 1244 treatment for losses on common stock acquired by the shareholder either as a nontaxable stock dividend distributed on account of section 1244 stock, or in exchange for section 1244 stock pursuant to a recapitalization or an F reorganization.[143]

An individual's ordinary loss on section 1244 stock is treated as a loss from the individual's trade or business for purposes of the net operating loss provisions (§ 172).[144] The significance of this provision is that nonbusiness deductions are deductible only to the extent of nonbusiness income for purposes of computing a net operating loss, whereas business losses are not subject to this restriction.[145]

---

138 Treas. Reg. § 1.1244(a)-1(b); and I.R.C. § 1244(d)(4).
139 Treas. Reg. § 1.1244(a)-1(b). Each partner who qualifies includes his share of § 1244 partnership losses with his other § 1244 losses, and the total is subject to the maximum dollar limitations.
140 Treas. Reg. § 1.1244(a)-1(b).
141 Id. Stock acquired from an investment banking firm will not qualify under § 1244, unless the firm was merely acting as an agent for the issuing corporation in selling an original issue.
142 Treas. Reg. § 1.1244(a)-1(b). This provision is reasonable where applied to a partner-distributee who was not a member of the partnership when the partnership acquired the stock. But, in view of the fact that a partner who was a member of the partnership when the stock was acquired could use § 1244 for his share of partnership loss recognized on account of such stock, it does not seem reasonable to bar that partner from using § 1244 when the stock is distributed to him and he personally suffers the loss.
143 Treas. Reg. § 1.1244(a)-3.
144 I.R.C. § 1244(d)(3).
145 I.R.C. § 172(d)(4).

2. The requirements of qualifying as section 1244 stock

Section 1244 stock must be common stock, whether voting or nonvoting, issued by a domestic corporation.[146]

The requirements of qualifying common stock as section 1244 stock are:[147]

(i) the corporation must adopt a written plan after June 30, 1958, to offer such stock for a period of no more than two years after the plan was adopted;

(ii) at the time such plan was adopted, the corporation must be a "small business corporation";[148]

(iii) at the time such plan was adopted, no portion of a prior offering can be outstanding;[149]

(iv) such stock must be issued by the corporation in exchange for money or other property (other than stocks and securities);[150] and

(v) for the five most recent taxable years ending before the year in which the loss is sustained (or for such fewer years as the corporation was in existence), the corporation must satisfy a gross receipts test, i.e., more than 50% of the corporation's gross receipts must have been received from sources other than: royalties, rents, dividends, interest, annuities, and sales or exchanges of stock or

---

146 I.R.C. § 1244(c)(1), and Treas. Reg. § 1.1244(c)-1.

147 *Id.*

148 A "small business corporation" is defined below.

149 In addition, if another offering is made subsequent to the adoption of the plan, no stock acquired after the subsequent offering will qualify for § 1244 treatment. Treas. Reg. § 1.1244(c)-1(h). Certain modifications of the plan under which the section 1244 stock is to be issued will constitute a subsequent offering and consequently will bar any stock acquired thereafter from § 1244 treatment. Treas. Reg. § 1.1244(c)-1(h). Similarly, the issuance of stock options, stock rights or warrants during the period of the plan will constitute a subsequent offering. Treas. Reg. § 1.1244(c)-1(h).

150 Thus, stock issued for services rendered cannot qualify as section 1244 stock. Stock issued in consideration of a cancellation of indebtedness of the corporation may qualify under section 1244 unless the debt was evidenced by a security or arose out of the performance of a personal service. Treas. Reg. § 1.1244(c)-1(f)(1). If a corporation plans to issue section 1244 stock in consideration of the cancellation of a corporate debt, the corporation should first carefully examine the nature of the "debt" to be cancelled, because if the "debt" is subsequently characterized as an equity investment in the corporation (i.e., hybrid stock), the stock issued in cancellation of that debt will not qualify under § 1244. Edwin C. Hollenbeck, 50 T.C. 740 (1968). *See also* Roland E. Scott, ¶ 68,148 P-H Memo T.C.

securities (only gains from such sales or exchanges are taken into account).[151]

(a) Requirement of a written plan. The common stock must be issued pursuant to a *written* plan adopted by the corporation after June 30, 1958, to offer only such stock during a period specified in the plan ending no more than two years after the plan is adopted.[152] The requirement that the plan be written is strictly enforced.[153]

To insure compliance, the plan should be formally adopted by the Board of Directors and included in the corporate minutes. The written plan should make specific reference to § 1244, and the plan should adopt such limitations as are necessary to comply: with the dollar limitations (imposed by § 1244(c)(2)) on the aggregate amount that can be offered under the plan; with the restrictions on the period of time during which such stock can be offered; and with the other requisites of § 1244.

(b) Definition of "small business corporation." A corporation qualifies as a small business corporation if at the time the written plan is adopted, the corporation complies with two conditions:

(i) the sum of the aggregate dollar amounts to be paid for stock which may be offered under the plan plus the aggregate amount

---

151 Since this test must be satisfied at the time that the loss is recognized, a shareholder cannot know with certainty when stock is issued to him whether it will qualify as section 1244 stock when a loss occurs.

152 Treas. Reg. § 1.1244(c)-1(c). For additional requirements of record keeping by both the corporation and the shareholder *see* Treas. Reg. § 1.1244(e)-1.

153 *See* Bernard Spiegel, 49 T.C. 527 (1968) denying § 1244 benefits; the court held that the written notes of the corporation's lawyer and accountant did not constitute a written plan adopted by the corporation. *See also* Sofie Eger, ¶ 66,192 P-H Memo T.C., *reversed,* 393 F.2d 243 (C.A. 2 1968). In *Eger,* the minutes of the corporation made reference to the adoption of a plan and stated that common stock would be issued under § 1244; but the minutes failed to state any details of the plan such as: the period during which the stock would be offered or the maximum amount of consideration payable for the stock. The Tax Court held that this was insufficient to constitute a written plan. While the Second Circuit reversed, the court emphasized that the stock was issued prior to the promulgation of the Regulations. The Tax Court pointed out in *Eger* that if the corporate minutes had contained the details of the plan, that would have been sufficient to satisfy the written plan requisite. Sofie Eger *supra,* note 7. For a recent decision stressing the significance of having the details of the plan in writing, *see* Pierre Godart, 51 T.C. 937 (1969).

of money or other property[154] which was received by the corporation after June 30, 1958, for its stock, or as a contribution to capital and as paid-in surplus, must not exceed $500,000;[155] and (ii) the sum of the aggregate dollar amounts to be paid for stock which may be offered under the plan plus the equity capital of the corporation as of the date of the plan's adoption must not exceed $1,000,000.[156]

It is noteworthy that unlike Subchapter S, for purposes of § 1244, the "small" attribute of a corporation refers to the size of its capital rather than to the number of its shareholders.

3. Usefulness of § 1244

One of the nicer aspects of § 1244 is that the failure to comply with its provisions does not cause any adverse tax consequences other than the loss of the benefits of that section. Consequently, there is every reason to have a corporation adopt a written plan in compliance with § 1244 whenever new common stock (voting or nonvoting) is to be issued for money or other property, if the conditions of that section will otherwise be satisfied or if it appears that they will be satisfied. It will be too late to elect § 1244 treatment after the stock is issued.

In determining the form of ownership of a corporate entity, the potential advantages of § 1244 must be considered. But it must be remembered that § 1244 is useful primarily where the business fails or at least is highly unsuccessful. It does not provide the shareholder with the advantage of a deduction of the operating losses of the corporation, as does Subchapter S. Nevertheless, more often than not, Subchapter S will not be a desirable election, and § 1244 is a useful hedge against failure.

---

154 The other property is taken into account at its basis on the date of contribution reduced by any liabilities to which it was subject. Treas. Reg. § 1.1244(c)-2(b)(1).
155 I.R.C. § 1244(c)(2); and Treas. Reg. § 1.1244(c)-2(b).
156 Treas. Reg. § 1.1244(c)-2(c); and I.R.C. § 1244(c)(2).

VI

Debt and Preferred Stock

A. ADVANTAGES AND DETRIMENTS OF DEBT INSTRUMENTS

When parties form a corporation, they must determine whether their contributions to the corporation should be made in the form of an equity investment or whether funds or property should be "loaned" to the corporation. A loan to the corporation may be represented by a security or by short-term notes,[1] both of which are debt instruments.

The question whether property contributed to a corporation should be an investment or a loan does not arise exclusively on formation of the corporation. Property is frequently contributed to a controlled corporation that has been in existence for some years, and the issue is also present there. It is possible for the question to arise in a reorganization setting, but the fact that securities may be treated as boot and that corporate notes will certainly be treated as boot will often discourage the shifting of equity interests into debt.

If the parties have decided to use debt instruments, they must give due account to the fact that while securities do not constitute boot in a section 351 exchange, corporate notes do not enjoy that exclusion. In a few circumstances the transferor may wish to recognize gain on the contribution of his property to the corporation, so that the corporation will enjoy a higher basis in the property received by it.[2] The distribution of short-term notes is one means of accomplishing that. In most circumstances the transferor will not wish to recognize gain at the time the transfer is made. However, when the transferred asset is sold by the corporation some

---

1 Other representations are also possible, but if long term notes are used, the possibility exists that they will be treated as securities. *See* Chapter V, pp. 260-261 *supra.*
2 I.R.C. § 362(a). *See* Chapter V, pp. 266-267 *supra.*

years later, the corporation may contend that the transferor received boot in order to increase its basis. The corporation is particularly likely to make that contention if the statutory period for assessing the transferor has expired.

1. Corporation's payment of interest and principal on a debt instrument

There are several significant tax advantages in using debt instruments. The corporation's payment of interest on the debt is a deductible expense.[3] In contrast, the corporation's payment of dividends on an equity investment is not deductible. The corporation's repayment of the principal of the debt instrument is a return of the capital of the bondholder or lender and usually will not cause him any tax consequences.[4] Again, in contrast, the corporation's redemption of its stock from a shareholder may be treated as a dividend to the shareholder.[5]

2. Hybrid stock and "thin incorporation"

A debt instrument will be treated as corporate stock where the attributes of the instrument more nearly resemble those of an equity investment than those of a debt, i.e., the so-called "hybrid stock."

When a debt is treated as stock, it may create unpleasant consequences. Interest paid on the debt is not deductible, and payments made in retirement of the debt may constitute dividends. If the parties have relied on a different treatment and acted accordingly, this change could prove to be financially embarrassing. As previously noted,[6] if the corporation has made a Subchapter S election, the presence of hybrid stock *may* cause a termination of that election.

Some characteristics which are examined in determining whether a debt instrument constitutes hybrid stock are: whether the debt is held proportionately by the shareholders; whether the corporation's capital was insufficient to conduct its business and the debt was an essential supplement; whether the debt is subordinated to the

---

3 I.R.C. § 163.
4 If the corporation had previously made an election under Subchapter S, the lender's basis in his debt instrument may have been reduced because of a pass-through of the corporation's net operating losses. *See* Chapter V, pp. 279-280 *supra*. In such event, the lender may recognize income on the repayment of the debt.
5 *See* Chapter I, pp. 11-26 *supra*.
6 Chapter V, pp. 268-269 *supra*.

claims of creditors; whether the debt has a fixed maturity date and bears interest which is actually paid; whether the lender intends to enforce the obligations even where it would be inconvenient to the corporation for him to do so; whether the corporation could have obtained the borrowed funds from outside lending institutions; and the debt-capital ratio of the business.

The debt-capital ratio is one of the single most important factors to be considered in determining whether debt is hybrid stock. Where the amount of a corporation's outstanding debt is disproportionately high with respect to the amount of capital invested in the corporation, the situation is described as a "thin incorporation." The thin incorporation concept is rarely applicable if the debt-capital ratio is less than 2:1, but that ratio should not be regarded as a bench mark.

In appropriate circumstances a very high debt-capital ratio has been sustained.[7] A thin capitalization does not require that the debt be characterized as stock; it is merely one factor, albeit a highly significant factor, in determining whether the debt is hybrid stock.[8]

Moreover, where an ongoing business is contributed to a corporation, good will of that business may be added to the corporation's assets in mitigation of an imbalance in favor of debt.[9]

An excessive amount of debt may constitute an intolerable burden for a burgeoning corporation. The corporation's interest payments on the debt may inhibit its growth and possibly even endanger its existence. If the lenders refrain from collecting the interest in order to permit the corporation to use the funds, and if they do not collect the principal on maturity, the risk of the debt's being characterized as hybrid stock is substantially increased.

---

7 *E.g.,* Baker Commodities, Inc., 48 T.C. 374 (1967) sustaining a debt-capital ratio of almost 700:1.

8 Baker Commodities, Inc., 48 T.C. 374 (1967); and Gooding Amusement Co., 23 T.C. 408, *affirmed,* 236 F.2d 159 (C.A. 6 1956), *cert. denied,* 352 U.S. 1031 (1957); and Lots, Inc., 49 T.C. 541 (1968), Acq., I.R.B. 1968-35. In *Lots* the Tax Court held that loans from a principal shareholder of the corporation constituted debt even though the corporation was thinly capitalized. *See* Berkowitz v. United States, 23 A.F.T.R.2d 69-1582 (C.A. 5 1969) affirming a judgment n.o.v. which had overturned a jury verdict granting interest deductions on loans made to a corporation by its shareholders when the debt-capital ratio exceeded 21:1. The Fifth Circuit emphasized, however, that no single test was conclusive in determining this issue, and the court listed eleven factors to be considered.

9 *E.g.,* Estate of Miller v. Commissioner, 239 F.2d 729 (C.A. 9 1956).

3. Loans guaranteed by shareholders

As an alternative to making direct loans to a corporation, the shareholders might cause the corporation to borrow the needed funds from a lending institution, and the shareholders could personally guarantee the repayment of the loan. Since such loans are usually made on reliance of the credit of the shareholders rather than the corporation, it is arguable that the substance of the transaction is a loan to the shareholder and an equity investment of the borrowed funds by the shareholders. If the transaction were so characterized, the corporation would not be allowed an income tax deduction for interest payments made on account of the loan, and all payments made by the corporation on account of the loan would constitute constructive dividends to the shareholders who guaranteed it.

The Service has raised this issue in several cases, but so far it has not achieved a significant victory.[10] However, the Service is not likely to abandon this contention so easily; and if the corporation has a high debt-capital ratio, any loans made to it pursuant to a guarantee of the shareholders is subject to some risk.[11]

In any event, even if the loan is not attributed to the shareholder, any loss suffered by the shareholder for repayment of the debt under his guaranty will usually be treated as a nonbusiness bad debt which is deductible as a short-term capital loss.[12]

4. Nontax use of debt

A shareholder may not wish to place more than a certain amount of capital at the risk of the business, but he may be willing to advance additional funds as a secured creditor. Debt may be employed to provide the lender with a senior interest—*i.e.*, a preference over shareholders for the return on his investment and for the return of his investment upon liquidation.

Debt instruments can be given by a shareholder to his family

---

10 The Service advanced this contention unsuccessfully in Murphy Logging Co. v. United States, 378 F.2d 222 (C.A. 9 1967), *reversing* 239 F. Supp. 794 (D. Ore. 1965); and again in a different context in Santa Anita Consolidated, Inc., 50 T.C. 536 (1968), Acq., I.R.B. 1969-8.

11 *See* Comment, *Guaranteed Loans and Direct Loans: Equal Treatment Under the Tax Law*, 16 U.C.L.A. L. REV. 421 (1969).

12 Putnam v. Commissioner, 352 U.S. 82 (1956). *See* I.R.C. § 166(d).

members or to a charitable organization without diluting the transferor's control of the corporation. Debt can be used in this fashion as a form of bail-out.

5. Losses incurred on worthless securities and bad debts

If a corporate business fails, the losses on the debt instruments will be treated as capital losses. If the amount loaned had instead been invested in common stock of the corporation, and if the stock qualified under § 1244, the loss on that stock would be an ordinary loss deduction.

If a Subchapter S election were made, the operating losses of the business are deductible by the shareholder to the extent of his basis in both stock and debt of the corporation. Thus, debt may be used in conjunction with a Subchapter S election; but if the debt is treated as hybrid stock, there is a risk that the election will be terminated.[13]

B. NONTAX CONSIDERATIONS IN THE USE OF PREFERRED STOCK

Preferred stock has many uses for both business planning and estate planning purposes. In some circumstances, however, nonvoting common stock or debt may serve a purpose equally as well as preferred stock. One advantage of preferred stock over debt is that the former can be acquired in a recapitalization or stock dividend without incurring tax liabilities while that cannot be done with debt instruments. Another consideration is that the corporation's burden of meeting interest obligations may become oppressive and stifle the company's growth; and a mandatory maturity for repayment of the debt may be burdensome to the corporation. An advantage of preferred stock over nonvoting common stock is that preferred provides more security to the holder and accordingly may be more marketable.

One of the useful attributes of preferred stock is that because of its preferential rights and because it does not usually participate in the growth of the business but instead provides a fixed rate of return and a fixed amount on liquidation, it can be valued more

---

13 *See* Chapter V, pp. 268-269 *supra.*

readily than common. Also, preferred stock can be issued in order to reduce the value of the outstanding common stock.

1. Estate planning considerations

(a) Gifts to the donor's family. The controlling shareholder of a closely held corporation may wish to divide corporate stock among members of his family, but he may also wish to retain control of the corporation during his life. Some of the advantages of giving away nonvoting corporate stock are that it will reduce the donor's estate tax liability; and if dividends are paid, it is a means of splitting the income among several members of the family. The shareholder could donate preferred stock[14] for this purpose, or he could give nonvoting common stock.

When contemplating making gifts of corporate stock for purposes of reducing the donor's estate, the provisions of § 303 should be considered.[15] When applicable, § 303 provides a valuable device for withdrawing funds from the corporation after the shareholder's demise. If the shareholder's stock in the corporation will likely qualify for § 303 treatment on the shareholder's death,[16] the gift of shares of such stock can endanger the availability of § 303 by reducing the percentage of the decedent's estate that is attributable to his stock. Conversely, if it is a close question whether the stock will qualify under § 303, gifts of other assets of the shareholder (*i.e.*, assets other than such stock) may reduce the size of his gross and taxable estates and thereby increase the percentage of his estate represented by the corporate stock.

A shareholder may wish to retain a fixed income from the corporate business and to divorce himself (and his gross estate on death) from the future growth of the business. One possibility is to recapitalize the corporation so that the shareholder acquires preferred stock having a value equal to a large percentage of the net worth of the corporation. The shareholder can then give his relatives

---

14 The gift of the preferred stock will not cause adverse tax consequences to the donor even where it is section 306 stock (§ 306(b)(3)); but if it is section 306 stock, it will maintain that taint in the donee's hands. § 306(c)(1)(C).

15 *See* Chapter I, pp. 31-36 *supra.*

16 Section 303 requires that the estate tax value of the stock included in a deceased shareholder's gross estate must exceed either 35% of the value of the decedent's gross estate or 50% of the value of the decedent's taxable estate. § 303(b)(2).

most of his common stock and retain the preferred. Thus, he will stabilize his interest in the business, since a subsequent rise in the value of the corporation will inure only to the benefit of the owners of the common stock. An added advantage to this arrangement is that the value of the gifts to the shareholder's family will be depressed, since most of that value will represent the company's potential for future growth rather than its present equity. Consequently, the gift tax cost of the arrangement should not prove too burdensome. A major obstacle to this arrangement is that the corporation may suffer from having to distribute large amounts as nondeductible dividends on the preferred stock. Thus, while preferred stock can be used for this purpose, moderation should be employed. On the shareholder's death the preferred stock can be redeemed pursuant to a complete termination of the estate's (or legatee's) interest in the corporation (§ 302(b)(3)) unless there are attribution problems that cannot be resolved.[17] If § 303 is applicable, the stock protected by that section can be redeemed without adverse tax consequences irrespective of attribution rules.

(b) Protection of surviving beneficiaries. It may not be feasible to have the shareholder's stock redeemed at his death, or he may prefer that it not be redeemed because of his faith in the business. In such event he may wish to provide his beneficiaries with some security that they will receive income from the business and will not be "squeezed out" of their investment.[18] Preferred stock may be employed as one step toward insuring that the beneficiaries will receive a minimum income from the business, but additional protections against squeeze-outs should be adopted.[19]

(c) Gifts to charitable organizations. Under present law, a gift of corporate stock to a qualified charity is a useful estate planning device.[20] One advantage of such gifts, whether inter vivos or testa-

---

17 Where the stock is included in the decedent's estate, it will lose any taint it may have had as section 306 stock. I.R.C. § 306(c). In any event, § 303 takes precedence over § 306; and a complete termination of a shareholder's interest (§ 302(b)(3)) is another exception to § 306 treatment. I.R.C. § 306(b)(1) and (2).

18 See Chapter IV, pp. 183-184 supra.

19 Id.

20 However, the reader should be on notice that there are many changes proposed in H.R. 13270 (the Tax Reform Act of 1969) affecting gifts of property to charities; and if that bill is enacted, it should be studied carefully before any gifts of stock are made.

mentary, is that the resulting reduction in the donor's estate tax liability may permit the donor's family to retain control of the corporation. The donee-charity may be a qualified private charitable foundation where that is desirable.[21] The Ford Motor Company, of which one-third of the outstanding equity is owned by the Ford Foundation, is a monument to the successful employment of this plan.

If a shareholder plans to make gifts of stock to a charity, there are advantages to making the gifts during his life rather than making testamentary bequests. An inter vivos gift to a qualified charity, where made properly, will not cause the donor any gift tax liability,[22] and the value of the stocks (including appreciation accruing after the gift) is thereby removed from the donor's estate. In addition, the donor will receive an income tax deduction, subject to the percentage ceilings on deductions for such gifts.[23] Precaution should be taken that the donated stock has such attributes that it can readily be valued.

Another use of charitable beneficiaries for planning purposes is to combine an inter vivos gift of a future interest to a member of the donor's family with a gift to a qualified charity of the income interest in the property. This arrangement utilizes the gift tax deduction for the charitable gift, thereby reducing the value of the gift to the donor's family which is subject to gift tax consequences; and if the donor precludes any possibility that the donated prop-

---

21 The Treasury has proposed amendments to the Code to limit some of the flexibility now available in making gifts of corporate stock to private charitable foundations, *i.e.*, it would limit the percentage of voting power and equity that a foundation could own in a corporation; it would require the management of the foundation to be separated from the donor and his family after a specified period of time; and it would limit tax deductions where the donor or his family retained control of the corporation. Sen. Comm. on Finance, 89th Cong., 1st Sess., Treasury Department Report on Private Foundations 36 (Comm. Print 1965). *See* Henderson, *The Use of Different Classes of Stock in Maintaining Control in the Close Corporation*, 24 N.Y.U. Tax Inst. 531, 550-552 (1966). Sec. 101(b) of the Tax Reform Act of 1969 proposes to add § 4942 (requiring that private foundations provide a minimum annual return for their beneficiaries) and § 4943 (imposing severe limitations on the percentage of stock of a corporation that can be owned by the private foundation) to the 1954 Code. H.R. 13270, 91st Cong., 1st Sess. At this writing, H.R. 13270 has been passed by the House and is pending in the Senate.

22 I.R.C. § 2522 provides a gift tax deduction for gifts to qualified charities.

23 I.R.C. § 170.

erty will revert to him,[24] he can also take an income tax deduction for the value of the charitable portion of the gift. Moreover, the gift removes the donated property from his gross estate, and any appreciation in the donated property is similarly excluded from estate taxation. However, the reader should beware that the proposed Tax Reform Act of 1969 (H.R. 13270) would amend §§ 170 and 2522 to preclude both an income tax deduction and a gift tax deduction for transfers of an income interest in a trust to a charity as indicated above.[25] Thus, this type of arrangement will not be useful if those amendments are enacted.

If the donated property is to be stock of a closely held corporation, the stock must be invested with guarantees that dividends will be paid; otherwise the value of the income interest in the stock may be incalculable, and accordingly no charitable deduction will be allowed for either income or gift tax purposes.[26] Preferred stock can be useful for this purpose, but additional guarantees that dividends will be paid must be provided, e.g., the preferred stock may be granted voting rights if dividends are not timely paid. The trustee should be an independent party, such as a corporate fiduciary, who cannot be regarded as under the control of the donor. The following hypothetical example illustrates this device.

B, a widower, is in a 60% income tax bracket. B is contemplating giving stock of the X Corporation presently valued at $30,000 to his son, S, who is 15 years old. However, B does not wish S to receive the property for 10 years. If B were to wait 10 years

---

24 I.R.C. § 170(b)(1)(D) denies a charitable deduction for gifts made in trust where the grantor has a reversionary interest in the income or principle, the value of which interest is greater than 5% of the value of the donated property. Thus, the donor should preclude any reversion to himself.

25 § 201(a) and (h) of H.R. 13270, 91st Cong., 1st Sess. As of this writing, H.R. 13270 was passed by the House and is pending in the Senate.

26 This is particularly true when the donor controls the corporation and therefore controls whether or not dividends will be paid. Treas. Reg, § 1.170-1(e). In Elsie McK. Morgan, 42 T.C. 1080 (1964), affirmed per curiam, 353 F.2d 209 (C.A. 9 1965), cert. denied, 384 U.S. 918, a charitable deduction was denied for both income and gift tax purposes where stock of a closely held corporation was donated to a trust, the income from which was payable to a charity for a period of 20 years. Cf. Leonard Rosen, 48 T.C. 834 (1967) for a similar result where the issue concerned the allowance of the gift tax annual exclusion (§ 2503) for the gift of an income interest of a trust. However, Rosen was reversed on appeal. Rosen v. Commissioner, 397 F.2d 245 (C.A. 4 1968),

and then make the gift, the stock may appreciate in value, thereby increasing the gift tax consequences; or B might die during the 10-year period, in which event the stock would be included in his estate. B could give the stock in trust for S to be distributed to S 10 years hence, but that would involve a gift of $30,000 and would exhaust B's lifetime exemption.[27] Alternatively, B could create a trust in which the income from the stock is payable to a qualified charity for 10 years and then the stock is to be distributed to S or S's estate. Assuming that the donated stock provides sufficient security of earning dividends that the income interest can be valued, the result could be as follows:

The value of a 10-year gift of an income interest for gift tax purposes is $0.291081 \times 30,000 = \$8,732.43$.[28] The value of the income interest is deductible for gift tax purposes,[29] and therefore the value of the gift of the future interest to S is $21,268, which may be offset by the donor's lifetime exemption if that is unused. The value of the 10-year interest for purposes of determining an *income* tax deduction for charitable contributions[30] is the same as its value for gift tax purposes.[31] Thus, B is entitled to an income tax deduction of $8,732.43, which at a 60% tax bracket nets him an after-tax savings of $5,239, *i.e.*, the deduction released $5,239 of B's funds which otherwise would be paid as taxes.

If B does not make the gift and retains the stock, which, let us assume, provides a 4% return, B would receive $1,200 per year of which he would retain 40% or $480 after taxes. Over a 10-year

27 I.R.C. § 2521. The gift can be designed to provide B with a $3,000 exclusion (§ 2503) which would reduce the amount of the gift that is subject to gift tax consequences.

28 Treas. Reg. § 25.2512-5, Table II. These tables are based on an assumed 3½% return, but the Government may challenge the use of the tables if the value of the income interest in the stocks is problematical.

29 I.R.C. § 2522. But no gift tax deduction will be permitted under the amended version of § 2522 proposed in § 201(h) of the Tax Reform Act of 1969. *See* note 25 *supra* and accompanying text.

30 Gifts in trust for the use of a qualified charity are deductible (Treas. Reg. §§ 1.170-1(d)(1), and 1.170-2(a)), but the deduction is limited to 20% of the donor's adjusted gross income. Treas. Reg. § 1.170-2(b). But no income tax deduction will be permitted if the amendment to § 170 proposed by § 201(a) of the Tax Reform Act of 1969 is adopted. *See* note 25 *supra* and accompanying text.

31 Treas. Reg. § 1.170-1(d) adopts the tables used for estate tax purposes (Treas, Reg. § 20.2031-7) which are identical to the gift tax tables.

period, B would have $4,800 compared to the $5,239 he acquired by giving the stocks to the trust. Moreover, the fact that he would receive the $5,239 in the year after the gift was made, while the income from the stock will be spread over a 10-year period, provides another small advantage in making the gift.

However, the primary advantage is not income tax savings, but potential estate tax savings. If B were to die during the 10-year period without having made the gift, the full value of the stock ($30,000) plus appreciation would be included in B's estate, and if we assume a 32% estate tax bracket, the tax on the stocks will be $9,400.[32] The relief from this tax is a substantial benefit.

Of course, where large amounts are involved, the savings will be more dramatic.

An alternative arrangement is to establish a trust with income to relatives for a given period and the remainder to a charity. In that event the income interest of the relatives may be subject to the $3,000 gift tax exclusion, and the remainder interest to the charity is deductible for both gift tax and income tax purposes.[33] Caution must be observed to insure that the value of the charity's remainder is not subject to diversion by the trustee to the income beneficiaries.[34] The proposed Tax Reform Act of 1969 contains provisions which would deny an income tax, gift tax and estate tax deduction for remainder interests in a trust given to a charity, unless the interest of the income beneficiary is for a stated number of years or for life and is a fixed dollar amount per year (an annuity) or a fixed percentage of the value of the trust's assets per year (a unitrust).[35] Also, the gift of stock of a closely held corpora-

---

32 If the stocks were removed from the estate, they would reduce the estate tax burden at the top bracket of the estate.

33 The Service initially issued (November 10, 1965) a proposed regulation stating that a remainder interest to a charity did not qualify for the 30% limitation (30% of adjusted gross income) on gifts to public charities but was limited to 20%. The Service withdrew the proposed regulation 30 days after issuance and announced that it would not take a position on this issue without first holding a public hearing. See DESMOND, HIGHER EDUCATION AND TAX MOTIVATED GIVING, pp. 51-52 (American College Public Relations Assoc., 1967). In Alice Tully, 48 T.C. 235 (1967), the Tax Court held that the value of a remainder interest to a charity was covered by the 30% limitation.

34 See William T. Grant, 48 T.C. 606 (1967) for an illustration of the problems that might be encountered in this plan, which, however, was successful in that case.

35 § 201(e), (h) and (i) of H.R. 13270, 91st Cong., 1st Sess.

tion to a charity remainder trust under the bill would probably not create any tax deductions unless an independent trustee has sole responsibility for determining the trust's net asset value each year.[36]

The gift of preferred stock to a charity can also be used as a form of bail-out of corporate earnings.

> **Ex.** The X Corporation has $200,000 accumulated earnings and profits. C is the sole shareholder of X, and C is in a 70% income tax bracket. If X were to declare a $100,000 dividend to C, C would retain $30,000 of it after taxes. Instead, C can have X declare a dividend of $100,000 par value 5% preferred stock with a fair market value of $100,000. The stock is to be redeemed 5 years after issue. There is no tax to C on receiving the stock dividend, but the preferred stock is section 306 stock. C then donates the stock to a qualified charity and takes a $100,000 charitable deduction[37] which reduces his tax bill by $70,000. Of course, the charity, a tax-exempt organization, recognizes no income when the stocks are redeemed 5 years later.
>
> Thus, C nets $40,000 more by donating the stock than he would retain by withdrawing the funds as a dividend. The cost of this savings is the payment of dividends of $5,000 per year to the charity, which total $25,000 after 5 years; that still leaves C $15,000 ahead, and the additional $25,000 cost is paid by the corporation.[38] There is a serious risk that the Service will attack the plan as a prearranged redemption made on behalf of the donor with the charity acting as his agent, but if the stocks are held for a 5-year period, that is a difficult argument for the Service to sustain.[39] Nevertheless, the plan is designed to provide the donor with a windfall by trading on the charitable status of the donee, and that invites attack. The proposed Tax Reform Act of 1969 would

---

36 H. Rept. No. 91-413 (Part 1), 91st Cong., 1st Sess. (August 2, 1969), p. 60.

37 Rev. Rul. 57-328, 1957-2 C.B. 229 provides that a charitable deduction will be allowed for such gifts, that the donor will not recognize income by making the gift nor will he recognize income when the stock is sold by the charity. Of course, C will lose the basis that was allocated under I.R.C. § 307 to the preferred stock when the dividend was made.

38 This cost can be halved by having the preferred stock redeemed seriatum over the 5-year period.

39 *Cf.* Chamberlin v. Commissioner, 207 F.2d 462 (C.A. 6 1953), *cert. denied*, 347 U.S. 918 (1954).

deny a tax deduction to C for the value of the preferred stock to the extent that its value exceeds C's basis therein.[40] Thus, if enacted, the proposed amendment would eliminate this loophole.

(d) Use of preferred stock in connection with a redemption of a decedent's stock under § 303. Section 303 provides that the redemption of stock included in the gross estate of a decedent will be treated as a purchase, rather than as a distribution essentially equivalent to a dividend, if the requisites of that section are met.[41] A potential obstacle to utilizing § 303 is the problem of valuing stock of a closely held corporation. An accurate valuation of the stock is essential in order to determine whether the 35%-50% test of § 303 is satisfied.[42] Consequently, the price at which the stock is sold to the corporation must be carefully set. If the parties executed a buy-out agreement before the decedent's death, the valuation problem may be resolved. It is possible for the buy-out agreement to establish the value of the stock for estate tax purposes if certain conditions are met,[43] and in any event the agreement will usually establish the selling price. The discussion below deals with the situation where the redemption price of the decedent's stock is not fixed by a buy-out agreement, and thus the price must be negotiated.

The decedent's personal representative may face some difficulties if he sells the decedent's stock to the corporation for an amount less than the value ultimately ascribed to it for federal estate tax purposes. In that case the estate will be taxed on a stock value in excess of the amount actually realized on the sale of the stock. If the selling price is substantially less than the estate tax value, the estate taxes imposed on account of the stock may approach or even exceed the amount realized from the sale; and in that event the estate may have a serious liquidity problem.

It would also be disadvantageous to sell the decedent's stock for an amount substantially in excess of the stock's estate tax value. In that case the Service might contend that the difference between

---

40 § 201(c)(1) of H.R. 13270, 91st Cong., 1st Sess.
41 *See* Chapter I, pp. 31-36 *supra*.
42 Section 303(b)(2) requires that stock included in the decedent's gross estate have an estate tax value which is greater than 35% of the value of the decedent's gross estate or alternatively is greater than 50% of the decedent's taxable estate.
43 *See* Chapter IV, pp. 184-185 *supra*.

the stock price and its value was not given in consideration for the stock and consequently that amount of the payment will not be covered by § 303 and may well be treated as a dividend to the recipient. Another possibility is that the excess payment will be treated as a gift from other shareholders of the corporation who will be subjected to gift tax consequences.

Thus, ideally, the price of the stock should approximate its estate tax value as closely as possible. One solution might be to defer the sale of the stock until the estate tax valuation is finally determined and then set the price accordingly. However, the Service's audit of the estate tax return may take several years; and in the meantime, the estate must pay its expenses, and an estate tax payment is required to be made within 15 months after the decedent's death. Consequently, the estate may need to consummate the sale before the audit is completed in order to meet its obligations. However, where stock included in a decedent's gross estate qualifies under § 303, it is likely that the estate will also qualify under § 6166 for an extension of time in which to pay the estate tax; and if so, this will mitigate the estate's immediate need for liquidity.

One alternative is for the fiduciary to borrow from the corporation the liquid funds needed by the estate. Such loans create tax risks: for example, the loan may trigger the imposition of an accumulated earnings tax;[44] or possibly the loan may be treated as a disguised dividend. If the loan is made on a short-term basis and if in fact it is repaid promptly, the risk of dividend treatment is not great.

Another alternative is to recapitalize the corporation within one year of the decedent's death, so that the estate receives preferred stock in exchange for its common or receives preferred and common stock in exchange for its common; or the corporation may instead distribute preferred stock to the decedent's estate as a stock dividend on the decedent's common stock. As noted in Chapters I and III, the recapitalization or stock dividend should not cause any recognition of income, since only stock of the corporation will be distributed or exchanged. Preferred stock usually is easier to value

---

44 I.R.C. §§ 531-537. The presence of loans to shareholders may invite an inquiry as to whether the corporation has accumulated earnings beyond the reasonable needs of the business.

than common because the return payable on the stock and the redemption value may be readily determined. The preferred stock received in the recapitalization or stock dividend will be section 303 stock because its basis is determined by reference to the common stock for which it was exchanged and the original common stock was covered by § 303.[45] It will not matter that the preferred stock is also section 306 stock if it is sold under the umbrella of § 303.[46] The preferred stock can thus be redeemed by the corporation under § 303 at values which can be determined with a reasonable degree of certainty. However, if the recapitalization is effected after the decedent's death, the basis of the common stock owned by him at his death must be allocated among the new shares of common and preferred stock issued in the recapitalization.[47] Similarly, if preferred stock were distributed to the deceased shareholder's estate as a stock dividend, part of the basis of the common stock would be allocated to the preferred shares.[48] Consequently, the basis of the preferred shares received in the recapitalization or stock dividend distribution will usually be less than the fair market value of those shares; and as a result, the estate will recognize a gain on the redemption of those shares to the extent that the redemption price exceeds its basis in the stock. If the redemption is effected within six months of the decedent's demise, the gain may be a short-term capital gain.

If the recapitalization or stock dividend were effected prior to the decedent's death, the estate's basis in the preferred shares would equal the estate tax value of those shares,[49] and thus the capital gains problem can be avoided when it is feasible to place the preferred shares in the hands of the decedent prior to his death.

Another solution (and perhaps the simplest) to the valuation problem is for the decedent's personal representative to sell the stock to the corporation at a price to be equal to the final determination of the stock's estate tax value. Thus, the sale will be consummated immediately, but the selling price will not be determined until the estate tax value is established. The corporation can

---

45 I.R.C. § 303(c).
46 Treas. Reg. § 1.303-2(d).
47 Treas. Reg. § 1.358-2.
48 I.R.C. § 307.
49 I.R.C. § 1014.

make a sizable down payment immediately, and when the estate tax value is determined, appropriate adjustments can be made.

2. Business planning considerations

Where there are several investors in a business, they may have entirely different wishes as to the nature and productivity of their investment, and different classes of stock can be useful in complying with their disparate goals. For example, one group of investors may desire substantial security for their capital investment and some assurance of a minimum return on their investment. Preferred stock or debt are means of accomplishing that. The other investors, who receive common stock, accept a greater risk; but if the business is successful, they are the principal beneficiaries of its growth.

(a) Allocation of stock between capital and services. The type of arrangement described above is useful when the primary contribution of one group of shareholders is capital and the contribution of the second group of shareholders is entrepreneurial talent, i.e., the latter group will operate the business and provide the management and expertise. The definitive treatment of this subject was written by Herwitz in his excellent article in the *Harvard Law Review*,[50] and the reader is urged to examine it carefully. The following discussion summarizes some of the considerations in using preferred stock or debt for this purpose.

S and C desire to form a corporation for the production and marketing of widgets. C will contribute $40,000 cash plus liquid assets having a fair market value of $20,000 and a tax basis of $5,000 to the enterprise. S will contribute services, including his expertise in the widgets business. S and C decide to form a corporation to conduct the business. S is not willing to join the enterprise solely for a salary; he demands a proprietary interest in the business so that he can share in its anticipated subsequent growth which will be due in large part to his efforts and expertise. C is willing to accept S as a co-venturer, and since he values S's services as approximately equal to his capital contribution, he agrees to an equal split of the profits.

Since S will need some of the profits of the business to meet his

---

50 Herwitz, *Allocation of Stock Between Services and Capital in the Organization of a Closely Held Corporation*, 75 HARV. L. REV. 1098 (1962).

living expenses, S will want a salary from the corporation. Instead, the corporation could distribute dividends to S, but that would be an extravagant waste of tax deductions, since reasonable salaries for employees are deductible and dividends are not. However, S will not wish all of his compensation in salary; since if the business is successful, his income tax burden would soon become excessive; and consequently S will wish part of his interest in the corporation to be reflected in growth common stocks.

On the other hand, while S is receiving a salary which constitutes a senior return on his investment of services, C has no comparable senior return on his capital investment. If S is paid a salary, and the net profits after payment of S's salary were then divided equally between S and C, the latter would be seriously disadvantaged. S and C might agree on an unequal distribution of common stock—i.e., 75% to C and 25% to S—to compensate for S's senior return via a salary; but the proper division depends upon the size of S's salary and the profits remaining after payment; and those figures are likely to change each year. It is difficult to estimate those figures with sufficient accuracy to arrive at an appropriate division of the stock. Moreover, an unequal division could provide C with voting control; but that can be resolved by creating two classes of common, each of which elects two Directors, and issuing one class to C and one class to S.

A more serious obstacle to using only common stock is the tax consequences. For example, using the 75%-25% ratio noted above, C will contribute property valued at $60,000 for his 75 shares of stock, and S will contribute a nominal amount of cash[51]—e.g., $500 —for his 25 shares. But S's 25 shares are worth at least 25% of the value of the assets of the corporation ($60,500) or $15,125. Since S paid $500 for shares worth $15,125, the difference of $14,625 will constitute ordinary income to S as stock distributed in payment for services rendered or to be rendered.[52] Moreover, since S's cash contribution is relatively small in comparison with the stock received for his services, S may not qualify as a transferor under § 351; and since S possesses over 20% of the corporation's stock, this may disqualify C from the protection of § 351

---

51 A nominal contribution may be required of S to comply with local corporate law prohibitions against issuing stock for services.
52 Treas. Reg. § 1.351-1(a)(1) and 1(a)(2) Ex. (3).

and accordingly C could recognize the $15,000 gain realized by him on the exchange of his appreciated liquid assets for stock.[53]

An additional problem created by using only common stock is that if the business is liquidated, S will receive 25% of the corporation's assets. C has invested $60,000 in the business, and he should be entitled to a return of his capital before any additional corporate assets are divided.

These problems can be resolved by using preferred stock or debt to represent most of C's capital contribution, and dividing the common stock equally between them. Then C will receive a senior return on his capital investment, in a similar manner to S's senior return on his services via a salary; and C will have a preference over S upon liquidation of the business so that C can recapture his investment before any assets are divided. Yet, the voting control of the corporation and the profits in excess of the senior interests of C and S will be equally divided.

The use of preferred stock or debt may also eliminate or mitigate S's recognition of income and may preserve the protection of § 351 for C's contributions. For example, if C contributed $59,500 for preferred stock and securities; and C and S each contributed $500 for an equal number of shares of common stock, S's shares will not reflect the value of assets contributed by C, and consequently S will likely be deemed to have paid fair value for his shares. Thus, S will not recognize income on the exchange. Even if S's common shares are deemed to be worth more than $500 because of potential future growth of the business (an unlikely event since C paid a like amount for his common stock), the difference should be relatively small and should not cause serious consequences to S or endanger the qualification of C's exchange for nonrecognition under § 351.

The question then remains whether C's senior interest should be represented by preferred stock or by securities, either of which could be issued tax-free under § 351 in exchange for C's assets. Debt (securities) possesses the tax advantages that interest payments are deductible and that the debt can usually be retired without risking dividend treatment. However, debt possesses a number

---

53 Treas. Reg. § 1.351-1(a)(1)(ii). I.R.C. §§ 351(a) and 368(c).

of disadvantages that must be weighed. In order to avoid hybrid stock treatment, the debt will need a fixed maturity date and probably should not be subordinated to the claims of creditors. If it is not subordinated, the corporation may find it difficult to obtain outside loans for additional capital. The corporation may not be able to afford the repayment of the debt at the maturity date; and S may not be willing to permit C to withdraw all of his capital from the enterprise while retaining a 50% interest in its profits. The required payment of interest may be harmful to the corporation, especially during the first few years of its operation. Also, if all of C's $59,500 contribution were represented by debt, the corporation would be thinly capitalized, and the debt would likely be classified as hybrid stock.

Thus, a sizable percentage of C's contribution should be exchanged for preferred stock. However, it is likely that a portion of C's contribution (*e.g.*, $20,000) could be exchanged for debt without causing significant difficulties.

(b) Division between junior executives and retiring management. When aging management commences to turn over the control of a corporate business to younger executives, preferred stock can be a useful device. The younger executives represent the future of the business, and any subsequent growth in the corporation's value will be due to their efforts. The retiring management will want a fixed secure return on the value of the business established by them during their tenure. The younger executives will desire voting control of the business as well as participation in its growth, but they may not have sufficient funds available to purchase the shares owned by the retiring management. One solution would be to have the corporation recapitalized into common stock and preferred so that the preferred shares represent the major part of the present value of the corporation. Thus, the common stock will have a relatively low value, but any future growth in the corporation will be reflected in the common stock and not in the preferred. The older management can then sell common shares to the younger executives at a price they can afford; the older members will retain a fixed return on their interests and will retain an interest in the corporation equal to its present value; and the future growth of the business will be enjoyed by the younger, active men.

It is noteworthy that preferred stock could be issued in a tax-free exchange pursuant to a recapitalization or could be issued as a tax-free stock dividend; but if securities were issued in exchange for stock pursuant to a recapitalization or were issued as a dividend, the shareholders would recognize income.

C. TAX CONSIDERATIONS IN ISSUING PREFERRED STOCK

Some of the tax considerations in determining whether to use preferred stock are:

1. Unfavorable considerations

(a) The issuance of preferred stock precludes an election under Subchapter S and will terminate an election that was previously made.[54]

(b) Dividends paid on preferred stock are not deductible expenses of the corporation.

(c) Nonvoting stock[55] will not qualify for redemption under the substantially disproportionate test (§ 302(b)(2)) unless the redemption of the nonvoting stock is made in conjunction with the redemption of voting stock;[56] and even then, if the nonvoting stock is section 306 stock, the substantially disproportionate test will be of no use.[57]

(d) Preferred stock cannot qualify for ordinary loss treatment under § 1244.[58]

(e) The sale or redemption of preferred stock may cause adverse tax consequences under § 306.

2. Favorable considerations

(a) Preferred stock can be exchanged by a corporation for its stock or securities pursuant to a recapitalization without causing the shareholder to recognize gain on the transfer.[59]

(b) Preferred stock can usually be distributed by a corporation as a stock dividend without causing recognition of income to the shareholder.[60]

---

54 I.R.C. §§ 1371(a)(4), and 1372(e)(3).
55 Preferred stock is usually nonvoting, but it need not be.
56 Treas. Reg. § 1.302-3(a)(3).
57 *Id.*
58 I.R.C. § 1244(c)(1).
59 *See* Chapter III, pp. 156-158 *supra.*
60 I.R.C. § 305.

(c) Preferred stock qualifies for the relief afforded by § 303 where the provisions of that section are applicable.[61]

(d) The redemption of preferred stock, whether voting or non-voting, in complete termination of a shareholder's interest in a corporation will qualify for redemption treatment under § 302(b)(3) even where the preferred is section 306 stock.[62] For purposes of determining whether the shareholder's interest was terminated, the attribution rules provided by § 318 are applicable, but the relief accorded by § 302(c) is available.[63]

3. Issuing preferred stock when the corporation is formed

There can be advantages to issuing preferred stock when the corporation is first formed, since preferred stock issued pursuant to an exchange covered by § 351 does not constitute section 306 stock.[64] However, if the preferred stock is subsequently redeemed by the corporation (when it has substantial earnings), the redemption must meet the not essentially equivalent test, or it will be treated as a dividend notwithstanding that § 306 is inapplicable. The preferred stock could be sold to a third party without adverse tax consequences, but it may be difficult to locate a purchaser unless the stock is invested with sufficient security that dividends will be paid thereon. It will often place too great a burden on the corporation to require that substantial sums be paid as dividends during the formative years of the business, and therefore preferred stock issued at that time may not contain sufficient security to make it a desirable purchase. If preferred stock does not meet the demand of a prospective purchaser, and if the stock is modified to meet the purchaser's demands, then the advantage of having issued the stock in exchange for property transferred to a controlled corporation may be lost.[65] However, the original preferred stock could contain provision for security of dividend payment that commences five years after issuance; and the stock might then be salable in

---

61 *See* Chapter I, pp. 31-36 *supra*.

62 I.R.C. §§ 302(b)(3) and 306(b)(1).

63 Treas. Reg. § 1.306-2(a).

64 The definition of section 306 stock refers to stock distributed as a stock dividend and preferred stock issued in a reorganization or corporate division. I.R.C. § 306(c). *But, note* § 306(c)(1)(C).

65 I.R.C. § 306(g).

five years, when the corporation hopefully has a substantial financial base, under its original terms without the need for making any modifications that would trigger § 306(g).

INDEX

TABLE OF CASES

INTERNAL REVENUE CODE CITATIONS

PUBLISHER'S NOTE

Basic Corporate Taxation *is set in Century Schoolbook, a transitional face, printed on Lock Haven cream white offset stock and bound with Riverside Linen.*

Originally intended for use in periodicals, Century Schoolbook, designed in 1890 by L. B. Benton especially for the American Typefounder's Company, now enjoys popularity as a fine text face as well.

DETROIT COLLEGE OF LAW